CALAMITY

CALAMITY

The Many Lives of
CALAMITY JANE

KAREN R. JONES

YALE UNIVERSITY PRESS
NEW HAVEN AND LONDON

For information about this and other Yale University Press publications, please contact:
U.S. Office: sales.press@yale.edu yalebooks.com
Europe Office: sales@yaleup.co.uk yalebooks.co.uk

Set in Adobe Caslon Pro by IDSUK (DataConnection) Ltd
Printed in Great Britain by Gomer Press Ltd, Llandysul, Ceredigion, Wales

Library of Congress Control Number: 2019950215

ISBN 978-0-300-21280-8

A catalogue record for this book is available from the British Library.

10 9 8 7 6 5 4 3 2 1

Dedicated to Irene Jones, Ismay Jones and Sheila Ditchburn
My heroines of the (Salisbury) plain

CONTENTS

CONTENTS

PLATES

1. Calamity Jane, General Crook's scout, 1895. Library of Congress, Prints and Photographs Division [reproduction number LC-DIG-ppmsca-50235].
2. Martha Canary (Calamity Jane), Black Hills, 1875. J. Leonard Jennewein Collection, Dakota Wesleyan University Archives, Mitchell, South Dakota.
3. Calamnity (i.e. Calamity) Peak. Near Custer City on B. & M. Ry. Title of the peak from the most noted character in the Black Hills. Library of Congress, Prints and Photographs Division [reproduction number LC-DIG-ppmsc-02658].
4. Martha Canary (Calamity Jane), Evanston, Wyoming, c.1880s. J. Leonard Jennewein Collection, Dakota Wesleyan University Archives, Mitchell, South Dakota.
5. Deadwood, South Dakota, 1876. Granger Historical Picture Archive / Alamy Stock Photo.
6. One and Original "Calamity Jane", Miles City, Montana. L.A. Huffman, c.1880–82. Montana Historical Society Research Center, MHS 981-573.
7. Martha Canary and E.C. (Teddy "Blue") Abbott, Gilt Edge, Montana, c.1887. J. Leonard Jennewein Collection, Dakota Wesleyan University Archives, Mitchell, South Dakota.
8. Martha Canary, Livingston, Montana, 1901. J. Leonard Jennewein Collection, Dakota Wesleyan University Archives, Mitchell, South Dakota.

INTRODUCTION

THE STORY OF CALAMITY JANE
TALL TALES, GENDER POSSIBILITY,
AND FRONTIER CELEBRITY

In spring 1877, Calamity Jane was out riding a trail and happened upon a runaway stagecoach from Wyoming that had been attacked by a Cheyenne war party. Promptly engaging in a breathless mounted pursuit of the careening coach, she leapt into the driver's seat in daredevil style, jettisoned all baggage (apart from the all-important mail), pacified the horses, and drove on to the safe confines of Deadwood City, whereupon she received a hero's welcome. A heady slice of all-action western adventure, the episode—known as the Rescue of the Deadwood Stage—was one of her most famous historical vignettes and was referenced in the opening scenes of the musical *Calamity Jane* (1953). In the Hollywood hit, a boisterous and bullwhipping Doris Day rode shotgun, as protector of the Deadwood stage, complete with Winchester rifle, fresh-faced athleticism, and catchy musical score ("Whip Crack Away!").[1]

Celebrated as a rootin' tootin' fixture of the frontier imaginary, one might be forgiven for assuming that Calamity Jane was a creature dreamed up by novelists and filmmakers, and regurgitated on demand as a stock western character. In fact, beyond the folklore is the story of one Martha Jane Canary, whose history speaks of complex gender identities, cultural representations, and the sinuous connections between lived and invented experience in the West. Indeed, on the matter of the Deadwood stage rescue, the local press painted a rather different story to that told by Canary and her latter-day celebrators. Covering the incident in March 1877, the *Cheyenne Daily Leader* failed to even mention her, identified bandits as the culprits in the ambush, and reported a driverless coach rolling into town courtesy of equine homing instinct. A few months later, Calamity Jane's name cropped up not as the savior of the hour, but as a likely member of a notorious band of outlaws, one eyewitness having identified a "woman dressed in men's clothes" among their number. Masculine disguise was successfully used by some of the West's most famous highwaywomen to evade capture (for instance, Pearl Hart, Sally Scull, and Laura Bullion), but in the case of Calamity Jane, her sartorial reputation made her prime suspect.[2]

The story of Martha Jane Canary/Calamity Jane is a dramatic tale of opportunity and oppression, masquerade and myth-making. The late nineteenth century brought far-reaching and rapid changes to the Great Plains—mineral strikes, railroad tracks, homestead booms, and territorial wars—and set the stage for Calamity Jane (along with a host of other characters, including Billy the Kid, Jesse James, and James Butler (Wild Bill) Hickok) to emerge as personifications of the West in its "wild and woolly" years. The period also saw an array of opportunities for women in the trans-Mississippi region, from running homesteads to entrepreneurship in service industries, including laundries, boarding houses, and brothels. At the same time, a heavily masculinized frontier culture left limited room for maneuver for an unconventional woman who inhabited what one early biographer called "the man-trails of the old West." Surviving photographs offer a tantalizing glimpse into the fluid identities of Martha Canary/Calamity Jane as she navigated between the assured swagger of a woman dressed as a man in theatrical stance and the abjections of a poor, alcoholic drifter eking out an existence at the margins of social acceptability. A masculine-clothed itinerant lounging on a rock (Plate 2); a confident army scout grasping a rifle in studio pose (Plate 1); a down-at-heel pioneer woman with a glass of beer held aloft in greeting (Plate 7); and a sepia-tinged mourner with flower in hand at Bill Hickok's grave (Plate 13): these scattered visual snapshots of "Calamity" tell a thousand words. Or rather, they do and they don't. Evident here are the swirling conceits that gathered around her as a frontier celebrity, as well as the hint of a hidden tale of personal struggle, storytelling, and gender possibility. How Martha Jane Canary came to be Calamity Jane, and how her story was successively recycled and repurposed over the span of a century or more, is the subject of *Calamity: The Many Lives of Calamity Jane*.[3]

Canary was born in Missouri in the 1850s and arrived in the West as a young child, traveling overland with her parents as part of the long procession of those taking to the mineral-rich lands of Montana in search of wealth and prosperity. She found neither. Orphaned and destitute by the end of the 1860s, she moved between railroad and mining camps, military stations and frontier towns, trying her hand at various jobs—some customary (cook, laundress, saloon girl, and prostitute), and others less typical (freighter, prospector, mule drover). Over these years, however, Martha Canary *did* make a name for herself. Well known in the rough and ready settlements of the western plains for dressing in men's clothes, a taste for liquor and wanderlust, and a tendency to shoot off her mouth and her guns, she became something of a regional curiosity. Quite unlike the pious school ma'am or the sun-bonneted "gentle tamer"—the stereotypical faces of the female frontier—here stood a maverick figure operating far beyond the boundaries of normative behavior and attracting local attention for her apparently wild ways, trigger itch, and insobriety. When she rode into Deadwood in July 1876, an arrival that symbolically marked the beginning of her ascent to frontier superstardom, the local press put it succinctly: "Calamity Jane has arrived." In the next few years, meanwhile, Canary went from being the subject of Black Hills gossip to national (and international) fame. Catapulting her onto this new stage were a number of literary renditions of her "story": newspapers, literary works, and a string of dime novels (cheap and sensationalist texts that reveled in the West and its colorful cast of characters) in which Calamity Jane played leading lady-in-buckskin to all-purpose frontier hero, Deadwood Dick. Representing a world of freedom and unfettered action, a "wild West" of the popular imagination that endures today, the "Heroine of the Plains" captured the public mood.[4]

Three years after Frederick Jackson Turner presented his famous frontier thesis to the American Historical Association, Calamity Jane addressed her own audience in print. Turner's 1893 essay, "The Significance of the Frontier in American History," argued the case for westward conquest as a foundational aspect of the American experience. *Life and Adventures of Calamity Jane, By Herself* (1896) offered a personal take on migration, settlement, and resilience in a trans-Mississippi theater. Like Turner, her rendition sprang from an acknowledgment of the West as a powerful and dynamic setting, as well as a sense of its potency as a dramatic device. Produced to accompany the dime museum show for Kohl and Middleton, in which Canary was performing, the short account presented a piece of staccato chronicle from a true-life frontier witness. In common with many journals of the westward journey, Canary's tale began with a potted genealogy, followed by a breezy narration of the dangers and thrills of a five-month overland trip across plains, rivers, and mountains. Describing herself as a "remarkably good shot and a fearless rider for a girl of my age," she noted being "at all times along with the men when there was excitement or adventure to be had." Briefly referencing her arrival at Virginia City, Montana, and the death of both of her parents, Canary focused on her work as a scout for General Custer, during which time she found a life "perfectly at home in men's clothes." The army years brought renown as a maverick "female scout," as well as the famous epithet "Calamity Jane, the heroine of the plains" (reputedly the words of one Captain Egan, after he was saved from an unceremonious dismount during an ambush). Thereafter, the narrative moved to Deadwood and her exploits as a Pony Express rider, the capture of Wild Bill's killer, and (naturally) the rescue of the Deadwood stage. All of these remained integral aspects of her legend in years to come. After a whistle-stop tour of her 17 years drifting from town to town, prospecting, mule-whacking and the like, Canary ended her tale by recalling a triumphal return to Deadwood as a famous character whose story continued to inspire fascination. With a nod to her authority as authentic narrator of the frontier experience, she closed with a message of humble assuredness: "Hoping that this little history of my life may interest all readers, I remain, as in the early days. Yours, Mrs. M. Burk. Better Known as Calamity Jane."[5]

Canary was not alone in wanting to commit her western story to posterity. Legions of female travelers and homesteaders eagerly wrote the frontier into ink, conjoining their own life stories with collective tales of manifest destiny and history in the making. As Dee Brown, author of one of the earliest academic treatments of westering women in *The Gentle Tamers* (1958), put it, female emigrants were eager diarists, who chronicled the everyday details of their experience, along with a sense of being part of something bigger than themselves. Their stories, however, were overlooked in a traditional narrative of westward conquest that concentrated on the white masculine hero, namely the cowboy, cavalryman, miner, sheriff, and desperado. Frederick Jackson Turner, for instance, stressed the role of the "over-mountain *men*" (my emphasis) in his celebration of American democracy and westward drive. Significantly, it was not until the rise of New Western History in the 1980s and its imperative to present a more crowded, complicated, and contested picture (what Elliott West calls "a longer, grimmer but more interesting story") that the "female frontier" was taken seriously as a historical subject. Thereafter, the excavation of a rich vein of first-hand testimonies produced by thousands of women as they encountered the West and made it their home illuminated a vibrant "Herstory" in a terrain that had hitherto appeared as "Hisland" (to use the terms of Susan Armitage). This freshly inscribed frontier revealed stories of domesticity, constraint, and hardship, but also social mobility, the invention of new identities, and a more flexible definition of "women's work." British-born émigré Evelyn Cameron, who went to Montana in the early 1900s with her husband Ewen to raise polo ponies, was one of those who documented daily life on the homestead and the hunting trail—from plugging walls with mud to prevent drafts, to pulling out a rotten tooth by wiring it to ropes thrown over a rafter. In one entry, she wrote: "Manual labour . . . is all I care about, and, after all, is what will really make a strong woman. I like to break colts, brand calves, cut down trees, ride and work in a garden." Such stories showed a diversity of experience on the female frontier that extended far beyond the Hollywood stereotypes of the domestic helpmate and the sassy saloon girl.[6]

Calamity Jane is a particularly intriguing figure in this story of women claiming authority and ownership over a history and a space traditionally occupied by men. For one thing, her autobiographical profile did not fit the model of the western authoress slaving over candlelight to compile a daily inventory of life (Evelyn Cameron found paper in such short supply that once one entry was finished, she turned the paper on its side and changed her ink color). Martha Canary was, in all likelihood, illiterate, her autobiography published to accompany a dime museum show in which she starred. As such, *Life and Adventures* was a co-production: forged both from the stories Canary had traded in saloon bars and around campfires, and from the designs of a literary agent tasked with writing into print the stage story of Deadwood's famed buckskin-clad raconteur. With its consciously theatrical delivery, it illustrated the connected contours of what feminist playwright Heather Carver calls "agency, spectacle, and spectatorship" in female autobiography. Boldly articulated and with a blustering sense of pace, *Life and Adventures* condensed Calamity Jane's westward rite of passage into seven pages (Turner's paper, incidentally, took 28). This was her script and her screenplay (which, according to period anecdotes, served as a useful prompt when Canary performed under the influence), and also served to provide visitors with a word-perfect souvenir of the show. In terms of style, it followed a general trend in frontier testimonials in emphasizing authenticity and escapade as critical ingredients of the frontier biopic (see, for instance, *The Adventures of Buffalo Bill Cody* (1904)) and favored a matter-of-fact prose that conjured the sense of a heroic geography roamed by luminous, yet straight-talking protagonists. This directness in writing, as early biographer Duncan Aikman noted, provided an all-important inference of truth: "when the autobiography is both exceptionally matter-of-course and exceptionally plausible, there is no reason for doubting it."[7]

In large part, however, *Life and Adventures* was hokum: an exercise in creative writing and myth-making, or, more accurately, in "writing" up the folklore of Calamity Jane as it had been laid out since the 1870s by Canary and others. The opening line contained two red herrings in the shape of her birth year (1852, rather than 1856) and surname (Cannary, i.e., with an extra "n" thrown in), both of which were faithfully reproduced as "truths." A good deal of the autobiographical detail was erroneous, to boot. Calamity Jane never rode with Custer, never served as an army scout or a Pony Express courier, and did not apprehend Bill Hickok's killer. As such, she presented something of a conundrum, in the words of early biographer Leonard Jennewein, "the hero who performed no heroic deeds." Believability and star appeal, it seemed, counted far more than hard evidence in supporting her claims to fame. As biographer Linda Jucovy notes, "the details about her exploits were rarely true, but no one cared. It was the story that mattered." Forget the finer points of historical accuracy: Canary's credentials came from being a credible western actor, in both senses of the phrase. She *had* traveled with army expeditions in 1875 and 1876, spent time in the railroad camps of the Northern and Union Pacific, participated in the prospecting boom in the Black Hills, and was a fixture of Deadwood in its embryonic years. A keen sense of theatricality (Jennewein remarked "she attracted attention in a dramatic manner, in episodes calculated to remain in the memory of the witnesses"), meanwhile, invested her grand tales with a veneer of authenticity. Calamity Jane walked the walk of the frontier hero, and, as bar-room storyteller, was well rehearsed at talking the talk. According to the Lander *Wyoming State Journal*, "she was proud of her cognomen and shrewd enough to utilize its possibilities"—a conclusion that raises interesting questions of agency, cultural resonance, and gender performance in explaining how a poor, itinerant woman became entangled in the heroic mythology of an imagined West.[8]

The process by which Martha Canary came to be Calamity Jane, I argue here, is best understood in terms of a wider culture of frontier celebrity under construction in the late 1800s—a heady time, in which those who had taken part in the western story were catapulted into the limelight as eyewitnesses to history and borderland entertainers. *Life and Adventures* mixed up the discrete elements of a nonconformist life with assumed "truths" and historical referents to create a potent frontier cocktail that spoke to period fascination with the wildest aspects of the "wild West." As the *Rapid City Daily Journal* put it, Calamity Jane was "the prickly cactus symbol of the pioneer days at the heart of their depravity." Feted as a frontier witness with star appeal, she joined the likes of Buffalo Bill Cody (whom Larry McMurtry calls one of "the first American superstars") in communicating the story of the West for the purposes of education, entertainment, and patriotic accounting. The fact that Canary's autobiography was factually light mattered little in an imaginative landscape of western myth-making, where granular realities were less important than satisfying cultural needs for a flamboyant and ideologically powerful American fable. Controlling this galloping beast of frontier mythology proved difficult. William Cody went bankrupt trying to make his "wild West" shows live up to their spectacular billing, and Canary, too, ran into problems trying to make sense of her public and private lives. Period accounts spoke of financial problems, mental and physical instability, a recurring drink problem, turbulent relationships, and an unsettled home life. In 1887, the editor of the *Livingston Enterprise* remarked: "A complete and true biography of the life of Calamity Jane would make a large book, more interesting and blood-curdling than all the fictitious stories that have been written of her." It would, the paper noted, "never find its way into a Sunday School library." Such editorial flourishes—glorifying Canary's "wildness" before shooting her down as social pariah, freak or eccentric—indicated the instabilities and inner contradictions of a frontier celebrity that at once celebrated and destabilized hegemonic masculinity.[9]

In fact, the contradictions and confusions in Calamity Jane's story raised considerable problems for would-be biographers. For many popular hagiographers, the solution was simple: merely accept her heroic mantle as "female scout" and weave her colorful history into the broader narrative fabric of the frontier imaginary. A number of scholarly works, meanwhile, went down the road of trying to separate fact from fiction, only to find the search for the *real* Canary both time-consuming and frustrating. Duncan Aikman, writing in the 1920s, surmised that "the nearer one comes to the actual scene of Jane's heroic performances, the more they vanish," while John E. Hutchens, commenting on the multiple tales (and the multiple Calamity Janes) that he heard about from old-timers, concluded "if they—who had experienced so much at first hand—could frequently disagree about this and that person or event, how was some Montana historian to arrive in the future at what he knew to be the truth?" Forensically focused historical biographies from James McLaird and Richard Etulain come closest to answering the plea of the *Livingston Enterprise* in assembling an exhaustive documentary trail of Canary's whereabouts from "bits and fragments" to picture a real-world existence firmly at odds with her legendary profile.[10]

Calamity: The Many Lives of Calamity Jane, on the other hand, steps beyond a search for "facts" and "truths" in favor of emphasizing story-telling, gender, and performance as a way of understanding the folkloric pageant that surrounded Calamity Jane in her life and afterlife. It sees her life and fable as necessarily and irrevocably entangled and, as such, builds on a number of recent biographies that focus on the complex constructions of frontier legends and their changing cultural representation through the twentieth century. Conceptually, it sits at the "and" point in *Life and Adventures*—the place where Canary's lived and invented experience meet. Integral here is the idea of locating Calamity

Jane in a powerful image culture in the throes of invention in the late nineteenth century, fed by technology and mass communications, the rise of consumerism, and the peculiar psycho-physical space of the West that seemed to invite dramatic rendition. In this regard, her invention as a frontier icon speaks not only of story creation, a forceful meta-narrative, and the potency of personality in the construction of an imagined West, but also of a modern celebrity culture predicated on famous-*ness*, a slow decoupling of fame from achievement, or what Amy Argetsinger calls the cult of the "famesque." A celebrity whose notoriety came from fabricated deeds, a striking profile, and a strong sense of performance savvy, Calamity Jane speaks in interesting ways to our present-day obsession with idols of various screen sizes, as well as providing an intriguing case study of a popular icon under construction. Approached in this vein, the fables and fascinations that grew up around the "heroine of the plains" are worth digging into, regardless of their relationship to fact. Meanwhile, in thinking about the entanglements of history, myth-making, and collective memory, what Shari Benstock refers to as the "matter and manner" of storytelling, is of value here. What was it that encouraged people to write Calamity Jane into *their* pasts, and what invited her successive recycling as a frontier eyewitness? Tall or otherwise, tales told and remembered, as historian Clyde Milner notes, "have their own value." Moreover, as Douglas Boyd points out, the mechanics of creating a collective past from gathering up a multitude of individual memories is a process that is "inherently complex, malleable and polyvalent." With various constituencies (including Canary herself) telling (and retelling) stories, the folkloric imprint of Calamity Jane inevitably contained a cacophony of voices. A storied presence of considerable import, we should not only accept, but also *expect* contested versions of her story.[11]

With such thoughts in mind, *Calamity: The Many Lives of Calamity Jane* tracks Calamity Jane from her birth in Missouri across a frontier space undergoing fundamental economic, social, political, and environmental change. According to historian Glenda Riley, as a historical figure, Canary represents little more than a whimsy, a cameo of the "wild woman" that distracts from, rather than informs, the representative history of women in the West. She belongs, Riley claims, to a redundant scholarship, one which focused only on "famous women who acted more like men" (see, for example, Ray Allen Billington's *Westward Expansionism* (1949)) or on hackneyed stereotypes (what Joan Jensen and Darlis Miller gather under the categories of "gentle tamers," "sun-bonneted helpmates," "hell-raisers," and "bad women"). I argue differently. By approaching Calamity Jane in terms of her unconventional lifestyle and gender identity, we can usefully destabilize the rigid assumptions around a monolithic "female frontier," as well as illuminate the West as a place of both opportunity and obstacle for women migrants who (either from necessity or inclination) challenged the boundaries of normative behavior. Feminist readings of Canary's life, as Richard Etulain points out in *Calamity Jane: A Reader's Guide* (2015), represent substantial "unfinished business" in her biographical case notes. Most significantly, her story speaks not just to the mechanics and practicalities of female empowerment in a "man's world," but also to an important sea change in modern understandings of sexual and gender identification. By reading her experiences as an unorthodox woman through the lens of gender possibility, in fact, we invite the prospect of redrawing the frontier binary in useful ways.[12]

Critical to the iconic reputation of Calamity Jane, of course, was the fact that she dressed as a man. This is where the threads of gender and performance are particularly instructive in unpacking her story and in finding a connecting path between life and legend. Through costume, gesture, and oratory, Canary navigated the contested terrains of frontier stardom, identity politics, and her restricted life choices. Indeed, a number of women in the American West (and elsewhere) took to adopting masculine garb in order to work and travel freely, to avoid sexual intimidation, or to engage in non hetero-normative lifestyles. As cultural theorist Judith Butler points out, gender is a fluid concept, one upheld and exercised by performative action. As a "female scout" known for her nonconformist ways, Canary was consistently read according to the rubric of what Butler later called "gender trouble." Canary's cross-dressing was salacious and subversive, an implicit disruption of dominant masculinity, and told an important "hidden history" of alternative gender identities in the West. Moreover, as a significant historical example of a woman exploring what Jack Halberstam calls "female masculinity," Calamity Jane was a radical figure who found a place of personal expression, celebrity power, and cultural purchase through an unorthodox gender performance. As Leonard Jennewein put it, she "combined flair with a native sense of show*man*ship" (my emphasis).[13]

When Martha Canary died in 1903, eulogies spoke of the glory days of old and the passing of one of the West's great personalities. She was buried in Mount Moriah cemetery, next to Wild Bill Hickok—itself a masterstroke of frontier myth-making and a signal of a community in the process of inventing a folkloric past. This was, however, far from the end of the story for Deadwood's raucous raconteur. Courtesy of literature, television, and film, Calamity Jane boasted an illustrious career in the twentieth and twenty-first centuries that embellished and reinvented the images crafted during her lifetime. *Calamity: The Many Lives of Calamity Jane* explores this posthumous landscape to consider how cultural representations of her story illustrated shifting views on westward expansion, gender politics, and social values. What remained a constant were two things: the ubiquity of her masculine costuming, and a resolute sense of her as a radical figure in the context of traditional gender roles. In the first wave of biographies, written in the 1920s and 1930s, Canary was cast as a kind-hearted oddball or a "gamey old bawd," as writers struggled to situate her in a world of frontier nostalgia and mid-century gender conformity. Visual media, too, toyed with how to present her as an acceptable or adventuring heroine, from the simpering theatrics of Cecil DeMille's *The Plainsman* (1936) to the wholesome notes of David Butler's 1953 musical starring Doris Day, whose depiction of "Calam" as a femme-faced tomboy remains the most popular representation to date. Later in the twentieth century, the dialectics of modern gender politics and the rise of the lesbian, gay, bisexual, and transgender (LGBT) movement saw Calamity Jane championed as a feminist incarnate and butch lesbian role model. Biographer Linda Jucovy in *Searching for Calamity* (2012) says of her subject: "She was a kind of hero to women like me who do not like being told how they are supposed to act." Stella Foote badged her as "our first liberated woman," while David Milch enlisted her in his *Deadwood* TV series (2004–06) as a grubby and profane sapphic storyteller.[14]

Successively recycled as a buckskin-wearing nonconformist idol, Calamity Jane swaggered across an expansive entertainment landscape that stretched from the nineteenth to the twenty-first century. Various different constituencies constructed their "wild West" hero(ine) to suit contemporary tastes, and, especially, as a conduit to ponder issues of heretical identity and non-normative lifestyles. A striking frontier celebrity, Martha Jane Canary stood tall as an iconic presence of the imagined West, combining lived and invented experience to create a powerful and lasting reputation that played with shifting understandings of gender, alongside more familiar themes of pioneer patriotics and nostalgic western adventuring. Her story speaks of *fin de siècle* myth creation, the complicated contours of identity politics, and the emergence of a modern celebrity culture. It seems only appropriate to circle the folkloric wagons, so to speak, by ending with a comment on the latest example of Calamity Jane myth-making in action, a tub-thumping quote emblazoned on internet sites and available for purchase on posters and t-shirts at the press of a button: "I figure, if a girl wants to be a legend, she should just go ahead and be one." Nowhere is there any evidence that Canary said such a thing. Much like the "Rescue of the Deadwood Stage," this apocryphal soundbite from the virtual frontier eagerly communicated the importance of performance, storytelling, and gender possibility in understanding the story of the famous "heroine of the plains."

CHAPTER ONE

"A FEARLESS RIDER FOR A GIRL OF MY AGE"
MARTHA CANARY GOES WEST (c.1852-70)

Life and Adventures of Calamity Jane, By Herself (1896) stated that Martha Jane Canary was born in Princeton, Missouri, on 1 May 1852. Some of this was true. Indeed, it is most likely that she was born on the first day of May, and that her early memories were forged in the rural hinterlands of Princeton, though there is no concrete proof of a birthdate or birthplace in official records. Muddying the waters of historical documentation were counterclaims that she was born in Iowa, to a Baptist minister, or was a "child of the West," raised at Fort Laramie by a soldier named Dalton. A raft of competing stories, meanwhile, touted birth years ranging from 1844 to 1860. Not until the 1940s, when historian Clarence Paine located a Mercer County federal census from 1860 that contained her name, was some clarity provided on the question of Calamity Jane's "origin story." According to these records, Robert W. Canary, his wife Charlotte, and their children (including an eldest daughter, Martha, four years old and recorded as Missouri-born) were living on a homestead in Ravenna Township, Missouri. Working backwards, Martha Jane Canary was most likely born not in 1852, as her autobiography claimed, but in 1856.[1]

Calamity Jane's family history was broadly representative of thousands of settlers headed westward in the late eighteenth and early nineteenth centuries. In a young country with a mobile demographic, betterment through migration represented foundational tenets of an emerging American ethos. The Canarys had started moving over the Appalachian Mountains in the late eighteenth century in search of fertile farmland. Martha's paternal grandfather, James, was born in Virginia in 1788, and by 1820 was living on a homestead in eastern Ohio with his wife, Sarah. Their son Robert—Martha's father—was born in 1825 and grew up in Monroe County, a rural community growing ever more populous with new migrants (it counted a population of 18,000 by 1840), which provoked many to move further west in search of productive frontier land. The extended Canary family moved on to Iowa, where Robert married Charlotte Bunge in 1855, only to up sticks again, this time to Missouri, where James Canary bought 320 acres in April 1856. Here, the documentary trail goes cold, with various uncorroborated accounts describing Robert and Charlotte Canary arriving in Princeton to live in a building near the county courthouse (another "birthplace" contender) and subsequently at James' log cabin. Over the next few years, James Canary divided up his land and sold it (at cost price) to his children, who, along with the influx of other settlers, set about eagerly transforming prairie into farmland. Documented in land agency records and tracked by various historians, the last part of the plot, some 180 acres, including the family cabin, was sold to Robert for $500 in December 1859. It was here that the 1860 census recorded the earliest biographical trace of Martha Jane Canary.[2]

Fragmentary testimonies from the Princeton years present a glimpse of Martha Jane Canary's childhood, but actually communicate much more about the importance of a credible and colorful backstory to her latter-day frontier celebrity. Robert Canary is presented as a somewhat lackluster farmer, and Charlotte as a firebrand, with a liking for liquor, cigars, gaudy dress, and fruity language—in other words, a worthy role model for her nonconformist daughter. *Life and Adventures* says very little about these years, beyond reference to outdoor exercise and adventure; but what Martha Jane left out, local hearsay and early biographers were happy to devise. Duncan Aikman, author of *Calamity Jane and the Lady Wildcats* (1927) visited Princeton and gathered (often salacious) tales from old-timers eager to regale him with stories of Charlotte Canary as a "Missouri exotic" and a "crazy, show-off, harum-scarum woman, drunk or sober." In common with the stories that swirled around her daughter in later years, and in keeping with the typologies of the stereotypical "bad woman," she was reputed to have a checkered past (gossips claimed she met Robert while working in a brothel) and a heart of gold. Recalling stories told by a friend, C.W. Ormsbey, a Princeton resident in the 1940s, told how Charlotte Canary had careered to a neighbor's house on a buggy and drunkenly thrown down 10 yards of calico with the instruction to "make your little sons of b-----s some shirts." In the 1950s, Doris Thompson, a local historian researching Princeton's most notorious daughter, suggested that the Canarys were regular fixtures in a landscape of local chatter, "a family the neighbors were not likely to forget" that continued to attract storytelling attention. Attesting to the importance of testimonial culture in stoking the fires of frontier celebrity, as well as the considerable prestige embedded in the mantle of pioneer witness, C.W. Ormsbey informed local historian W.W. Morrison: "I could talk for hours telling you everything you need to know" about Calamity Jane, all of which "is every word true." Ormsbey had lived in Princeton for 78 years (arriving in 1870, several years after the Canarys left) and "had seen the cabin many times." He knew where to locate Calamity Jane (though all that remained of their home by the late 1940s was the rock under the fireplace), though the veracity of his claims rested on *knowing* those who had *known* her. Such assertions of authority revealed much about the connected threads of conversation, memory, and frontier identity in the evolution of the Calamity Jane legend. Moreover, while some recounted a "nice child" who played with their children and attended the local school, most early biographers were wont to present Canary as a youthful version of her folkloric persona. According to historian Ronald Lackmann, she had a reputation as a "wildcat" by the age of 10, while Aikman painted a lively tapestry of a miscreant and "untutored rebel" roaming fields and farms, and finding "awe-inspiring secrets of country depravity" in a neighborhood "full of admirably grotesque characters." Biographer Leonard Jennewein saw her future course already set: "she was off the beaten path before she ever got on it."[3]

THE TRAIL FROM PRINCETON: WESTWARD JOURNEYING AND MARTHA CANARY'S RITE OF PASSAGE

The demographic mobility of the Canarys was typical of period emigrants, who bounced from farm to farm seeking a prosperity that seemed to lie ever westwards. This story of movement also fitted well with the restless and rootless lifestyle favored by Calamity Jane in later years, though her inclinations for itinerancy took her not to the idealized domesticity of the homestead, but (in line with her unorthodox approach to the usual fixings of the "female frontier") to the transient spaces of a West under processes of incorporation. It was in the early 1860s that Robert and Charlotte Canary, together with their children, left the mid-West for the Rocky Mountains. In common with most westward migrants, there were push and pull factors behind their decision. James Canary died in 1862, and his successors fell to wrangling about the estate (including court proceedings brought against Robert by his siblings over the matter of an unpaid $600 loan). Discord was also brewing in Missouri about the politics of slavery, and some have contended that Charlotte had secessionist sympathies. Stories of mineral strikes in Montana also fired the imagination with promises of another western dream, and, by the end of 1862, the farm had been sold in preparation for a new journey. The family most likely set off sometime in early 1863 (though *Life and Adventures* claims 1865) and may have spent time in Iowa before traveling to the goldfields in 1864. In her autobiography, Canary noted taking the overland route to Montana, a trail that snaked from Independence along the banks of the North Platte River to Fort Laramie (established by the US Army in 1849), before tracking through the Rockies at South Pass (a route discovered by fur trappers in 1812), and joining a wagon route to the mining camps further north. The trail through Wyoming took in Independence Rock, dubbed by Jesuit missionary

Pierre-Jean de Smet "the register of the desert" for the signatures of emigrants carved on its granite face. In 1846, fur trapper Rufus B. Sage noted that the rock was "covered with names of travelers, traders, trappers, and emigrants, engraved upon it in almost every practicable part." The Canarys, it seemed, did not participate in this tradition.[4]

By the time the Canarys headed westwards, these overland routes were well trod, having been traversed by wagon trains for nigh on two decades. A total of 400,000 emigrants took the Oregon Trail to the Pacific between 1834 and 1869 (the latter date marking the opening of the First Transcontinental Railroad). Travelers made use of guidebooks (*The Emigrants' Guide* provided the first *Lonely Planet* precursor in 1845), military and trading posts, ferries, mapped shortcuts, and seasoned scouts to assist their passage. Twenty years before, things had been rather different, with wagon trains heading cross-country with little knowledge or preparation, eyewitnesses describing abandoned family heirlooms and broken equipment strewn along the route, and communicating disastrous tales of lost parties (notably the Donner Party, most of whom succumbed to the cold of the Sierra Nevada winter of 1846–47, while the remainder survived by eating the flesh of their compatriots). By the early 1860s, however, the main trails were more like demographic and information superhighways (by the standards of the day), serviced by the Pony Express (1860–61) and the First Transcontinental Telegraph (1861). Historian Richard White goes so far as to say that trail migrants met society "at virtually every turn." That said, even in the high days and hubbub of the wagoneering era, one might still pass relatively anonymously through transient camps and military posts. The only anecdotal account of the emigrant Canarys comes from an associate of Buffalo Bill Cody, a man known as Boney Earnest, who claimed to have seen the family at Fort Steele, en route to Salt Lake City, poor and hungry, but still fired by dreams of striking it rich in the Montana mining boom. Earnest's testimony was riddled with inconsistencies (Fort Steele was not established until 1868, Martha Canary's age was listed as 15, and the encounter was dated to 1872), but recent biographers have seen no reason to doubt the general tenor of his commentary.[5]

A 2,000-mile journey from Missouri to Montana, as Martha Canary accurately recalled, took five months. Highlighting the process by which fragments of authentic testimonial—the lived experience of Martha Jane Canary—served as useful "building blocks" around which her legend could be constructed, *Life and Adventures* reveled in this as a time of unbridled excitement. Canary spoke of hunting with the men and always being around when adventure was to be had, a motif that served as a foundational aspect of her frontier celebrity. As such, the overland trip was a rhetorical as well as a physical one, a journey of discovery that marked the entry of Calamity Jane into a dynamic "wild West," and a performance landscape that allowed for the exercise of an unconventional gender identity. With a distinctly Turnerian twist, Aikman effused about the impact of this new land on the youthful Canary: "the wild country claimed her, then. It gave her a beautiful, a flamboyant vocation, sensually rich and ecstatic." Significantly, this attraction for an untamed frontier ascribed to Calamity Jane a traditionally masculine outlook. Women, it was assumed, typically approached the West with reluctance and saw few redeeming aspects to the drudgery of a migrant life. Revisionist historians writing with a feminist bent have refined this story considerably, finding complex cognitive responses among women travelers that include an abiding concern for the integrity of the family unit (articulated, especially, in diary accounts of illness and death), expressions of wonderment at the natural features before them, and an eagerness to embrace the opportunities that the region offered in terms of female empowerment (one homestead claim in ten was filed by a single woman). Twenty-two-year-old Sarah Raymond Herndon, who traveled to Virginia City in 1865 with her family and wrote of her travels in *Days on the Road: Crossing the Plains in 1865* (1902), talked exuberantly about picking wildflowers, learning to fish, and riding out in advance of the train on her horse. Survival on the trail demanded that gender norms, like old furniture, be cast off in favor of a resourceful mentality. Some women relished the chance to drive wagons and to dispense with long skirts (Herndon spoke in such terms), while others expressed discomfort at the falling away of social conventions and typically feminine behaviors in a place "beyond civilization."[6]

It is worth remembering at this point that Martha Canary would only have been about eight years old when the events she related occurred, thus suggesting an element of conflation to her boisterous retrospective. At the same time, while traditional treatments of the frontier story presented children as invisible or incidental, the act of rescuing them from "historical limbo," as Elliott West notes in *Growing Up with the Country* (1989), revealed them to be highly visible and engaged presences. Some 40,000 traveled the overland trails, and, of those children who wrote up their experiences in diaries and journals, many spoke of excitement and adventure. D.B. Ward, writing in 1911 of his journey to Oregon some 60 years before, recalled "It was a long, long journey; full of grave responsibility to the older members of the family . . . But for me, a lad of fifteen, it was . . . the most interesting six months' period of my life." Many adults saw danger in fording ravines and crossing swollen rivers, but a child's-eye view was often more carefree. Whether turned loose or put to work, children on the trail found fresh spaces for exploration and entertainment (competitive buffalo dung collection—a product which travelers burned as fuel on campfires—being a popular game). Significantly, this embracing of westering chutzpah was not exclusively confined to young men. As Sarah Cummins pointed out: "Being naturally 'full of curiosity' and roving in mind and disposition I would mount my riding nag and employ every spare moment in feasting my eyes and my 'mind's eye'." Scattered across the written West in diary and chronicle, then, were examples of girls and young women riding, shooting, and driving wagons, in addition to participating in more customary chores of cooking, mending clothes, and looking after siblings. Accordingly, while Martha Canary's tall tales about her trailside appetite invariably contained a dose of artistic license, the gulf between her lived and invented experience may not be as large as one might think.[7]

VIRGINIA CITY TO PIEDMONT: GOLD STRIKES, STORIES, AND PATHWAYS TO CALAMITY JANE

Virginia City was the destination of the Canarys and the site of Montana's latest mineral rush. In common with many of the mining boomtowns of the West, its early history was a somewhat accidental one, with prospectors heading to the Yellowstone River in early 1863 stumbling upon gold in nearby Alder Gulch. Word spread quickly, and, in common with a pattern repeated from California (1848) to the Klondike (1896), a frenzy of eager prospectors descended on the region hoping to find their fortunes in mountain streambeds and shallow seams. A year after the strike, 10,000 people were perched in tents, shacks, and caves in nearby hillsides. Some came from farms back east (Missouri, in particular), while others had jumped from western mining camp to mining camp in search of the "big strike." For Sarah Herndon, this world was lively and dynamic, with men like "bees around a hive" and "the ground literally turned inside out," with "great deep holes and high heaps of dirt." The mines, she noted, were "said to be very rich." For early arrivals, in fact, there was a good chance of making money from placer mining (extracting surface ore using pan, pick, and shovel). Some $30 million worth of gold was discovered in the first three years. With its stories of colossal nuggets and "gold fever," the mining frontier boasted a heady romantic iconography and played an instrumental role in nineteenth-century western conquest, particularly in terms of demographic consolidation, urbanization, and the development of political structures. Montana Territory was created in 1865 on the back of the Alder Gulch claim, and Virginia City became its capital.[8]

Like most mining towns, Virginia City was notable for its homo-social culture: the early western mining towns were populated by large numbers of transient young men, and women were frequently outnumbered 10:1.

Recalling his mother's account of the California mines, Josiah Royce described the typical camp as a place of "unattached men who sojourned within it while their luck was good and who quit it without a thought upon news of a new strike elsewhere." The rapid nature of their establishment made these ramshackle places, sprawling shanties with little civic authority or social rules. Herndon described Virginia City as "the shabbiest town I ever saw." A number of factors contributed to the lawlessness and sporadic violence of the average mining camp, including the competitive nature of mining as an enterprise, a young male populace, and a "code of the West" that prized defense of property and honor. Virginia City became notorious for its criminal activity perpetrated by "road agents" (bandits) and for the vigilance committees (1863–64) that imposed order with impunity and trod a fine line between the use and abuse of authority in carving a community out of the rough and ready settlement.[9]

Civic boosters had big plans for Virginia City and set about an ambitious building program of residential, commercial, and official buildings that numbered some 1,200 structures by 1868. As with many western mining settlements, however, the promise of vast and sustained mineral wealth was illusory. When gold was discovered at Last Chance Gulch (Helena, Montana) in July 1864, most prospectors upped sticks and went in search of glittering nuggets. By the early 1870s, only a few hundred residents remained in Virginia City. The town remained largely abandoned until the 1940s, when Montana ranchers Charles and Sue Bovey began buying and restoring properties. Today, the old mining settlement remains one of the better-preserved "wild West" ghost towns (which number some 8,000), and a monument to the greenback allure of the mining era, the optimism of early residents who staked a claim to wealth and permanence in their grand buildings, and the precariousness of a community dominated by industrial risk and stark environmental realities.

Just one piece of documentary evidence attests to the presence of the Canarys in Virginia City: a press article from the *Montana Post*, dated 31 December 1864. Discussing "provision for the destitute poor," the editorial mentions three young girls by the name of Canary who appeared on the doorstep of James Fergus, county commissioner, looking for charitable relief. Described, respectively, as a gambler and a "woman of the lowest grade," Robert and Charlotte Canary came in for fierce criticism for sending their children out in the depths of winter wearing only calico slips. The *Post* saw this as "a most flagrant and wanton instance of unnatural conduct on the part of parents to their children." The goldfields, it seemed, had not delivered prosperity to the struggling family and, in common with other prospectors, they lived a hand-to-mouth lifestyle, hopping between different strikes in pursuit of fortune. Period testimony records them as living in nearby Nevada City, and also at Blackfoot City, where gold was struck in May 1865, and where Charlotte took in laundry to make ends meet. Things became yet more desperate in 1866–67, when both Charlotte and Robert died—the former, most likely, of typhoid in Blackfoot, Montana, and the latter in Salt Lake City, though no official records exist for either death. In the many fictions of Calamity Jane, various alternative "versions" exist of this time, including her parents being killed in an Indian attack, and Charlotte Canary running a brothel in Virginia City called the Bird Cage.[10]

What did life in a mining camp offer for an uprooted, destitute young woman without support networks? Stories from Virginia City's "female frontier" in the 1860s highlight both opportunities and limitations to action. Twenty-year-old Mathilda Dalton, a migrant who had come west with her family in 1862 and was hailed as one of Virginia City's "belles," lost both parents in a typhoid epidemic in January 1864. A single woman left alone with three younger siblings to support, she had little recourse but to marry a local miner, Zebulon Thibadeau, with whom she later moved to Wisconsin, and eventually to Idaho. For Virginia Slade, meanwhile, the laxity of social conventions in the mining town allowed a degree of independence and space to operate beyond the usual confines of gender orthodoxy. Resident of the Elephant Corral and wife of Jack Slade (the last man to be hanged by the Vigilance Committee, in

March 1864, for drunk and disorderly offences), she enjoyed riding her Kentucky stallion astride, and carried a concealed revolver under the glamorous dresses she made for herself. After burying Jack (reputedly in a tin coffin full of liquor), she remarried—this time a man named Jim Kiskadden—and opened a millinery shop. The pair divorced in 1868, local gossips reporting Virginia's fierce temper as a main driver in the estrangement.[11]

If Virginia Slade highlights the possibilities for unconventionality and flamboyance in the mining camp environment, then the example of Harriet Sanders illustrates an equally potent tendency for frontier myth-making. Wife of Wilbur Fisk Sanders (founder member of the Montana Historical Society, vigilante, prosecutor, and territorial delegate), she arrived in Montana in 1863. Settling first in Bannack, the family moved to Virginia City soon after. Their residence was built a half mile out of town to keep the Sanders' sons away from the influence of dissolute miners. A few years later, once the town had become less riotous, log rollers were used to move the house closer. Sanders wrote a memoir of her life in the 1890s that placed heavy emphasis on reminiscences of the overland trail and early life in the mining camps. In focusing on this 1863–65 period, as historian Clyde Milner notes, she positioned herself as a "true pioneer," a label of some portent and one that communicated a sense of standing in the community, something especially important as Sanders assumed the presidency of the Montana Women's Suffrage Association. Meanwhile, the narrative disconnect between trailside diary and published autobiography implies that the past might be easily rewritten to fit a preferred "shared memory" of Euro-American settlers. As Milner points out, comments on "hostile Indians" had not been part of Sanders' personal experience as an emigrant, yet made it into her book as something "she and her fellow pioneers had told each other . . . for decades." This bending of individual testimony to fit the needs of collective memory usefully sheds light on Canary's telling of *Life and Adventures*, as well as the folk-loric landscape others constructed around her. Exchanged, assimilated, and recycled to suit the needs of the frontier community, tall tales could be deftly woven to create a patchwork useable past.[12]

Details of Martha Canary's movements through the late 1860s remain sketchy, but she seemingly left Virginia City in favor of a nomadic life, roving between what historian Richard Etulain calls the "half-formed and male dominated" settlements—mining camps, military forts and railroad stations—that became her lifelong natural habitat. *Life and Adventures* told readers that she went to Salt Lake City with her father in 1866, and, when he died, moved on to Fort Bridger, and then to Piedmont, Wyoming. Anecdotal accounts from the period place her in various locations: in Bannack, working in a brothel run by Madame Mustache, a moniker given to Eleanor Dumont due to the hair on her upper lip (1865); robbing a grocery store at Confederate Gulch, Montana, to buy supplies for sick miners (1866); as the ward of Major Gallagher, who took her under his wing at Fort Bridger and brought her to the town of Miner's Delight (1868); running freight teams for the Union Pacific on the Montana–Utah line (c.1868–69); working as a "prairie queen" in Kansas (1868–70); as saloon girl or prostitute at the stage stops near Cheyenne (1868–69); and residing at a boarding house in Piedmont (1871). This breathless inventory of supposed sightings attests to the pathologically itinerant lifestyle adopted by Canary, as well as to her installation as a person of interest in networks of frontier gossip. Importantly, her only documented appearance comes in an 1869 census for Carter (now Sweetwater) County, Wyoming, where she was listed as a 15-year-old resident of Piedmont, a Union Pacific stop that was used as a transit station for the provisioning of rail crews (and is now a ghost town). The Piedmont data offers only a fragmentary glimpse of Canary, but it does suggest a lonesome and somewhat precarious existence. Of the 90 residents in the transient settlement, 16 were female. Canary, who had arrived five months previously, was recorded as the only single woman.[13]

According to historian James McLaird, the documentary record of Martha Canary in these years was, to a great extent, erroneous and embellished, serving principally to dispel any "remaining doubts that Martha's *Life and Adventures* includes any reliable biographical information." *Calamity: The Many Lives of Calamity Jane* instead reads in the errata of the testimonial trail a useful mapping of the contours connecting Canary's lived and invented experience. A fuzzy narrative cartography, these scattered accounts (while questionable on precise factual content) convey an important sense of located-ness in situating Calamity Jane in a temporal and geographical space, namely Montana and Wyoming in the 1860s. Given her personal circumstances, the fact that she tried various ways to earn money seems a salient survival strategy. Multiple period witnesses suggested that Martha Canary was willing to turn her hand to various occupations in order to satisfy the basics of subsistence. John McClintock, resident of Deadwood in its early years, described her as a woman "ready to take hold of any kind of work." Also worth noting is that the male-dominated camps that Canary frequented were hotbeds of storytelling and exaggeration, where populations were transitory and identities uncorroborated. It is thus no surprise that evidence of her whereabouts is elusive—or, indeed, that she was the subject of so many yarns. Moreover, while the testimonial trail falls short of confirming the truths of a historical existence, it firmly substantiates her residency as a frontier celebrity in the making.[14]

In plotting the process by which Martha Canary became Calamity Jane, a number of folkloric threads are worth teasing out at this point. The various "versions" of Canary's life in this period are fragmentary, contradictory, and often sometimes downright absurd; yet all survived in collective memory. Afforded a starring role in the region's storied past, Canary served as a multipurpose frontier artefact. She was, in no particular order, an abandoned youth, charismatic renegade, dissolute woman, and authentic eyewitness to a landscape under dynamic transformation. Ben Arnold described her as a "picturesque character of the Old West" who ran away to the freighting camps after being "led astray by a ruffian miner" at Virginia City. Possessing a "constitution of iron" and being a "good teamster, a skillful roper, and a crack rifle shot," she seems even here to have channeled a sense of female masculinity in action, having qualities "admired by western men." Arnold labeled her a "strange mixture of the wild and the wayward, the generous and unselfish." He also noted that her rough-hewn quality made her appealingly authentic: "she never posed, her personality was her own."[15]

Needless to say, many chroniclers of Calamity Jane have written up her formative years through the lens of latter-day notoriety. Some have tried to locate her (often uncomfortably) in the usual categories of female stereotype. Others have pointed to youthful moments that augured a deviant path. In the Gallagher story, for instance, Martha Canary was presented as a "pretty and vivacious" young woman until she rebelled against her guardians to commit such "depraved escapades" that locals raised funds to banish her to the Union Pacific camp. "A stray from infancy," according to the *Cheyenne Daily Leader*, she was sent to reside with "the most degenerate railroad workers and other elements of the motley population." Reminiscences of childhood from Charles Andrews, meanwhile, placed Canary as a babysitter at Emma Alton's boarding house, where she provided a sneak preview of her later costuming, "dressed in a soldier's uniform at some party." According to Etulain, such tales projected the idea of Calamity Jane as a "modern day homeless waif" who invited the generosity of westerners, but whose unruly behavior often meant she was seen as a pariah. The most leftfield account of this type came from Hays City, Kansas, where Canary appeared as an attractive 20-year-old who demonstrated a little of her latter-day bravado in a riposte to a local man who asked her about her underwear, whereupon she "filled the air with shrill and slightly obscene rebukes for his bawdiness, and his sombrero with warning bullets."[16]

Light on accuracy and heavy on stage presence, the vast majority of these fanciful tales of Calamity illuminate a frontier celebrity in the making. Underneath the performance flourish, however, was the sense of Canary as a strong-willed young woman who lived hand to mouth and balked at the constraints of normative feminine behavior. As the *Lusk Herald* put it many years later:

> at the age of 18 she had run the scale of all human emotions, and her rough life had left its stamp indelibly upon her. At this age she could fill a can tossed in the air with lead bullets from her six-shooter and could flick a fly from the back of a mule with a sixteen-foot whiplash.[17]

Equally worthy of note was the fact that so many westerners chose to position her in *their* frontier stories. For many, it seemed, an encounter with Calamity Jane was a signal of being "part" of the pioneer community in its formative days. As her celebrity reputation was affirmed, so too was the frontier pedigree of the teller, thereby creating a powerful rite of association, and a potent and collective landscape of storytelling. Arnold, for instance, was keen to debunk Canary's scouting claims—inventions, he said, of those "who never knew her"—while at the same time championing his own intimate and authentic testimony containing "many stirring adventures." Fragments of manufacture and memory, scattered tales of Calamity Jane told of the germination of her folkloric identity as an enigmatic product of the West. Much of the work in revisionist historiography has sought to move away from stereotypes of the "gentle tamer or wild temptress" in favor of "seeing women as they really were." In the case of Calamity Jane, history, fable, and reminiscence meshed together, so as to make such extrications impossible. This should not, however, encourage us to leave her well alone. In fact, the combination of a transient existence, an unorthodox gender profile, and a chorus of competing cultural representations makes for a fascinating study in the cultural mapping of frontier mythology from frontier memory.[18]

CHAPTER TWO

"I NAME YOU CALAMITY JANE"
CROOK, CUSTER, AND CROSS-DRESSING IN
THE US CAVALRY (c.1870-76)

It was in the early 1870s that emphasis in the Calamity Jane story shifted to the US Army. *Life and Adventures of Calamity Jane, By Herself* (1896) contended that she joined General Custer at Fort Russell, Wyoming, in 1870 and journeyed with his entourage to Arizona, where she worked as a scout. Here, she described turning away from "the costume of my sex" to wear a cavalry uniform. According to Canary, "it was a bit awkward at first, but I soon got to be perfectly at home in men's clothes." Thereafter, military service took her to a string of forts across the West, including Sanders, Custer, Russell, and Laramie, from where she was deployed in various campaigns, including the Nez Perce (dated as 1872) and Black Hills (1875–76) expeditions. Ever present in the autobiographical imprint was the idea of adventure and excitement, now expressed in terms of "dangerous missions" against indigenous insurgents, the protection of miners, and the fearless delivery of military dispatches. Calamity Jane talked of swimming the Platte River in 1876 to bring vital intelligence from General Crook to Fort Fetterman, an exhausting 90-mile ride that saw her ambulanced for two weeks. Narrated as an all-action gallop across a western theater of conquest, Canary's memoir of life in the army made a seamless leap from her overland rite of passage into a soldierly world of homo-social fraternity. Most significantly, in the masculine culture of the US military, Calamity Jane seemed to find a degree of social communion and peer endorsement. "By this time I was considered the most reckless and daring rider and one of the best shots in the western country," she recalled.[1]

Confidently parading as a frontier heroine clothed in bravado and buckskin, "the female scout" presented a striking border character to match the likes of Buffalo Bill Cody, who made his fortune (and legend) procuring bison for the US Army and guiding hunting parties in the 1860s. Corroborative evidence of Martha Canary's illustrious military career, however, is hard to come by: Custer never fought in Arizona, the Nez Perce campaign was in 1877 (not 1872), and Canary's boast of protecting miners during the Newton–Jenney Expedition was erroneous. At no point in these years was she listed on the official army payroll as a scout for Crook. Instead, contemporary testimony placed her in various occupations: freighter, teamster, laundress, cook, barkeep, and all round "camp follower" (using the pseudonym "Frank Marden" to stow away with the military train). John Hunton described her as a "sporting" woman (by which he meant a prostitute) who never, as far as he could recollect, ever shot at an object, though he admitted seeing her "fire her pistol into space." She was not, as Bill Cody sternly asserted, a fellow pathfinder. Canary's lived experience in these years, nevertheless, was close enough to the general details of *Life and Adventures* to make her creative biography appear authentic. While Hunton derided Calamity Jane as "among the commonest of her class" and lampooned any claims to fame, he did admit her a certain theatrical quality. She was, he noted, "of the type generally given her by magazine writers and newspaper correspondents." In telling her story, Canary spoke of known figures, dates and places, thereby lending her testimony a patina of plausibility, forged from direct engagement with frontier geography. Tales told by others likewise provided corroborative evidence of her antics in camp and, most significantly, revealed that she was operating beyond the usual boundaries of feminine behavior. Cody agreed that she was a crack shot, "perfectly at home in wild country," and, while more of a "hanger on" than a formal scout, did serve as a kind of "mascot" that everyone was "glad to have . . . around." A raconteur with a tendency for unorthodoxy, Calamity Jane was certainly memorable and entered collective memory as a witness to extraordinary times. A colorful border character with stories to tell, she was ideally placed in a landscape of western conquest that was steadily being written up as American fable. Calamity Jane may not have been formally employed as an army scout, but in the performance landscape of the West, she played figurative guide with aplomb.[2]

JANE GETS HER NAME: THE CALAMITIES OF CALAMITY

Life and Adventures was absolutely right in locating her army years as formative ones for the construction of Calamity Jane as a frontier celebrity. It was particularly pertinent that the period in which she traveled with the military provided the occasion for her naming. As recited in her autobiography, the most popular version of how Canary came to be Calamity involved an incident at Goose Creek, Wyoming, in 1872–73, when a gutsy young woman dressed in soldier's clothes saved Captain Egan from ambush. In Canary's narrative, the officer was surprised by a Nez Perce raiding party (she says "Nursey Pursey") and was about to be thrown from his horse, when she rode back from her position in the advance of the train to save him. After carrying him to the safety of the nearest fort, he reputedly named her "Calamity Jane, the Heroine of the Plains." James Egan, it should be noted, denied all knowledge of this incident in later years, although his stations at Fort Sanders, Russell, and Laramie in the period 1868–76 located him in the right area. Egan's wife later contested the story, on the basis that a woman would lack the physical strength to perform such a feat. Canary, however, was tall by contemporary standards (just under six feet in her boots), was robust in stature (described by Jennewein as "long armed, big boned and muscular"), and had lived an outdoors life. As latter-day biographers have pointed out, the fact that Egan was a flamboyant character marked him out as someone with whom she would want to be "permanently linked" in the folkloric record. Such conclusions suggest an element of strategic maneuver to Canary's storytelling, and a sense of marketing savvy that inferred an element of celebrity construction at play.[3]

Muddying this narrative landscape of cultural representation and folkloric layering were alternative accounts of her christening. Questions as to the provenance of the Calamity Jane label at once raised suggestions of inauthenticity, subterfuge, and lack of mettle to her frontier heroism, potentially unseating her as a sham and "famesque" celebrity. At the same time, these competing claims also served to add a whiff of enigmatic presence to the Canary story. That she was mysterious, unfathomable, and unknowable added a puzzling element that, at the very least, ensured that people kept talking about her. In some of these stories, it was not Egan who was saved, but Antelope Frank, a western scout with whom Canary was working a trail. Others blamed journalists for her title (a plausible suggestion on the face of it, given their role in fanning the fires of fame in the latter 1870s, but rather undermined by the fact that the papers in question didn't yet exist). A further coterie of period witnesses, including George Hoshier, a pallbearer at Canary's funeral, submitted that her name related to a general tendency to attract trouble. "Calamity," he said, "followed her everywhere." Some claimed that she was named for her endeavors in tending to the sick in General Crook's command in 1876, while others related a tawdry tale of her being discovered swimming nude with a group of soldiers. Playing fast and loose with the finer points of historical dating, residents of Deadwood transplanted her "moment" of naming to when she played nursemaid to those in the town who had been stricken by the smallpox epidemic of 1878. Even Wild Bill Hickok weighed in on the question, claiming that he coined the phrase when she tipped him off about some poker-playing cowboys bent on revenge. Army surgeon Valentine McGillycuddy, an important early chronicler, took a more sanguine perspective, assuming that her name reflected her backstory as an orphan and overall "bad luck."[4]

What each of these narratives shared was the idea of someone who either invited or avoided calamity by her presence, suggesting a magnetic quality to Canary's persona that placed her as a critical actor in the frontier imaginary. In these contested tales of how Jane became Calamity lay the essential elements of a frontier celebrity written into textual weave: brash female scout, angel of mercy, unorthodox firebrand, and cross-dressing oddball. Canary, for her part, appeared to recognize the furor that surrounded her (as well as the gains to be had by cultivating a sensationalist persona), when she noted that her name came as a result "of all the trouble I always seemed to get mixed up in." Speaking to a journalist from the *Billings News*, she even claimed to have been minutes away from the Little Bighorn battlefield (other sources placed her as a cattle driver in Wyoming and in hospital with pneumonia at the time), thereby raising the specter of a counterfactual history, in which Calamity Jane swooped in as *scout ex machina* to either prevent or participate in the collective martyrdom of the Seventh Cavalry. As she put it: "I was with Custer for several months and in different engagements, but if I had been with him in his last battle, I would probably be with him now . . . On the other hand, had Custer paid attention to warnings and a message sent him he and his brave band might be now in the land that I am in." Playfully invoking her name as and when required (Aikman claimed she frequently announced herself when entering bars), the performance routine of Calamity Jane began to take shape. George Hoshier pointed out that she "got so much notoriety . . . partly because she was always doing some crazy thing, and partly because she wanted to be notorious." Aikman, likewise, saw star power embedded in the Calamity Jane brand, concluding that "Celebrity, flamboyance, notoriety would grow up around it even if she did not trouble to invent legends herself."[5]

Further complicating this "origin story" was the fact that there were *other* "Calamity Janes" operating in the West. Although we cannot be sure why these people were so named, a common thread seems to have been a sense that they were inhabiting a space of non-traditional gender expression. Quite possibly they were christened with specific reference to the original "heroine of the plains," based on being similarly prone to misadventure, excessive drinking, and fiery interpersonal relationships, or for their preference for nonconformist lifestyles. As the *Montana*

Standard commented in a 1941 editorial, "Every boom town had its Calamity Jane in Old Days," a title favored by western "trail blazers" to describe women of "picturesque profanity," who had an "originality" in dress code, or who were possessed of "a tall, angular form and a pair of cross eyes." One of the pretenders to the title—or, as the *Standard* called them, "pseudo Calamity Janes"—was Mattie Hamilton from Pueblo, Colorado, who narrowly escaped death in 1875 when her abusive husband George (who also acted as her pimp) aimed a pistol at her at close range. Another, Mattie Young from Denver, had a liking for liquor and died in a traffic accident while under the influence. As reported in the *Cheyenne Daily Leader* in August 1878, Young was a "well-known" presence in the town; the roots of her name were explained thus: "Calamity Jane, it is hardly necessary to say, is a nick name which was acquired during a somewhat eventful career by the calamity she wrought wherever she moved."[6]

The fact that Canary was in the habit of using pseudonyms and different surnames only added to the confusion. Under the title of Mrs. King, she found her way into the *Rock Springs Miner* as "one of the most widely known characters in this western country," and was known both for frequenting the Union Pacific camps in the "days of tents" and as a horse wrangler without parallel. For the Deadwood *Black Hills Daily Times*, the idea that other towns were trying to cultivate derivatives of "their" home-grown star provoked a sense of proud amusement, one editorial noting how "every one-horsed city in the country is claiming the veritable Calamity as a resident." This sentiment was also demonstrated in the reportage of the *Cheyenne Daily Leader*, which ventured that the "Calamity" killed in Denver was "*not* the Calamity Jane so extensively known in the Hills." It went on to describe Annie Filmore of Livingston, Montana—in the news after being beaten up by a male partner—as "Calamity Jane Number Two." Making merry with this apparent multiplication of "Calamities," the *Cheyenne Daily Sun* ran a short news story entitled "Where is Calamity Jane?":

A woman of that name died last summer in Denver. Now Calamity Jane is reported to have walloped two women in Sturgis City the other day. And on the same day her name is gazetted among the departures from Deadwood en route to Leadville.[7]

The report concluded that "Jane is evidently ubiquitous, as well as a tough case." For the Denver *Rocky Mountain News*, meanwhile, the "ill omen" attached to the "Calamity Jane" epithet connoted a string of historical figures suffering similar fates, from Jane Seymour to Jeanne de Valois. To further complicate the nomenclatural trail, it is worth noting the common use of "Calamity" throughout the West as slang for venereal disease. "Jane," meanwhile, was often used as a "catch-all" term for women.[8]

SCOUTING AND STORYTELLING: CALAMITY JANE ENTERS THE BLACK HILLS

The principal setting for the grand entrance of Calamity Jane, frontier celebrity, was the Black Hills—to the Lakota, a bountiful and sacred landscape that was catapulted to prominence in the history of westward conquest with the discovery of gold in 1874 by a survey expedition led by General Custer. The Hills had been given to the Lakota under the terms of the Fort Laramie Treaty (1868), and now prospectors flocked there in droves, causing tensions and fracturing the uneasy peace that existed between the US Army and plains nations. Martha Canary, in fact, was neither the first non-native nor the first white woman to set foot in the Hills (though the *Cheyenne Daily Leader* labeled her "the first woman who ever penetrated that reckless region"). Accompanying Custer's expedition party had been Sarah Campbell, an African-American woman from Kentucky who became known as "Aunt Sally." Campbell was born into slavery in 1823, but successfully contested her status in a legal case, citing "unlawful detainment." Through the 1830s, she worked on steamboats out of Missouri that catered for the fur trade, before marrying one of the workers. Widowed soon after, she migrated to Dakota Territory to run a club, serve as midwife, and operate a laundry. Appointed cook for Custer's Expedition in 1874, Campbell turned her hand to prospecting, and filed a mining claim as one of the founder members of the Custer Park Mining Company. A colorful example of female agency and the mechanics of frontier invention in the West, she played to visiting journalists eager to report moments of historical providence with the assertion: "I'se the first white woman as ever entered the Hills." In all likelihood a tongue in cheek remark, Campbell's comment usefully highlighted the complex hierarchies of race, community, and social acceptance in nineteenth-century America. William Curtis, embedded journalist with the Custer Expedition, labeled her "an old frontiersman," a phrase that alluded to the flexible boundaries of gender normativity for those seen as part of the "rough and ready" pioneer vanguard.[9]

Another woman seeking opportunity in the Black Hills (who also garnered fame as the first "white woman" in the country) was Annie Tallent. Born in New York in 1827, Tallent was a member of one of the illegal mining outfits entering the Black Hills in the grip of "gold fever." Setting off in August 1874 within a party led by John Gordon, the entourage included 26 people and two greyhounds, Dan and Fan. The group ran into difficulties when it became clear that Gordon did not know the country as well as he claimed. Luckily, the party was well armed, well provisioned, and in possession of a compass. In an indication that women as well as men bought into the western dream of adventuring across strange terrain, Tallent talked fondly of the "social hours spent around the smouldering [*sic*] camp-fire after our days' journeys were ended." On leaving "civilization," she was not tempted to turn back, although the daily trundle of wagoneering soon lost its novelty, to become "painfully realistic and prosaic." Like Canary, she spoke of treacherous river crossings, and made a point of criticizing the men for their macho approach to travel. In an exasperated tone, she complained "how prone some men are, when vested with a 'little brief authority,' to become arbitrary and domineering . . . it is enough to make the angels weep." Entering the Black Hills in December, the party made camp for the winter at French Creek, "wearied and worn," but with the presence of mind to build a stockade and cabins. The US Army arrived the following April to evict the prospectors, and Tallent was taken to Fort Laramie on the back of a mule. She later settled in Deadwood and Rapid City, becoming a key figure in the fledgling education system and first superintendent of schools in Pennington County, South Dakota. Her frontier memoir, published as *The Black Hills, or the Last Hunting Grounds of the Dakotahs* (1899), was notable for its anachronistic views of American Indians, though in the introduction it did acknowledge the habit of collective frontier memory to embellish the past in favor of "the glamour of romance."[10]

Following in the footsteps of Campbell and Tallent, Martha Jane Canary was an early contributor to the female frontier in the Black Hills, arriving in 1875 with the Newton–Jenney Expedition, and returning the year after with General Crook's 883-strong force sent to pacify the plains tribes. *Life and Adventures* talks in general terms of being part of a dispatch to protect emigrant miners (in fact, the Newton–Jenney Expedition was charged by the Office of Indian Affairs and the Department of War with making a scientific inventory of the region, especially its minerals, though some might well point to fecund links between exploration and empire), and outlines her work as a frontline scout for Crook during his mission to rendezvous with Custer, Miles, and Terry at the Bighorn. Conveying the narrative of a dynamic US Army in the action of defending its own, Canary's version of the historical threads of westward expansionism presented a salutary narrative that emphasized what historian Richard White has called an "inverted" view of conquest: triumphal, all-action, and morally unproblematic. Moreover, in presenting herself as part of this cadre, Canary effectively championed her credentials as an authentic pioneer and a heroine of the plains (as she said much later to a journalist: "Wa'n't nothin' here but a few miners, an' they wouldn't have been here if me an' the soldiers hadn't come an' took 'em away from the Injuns"). Much of what was claimed here bore the hallmarks of performance bluster. However, it is indeed true that when the Expedition snaked out of Fort Laramie for the Black Hills on 25 May 1875, under the command of Colonel Dodge, at the back of the train was a group of stowaway camp followers, including Martha Jane Canary.[11]

As the military caravan made its way across the plains, slowly a picture began to emerge of the curious woman among its number. Recorded by soldiers, freighters, and embedded journalists, these testimonials provide the first evidence of Canary's metamorphosis into a frontier celebrity. The first definitive mention of "Calamity Jane" came in an article in the *Chicago Tribune* of 19 June 1875, in which acting assistant surgeon and reporting journalist J.R. Lane talked about an unusual apparition at camp: a woman who had drawn the attention of military chatter during the Powder River campaign the previous year for her sartorial habits and her tendency to wander. One of the scouts had supposedly remarked: "it would be a great calamity if she should be captured and killed by the Indians." This comment at once presented the possibility of another "origin story" and implied that Canary had become a familiar fixture among the ranks. Lane said she was in the West because of "yielding to drink" and was subsisting at the social margins: a nomadic, occasional worker known for her unorthodox gender identity, who held down a job for a few months only to fall off the wagon. Lending pathos to the story, he added that once she was a "good looking woman" and a successful milliner in Omaha, Nebraska (again, further variations on her past). Turning to her presence in the Black Hills entourage, he wrote:

> is it at all strange, then, that CALAMITY JANE should be here. Calam is dressed in a suit of soldier's blue, and straddles a mule equal to any professional blacksnake swinger in the army. Calamity also jumps upon a trooper's horse and rides along in the ranks, and gives an officer a military [salute] with as much style as the First Corporal in a crack company. Calam is often taken for a trumpeter, or a bugler,

but Calamity isn't any such thing. For Calamity Jane, or rather Jane Canary, is a female.

Lane ended with a powerful point of inquiry: "Who says women cannot endure hardships equal to a man?" Although couched as a piece of playful rhetoric, the editorial posed salient questions about the capabilities of women to perform roles usually reserved for men, and firmly connected the historical and folkloric tracks of Canary and Calamity. Also significant was its citation of female masculinity as an essential marker of her personal and public identity.[12]

Camped at French Creek (at the site where Annie Tallent and her party had spent the previous winter), correspondent Thomas C. Macmillan penned an article for the *Chicago Inter Ocean* on 3 July 1875 that talked about a "strange creature" who had traveled with the train since Fort Laramie and seemed, in his estimation, to be a "real-life" version of Bret Harte's colorful heroine "Cherokee Sal" in *The Luck of Roaring Camp* (1869). Macmillan's reference illustrated the importance of the frontier imaginary in the minds of those encountering the West in the late nineteenth century. Sal, of course, had been the hapless lone female in Harte's mining-camp tale, described as "dissolute, abandoned, and irreclaimable," who died in childbirth, leaving her son, "Tommy Luck," to be raised by prospectors. This "Calamity," which is what, Macmillan noted, the "high latitude nomenclature" called her, was a young woman with a preference for wearing the uniform of "Uncle Sam's boys" and riding astride. Describing an apparently effortless residency within the masculine culture of the freighting teams, he pointed out that " 'Calamity' has the reputation of being a better horseback rider, mule and bull-whacker and a more unctuous coiner of English, and not the Queen's pure, either, than any man in the command." Just as Campbell had been labeled a "frontiersman" by her chronicler, so Canary, too, found herself included in the roll call of western masculinity.[13]

Corroborating the presence of Martha Canary at French Creek is photographic evidence: the earliest known visual record of her, and a valuable source for excavating Calamity Jane as a historical and theatrical subject (Plate 2). Taken by official expedition photographer A. Guerin in July 1875, it depicted her lounging on a rock, wearing a wide-brimmed hat, boots, rough trousers, and a neckerchief. The modish technology of photography was widely used as a device to create a documentary record in (and of) the West. The camera was utilized by survey and military teams to document their explorations, by settler communities eager to confirm their new western lives and identities, and by sport hunters who used it to ritually claim game trophies. As Martha Sandweiss puts it, a "new medium and a new place . . . came together" to fashion the West as the "most distinctive subject" of nineteenth-century American photography. Under the gaze of practitioners such as Timothy O'Sullivan, Frank Jay Haynes, and Laton Huffman (as well as lesser-known women photographers, including Sarah Ladd, Jane Gay, and Evelyn Cameron), the historical thrust of westward expansionism was committed to the collective memory in a process that preserved an imprint of moments "frozen in time," and communicated a panoramic frontier story that bore witness to the imaginative fancy of its producers, actors, and consumers. Enticingly real in its presentation, the visual rendering of Calamity Jane afforded a sense of corporeality, as well as physically locating her in the craggy setting of the western frontier. Entitled "Martha Canary (Calamity Jane), Black Hills, 1875," the impression given is one of eyewitness chronicle, raw and unmediated. At the same time, the photograph communicates a sense of its subject's emerging frontier celebrity, as well as her eye for staging and performance. Looking directly at the camera's eye, Canary sports a casual and assured countenance that is very different from the formal portraiture of period studio work and much more akin to the "landscapes and life" format which came to dominate the nineteenth-century photographic genre of male westerners at labor (cowboys, soldiers, farmers). At home in the Black Hills, and attired as a man, this inaugural image of Calamity Jane established her at ease in an expression of female masculinity.[14]

As the Expedition moved to inventory the Black Hills, testimony from the ranks fleshed out a sense of the developing profile of Calamity Jane. *McGillycuddy, Agent* (1941), which was compiled by the second wife of Valentine McGillycuddy, surgeon-surveyor, from his notes of the time, devoted an entire chapter to Calamity Jane that affirmed her status as a "child of the regiment," comic foil, hard worker, and entertainer. Harry Young, teamster and author of *Hard Knocks: A Life Story of the Vanishing West* (1915) labeled her a "pet of the fort" and (somewhat specifically) as "the great female character of Wyoming from 1875 to 1906." Both men reported her birth not in Princeton, but in Fort Laramie, born to a soldier named Dalton. Allegedly, Dalton took his young family to a ranch when he was discharged from duty, only to be killed during an attack by American Indians. Dalton's wife (who had been shot in the eye by an arrow) made a harrowing eight-day journey to deliver her daughter to the care of the fort, before dying. Thereafter, "Calamity" Jane Dalton became a ward of the military camp and was adopted by one of the other officers. Faithfully reproduced by early Canary biographers Estelline Bennett and Dora Du Fran, this story lived on in a process of narrative recycling that allowed for competing versions of Calamity Jane's past to survive well into the twentieth century.[15]

Ideas of gender masquerade and mobility featured prominently in these accounts. Young claimed that the youthful Calamity had been "enamored" with a Sergeant Shaw, who persuaded her to go on the Newton–Jenney Expedition and to dress as a man, adding "one not knowing her would never have taken her for a female." McGillycuddy spoke of his first encounter with a youth, roughly 16 years of age, wearing chaps, spurs, and a sombrero at the parade grounds just before the train left for the Black Hills. Drinking that evening with Colonel Dodge and his entourage, he was told "that was Calamity Jane, regimental mascot in spite of her name." Dodge's autobiography, interestingly, failed to mention her, though according to McGillycuddy, on the night in question, he described her as "a queer combination" of domestic aid (nurse, cook, laundress) and frontier firecracker, "crazy for adventure." Once on the trail, McGillycuddy argued, Calamity Jane became ever more emboldened (here the performance codes of a retrospective frontier story were clearly evident: writing a memory of a character made true to her "wild" self). Four days out of Laramie, the inevitable gender reveal took place, and was recounted by both memoirists in the manner of frontier farce. According to the story told by Young and McGillycuddy, Calamity Jane walked to the army store to buy cigars, only to encounter a group of officers. They vowed to keep her identity secret, but when she chose to deliver an ostentatious salute in "true soldierly style" before an officer in command, one A. von Luettwitz, the illusion was shattered. When Luettwitz returned salute, the men fell about laughing, and Calamity Jane was reported to Colonel Dodge as an interloper. Here, at the moment of banishment, she made a trickster move, turning her pony in behind the last wagons and ducking under the bars to re-join the rear of the train. According to McGillycuddy, this "ceremony was repeated daily, as she obeyed the order to leave camp, returned promptly and joined the day's march." In between times, Canary reputedly moved from camp to camp, sometimes hunting deer and antelope for the table, caring for sick soldiers, and mending clothes. "She was not quarrelsome," he noted, "and continued to be a valuable but unauthorized member of the wagon train." Young, likewise, saw Calamity Jane as a useful person to have around: entertaining the teamsters with japes and helping out with camp duties.[16]

In March 1876, General George Crook led two cavalry and ten infantry companies from Fort Fetterman, Wyoming, on a mission to forcibly remove "hostile" tribes from the Black Hills. As a response to the increasing incursions of white settlers, as well as mounting pressure from political and military circles for action against the so-called "Indian Problem," the US Government issued a decisive proclamation that mandated all tribes to return to their reservations or face martial consequences. Isaac Bard wrote in his journal that Canary (who had cultivated a nomadic existence after leaving the Newton–Jenney Expedition to frequent the road ranches and saloons from Cheyenne to Laramie) planned to join what became known as the Yellowstone and Bighorn Expedition. Illuminating the developing interest around her as a cross-dressing curiosity who seemed to invite mayhem, he noted: "Calamity Jane is here going up with the troops. I think there is trouble ahead." Evidence, too, of her status as a "mascot" for the US Army could be found in the rank-and-file chatter, where troops were apparently excited to hear that she was traveling with the train. Just as on her previous military outing to the Black Hills, the collective memory of the Yellowstone Expedition resonated with narrative encounters with "Calamity" at camp or on the road. Teamster Jesse Brown recalled pausing at a rest stop in Custer to see her driving a government mule team, "dressed in a buckskin suit with two Colts [*sic*] six shooters on a belt." Headed straight to the saloon, she "was soon made blind as a bat from looking through the bottom of a glass." In Brown's estimation, she was "the toughest looking human that I ever saw."[17]

By May 1876, Canary had left the military caravan. Sighted in Cheyenne, she was arrested under the pseudonym "Maggie Smith" on a charge of grand larceny (for stealing a woman's shirt, petticoat, stockings, hat, dress, and other sundries). After she had served three weeks in jail, a jury found her not guilty: testament to the affection with which she was held in local circles, as well as her convincing oratory. Lent a dress to wear in court by the wife of the deputy sheriff, she proceeded from her acquittal down Main Street to hit the saloons. The local press reveled in her antics, the *Cheyenne Daily Leader* reporting in "Jane's Jamboree" how she commandeered a horse and buggy after taking "frequent and liberal potations" that "completely befogged her not very clear brain." Stopping at Chugwater Ranch, 50 miles away, she imbibed more "bug juice," then headed on to Fort Laramie, a further 90 miles. The entry of Calamity Jane into the world of the press release was significant. In later years, reportage on her behavior was a staple of local newspapers, which delighted in her anarchic and easily sensationalized performance. Evidence of the vibrant threads that tied towns together in a network of regional hearsay and gossip, the Denver *Rocky Mountain News* reported on her trip in an editorial entitled " 'Calamity Jane': A long and lonely journey into the Indian Land—An unprotected female rivals Sheridan's ride." Noting her place among famous patriotic riders, including Paul Revere and Kit Carson, the paper talked of the "eccentric female resident" with a weakness for "strong drink" and "profanity." "In her case, however," the editorial related, "they are not unmixed evils; sometimes they compensate each other. One oftentimes delivers her from scrapes into which she has been precipitated by the other." Readily stoking the furnace of frontier celebrity, the *News* narrated Canary's frenzied saloon crawl, and situated her as an important subject of storytelling interest and sardonic refrain. The paper closed by noting that "it is not known" whether she met "hostile Indians," but, when asked by the correspondent, she replied in the affirmative, gesticulating "that a party of howling devils swooped down upon her and tried to capture her outfit, but she swore at them till they left." With mordant tone, the reporter noted: "The guileless Sioux [Lakota] were probably awed by her profanity, or, being exceedingly superstitious they may have taken Calamity Jane for Belzebub himself, in the disguise of a Cheyenne beer-jerker."[18]

Period witnesses had Calamity Jane re-joining Crook's military command in mid-June, just after the Battle of the Rosebud. Again, the testimonial trail is complicated both by chronological inconsistencies and biographical reminiscences compiled many years later. Significantly, it is here that the only record of her employment as a scout can be found. According to Frank Grouard, chief scout and interpreter for the second Yellowstone Expedition, Calamity Jane joined his crew in late summer 1876, after several men left their posts. Grouard's narrative, however, is shot through with inaccuracies in terms of timeline, and is contradicted by the accounts of others on the campaign. A contemporary account from Captain Anson Mills, meanwhile, points to Canary's scattergun navigations of gender concealment and performance, as well as the well-oiled mechanics of the army gossip network. In *My Story* (1918), Mills described Calamity Jane as "a national character . . . a woman of no mean ability and force even from the standard of men." One story was particularly instructive in revealing the army's response to finding a stowaway female "unintentionally employed" as a teamster on the trail to Reno. Leaping from a wagon to announce that she "knew" Mills as he walked by, gossip swiftly spread through camp as to the nature of the captain's liaison (the implication being that he "knew" her as a prostitute), whereupon Canary was arrested and "placed in improvised female attire under guard." Offering a rare (and documented) insight into the power dynamics and destabilizing sexual politics of a woman dressed in male clothing on the military train, Calamity Jane was shipped back to Fort Fetterman with the wounded, though not one of their number, as *Life and Adventures* claimed. Costume was vitally significant, both as a symbol of alternative gender expression and as something which, when removed, stripped Canary of her identity and power.[19]

The dubious provenance of Canary's scouting credentials, it seemed, was irrelevant. The fact was that Calamity Jane had become a subject for discussion and was being steadily written into the collective memory of the region. One of those complicit in this endeavor was Captain Jack Crawford, whose newspaper prose and poetry wove her into the literary fabric of the Black Hills (even signing his own writings "Calamity Jack"). Samuel Smith, speaking later of his time as a freighter in the 1870s, referenced the significance of Canary's dress code in defining her unorthodox reputation and communicated the sense of a frontier idol under construction. He remembered Calamity Jane as a freighter based near Fort Fetterman, known for her drinking, swearing, and chewing of tobacco. In his narrative landscape, "she always dressed in men's clothing when scouting," and otherwise "assumed this costume about half the time." John Bourke, in *On the Border with Crook* (1891), similarly described an individual with a reputation founded on mannish gesture and attire: "it was whispered that one of our teamsters was a woman, and, no other than 'Calamity Jane' . . . she had donned the raiment of the

alleged rougher sex, and was skinning mules with the best of them."
Depicted as "rough and burly as any of her messmates," Canary seemed
to successfully inhabit a homo-social world. Arriving in the West as a
young woman, but often passing as a man, she was at home in the fixings
of female masculinity and in her adoptive western geography. "It was not
an unusual thing for her to put on men's clothing, take three or four yoke
of oxen, go out into the woods alone, and stay several days, chopping and
hauling in wood from the mountains," he mused. Her emerging fame
also found articulation in the names given to regional landmarks by
military and prospecting parties. Crawford reported "Calamity Bar" as a
lucrative mining claim three miles from Custer, named after "a woman
who accompanied the soldiers," while "Calamity Peak" was the title given
to a mountain by McGillycuddy's survey (Plate 3), situated three miles
from French Creek and christened, according to *Andreas' Historical Atlas
of Dakota* (1884), "in honor of a sporting woman, familiarly known as
'Calamity Jane'."[20]

PASSING AS A MAN: CROSS-DRESSING AND GENDER POSSIBILITY

The military costuming of Calamity Jane was an essential part of her
origin story as "female scout," and an intrinsic part of her frontier celebrity. In turn, this located her as an important character in a wider landscape of nineteenth-century transgressive gender politics. In *Life and
Adventures*, Martha Canary talked about donning masculine attire,
feeling awkward at first, but then becoming entirely "at home." Comments
made at other times saw her appropriate a masculine identity as her own:
"Yes, I was a regular man in them days. I knew every creek an' holler
from the Missouri to the Pacific." Canary's juxtaposition of a male character type with freedom of movement and an expert knowledge of
western geography was important. Not only did it assert her claim to be
a frontiersman of the heroic archetype, but it also pointed to the ways in
which dressing as a man allowed latitudes otherwise impossible for a
woman in those years. While the traditional story of westward move-

ment championed men in valiant garb and sidelined women as absent or supporting players, histories of "passing" women serve to illustrate the diversity of experience on the female frontier, and point to important renegotiations of the gender binary at play. By masquerading as men, women were able to hold jobs, vote, go to war, and travel without the threat of sexual intimidation: using costume as a tactic to claim economic opportunities and articulate a freer sense of individual agency. The world of military service, in fact, boasted a distinguished tradition of cloaked women (recruits to Nelson's navy and famous privateers such as Mary (Mark) Read and Anne Bonny; or Mary Galloway and Jennie Hodgers (Albert Cashier), two of more than 400 women who fought as men in the American Civil War) whose motives were various: patriotism, adventure, revenge, financial gain, or love.[21]

Threaded with patriarchal motifs of autonomy and authority, the adoption of male costume was (either consciously or unconsciously) a political statement. Demonstrating a clear understanding of the politics of dress, Cora Anderson (who passed as Ralph Kerwineo in Milwaukee at the turn of the twentieth century) explained her decision to adopt male clothing in terms of a conscious desire to enjoy benefits claimed exclusively by "the privileged sex." When arrested in 1914 for disorderly conduct, Anderson adopted an activist tone: "Do you blame me for wanting to be a man, free to live life in a man-made world?" Such assertions suggested a tension between keeping one's identity secret in order to claim rights and privileges, and using a sartorial reveal as a platform for a gesture politics that disrupted cultural hierarchies to show women prospering in masculine realms. Certainly, the liberties gained by presenting as a man were not lost on prominent female rights campaigners. Costume brought the possibility of renegotiating gender opportunities, as well as demonstrating the convictions of a "new woman." As campaigner Elizabeth Cady Stanton posited in the suffrage newspaper *The Revolution* (1869), the "true idea" was for "the sexes to dress as nearly alike as possible." Men's clothing, she noted, offered three benefits: convenience, equality, and security.

Masculine masquerade was, therefore, both sensible recourse and political necessity. "If," she stated, "by concealing our sex we find that we, too, can roam up and down the earth in safety, we shall keep our womanhood a profound secret" until such a day when "we shall dress as we please." Others pointed to the entrenched networks of clothing and power that stitched women's rights and sartorial choices firmly together. As one delegate to the National Women's Rights Convention (1850) put it: "What are the proper kinds of clothes for a free woman to fold about her limbs? . . . Does a man owe nothing to his hat, his coat, his pantaloons, his boots? Can a female be considered as equal to a male until she has won the right to wear his garb?" Such extrapolations illuminated a nineteenth-century landscape in which clothing choice was deeply politicized.[22]

The West was particularly interesting terrain in this story of costuming and cross-dressing. A place of escapes, new starts, rapid economic and social change, and loosened cultural conventions, the trans-Mississippi landscape offered fertile ground for those wishing to assume a different persona and a narrative disguise. "One Eyed Charley" (Charlotte Parkhurst) took to dressing as a boy when orphaned in Vermont, came to the California Gold Rush in 1849, worked as a stagecoach driver, voted in the presidential election of 1868, and became well known as a "famous coachman, the fearless fighter, the industrious farmer and expert woodman." His "thirty years in disguise" (as the *New York Times* put it) was only discovered when locals began preparing Charley's body for burial in 1879. Charley's case, as it turns out, was less unusual than one might think. As historian Peter Boag writes in *Re-dressing America's Frontier Past* (2011), cross-dressers were not "simply ubiquitous, but were very much a part of daily life on the frontier." In 1878, the *Central City Weekly Register* proclaimed that a "mania for females to appear in male attire has struck . . . the state in a bad way." Concealed in some of the most famous period narratives, in fact, were stories of passing. Horace Greeley (to whom is popularly attributed the phrase "Go West Young Man") recounted a pleasant conversation with a young male prospector leaving the goldfields on the Pikes Peak Express (1859) who, the conductor later told him, was a woman.[23]

Women elected to adopt the guise of men for various reasons. Albert Richardson, writing of his travels in the Colorado mines in the late 1850s, attested to the fact that passing was often undertaken out of economic necessity, or with ideas of exploration or adventure in mind (all with their own storytelling possibilities): "I encountered in the diggings several women dressed in masculine apparel, and each telling some romantic story of her past life." Adding that, "Some were adventurers; all were of the wretched class against which society shuts its iron doors," Richardson highlighted the common assumptions of passing women as desperate or deviant for their rejection of the traditional female frontier. Cross-dressing, indeed, often went hand in hand with an itinerant lifestyle (what Boag calls "hoboing"). Often colorfully extrapolated on in popular literature, some women took to masculine garb for the purposes of subterfuge and revenge, to seek out errant lovers or (often) to escape from abusive relationships. In other cases, criminal activity was a driver. Broncho Liz (*sic*) disguised herself as a man to flee from the law after murdering her husband, Charles Skeels, in Coeur d'Alene in March 1889; while Jennie Stephens donned male attire to lead a gang of bandits in 1890s Oklahoma. Providing firm evidence of the connections between frontier celebrity and mannish masquerade, Pearl Hart gained an illustrious reputation, later laid out in dime novels, for her habit of dressing as a man to hold up stagecoaches (fame as a "girl bandit" nonetheless had its pitfalls, not least in terms of evading capture). Important in all this, of course, was performance code: a successful presentation as a "man of the West" was contingent on mastering a range of masculine gestures and activities. A woman who passed as "Bill" in Missouri and worked as a laborer thus "drank, swore, flirted with women, fished, camped and even chewed tobacco." Particularly intriguing in terms of the theatrics of cross-dressing was the community of prostitutes in Williams Creek, Cariboo, California, who dressed as men to "swagger through the saloons and mining camps with cigars or huge quids of tobacco in their mouths, cursing and swearing." Sporting Bowie knives and revolvers, and in the habit of card playing and whiskey drinking, they performed a hyper-masculine role-play in the act of promoting their sexual services.[24]

While the first tranche of western women's histories was keen to find proto-feminists hiding in every gulch (a necessary counterpoint to what Susan Johnson calls the traditional "western-history-as-usual" paradigm that traded almost exclusively in heroic white men), recent work in gender and queer studies points to a need for further interrogation of the frontier gender binary. Inhabiting a world of gender masquerade was not always about safe travel, employment or a cloaked opportunity for female empowerment. As Peter Boag notes, passing was sometimes a consciously performed choice to present according to a lesbian or transgender identity. San Francisco, in particular, became a center of alternative lifestyles a full century before Haight-Ashbury made it famous for "flower power" counterculture. Documented by the "She Even Chewed Tobacco" Project in the 1980s, the city boasted a subculture of passing women with vivid histories of diverse gender expression and same-sex desire. Jeanne Bonnet, whose story made headlines as a salacious tale of fraud, violence, and passion, was born in Paris in 1849 and came to the city as part of a theater troupe. After spending time in a reformatory for theft, she ran a crime ring of young male thieves, before graduating to an all-women gang, the members of which she recruited from brothels. A colorful figure, Bonnet was shot in the bedroom of a San Miguel saloon in 1876, while waiting for her lover, Blanche Buneau. Newspapers reviled her as a "man-hater" with "short cropped hair, an unwomanly voice, and a masculine face," and complained of her "nonsensical notoriety" for dressing in man's clothes. Despite its social latitudes, the West was not entirely out of step with the rest of the country in championing sartorial and sexual orthodoxy.[25]

Press sensationalism surrounding the Bonnet case attested to popular interest in those who passed as men, especially when it promised the frisson of a true-life dime novel tale of spurned lovers and gunplay. Such stories depicted the riotous days of the frontier in all its glory. Passing women were categorized as bold, eccentric, aberrant, or dangerous: vibrant symbols of the "wild and woolly" West. Cross-dressing celebrity, however, was not the same thing as social acceptance. While sometimes playful and triumphant, media interest was also fickle and judgmental: an emerging celebrity culture in which the infamous and the "famesque" were gossiped over and gawked at, celebrated, and condemned. Emerging pseudo-scientific treatises from sexologists and psychologists, meanwhile, constrained opportunities for gender unorthodoxy by demanding "normalization" as a critical component of societal development. Cross-dressing, they contended, had no place in a civilized, post-frontier West, where womanly dress and lifestyle served as a barometer of progress. Accordingly, by the end of the nineteenth century, a raft of legislative measures had been passed that wrote gender conformity into civic code. Keen to impose visions of respectability, decency, and prosperity on developing western centers, some 45 cities passed laws against cross-dressing in the period 1848–1914. Statutes from the San Francisco Board of Supervisors (1863, 1866, 1875) resulted in more than a hundred arrests in the years to 1900, while in Denver a new statute against lewd behavior in 1875 banned anyone appearing "in any public place within this city in a state of nudity, or in a dress not belonging to his or her sex." Being caught subverting this "moral" regulation meant a fine of between ten and a hundred dollars. Other cities introduced fines, jail sentences, psychiatric admissions, and deportations.[26]

The story of Babe Bean, arrested for cross-dressing in Stockton, California (1897), illustrates the dynamics of salacious interest and moral propriety in shaping cultural attitudes towards those whom contemporary psychologists termed "sexual inverts" (a blanket term that captured homosexuals, cross-dressers, and transgender individuals). "Telling all" in a biographical exposé printed in the local newspaper, Bean explained how she was of a good family, had been sent to a convent because of her "rough ways," and rendered mute in an accident. Aged just 15, Bean escaped by marrying her brother's best friend (and promptly securing a divorce), before assuming an itinerant lifestyle. Passing as a man by the name of Jack Garland, Bean sought the "liberty the world sees fit to allow a boy . . . [for] as a man I can travel freely, feel protected and find work." Finding a houseboat on McLeod Lake, Garland settled into a local community, which, once the grand masquerade was revealed, warmed to her traumatic story and endearing personality. Careful (and theatrical) in her navigation of legal acceptability, Bean freely admitted to being a woman, but noted a preference for dressing as a man. In this, there was no attempt at deception. Inducted into the local bachelors' fraternity and working as a press writer, she earned a local following based on "affectionate curiosity." On one occasion, however, the "Girls of Stockton" balked at Bean's status as sartorial exception, writing to the local paper that, "if the rest of us wanted to walk out in that kind of costume for a change, we would be arrested quicker than quick." This incident indicated a broader questioning of costume and gender rules among western women, and hinted at the importance of charisma and performative flourish in the stretching of legal ordinances. Garland riposted with an invitation to all to find agency in clothing choice: "It is your privilege to dress as you see fit, whether it is after the fashion of Venus, or after the fashion of Babe Bean." In subsequent years, the shifting contours of tolerance and reprimand saw the so-called "Trousered Puzzle" write up a biography in the Stockton *Evening Mail* and, after a stint in the Spanish–American War, work as a journalist for the *San Francisco Sunday Examiner*. Garland was forcibly admitted to a psychiatric hospital in 1917 for refusing to adopt hetero-normative clothing, before working as a male nurse and social worker in San Francisco. When Garland died in 1936, a further secret was revealed: Bean had been born Elvira Virginia Mugarrieta, daughter of the Mexican consul and granddaughter of a Louisiana Supreme Court justice.[27]

Tales of Babe Bean and Jeanne Bonnet pointed to complex social renegotiations at work in frontier culture. Read in terms of gender possibility, the nineteenth-century West was a landscape of flux, reinvention, and what Susan Johnson usefully defines as "a place of disrupted gender relations." The case of Calamity Jane usefully informs this story of alternative gender expression, as well as cementing the importance of the frontier as a rhetorical stage for living out fresh identities. How we might read the experience of Martha Canary within this re-dressed history is nonetheless complicated—not least by the repressive sexual politics of the age and by Canary's lack of discussion of such matters.[28]

On one level, Calamity Jane's choice of manly gestures and military vestments was pragmatic, a logical extension of the mentality that saw women on the overland trails discard petticoats and side saddles, and a necessary recourse for those wishing to travel alone without fear of sexual harassment. Bourke noted that Canary's ways were "eccentric and wayward rather than bad," and that she had "adopted male attire more to aid her in getting a living than for any improper purpose." George Hoshier suggested that she adopted men's garb "because it was easier for her to ride and also made the trip a little safer for her." Camp followers, it was widely known, took to wearing army uniform as a way of ensuring clandestine passage. Equally, it is entirely plausible to see Canary's behavior as (at least in part) political in design. Her travels in the early 1870s attested to the freedom of movement afforded by the sartorial threads of masculinity. According to Hoshier, Canary wanted to go freely to the Hills, and the wearing of male attire allowed her full rein. Though hard to place explicitly in an activist vein, Calamity Jane did speak to questions of female empowerment by her actions (i.e., in showing the capabilities of a woman in successfully fielding "man's work"), and even made occasional orations to that effect. Speaking to Horace Maguire, who faithfully reproduced the conversation in *The Coming Empire* (1878), she "protestingly" queried: "Hasn't a poor woman as good a right to make a living as a man?"[29]

Digging deeper into the story of Calamity Jane's unconventional identity and masculine costuming, meanwhile, reveals further contours of gender possibility. In *Life and Adventures*, Calamity Jane talked of a tomboyish upbringing, her liking for boisterous pastimes, and comfort with the homo-social culture of the trans-Mississippi. For Lou Sullivan, a biographer of Jack Garland, such articulations suggested not a "dissatisfaction with the way society expected women to dress," but an unorthodox gender identity: the wish to live as "a man among men." Significantly, in passing from Canary to Calamity, Martha Jane took on masculine fixings to inhabit an environment in which she felt (in her own words) naturally situated. At this point, it is helpful to recall Judith Butler's categorization of gender as an unstable classifier dictated by action: what one *does* rather than what one *is*. This notion of a cultural identity secured by repetitive performance is particularly intriguing when we consider the tangled layers of Canary's lived and invented experience, as well as the fact that gender identity is inevitably cloaked in masquerade because, as Butler puts it, it "involves impersonating an ideal that nobody actually inhabits."[30]

Central to Calamity Jane's emerging reputation as a "female scout" was a performance swagger founded on female masculinity, the term coined by Jack Halberstam to describe a subversive masculinity appropriated by women. Canary herself spoke of a transformative process as she became "perfectly at home in men's clothes," while period testimony spoke of (often with a prurient or pejorative gaze) her "mannish" appearance and ways. Contemporary narratives routinely referenced her as a "woman-man" or a "man-woman," suggesting at once a radical challenge to the frontier binary, as well as popular interest in pondering the mysteries of gender fluidity. According to Agnes Spring (born in 1894), librarian and state historian for Wyoming and president of the Colorado Historical Society, she was frequently seen in Cheyenne, where "she used to dress in men's clothing and often got by as a man." In trying to make sense of Canary's cross-dressing behavior, Richard Etulain sees a firmly hetero-normative heroine, whose theatrics obscured her ultimate aspirations for a traditional pioneer life as wife and mother. *Calamity: The Many*

Lives of Calamity Jane suggests, instead, a more complicated picture that at least invites alternative readings.[31]

An unconventional, itinerant woman, Calamity Jane not only made her way in a patriarchal world, but also found her place through spoken and sartorial demonstrations of gender unorthodoxy. This performance was an act (in the sense of being instrumental to her celebrity persona), but might equally be viewed as an act of self-expression. Indeed, cultural representations of her through the 1870s focused overwhelmingly on her masculine traits and dress code as an intrinsic part of who she was. In her afterlife, too, successive commentators wrestled with Calamity Jane as a "female scout" who conjured various heretical prospects. Writing in *Frontier Magazine* (1925), Francis Hilton concluded she was "one of the thousands of women whose misfortune it was not to have been born a man," remarking on her "complete metamorphosis" in the army years to embrace a masculinized identity. Standing before the Chicago Corral of the Westerners in 1945, Clarence Paine offered a clunky analysis of her as "Man, Woman . . . or Both?," while more recent works have presented Canary in a sympathetic light and within an activist frame of reference. For Linda Jucovy, the young Calamity Jane was both inspirational and demonstrative in her gender nonconformity, struggling to be "a woman being a man, and . . . not sure how to be." Playwright Carolyn Gage sees Canary's cross-dressing inclinations as evidence not only of a desire to claim the privileges of a male vantage, but also of the natural inclinations of "a butch woman who had the misfortune to be born in an era before lesbian culture." Hence, while Calamity Jane did not address such questions directly, her vivid performance of female masculinity communicated a powerful message of alternative gender expression and complex social identities. Canary habitually situated herself as being "a regular man," while at the same time orating her defiant sartorial choices as a rejection of the costume of her sex. Performing masculinity with a frontier flourish, she offered a sophisticated take on modern understandings of gender identification as fluid and negotiable.[32]

CHAPTER THREE

"CALAMITY JANE HAS ARRIVED!"
FROM DEADWOOD TO DIME NOVEL (1876-95)

With credentials such as "Calamity Jane, female scout" safely tucked under her (buckskin) belt, *Life and Adventures of Calamity Jane, By Herself* (1896) moved out of the martial terrain of the Black Hills to its next site of frontier celebrity: Deadwood. Sporting a keen eye for theatrics, Canary began by narrating the famous wagon ride into the city from Fort Laramie in June 1876, before detailing her subsequent work as a Pony Express rider. The 50-mile route from Custer to Deadwood was not only "one of the roughest trails in the Black Hills country," but also "the most dangerous," thanks to bandits who regularly held up the mail and extorted money from travelers. Calamity Jane, by her account, had little trouble on the route. Safe passage was assured by equestrian skills, well-known abilities as a "quick shot," and an all-round reputation as a "good fellow" (each markers of her successful navigations of frontier masculinity). Continuing the themes of mobility and freedom which had run through her earlier storied years, the period from the late 1870s until the mid-1890s was defined by a sense of mobility: a whistle-stop listing of residencies and vocations and an overall sense of restlessness befitting a "heroine of the plains" who couldn't quite relax in a frontier world steadily moving from conquest to consolidation. The first year, she noted, was spent around Deadwood, riding an expansive territory to frequent various mining camps (while still holding her mail delivery every two days), and returning to town in time to capture Wild Bill Hickok's killer, Jack McCall, at a local butcher's shop in August 1876 (she reputedly threatened him with a meat cleaver), and secure the rescue of the overland stage the following spring. The fall of 1877 brought a return to service with the Seventh Cavalry, before a temporary return to the life of a prospector the following year. Calamity saw out the decade in Fort Pierre as a freighter. In the early 1880s, Canary said, she ranched cattle and ran an inn in Yellowstone County, before making an extended trek across the trans-Mississippi landscape to tour California, Texas, and Arizona. After a life spent roaming, she mused, "it was about time to take a partner for the rest of my days," and so she married Texan Clinton Burke (1885), giving birth to their daughter two years later. This "quiet home life," she said, lasted until 1889, when more nomadic wanderings through old haunts in Wyoming and Dakota carried Martha Canary through to the mid-1890s.[1]

Focusing on this 20-year period, this chapter explores Canary's life and adventures to highlight the ways in which lived and invented experience conspired. The emerging picture is of a complex character—troubled, energetic, vulnerable, and restive—who grappled with the contested terrains of gender orthodoxy and opportunity in the West. Evident, too, are the powerful threads of storytelling and narrative pathways through which communities "became western," alongside the nuts-and-bolts socio-economics of frontier assimilation. Usefully bookmarked between Canary's famous ride from Fort Laramie to Deadwood in June 1876 and her triumphal return to the "magic city" of the Black Hills 19 years later, these years saw Martha Canary catapulted from object of local hearsay to national fixture of the frontier imaginary. Here, in the dusty confines of Deadwood and its western hinterland, the iconic persona of "Calamity Jane, heroine of the plains" was comprehensively played out. Period oratory (often critical in tone) ruminated on Canary's everyday existence as a poverty-bound drifter who struggled with a drink problem. Looming much larger, however, was regional chatter that championed her as a buck-skin-clad bull-whacker, party animal, and redoubtable frontier eyewitness. This heroic persona, cultivated by Canary and others, used gesture (manly swagger and repertoire), props (firearms and firewater), and worthy associations (with people and places) to establish a patina of credibility. That much of this "famesque" mantle was fabricated suggests that truth was a less important ingredient than convincing performance in creating a popular idol. For newspapers, literature, and dime novels, there was much to chew over in the intriguing gender possibilities of the "female scout." Cast in the role of authentic and unorthodox frontier celebrity, various constituencies saw fit to invest in the folkloric capital of Calamity Jane.[2]

DEADWOOD: COMMUNITY AND CELEBRITY IN A FRONTIER TOWN

It is pertinent that this story of threaded history and hearsay started with a grand entrance. Here, in the rough-hewn town that was busily taking shape in the Black Hills, the stage was set for the meteoric rise of Calamity Jane. Fueled by news of mineral strikes, Deadwood had been established as an illegal encampment on Lakota land, and grew swiftly to accommodate 5,000 gold seekers (Plate 5). Talking of the city's reputation for lawlessness, the *Laramie Daily Sentinel* pointed out that it "does not present a very inviting appearance. The street is nothing but mud ... about one half of the business houses in the town are liquor stores, saloons and gambling houses." True to her reputation for being in the right place at the right time, Martha Canary rode into the fledgling settlement after her release from Fort Laramie in summer 1876 as part of a wagon train that included Charlie Utter (a trapper and prospector known by the moniker Colorado Charlie) and Eleanor Dumont (gambler and brothel owner popularly known as Madame Mustache), both of whom played formative roles in Deadwood during its inaugural years. Particularly significant was the throwing together of Calamity Jane with gunslinger, gambler, and western hero Wild Bill Hickok, an encounter that allowed Canary to effectively ride shotgun on his already ascendant frontier celebrity.[3]

Born in 1837 in LaSalle County, Illinois, Hickok journeyed west, aged 18, after a fight with Charles Hudson, whom he assumed he had killed, after both fell into a canal. At Leavenworth, he joined the Jayhawkers, a partisan vigilante group fighting for the Union, and met a youthful Bill Cody, about to embark on his scouting career for the US Army (the West, despite its spacious confines, witnessed an uncanny ability for having its rising stars just "happen" upon one another). Still in Kansas, and working as a wagon freighter, Hickok was involved in a fracas at the Rock Creek stage station in 1861 with David McCanles, an alleged gang member, who was trying to buy land. In the stories that soon swirled around the incident, it was maintained that Hickok shot McCanles from behind a curtain, though corroborating evidence was scant. Much like Martha Canary, Hickok cultivated a striking presence as a frontier hero with an imprecise historical pedigree. In the Civil War, he was variously spotted as a teamster, scout, and spy for the Union Army, before making a living as a professional gambler. Along the way, he acquired a reputation as a sharpshooter (engaging in at least one duel, with Davis Tutt in Springfield Square in 1865) and (in the way of things) this segued into a career as lawman, deputy marshal, showman, and scout for Custer's Seventh Cavalry. Capitalizing on a growth industry in frontier entertainment—which would only grow more capacious as the century played out—Hickok took six American Indians to Niagara in 1865 as part of a theatrical review entitled "The Daring Buffalo Chasers of the Plains," before making his way back west when financial disaster ensued. He became marshal and sheriff in Kansas City in 1869, and Abilene in 1871.[4]

Hickok's ascendancy to frontier stardom came from a colorful personal story that was vividly expressed in period media. In *Harper's New Monthly Magazine* for February 1867, George Ward Nichols had him single-handedly kill the nine desperadoes known as the McCanles Gang in a rip-roaring, gun-smoked showdown. A lawman known for his gun skills, Hickok proved ideal fare for the emerging dime novel market, making his entrance in *Wild Bill, The Indian Slayer* (1867), and played himself in the stage play *Scouts of the Plains* with Cody in 1873. Prior to his triumphant entry into Deadwood in summer 1876, he married circus owner Agnes

Lake (another keen demonstration of his connection to the world of entertainment) and set off for the goldfields with Charlie Utter, hoping to secure his fortune. Having been diagnosed with glaucoma in Abilene, Hickok had to content himself with talking about his life as a sharpshooting lawman, instead of serving as one. As the *Cheyenne Daily Leader* saw it, Hickok's time was gainfully occupied "stuffing newcomers and tenderfeet of all description with tales of his prowess and his wonderful discoveries of diamond caves, etc., which he describes as being located 'up north'."[5]

Hickok and his party reputedly encountered Calamity Jane at Fort Laramie, where one of the officers pleaded with them to take her to the Black Hills. According to Joseph "White Eye" Anderson, Canary had been carousing with soldiers, had got drunk on a recent pay packet, and was sobering up, near naked, in the guard house. Steve Utter, Charlie's brother, accepted. Once she was furnished with some clothes from the officer and members of the group, including a broad-brimmed hat and buckskin outer garments, Anderson thought she scrubbed up pretty well. Over the next fortnight, the motley band of prospectors, drifters, and camp followers made their way to the Hills, their journey (or more accurately, social interactions) dutifully recorded in Anderson's memoir. Calamity Jane appeared here as a young woman (he put her at 25), with keen skills as a muleskinner and teamster. Her abilities to wield a rope and a rifle were noted, as was her penchant for profanity. Anderson recalled one occasion when she shot a coyote with a pistol from a distance of a hundred yards (a feat described as "masculine"), and she was said to be useful in helping prepare camp meals. A "big-hearted woman," she was particularly visible at the close of the day, drawing an audience around the fire and telling "some of the toughest stories I ever heard." Anderson's account suggested that the essential ingredients of her famous identity (a drinking, buckskin-wearing, pistol-packing female masculinity) were all in place as the party approached Deadwood. Significantly, in recounting his memoirs, he felt it important to situate his own story within Calamity Jane's developing folkloric landscape.[6]

Their arrival in Deadwood was in true theatrical style: Hickok and his entourage paraded through the town, a signal of the performativity of the aspiring frontier celebrity, as well as the functionality of western terrain as a grand stage for the conscious exercise of heroic identities. Richard Hughes, local newspaper editor, noted that Hickok, the Utter brothers, "Bloody Dick" Seymour, and Martha Canary "rode the entire length of Main Street, mounted on good horses and clad in complete suits of buckskin, each suit of which carried sufficient fringe to make a considerable buckskin rope." The Deadwood *Black Hills Pioneer* saw a good story brewing, and eagerly vociferated "Calamity Jane has arrived!"—seemingly elevating her above other members of the party in a roll call of the frontier "famesque." Accordingly, while many commentators have alluded to the benefit Canary derived from hitching her celebrity to Hickok's folkloric wagon, it is also possible to make the reverse argument. Calamity Jane carried a certain cachet, a nonconformist glitz that meant that Hickok might well have seen the added value in having her around as sidekick. According to contemporary Charles Bocker:

> It stood Bill in good stead to "stand in" with her and share her earnings. Deadwood at this time was wide open—there was no law except the law of the six shooter, the law of gamblers, miners and prostitutes who took the law in their own hands.[7]

Such comment was interesting, not least for the fact that it suggested the performance appeal of gender unorthodoxy, as well as the media-savvy nature of those seeking to cultivate a heroic reputation. As historian James McLaird points out, by the mid-1870s "Calamity Jane" was "more attractive a personality than critics suggest."[8]

At this point, period testimony reveals a blatant collision between the autobiographical terrain of *Life and Adventures* and eyewitness accounts of how Canary made a living during her residency. In assembling her own history years later, of course, it was hardly a surprise that she chose to skirt over her working days in the dance hall. Society was enthralled by the idea of the "wild woman" who transcended normal rules, but chasing American Indians and delivering mail was wholesome heresy. Talking about making ends meet by working in a bar or brothel carried not the luster of western legend, but a sense of grim frontier reality, with the added gamut of moral indignation. Standing pre-eminent in the flamboyant landscape of Deadwood's dancing halls was the Gem, established by entrepreneur and opportunist Al Swearingen when he arrived in the town in May 1876. It was here, reputedly, that Canary plied her trade as saloon girl and prostitute, along with Kitty Arnold (who traveled with Hickok's party and had, according to period accounts, also taken to wearing "the regular buckskin suit, trousers and all"), and Al Swearingen's wife. Joseph Anderson recalled that, soon after their arrival in the town, Canary borrowed money from the party to buy feminine clothes and pay for a bath. "I can't do business in these old buckskins," she remarked, "I ain't got the show the other girls have." A few days later, she showed up at their camp, "pulled up her dress, rolled down her stocking and took out a roll of greenbacks." For many single women traveling to the West, saloon and sex work indeed proved a common recourse. Most prostitutes on the frontier were under 30, illiterate, and traveling alone. Often, they were runaways, orphans or widows, refugees, or individuals escaping from dysfunctional or abusive relationships. Meanwhile, the fact that a young man dressed as a woman and working at the Gem proved every bit as effective in parting men from their coin as his female peers gave a hint as to the fluid gender boundaries of frontier space. Further complicating this landscape of sexual ambiguity, barkeep Harry Young (who remembered Martha Canary from the Jenney Expedition) described her as a "thoroughly masculine" individual, who danced with the dance-hall girls as readily as the customers.[9]

Harry Young further contended that Calamity Jane roved the plains as a recruiting sergeant for the Gem. For young women living hand to mouth in the forbidding landscapes of the high prairie, the dance hall offered a veneer of glamor and a wage packet higher than other domestic work (and, in fact, the average monthly salary of a cowboy). Meanwhile, for those in possession of entrepreneurial acumen, or with financial collateral to their name, the sex industry held out the prospect of a lucrative career. A migrant from Liverpool, Amy Helen Dorothy Bolshaw (later known as Dora Du Fran) came to the United States with her parents in the 1860s, living first in New Jersey and then in Nebraska. Traveling west as a young woman, she found work in Rapid City as a dance-hall girl and, after marrying local gambler Joseph Du Fran, forged a successful career as a madam, with a string of brothels across Montana and South Dakota. In Deadwood, she operated a particularly successful outfit on Fifth Street (known colloquially as Saloon Street) called "Diddlin' Dora's," famous as "the three D's: Dining, Drinking and Dancing." Du Fran's principal competitor in the town, Alabama-born Mollie Johnson, graduated from work as a teenage prostitute to manage a profitable brothel on the corner of Sherman and Lee Streets. Attracting attention for her marriage to African-American entertainer Lew Spencer (who turned out to be not only a bigamist but a wife-killer), she was known for her lavish parties and conspicuous consumption, regularly parading down the streets in a carriage as "Queen of the Blondes."

Beneath the stories of colorful characters, of course, the frontier sex economy relied on a network of sexualized power relations, in which women were routinely subjected to violence, disease, and substance abuse. For many madams, too, the nature of the industry often meant that success was ephemeral and subject to moral sanction. Eleanor Dumont (Madame Mustache), with whom Calamity Jane traveled into Deadwood in 1876, boasted a typical "rags to riches to rags" story that began with humble beginnings in New Orleans, included success as a professional gambler in San Francisco and proprietorship of the Vingt-Et-Un gambling hall in Nevada City. Made destitute by lover Jack Knight (whom she pursued and dispatched with a shotgun), Dumont traded in card gaming and sex in various mining towns across the West, before ending up in Bodie, California, where she lost all her money in a bet and committed suicide.[10]

As for Martha Canary, regional chatter placed her firmly in Deadwood's saloon culture in various capacities as worker and customer. Young recalled a meeting in Jim Pencil's bar, where a buckskin-clad Canary, whose "language was very profane and her love for whisky equaled that of any hard drinker," borrowed money for a drink and was soon "in a wild state of intoxication." Providing evidence of the importance of homosocial bar-room oratory in the early incubations of community on the mining frontier, he recalled that "she was then dubbed a good fellow and admitted as a member of the pioneer characters of Deadwood." Likewise, when the Crook caravan returned to Deadwood in fall 1876, Calamity Jane assumed (at least in McGillycuddy's retrospectively written drama) the role of embroidered border scout to serve as "life and soul" of the welcoming party. "Dressed in her usual cowboy costume, Winchester rifle slung across her saddle, the saddlebags vibrating with the bucking of her bronco," she escorted the troops to the McDaniels Theatre, where she danced with McGillycuddy (and drank him under the table) and reacquainted herself with the teamsters, "shrieking at old pals and slapping them on the back as they passed."[11]

As Canary stumbled and serenaded her way through Deadwood's hostelries, the narrative thrust of local testimonial culture told a story later laid out in *Life and Adventures*. Emphasizing masculine attire, gunplay, and all-action swagger, it conspired in the creation of a regional frontier celebrity, while alluding to the complicated life of an individual grappling with a transient existence, unorthodox gender profile, and economic and social vulnerability. With the antics of Calamity Jane recited in theatrical tone, the impression was of Deadwood as a place of dramatic flourish, and Canary as a conscious performer of frontier repertoire. In a piece for the *New York Graphic* entitled "A Lady Among the Miners: The Experience of a New York Belle in the Black Hills," Adrienne Davis narrated her encounter with a character noted for riding "on horseback without a side saddle . . . a good shot, and . . . a frontierswoman . . . better than a good many men." Charles Bocker, likewise, described a figure very much in the foreground, the "main 'woman' and an 'old timer'" always with plenty of money from the men she was with, "on a carousel," and hitting the saloons in buckskin costume specifically to capitalize on her fame. With a nod to her performative bent, he described her behavior as "in the nature of a burlesque." As usual, however, there was a sting in the testimonial tail: "everyone knew she wasn't virtuous and she could not pass herself for other than a prostitute. Decent women had nothing to do with her." For Seth Bullock, recently arrived in Deadwood, Canary was a "star performer—as tough as they make them but with the tenderest heart in the world." Such observations, like much period chatter around Canary, played fast and loose with details, dates, and definitive truths, making the trajectory of her frontier fable far easier to plot than day-to-day happenings. In affixing her storied past to their own biographical reminiscence, meanwhile, late nineteenth-century story-tellers embellished their own pioneer credentials by a located-ness to Canary. She was of the time and so were they. Deployed as folkloric capital, Calamity Jane went from being a star of the Deadwood saloon to a legend in the frontier imaginary, transmitted into collective memory by rite of association and a widespread culture of old-time recollection that focused on memorable encounters with an unconventional woman.[12]

READ ALL ABOUT IT! CALAMITY JANE IN BLACK HILLS NEWSPAPERS

Biographers have typically labeled the dime novel as a critical ingredient in transporting Canary/Calamity from regional curiosity to national icon. Significant in this regard, however, was the legion of local newspapers that proved important conduits in establishing and circulating the Calamity Jane story. News and westward expansion were synchronous forces. The press advertised the West from afar, while, as Frank Mott points out, "Wherever a town sprang up . . . a printer with a rude press and a 'shirt-tail-full of type' was sure to appear." Regarded as beacons of modern communication, news media were often seen as agents of civilization and essential to an infrastructure of civic improvement. That is, however, not to say that the press shied away from indulging in wild tales of the western frontier. For one thing, such tales sold copy in a competitive market. Moreover, in the dynamic environs of early western communities there was a sense, as Deadwood pioneer John McClintock put it, of "a state of expectancy and wondering what would happen next" that fostered a media culture predicated on dramatic disclosure. In this climate, Martha Canary provided useful grist: her performance of female masculinity was colorful, demonstrative, and highly reportable. Offering potential for prurient interest, moral judgment, and the exercise of sardonic wit, the deeds (real and imagined) of Calamity Jane were reported as part of frontier whimsy and local flavor.[13]

According to William Allen White, editor of the Kansas-based *Emporia Gazette*, local print media in the nineteenth and early twentieth centuries were "drab and miserably provincial to strangers," their "sweet, intimate story of life" of inestimable value in fostering local community, but otherwise lacking in translatable value. In the case of Martha Canary, however, the "larger than life" antics reported by the likes of the *Cheyenne Daily Leader* not only showed the mechanics of community formation on the frontier, but provided Calamity Jane with an opportunity for a more expansive broadcast of her tall tales. These stories were widely recycled across regional media, courtesy of word of mouth and the "newspaper exchanges" fed by railroad and telegraph technology, and local presses were eager to convey the westering story in all its illustrious detail. Corroborated and communicated on the news circuit, a tabloid imprint of Calamity Jane helped lay the groundwork for a frontier celebrity that was augmented by the dime novel. Meanwhile, once a buckskin-clad Canary had been established as a character of interest in pulp fiction, the local press eagerly participated in a textual dialogue, either by way of embellishing her reputation for gender unorthodoxy, or by pointing out where everyday reality hit her dime novel persona square in the face.[14]

Presenting Calamity Jane as a many-sided raconteur—flamboyant, comic, tragic, and vulgar—the local press not only paid heed to the complexity of Martha Canary's story, but also revealed an unstable relationship between media and subject that hinted at a modern celebrity culture in the making. Infamy, drama, and mass communication were all critical elements in the forging of a "famesque" Calamity Jane. It was, arguably, this very *public* articulation of her life that set her apart from other frontier women striving to make ends meet and engaging in various kinds of gender transgression in the late nineteenth-century West. As McLaird points out, "What most separated Martha from her female companions in the West were her charisma and bold actions that gained attention from the press." Running through reportage was the sense of a person of inimitable qualities, but not an unblemished heroine. Her unconventional behavior, drinking, swearing, and other traditionally masculine mannerisms invited a degree of voyeuristic review, but also a rebuking tone. Combining an attack on its rival paper with an exposé of Canary, the Deadwood *Black Hills Daily Times* contended that the " 'heroine of the hills,' who figured so largely in the local columns of our contemporary this morning, didn't 'man out' very well upon investigation." Castigating Canary as a common prostitute (and the editor of the competing tabloid as one of her customers), the *Times* reveled in proclaiming

> the statement that she is pre-possessing in appearance is the merest balderdash. She looks more like the result of the gable end of a fire proof [*sic*] and a Sioux Injun, than anything we can think of at the present writing. She contains mighty thin stuff for a heroine.

Combining repartee and riposte, early press treatments of Canary showcased a rehearsal of the axioms of spectacle and shame intrinsic to modern celebrity culture. Moreover, by taking this tack, normative standards and the peccadillos of deviant behavior could be usefully contained within a cloak of frontier performance. Canary's eye-catching personality could thus be enjoyed as a throwaway slice of western libertarianism, even as her nonconformist ways cautioned against any notions of social acceptability.[15]

Running through press accounts was a sense of the marketability of the West as prime site for the exercise of heroic imaginings. Adopting the tone of the knowing insider, the *Cheyenne Daily Leader* chided Bill Hickok as a "very tame and worthless loafer and bummer," whose legend had been resoundingly "spun" by the " 'scare-heads' of the border press." According to the *Omaha Daily Herald*, meanwhile, the opening of transport networks and lines of economic opportunity had brought a raft of new arrivals to the West, each of whom adopted the costume and gestures of the frontier hero: "now that the trees are blazed and roads made, we see quite a number of the knights of long hair and buckskin, charging along the line, whose glory and aspiration seem to be in a name." A signal of her growing status as cross-dressing curiosity, the *Daily Herald* pointed out: "As Calamity Jane has donned the Buckskin, she too is entitled to honorable mention along with the boys." The *Cheyenne Daily Sun*, in its "Pictures of Life in the Black Hills," likewise presented a landscape of folklore, with characters parading on a western stage crying out for literary imprint: "the poet-novelist … will find in the Black Hills characters for his romance sitting astraddle of stumps, dealing cards or shooting anybody down on the spot." Calamity Jane was identified as a person of particular interest:

> A little creature of 22, whose movements have an unstudied grace, and whose eyes emit a greenish glare whenever she is very mad. She has been a scout in the army, has dressed in soldier clothes, has gone on horseback over mountains and fought with Indians, and is now dancing in a hurdy-gurdy house in Deadwood.

As the *Sun* asserted, "the rising young genius who wants to achieve fame in literature at one yellow cover, will please take the first train for the Hills."[16]

Glorying in Calamity Jane as a character of western fancy, local press played a significant role in disseminating her legend. In a pertinent signal of her burgeoning reputation, the *Cheyenne Weekly Leader* pointed out that Canary was "a lady not unknown to fame." Spoken of without need for any kind of elaboration, the *Weekly Leader* claimed, Canary had entered the realms of those who were famous *for* being famous. That said, the imprint in tabloid news was not without frequent (and often relished) notation of her idiosyncrasies and shortcomings. Thus, the *Cheyenne Daily Leader* finished its coverage of the "heroine of more adventures than any woman of her age and weight in the West" with a story detailing how Canary had hurt her foot in Deadwood during a wagon accident. A week later, it reported that she had recovered enough to dance. If newspaper coverage served as a willing accomplice in elevating Calamity Jane as a frontier idol, it equally affirmed her status as a social pariah.[17]

In an indication of the collaborative forces at work in the construction of frontier celebrity, Canary seemed to seek out the press when it suited her. Journalists, for their part, greeted her latest appearance with narrative playfulness and grisly relish. On occasion, they invented scenarios to appeal to popular tastes for the latest scoop in Canary-ana. The *Cheyenne Daily Leader* usefully illustrated these blurred lines of news and fictional reporting in a spectacular article headlined, "Calamity Jane. Her Unannounced Call at the *Leader* Office—An editor bulldozed." The article began with a slow and stifling summer afternoon in Cheyenne and a purposeful step upon the stair. The culprit appeared, "a presence at once awful and ludicrous," and announced in "sepulchral falsetto," bullwhip in hand and smelling of gin: "I want to see the fighting editor. I am Calamity Jane. I'm just in from the Black Hills. Be you the fighting editor?" The editor, reputedly, played dumb and promptly jumped out of the window, returning later to find the office turned upside down and a note pinned to the door saying:

Print in the LEADER that Calamity Jane, the child of the regiment, pioneer white woman of the Black Hills is in Cheyenne, or I'll scalp you, skin you alive and hang you on a telegraph pole. You hear me, and don't you forget it. Calamity Jane.

The piece ended by noting that the city editor, somewhat incongruously (not to mention implausibly), had fled to Borneo. On one level nothing more than puff journalism, the success of the article relied on the average *Leader* reader being familiar enough with the performance routine of Calamity Jane to find it suitably entertaining. Moreover, as Wyoming archivist Lola Homsher noted, the emerging folkloric landscape growing around Martha Canary proved an excellent fit for the "unrestrained and exaggerated style of writing of editors in the late 1800s."[18]

If toying with the "terrifying" presence of Calamity Jane was one approach of the local media, another was the search for her "authentic" backstory. The *Cheyenne Daily Sun* adopted the cynical tone of the western insider in commenting on the multiple claims to the "Calamity Jane" birthplace: "A few days ago Iowa claimed her for its own; then Illinois; then Missouri. And now a Virginia City paper says she was born there, and that her father is a well-to-do banker of that city." The next month, it ran an enticing editorial "Calamity Jane—The True History of Her Life," which used the occasion of "the return of the well-known frontierswoman, 'Calamity Jane'" as a vehicle to explore her striking life history. As the paper noted, here was a character whose public persona was known to many, yet the details of her real life remained mysterious. Aiming to rectify this, a *Sun* reporter had interviewed one A.R. Hendricks, who traded a tall tale of Jane Coombs, daughter of an Iowan Baptist minister, who eloped with a military suitor and took to masculine dress and a scouting career when he was killed. Calamity Jane, it argued, easily held her own, both in gesture and garb, with the canonical male heroes of western myth:

> she has hunted the red man of the plains and the buffalo; served as a
> guide to the inexperienced miners and trappers and dresses in buckskin

from top to toe a great portion of her time. She is one of the best horse-back riders in the west, plays a good game of cards or billiards, and is at all times competent to get away with her allowance of sporting suste-nance. All together she is a remarkable subject for the basis of a novel in the hands of Ned Buntline, Dr. Beadle or Sylvanus Cobb.

Reprinted in various regional papers, the article illuminated public interest in the "true" Calamity Jane, as well as elucidating how competing tales of her past made their way into popular circulation.[19]

THE FEMALE SCOUT TAKES HOLD: THE TEXTUAL WEST AND THE WRITING OF CALAMITY JANE

The literary rendition of Calamity Jane began in earnest with journalist Horace Maguire's *The Black Hills and American Wonderland* (1877), a treatise based on the author's "personal explorations" as a journalist for the *Montana Post* in the mid-1860s, and thereafter in the Dakotas. Featured on horseback and mistaken for a "dare-devil boy," she appeared first on the fringes of Deadwood. Describing Calamity as a wayward soul in possession of a "remarkable career of ruin, disgrace and recklessness," Maguire adopted a moralistic tone, yet toyed with a romantic character to which he was strangely drawn. Her disguise was convincing, with "nothing in her attire to distinguish her sex . . . save her small neat-fitting gaiters and sweeping raven locks." Canary cut a striking impression in a buckskin suit, with an antelope vest and a broad-brimmed Spanish hat, riding "with the daring self-confidence of a California *buchario*." Dynamic in style and in motion, she was both exotic and feral, a creation of the borderlands who could give "as good an imitation of a Sioux war-whoop as a feminine voice is capable of." This striking (and genre consistent) visual picture was embellished with a short biography that set the stage for the idea of Calamity Jane as civilized, tender, and (most importantly) feminine under her masculine costuming. She came, said Maguire, from Virginia City (mistakenly listed as Nevada and not Montana) and was of respectable family, but had since pursued a deviant lifestyle: "Donning male attire in the mining regions where no restraints were imposed for such freaks." An accomplished hunter, miner, freighter, scout, and stage driver, Maguire's Calamity successfully carried an alluring masculine frontier identity, but at the same time retained a residual femininity. A final literary flourish thus pointed out that she was "still in early womanhood," and her "rough and dissipated career" had not yet, in the words of Lord Byron, "swept away the lines where beauty lingers."[20]

Maguire fleshed out his description of Calamity Jane in *The Coming Empire: A Complete and Reliable Treatise on the Black Hills, Yellowstone and Big Horn Regions* (1878). Here she was illustrated for the first time as "Miss Martha Canary (Calamity Jane), the female scout," on horseback, wearing men's clothing, and brandishing a pistol. A few pages on, Maguire delved into her backstory, a one-time "sporting woman" of the Black Hills who was fast becoming a regional luminary. Calamity Jane was one of the "noted characters in the old mining regions," a woman of considerable pioneer provenance who enjoyed a "wide notoriety." At this point, the narrative switched to focus on defense of honor and a woman whom Maguire described as "shamefully abused" by the press, and about whom all kinds of lies had been told (all of which he reproduced for the benefit of reader intrigue—highwaywoman, horse stealer, card sharp, minister's daughter). Placing himself in the role of trusted confidant, he pointed out that Calamity Jane had freely confessed to her infelicities: "she admits . . . that she has dressed in male attire manufactured out of buck-skins, acted in the capacity of a scout in the Indian service; been a stage-driver; and made several long trips as a bull-whacker." Here was a useful clue as to the performance mechanics at work in constructing Calamity Jane as an authentic frontier celebrity. Not only did Canary (and her proxies) skillfully create history from story, but they also cultivated a sense of truthful authority by lambasting those who spread tall tales. Moreover, by positioning uncorroborated details of Calamity Jane's past (e.g., scouting) alongside firmly authenticated aspects (e.g., traveling with the army), a sense of credibility was affirmed. Maguire concluded his study with a character endorsement based on survival need ("she charges—probably with much truth—that if she has done anything wrong society, and not herself, is to blame, as she always came near starving to death when she tried to support herself in a more womanly way"), before finishing in the familiar territory of masculine bragging rights: " 'Calamity Jane' can throw an oyster-can into the air and put two bullet-holes into it from her revolver before it reaches the ground, and offers to bet she can knock a fly off an ox's ear with a sixteen-foot whip-lash three times out of five."[21]

Maguire's role in fanning the fires of frontier celebrity was significant. Not only did his depictions of Calamity Jane enter public discourse as a stock rendition, but his narrative locutions also inspired others to tackle the West as dramatic subject. For many novelists and scriptwriters (some of whom were writing the frontier from afar), Maguire was regarded as a first-hand witness, and was thus repeated verbatim or with little critical interrogation. Thomas Newson's *Drama of Life in the Black Hills* (1878) devoted considerable space to Calamity Jane, and used both Maguire and local newspaper copy to supplement information gained from the author's trip to the region in the mid-1870s. Presenting a character both kindly and capricious, Newson's Calamity was strong-minded and of generous heart, yet possessing "all the daring and courage of the lion or the devil himself" when enraged. A person of enticing gender possibility, she fought American Indians, got drunk in bars, and scouted for the army during the day, before changing into feminine costume for the evening. "When dressed in her own garments she looks comely; when equipped as a man she has all the characteristics of the sterner sex, with the pistols, bowie-knives and other weapons of death," he noted. Here, too, was the idea of Calamity Jane as a character of gender masquerade who conformed to feminine codes underneath her buckskin coat. Championing a figure both exceptional and authentic in her frontier costuming, Newson proclaimed: "she imitates no one; is an original in herself."[22]

ON THE TRAIL OF DEADWOOD DICK: MASCULINITY, MASQUERADE, AND
TRANSGRESSION IN THE DIME NOVEL

Adding a fresh layer to the mythology of the "heroine of the plains" was Calamity Jane's burgeoning career as a dime novel star. Popular from the 1860s until the turn of the century, and consumed by a largely male, adolescent readership based in the urban industrial East, these publications were cheap to buy and were marked by their lurid covers, salacious tales, and byzantine plot conceits. Stories of disguise and mistaken identity were common, as were narrative devices of hero–villain face-offs, all-action set pieces, moral quandaries, and a predilection for (what would later become known as) "Hollywood" endings. Urban crime, military campaigns, and tales of revolutionaries and foreign spies were all popular topics of storytelling, though dominating the genre (especially in the 1860s and 1870s) were frontier yarns. Churned out in their thousands by authors who wrote a novel a night at the height of their popularity, the dime novel played a significant role in confirming the power of the West as mythological terrain.

The western dime novel typically followed a specific formula. Pitting good against evil, framed around a series of fights and other action sequences, and featuring larger-than-life (often eccentric) characters that were invariably clad in buckskin, the genre boasted a common narrative architecture that still left room for authorial extrapolation. According to Daryl Jones, there were six model "heroes" in the dime novel: the backwoodsman, the miner, the outlaw, the plainsman, the cowboy, and the rancher. Each of those sat comfortably in the category of frontier champion. Literary engagement with the West had a lengthy lineage, most notably expressed in James Fenimore Cooper's *Leatherstocking Tales*, and the pulp fictions of the 1860s bore witness to this ancestry, as well as taking their cues from contemporary news of dramatic and break-neck expansion in the trans-Mississippi theater. Audiences were firmly interested in the "real-life" account, attested to by the popularity of stories on Buffalo Bill, Jesse James, Wild Bill Hickok, and Kit Carson. Significantly, the burden of truth in these supposedly accurate biographical vignettes seemed far less important than a vague notion of believability in framing the narrative arc of the flamboyant frontiersman.[23]

Pennsylvania-based pulp fiction writer Edward Wheeler chose Calamity Jane as a key character for his new "Deadwood Dick" series, set squarely in the territory of the Black Hills. Central to her appeal was a whiff of western authenticity, a ready-made celebrity status, and an enticing line in gender possibility. Her story, in fact, was ideal fare for the dime novel world and its interest in boisterous adventuring and epic face-offs, even down to the right attire. Most intriguing was the way in which the world of pulp fiction grappled with the issue of gender fluidity and masquerade. As Nancy Chu notes, while the western dime novel presented strong and prominent female characters, it typically upheld the "Cult of True Womanhood" in promoting piety, purity, and submissiveness towards men. At the same time, dime authors were attracted to the West as a place beyond the boundaries of normativity, a space where the spectacular "writeability" of nonconformist protagonists such as Calamity Jane satisfied audience demand for a dose of the wild and sensational. A frontier curiosity performing a trademark line in female masculinity, she allowed writers to play with the idea of transgressing cultural boundaries without being *too* radical. In a complicated sleight of hand, Calamity Jane could be an aberrant "other" who reinforced traditional roles, and a heretical role model through whom audiences vicariously imagined flouting established gender boundaries. Wheeler, in fact, had included a cross-dressing heroine in his first novel. *Hurricane Nell, the Girl Dead Shot; or the Queen of the Saddle and Lasso* (1877) served as a useful dress rehearsal for Calamity Jane, riding the West clad in buckskin, grasping a rifle, and seeking revenge on outlaw Bob Woolf for killing her parents. Able to "out-run, out-ride, out-shoot, out-lasso and out-yell any man in town," Nell galloped through the storyline, rescuing a Philadelphia lawyer from Indian attack, and winning out in a shooting competition. Seen in this frame, Wheeler found (like many others in his time and in years since) something compelling in the character of a woman clothed in masculine garb and touting the usual skill set of the male hero. With her distinctive western identity, the hint of a traumatic backstory, and the cloak of gender masquerade, Calamity Jane was ideally suited for a starring role as a dime novel hero(ine).[24]

Calamity Jane made her dime novel debut as sidekick to Deadwood Dick, the star of 22 novels between 1877 and 1885—a bristly and suitably enigmatic masculine hero, who upheld law and order through righteous violence. In her first outing, *Deadwood Dick, The Prince of the Road; or, The Black Rider of the Black Hills* (1877), she appeared as an intrinsic part of the frontier imaginary, someone "here, there and everywhere, seemingly all at one time." Wheeler's romantic heroine was "dressed in a carefully tanned costume of buckskin; the vest being fringed with the fur of the mink; wearing a jaunty Spanish sombrero; boots on the dainty feet of patent leather, with tops reaching to the knees." While Hurricane Nell was neither rough nor unattractive, Calamity Jane bore the scars of a difficult past and an outdoors life, yet retained vestiges of femininity: "a face slightly sunburned . . . eyes black and piercing; mouth firm, resolute and devoid of sensual expression," but "showing the traces of beauty that even excessive dissipation could not obliterate." Much like Maguire's depiction, this Calamity Jane was deviant not by design, but by difficult circumstance, born of respectable parents in Virginia City and damaged by a "foul wretch" who "stole away her honor." A character that invited sympathy and prurient fascination, but not emulation (one of the novel's protagonists hoped his daughter would never turn out like her), her narrative imprint alluded to the traditional moral conservatism of the dime novel genre. That is not to say that there were not alternative readings to be made of female agency and gender ambiguity in action. After all, Calamity Jane could "ride like the wind, shoot like a sharp-shooter and swear like a trooper." Even Deadwood Dick valorized her rightfully brave and independent disposition. Meanwhile, as the plot twisted its way through kidnaps and card games, routs and rescues, it seemed the job of Calamity Jane to pop up on the trail, offering ambiguous gender interventions of a six-gun variety. In one savior-of-the-saloon set piece, she wielded "a cocked six in either white, shapely hand," while hollering "Come! . . . It's every man for himself." The novel ended with Deadwood Dick proposing marriage, whereupon Jane quipped: "No . . . I have had all the *man* I care for. We can be friends, Dick; more we can never be!"[25]

The Double Daggers; or, Deadwood Dick's Defiance (1877) was published just two months later. A signal of the recent arrival of Calamity Jane on the national stage and of the immaturity of the Deadwood Dick franchise, Wheeler offered a quick biographical recap that described her male attire, buckskins, pistols, and itinerant life ways. A local of the hills, she was abandoned by her family in Nevada, found wealth in mining claims and saloon games, and betrayed a social conscience in helping out the unfortunate. Her character, beyond that, gained little elaboration, though the novel ended with the observation that Calamity Jane was a loner, "daredevil," and "reckless adventurer" destined not to marry. After a number of issues that failed to mention Calamity Jane in any discernible way, she received substantive development in *Deadwood Dick on Deck; or, Calamity Jane, the Heroine of Whoop-Up* (1878). Here, Calamity Jane swaggered through the narrative landscape as leading protagonist, again appearing always at the right moment to rescue the hapless and mistreated, and generally save the day. The cover image, too, was important, not only for placing her center stage, but also for communicating a more conventionally feminine imprint of frontier heroics. With flowing hair blown back by the wind, wearing a broad-brimmed hat, a blouse, and neckerchief, rifle over shoulder, and grasping the reins of a horse, Wheeler's Calamity offered a softer, less heretical, inscription of female masculinity.[26]

Calamity Jane's entrance in *Deadwood Dick on Deck* was a sonic one: "a wild rollicking harmony of weird music, such as none but a cultivated voice could produce" that enlivened the campfire of Sandy and Colonel Tubbs. The pair deliberated on who could be producing the song, decided that it was Calamity Jane, and proceeded to chew over her character traits. Both ventured that little was known of her, aside from her title (another hint at Canary's "famesque" celebrity status), before using their camp conversation to deliver a potted biography in frontier dialect. Sandy questioned why any woman would "lower" herself to dress as a man, and assumed her to be an "eccentric creature." Tubbs described Calamity Jane as "the most reckless buchario in ther Hills," who "kin drink whisky, shute, play keerds, or sw'ar," but stayed true to the narrative thrust of the series in marking her as a good-hearted survivor: "Janie's not as bad as ther world would have her; because she's got grit an' ain't afeard to shute ther galoot as crosses her, people condemn her." Making an assertion of gender equality in tune with the modish "new woman" of the late nineteenth century, he proclaimed: "ef a female ken't stand up an' fight fer her rights, et's durned little aid she'll git."[27]

When Calamity Jane finally appeared in person, Wheeler took the opportunity to run with a breathless description of a free spirit standing upright in the saddle of her charging horse and whooping with feral abandon. A personification of the energy of the West, she rode "madly," her eyes "dancing with excitement," entirely attuned to her steed and environs. There was, however, a clear sense of base femininity in play, a presence "graceful and womanly" with "long, raven hair that reached below a faultless waist," "a breast of alabaster purity," wearing a velvet jacket and Spanish hat, diamond rings, and a gold chain won from the gambling tables of Deadwood. This all-action, soft-focus Calamity was heavy on romantic allusion, yet Wheeler was also keen to stress her authenticity, remarking in anecdotal fashion that it had been "ever my fortune to see her . . . when Deadwood was but an infant city." Later on, however, there were hints of a more radical re-ordering of gender codes at work. Asked why she wore manly attire, Calamity Jane stressed both practicality and fraternity: "I don't allow ye ken beat men's togs much for handy locomotion an' so forth, an' then, ye see, I'm as big a gun among the men as any of 'em." In another passage, she presented her passing as a man as evidence of gender dysphoria: "Ye see, they kind o' got matters discomfuddled w'en I was created, an' I turned out to be a gal instead of a man, which I ought to hev been." Such comments, of course, served to heighten the performance value of a topsy-turvy frontier world, where social conventions were loosened, but always enacted with chivalric honor in mind; a "rough Paradise," where Wheeler could indulge his readers in a heroine who was full of delicious ambiguities. His Calamity was deviant and just; proficient with firearms, but never a cold-blooded killer; swaggering with performative masculinity, but contained by a safety net of womanly affections. Presented as a dynamic and unorthodox idol, she galloped across the pages at full speed, exhibiting both a feminine eye for detail and a full gesturing of frontier machismo. This sense of gender ambiguity was a critical ingredient in Calamity Jane's literary appeal, carefully joined to which was the idea of narrative mystery. Hence, as the novel unfolded, a clandestine past was unveiled, including a birth-name of Jane (Jennie) Forrest, events surrounding her traumatic assault (which was implied to be sexual in nature, but was not discussed), and a subsequent quest for vengeance on the perpetrator, Arkansas Alf Kennedy. The story ended with Kennedy killed by vigilantes, Sandy taking an eastern, sophisticated bride (despite finding Calamity Jane "exceedingly strange, and wonderfully beautiful" when she saved him from being mauled by a bear), and Jane wandering the trails alone. Wheeler judged it unlikely she "will ever marry, especially since Sandy is gone."[28]

Calamity Jane's only other cover appearance was in the tenth instalment of the series, *Deadwood Dick in Leadville; or, a Strange Stroke for Liberty* (1879), where she was illustrated brandishing two cocked pistols at outlaws in a saloon. A visual lure to cash in on the popularity of the armed western heroine, the dime novel actually contained very little material on her, aside from reference to "the Girl Sport," who was known throughout the Rocky Mountains and defined by her buckskin look and revolvers (what Wheeler labeled "the principal items of her make-up"). Villain Ralph Gardner admitted to being particularly enraged at being "knuckled under" by a woman, and Calamity Jane confirmed her position as a defender of justice and of poetic flourish by asserting "You may think me a strange character, and perhaps I am, but I enjoy a free fight, when it is for the right." Deadwood Dick was hanged at the end of the story—though this was not the barrier to plot development one might expect.[29]

In fact, for the rest of the dime novel series, Dick and Calamity danced a circuitous storyline in which they were successively killed, estranged, and reunited. Tensions of gender conformity and transgressive possibility marked their (increasingly miraculous) engagements. A romantic future looked promising for the pair in *Deadwood Dick's Device; or, the Sign of the Double Cross* (1879), where the eponymous hero returned from the dead, courtesy of secret "remedies" applied by ministering seraph Calamity Jane. While Jane had so far refused Dick's matrimonial overtures, she continued to "hover around" him as a sort of guardian angel. "Some would laugh were they to hear me call *her* an angel," he joked. A signal of her recurring roles as righteous eccentric and mysterious westerner, Dick pondered on Jane's nature thus:

> A wild, strange creature she is—virtuous, and true as steel beyond peradventure, yet so wild and strange as to seem a part of the wilderness through which she roams. *Has* she a heart? If so, it is buried deep under a cloud of past obscurity.[30]

By the end of the novel, relations between the buckskin-clad pair were looking decidedly fractious. Dick had married a new belle, Stella, who failed to survive her wedding day, on account of a poisoned cup of tea, for which he erroneously blamed Calamity Jane (the poisoner was later revealed to be one of Dick's ex-lovers, Fanny Farron). Then, in *Blonde Bill; or, Deadwood Dick's Home Base* (1880), Dick vowed to leave behind his outlaw life and become a prosecutor, while a villain offered Calamity Jane $1,000 to kill her erstwhile partner. In a heart-to-heart address to the audience, she pointed out that underneath all the masculine performance, all she truly wanted was heterosexual love and affection. The barriers, she said, to her embracing a world of civility and romance were not cultural (she noted "Knowledge of manners, education, intellect—all are mine"), but came instead from a life of lonesome desolation and (interestingly) the sheer weight of the mantle of *being* Calamity Jane. According to historian Peter Boag, the cross-dressing dime novel star was "above sexual suspicion," and thus able to romp across the frontier imaginary with impunity. That said, Calamity Jane's soliloquy, at the very least, invites alternative readings. Was it even possible that a character whose identity rested on gender unorthodoxy and a transgressive performance of frontier masculinity could find her place in a life of settled domesticity? Further excavation of what this said about sexual and social conventions remained (predictably) undeveloped in the dime novel. For the twenty-first-century reader, however, there remain interesting angles of gender possibility.[31]

Even when his heroine had realized her adoration for Deadwood Dick, Wheeler did not make things easy for the pair. Calamity Jane disguised herself as Little Toothpick in *A Game of Gold; or, Deadwood Dick's Big Strike* (1880) to check on her paramour's fidelity. More emotional trauma ensues in *Deadwood Dick of Deadwood; or, the Picked Party* (1880), as a tearful Jane mistakenly assumes Dick to be cheating. Once his honor is restored, she assumes the buckskins of her "old style" to rescue Dick from prison and marry him in the final lines of the novel. Wedding bells sound again (proof that even in a series, plotlines were not automatically sequential or consistent) in the very next issue, but not before the usual round of kidnaps, brawls, and near-death experiences. Here, in *Deadwood Dick's Doom; or, Calamity Jane's Last Adventure* (1881), "the notorious free-and-easy, reckless waif of the rocky Western country" features prominently in a tale that focuses on a mining camp run by the nefarious Piute Dave. Calamity Jane receives most textual screen-time in Chapter VI, entitled "A Very Singular Performance," in which Wheeler demonstrates a keen authorial affection for his cross-dressing lead:

Calamity had changed but little since the time when this pen last introduced her: she was the same graceful, pretty girl-in-breeches that she had always been, but if there was any change it was in the sterner expression of her sad eyes.

Here, too, is a sense of the underlying friction between gender conformity and heresy that runs through Wheeler's dime novels. Calamity Jane arrived in Deadwood having "never quite given up the hope that Dick would, at some distant day, recognize her devotion to him, and take her as a wife." The idea of heterosexual courtship, reputedly, had quietened her demons, "the bitterness of her strange young life had seemingly melted into glorious sunshine." At the same time, significant barriers existed to consummating the romance, from her kidnap by "a Mormon devil" to Piute Dave throwing Dick in a pit of quicksand and leaving him for dead.[32]

Ultimately, a blissful "happy ever after" for Deadwood Dick and Calamity Jane was not part of the melodramatic trajectory of Wheeler's dime landscape. Jane was abducted and rescued in *Captain Crack-Shot, the Girl Brigand* (1881), only to fall prey to the dastardly designs of gambler Tra-La-Lee Charlie, who imprisoned her for refusing to become his partner in *Gold Dust Dick, a Romance of Roughs and Toughs* (1882). With a highly contorted plotline, this novel tale saw Jane taken captive by a band of Aztecs, escape with the help of a like-minded cross-dressing protégé called Roxey Ralph, and rescue Deadwood Dick from being burned at the stake by Ponca Indians. In a salient morality tale on the pitfalls of frontier celebrity, Wheeler had his heroic duo repair to a remote location "wherein to hide their identity." The allure of the theatrical frontier, however, was too much to resist, and Calamity returned in *Deadwood Dick's Divide; or, the Spirit of Swamp Lake* (1882) as a spectral presence with a propensity for climactic fits of anger: "when I get mad, I make smoke rise above the hills, I tell ye." In *Deadwood Dick's Big Deal; or, the Gold Brick of Oregon* (1883), Jane and Dick have a baby boy, only to fall out after Dick sees Jane embrace another man (who turns out to be her evil brother, Ralph Chester). Settling the issue of parental custody over a game of cards, and in Dick's favor, Jane attempts suicide, only to have a concerned citizen intervene and discharge the fatal shot into Ralph. Wheeler concludes that Deadwood Dick and Calamity Jane's "paths in life" were destined to be "wide apart." Sworn enemies by the time of *Deadwood Dick's Claim; or, the Fairy Face of Faro Flats* (1884), Wheeler turns somersaults on romantic resolution to reunite them in *Deadwood Dick's Diamonds; or, the Mystery of Joan Porter* (1885). In the final episode of the series, *Deadwood Dick's Dust; or, The Chained Hand* (1885), Calamity Jane strides onto the western stage as fresh faced and vibrant as in her first outing, only for her and Dick to be killed by reprobates and buried side by side.[33]

Wheeler was not the only pulp fiction author to feature Calamity Jane, though his character development was the most extensive. For other dime novel authors, too, the "heroine of the plains" appeared as a redoubtable frontier celebrity and character of intriguing gender masquerade. She earned top billing in *The Beautiful White Devil of the Yellowstone* (of which no copy survives) and in Reckless Ralph's *Calamity Jane: The Queen of the Plains*, serialized in *Street and Smith's New York Weekly* in 1882. Appearing in an illustration for the *Weekly* in classic "hold-up" pose, pistols drawn at four bandits, with determined stare, long tresses, and in skirt and blouse, this Calamity—like Wheeler's—is a tumbled mixture of frontier machismo and feminine charm. An advertisement for *The Queen of the Plains* in the *Cheyenne Weekly Leader* shows the popularity of the genre both *of* the West and *in* it, promising readers "a strangely real and powerful story," replete with "daring deeds by a brave woman's hands." Stressing the accuracy of its presentation, it claimed authorship by a true westerner, "a man who lives amid the scenes he describes, and knows the men and women he writes about." Readers were promised "Wild Reality, Truth, Originality and Power of Description." Over several instalments, *The Queen of the Plains* communicated a tale of trauma, revenge, and glorious reunion. Raised in a remote cabin by Mountain Jim, an old trapper she took to be her father, the young Calamity Jane was orphaned when a gang of bandits attacked (but not before a "grand deathbed reveal" as to the whereabouts of her real father). Well armed and fueled by avenging fury, she went on to take down all 26 outlaws, before easing into a glamorous existence running a gambling hall in Deadwood. A "wonderfully beautiful woman" with bejeweled fingers and pearl-handled revolvers, this Calamity found time to ride with Jesse James and locate her father, with whom she started a new life in Colorado.[34]

Also notable was the international reach of Calamity Jane as a dime novel heroine, proof of the broad appeal of the western brand and of stories of gender unorthodoxy. The British equivalent in lurid pulp fiction, the "penny dreadful," had captivated working-class audiences since the 1830s, regaling readers with action and romantic tales and the "real-life" exploits of Dick Turpin and Sweeney Todd, alongside reprints of stories featuring American western heroes, including Buffalo Bill and Jesse James. Mindful of the potency of frontier mythology, the *Boys of England* series (established in 1866) focused on Calamity Jane in an 1881 story called "A Strange Woman." Told in the form of an autobiographical reminiscence, it narrated the author's prospecting trip to Rapid City, Dakota, and was interwoven with a beguiling question: "Is Calamity Jane a real character in the mountains?" A rude saloon provided the point of encounter, into which Calamity Jane walked, complete with signature fringed buckskins and marked by her "lithe, graceful form, the long raven locks, the diminutive moccasined feet, and the smooth, sun-browned face of the stranger." When the barkeep refused to sell her whiskey, she cocked her revolvers and, with a "fear-inspiring magnetism," procured a drink. Delivering a rousing oration on female empowerment, she railed: "Don't think, because I'm a woman, I can't protect myself; and I don't want you to make this crowd believe a lie about me, either. I don't make disturbances anywhere: I just protect myself, that's all." In a testament to Canary's growing celebrity status, the author remarked that he had long been trying to solicit an interview with her, and could not believe his luck. Offering a cigar (which she lit by striking a match on her hip),

Calamity went on to provide a "heart-to-heart" testimonial—faithfully printed—that spoke of her honesty, her preference for traveling in masculine worlds where she received fairer treatment, and her nomadic existence. Attributing her name to the fact that her "whole life" had been a calamity, she spoke of the death of her mother in Alder Gulch, life in the company of miners, and travels with the army in the Black Hills. The story here, interestingly, is much closer to the narrative landscape set out in Canary's orations, and later laid out in *Life and Adventures*, suggesting, perhaps, that the author had picked up on regional testimony more than pulp fiction fare. Accordingly, "A Strange Woman" located Calamity Jane "at home" in buckskins, at the head of the military train ("the boys will tell you I always ride ahead with the scouts"), and in possession of a good heart and a "womanly nature."[35]

Another British offering, Henry Llewellyn Williams' *Buffalo Bill*, published in London in 1887, presented a book-length frolic based on the dime novel formula that cherry-picked elements of Canary's folkloric fable with added artistic license. Here, a character called Calamity Sal was ambushed by bandits on a stagecoach, but gainfully "seized the reins from the dying driver's grasp and drove off through a hail of bullets." As literary critic Ramon Adams notes, "The author had evidently read in some dime novel about Calamity Jane performing such a stunt" and borrowed the scenario for a stock storytelling exposition on the frontier. In fact, Williams' heroine not only seemed to borrow from the mythological feats popularly attributed to Canary, but also bore a similarity (in name and attitude) to Cherokee Sal, heroine of Bret Harte's *The Luck of Roaring Camp*. This "pick-and-mix" quality to the stars of the frontier imaginary saw their easy deployment across popular literature. Asserting national ownership over the West as a patriotic landscape, one American commentator snubbed it as "a ludicrous attempt of an Englishman to write of the American West about which he knew nothing."[36]

With its serpentine plots, grand flourishes, and masked identities, the dime novel genre was well placed to choreograph Calamity Jane from regional curiosity to frontier superstardom. Here, in this landscape of western dramatics and inscrutable plotlines, her evolving reputation as a cross-dressing adventurer found a suitable performance habitat. She was mysterious, extraordinary, and glamorous, yet at the same time knowable, fallible, and plain spoken—all critical points of reference in a culture of modern celebrity. As such, the dime novel built on a growing storytelling buzz around Canary/Calamity, and repackaged it for a national (and, indeed, international) audience. Encapsulated as a swaggering, pistol-packing frontier icon, the unconventional heroine imagined by Wheeler and others cut a striking presence as a personification of the wild frontier. A brief examination, however, of the actual details of her dime novel imprint finds little that translated beyond the pages of nineteenth-century pulp fiction. None of the feats which lived on as defining aspects of the Calamity Jane story (the Deadwood stage rescue; connection with Bill Hickok; scouting with Custer) featured as part of the dime novel-scape, while the series of events laid out by Wheeler (the search for Arkansas Alf; kidnap by Tra-La-Lee Charlie; and on/off romance with Deadwood Dick) each failed to make a lasting imprint in popular mythology. What the medium *did* do was deliver the "heroine of the plains" onto a more expansive stage, making the contribution of the genre less about its stories (which were generally confounding, hard to follow, and derivative), and more about its broad-brush character development. Wheeler's Calamity was tangible and intangible, a spirited personality of intriguing gender masquerade. Deadwood Dick described her as "perhaps the queerest character to tame or coax, that you could find in all the Western mining country." Also significant was the way in which the dime novel Calamity both valorized and destabilized hegemonic masculinity. While other commentators have seen the dime novel as an essentially conservative medium, *Calamity: The Many Lives of Calamity Jane* suggests the possibility of a more radical reading. Successfully inhabiting the garb of the male frontier hero, pulp fiction Calamity presented a vibrant snapshot of gender possibility. If we assume that popular literature has the potential to subvert social norms in its parodies and plays, then the flourishes of a buckskin-clad heroine could also redraw the lines of sexual politics. As Lillian Craton points out in her study of cross-dressers in Victorian literature, "sensational female masculinity provides a basis for the renegotiation of feminine identity." Leaving aside its less than memorable narratives, the enduring contribution of the dime novel thus lies in its rendering and reiterating of Calamity Jane as an enigmatic and activist personality, one that chipped away at the idea of masculinity as a category owned exclusively by men.[37]

CONJURING WITH CALAMITY: LITERATURE AND GENDER POSSIBILITY IN THE FRONTIER IMAGINARY

Fault lines of gender possibility could also be found in the first full-length novel about Calamity Jane. Authored by Mrs. William Loring Spencer, serialized in the *New York Tribune*, and collated in book form as *Calamity Jane: A Story of the Black Hills* (1887), this work was important both for its female authorship and as the only fulsome (semi-)biographical work to be written during Canary's lifetime. Set in Deadwood and its environs, the work drew heavily on the genre conventions of period literature to present a sprightly romp through a part-fictive, part-for-real frontier landscape. Spencer and her husband had honeymooned in the Black Hills in the spring and summer of 1877, though no evidence exists that she encountered Canary in person. Pitched as "a thrilling story of the dime novel order," the book offered a nod to the contemporary popularity of pulp fiction, the appeal of sensationalist western biographies that were heavily creative in design, and of gathering national interest in Calamity Jane. In somewhat caustic tone, the *Livingston Enterprise* placed it firmly in the category of "novel," while the *New York Times* was rather more effusive in praising the tale of a "gentle highwayman" dressed as a man and falling in love.[38]

Spencer's work took the form of light-hearted fancy (her third novel in the style), and reflected its author's captivation with the Black Hills, as well as her theatrical background. None of the historical staples of *Life and Adventures* appeared here, although she did borrow from the narrative contours of the dime novel in constructing a lead actor whose gender identity was colorful, captivating, and confounding. The plot of *Calamity Jane* revolved around an evolving relationship between a cross-dressing outlaw and the "tender creature" Meg, who arrived in Deadwood to start a new life with her new husband. "Tired of this conventional life," mining magnate Charles had struck west in the hope of living out dreams of becoming a frontier hero, only to be thwarted at the first turn when his wife disapproved of him buying weaponry. A stereotype of the cowering female emigrant, Meg was presented as ever fearful, balking at the smell of "frontier life" as an olfactory assault of burning beef and dirty blankets. Calamity Jane, meanwhile, swaggered onto the stage at a women's fete in Deadwood—an enigmatic interloper who held up the party with pistols drawn and the words "Stop! I'll have no run-a-ways from this camp. I'm a woman." Wearing a broad hat, leaning on her rifle, a "mannish jacket and powder horn slung over her shoulder," Spencer's heroine bore more than a passing resemblance to the incarnations of contemporary fiction. True to the author's dime novel leanings and penchant for the literary titillations of gender masquerade, this Calamity was both boyish and "delicately pretty." Meg, for her part, knew exactly who this stranger was, a western prodigy "whose eccentricities were so numerous and daring, so remarkable, that she was suspected to be in every deviltry from robbing trains to playing faro." With an intriguing nod to Calamity Jane's developing cult of frontier celebrity, the local ladies' group had long hoped to encounter this "character of romance," yet struggled to deal with her in the flesh. She seemed equally awkward, enticed by the picnickers in the hope of "capturing" a female kinship from which she had been estranged, before springing to her feet, analogizing women to game birds, grabbing her rifle "as boys do," and demanding a lock of hair from each of them.[39]

The rest of the novel focuses on the interaction between Calamity and Meg as they flirt with one another as polar opposites (genteel eastern wife and rough western vagabond), empathetically drawn members of the sisterhood, and, at times, aspiring sapphic lovers. In one particularly striking scene, Spencer evokes the "irresistible natural attraction" between Meg, "gentle, timid, loving, whose strength was of spirit, of soul" and "that wild, reckless creature, breaking laws as she would snap a straw, laughing at dangers that men would but care to face; yet with a passionate heart, calling out in the wilderness of her life." Inviting Calamity to return to her cabin, Meg cries out: "It may seem strange, yet so it is, that except my husband, no one touches my heart, rouses my interest, as you do Jane!" Then the two women share an intimate moment: " 'Oh! Sweet soul!' Calamity shivered as the words came forth, and trembled as she caught Meg's soft breath, and then, pulling herself away, kissed both of the white hands that Meg had clasped about hers." Spencer destroyed any chance of the romance being consummated by having Calamity Jane killed off (a typical conclusion to frontier romances, and, indeed, early lesbian fiction), but the nature of the relationship between her two leads is worth speculating on. Their liaison may have illustrated a tendency in period fiction to write intimate female acquaintance as intrinsically platonic and asexual, or as innocuous practice for heterosexual romance. Equally, motifs of masquerade and gender deviance might have been used to pique audience interest. Thinking of more heretical possibilities, this might reveal a "hidden history" of same-sex desire—a dress rehearsal for the cabin talk between Doris Day's "Calam" and Katie and its multiple queer interpretations.[40]

Modern biographers have largely avoided such considerations, preferring to write it off as figurative fancy. Those who have given Spencer's work critical attention have typically employed a pejorative tone or positioned her authorial voice within the framework of conventional female camaraderie and ambition. Speaking before the Chicago Corral of the Westerners in 1945, Clarence Paine concluded that "even in melodrama those are hardly scenes between two normal women," before using Spencer as a vehicle to speculate on Canary's possible hermaphroditism.

Writing early in the twenty-first century, Richard Etulain described the work as "hackneyed" and "shallow," though a salient example of how a "sympathetic author" might tap into the "residual femaleness" of Calamity Jane. Elsewhere, he pointed to the novel as strongly indicating Jane's aspirations to be a "typical pioneer woman." For Linda Jucovy, it was an "interesting . . . darker" take that reflected both the proclivities of "fan fiction" and a uniquely female perspective ("being a woman helped Spencer think about Calamity as a real person"). What has been so far missing from literary commentary is attention to the importance of gender difference and disruption in Spencer's narrative. Within the whimsical plotline was a powerful and subversive thread of sexual trans-gression. For some readers, Spencer's take offered escapist and sensation-alist pulp fiction: the usual masquerades in a frontier world turned upside down. Hiding in plain sight, though, was at least the possibility of an alternative reading of a fictive Calamity. If Jane was drawn to the aura of domestic civility that Meg represented, as Etulain alleges, then surely we must acknowledge the novel's natural corollary: that Meg was equally attracted by Jane's frontier-branded unorthodoxy. There are complexities to approaching a nineteenth-century protagonist through the lens of twenty-first-century understandings of sexual and gender identification. However, Spencer's heroine, in common with most contemporary depic-tions of Calamity Jane, was founded on a performance of female mascu-linity. Thinking of how we might locate her story within a frontier imaginary of gender possibility presents a new, and valuable, point of entry for the next generation of Calamity Jane-ologists.[41]

MAKING SENSE OF CALAMITY: "WHO HAS NOT READ OF THEE AND WONDERED AT THY STRANGE STORY?"

As Calamity Jane, literary heroine, roamed the pages of the textual fron-tier, Martha Canary, too, was on the move. The late 1870s through to the mid-1890s placed her in a variety of locations across Wyoming, the Dakotas, Montana, Utah, Idaho, and Nebraska. As plotted on a map by

Linda Jucovy, the scale of her geographical mobility in these years was astonishing: a network of crossing trails that amounted to nearly 10,000 miles of road and rail. Canary's motivation for wanderlust was pathological and pragmatic. She had been living a transient life since childhood and, as a vulnerable woman, the mobile life delivered opportunities for subsistence and a kind of security in traveling light. The bright lights of dime novel fame had brought some benefits in the way of work, drinks tabs, and adoration; but Martha Canary otherwise received little pecuniary advantage. As the *Billings Gazette* put it, "Buffalo Bill Cody is said to be worth $250,000. Calamity Jane, his old associate, is not worth $2.50." Her unconventional lifestyle, meanwhile, invited notoriety and also an itinerant existence. As Jucovy put it: "it was when she stopped that trouble found her." Across the grubby settlements of the nineteenth-century frontier, Canary seemed to lurch from town to town, working as a teamster, hauling wood, cleaning and doing laundry, cooking, and serving in bars and hostels. Sometimes she spent a few days in a location; sometimes several months. She would live on the margins of a sedentary existence, before heading for the road, sometimes sleeping rough, often engaging in drunken rants and spending time in jail. Along the way, she was reputed to have taken a number of husbands or male associates— bull-whackers, cowboys, and outlaws—before becoming a "virtuous wife" with rancher Frank King in the Yellowstone Valley and bearing a son called "Little Calamity."[42]

Much of this narrative trail has been assembled from uncorroborated (and often contradictory) testimonial accounts. Albeit fragmentary, these nuggets of documentary evidence provide a hint as to the turbulent existence of Martha Canary in these years, as she entertained her growing performance identity as a cross-dressing frontier celebrity, and struggled to sit comfortably in a hetero-normative life of settled domesticity. According to the marriage records of Bingham County, Idaho, on 30 May 1888 she was legally wed to William Steers, the father of her baby daughter Jessie, having lived with him in Rawlins for several years. Marked by bouts of drinking and domestic violence, Canary's relationship with Steers was an abusive one (though the *Sundance Gazette* chose to present a capricious partnership akin to dime novel Calamity Jane and Deadwood Dick). Canary instigated several warrants for his arrest and, according to a later editorial in the *Livingston Enterprise*, duly filed for divorce, pertinently telling the judge "the law ain't givin' me a square deal—it never gives a woman a square deal." Eyewitness accounts of her "settled life" with Clinton Burke (whom, according to Etulain, she met at a logging camp in the early 1890s and with whom she lived intermittently until 1895/96) also communicated a sense of disconnection at play, with Canary costuming herself in work overalls, play-fighting with ranch hands, chewing tobacco, and getting into scrapes with the law. Enticed by the latitudes of frontier performance, Canary wrestled with the harsh everyday realities of making ends meet, alcohol addiction, and (quite possibly) complex psychological issues of gender or sexual identity. One ex-cowboy, W. Newcom, who was working in a stable near the run-down cabin at the back of a saloon in Miles City where she lived in the mid-1890s, recalled being woken by her one night in a panic. The local judge, she said, wanted to imprison her simply because she was "a celebrity" and she had no money to bail herself out. Her solution: run away. After swiftly packing her belongings in what Newcom called "her war bag" and "a cheap suitcase," Canary vowed to "whip h--- out of" the judge, before stealing off into the night bound for Deadwood.[43]

The construction of Calamity Jane as a frontier celebrity in the two decades from the mid-1870s involved a complicated interaction between the worlds of fantasy and reality. From her ride into Deadwood in 1876, Martha Jane Canary traveled the trail from regional misfit to western legend thanks to various constituencies: local news press, town gossips, literary works, and the actions of Canary herself. A key element in this ascendancy was a culture of frontier storytelling. Everyone, it seemed, had a yarn to draw on—a figuratively loaded Colt .45 that was light on accuracy but heavy on impact potential. The *Rock Springs Miner* pointed out that "there is scarcely an old-timer in Wyoming and the Black Hills who has not a tale to tell about 'Calamity'." The *Bighorn Sentinel* noted that she was "well known by many of the old timers of the Black Hills, Cheyenne and Sweetwater mining country, and many other places of the wild and woolly West." Essential here were the conjoined forces of performance and provenance: of Calamity Jane as an authentic and convincing western actor.[44]

Embellishing this storied past of authenticity and invention was a photographic record. From the earliest known image of Calamity Jane, which had her dressed in masculine clothes and draped over a rock in French Creek in 1875 (Plate 2), the visual trace through to the early 1890s attested to a woman navigating the worlds of borderlands celebrity and western chronicle. She was depicted by others as part of a process of frontier witness and, at the same time, toyed with her entertainment potential as a "female scout." Attired in the sartorial threads of the western path-finder, with a Winchester at her side, Calamity Jane was image-captured by an unknown photographer in Deadwood in 1876, a visual marker of a female masculinity that formed a lasting cornerstone of her identity (see Plate 1 for a later example). Sitting for famous photographer, L.A. Huffman, sometime between 1880 and 1882, however, Canary sat stoically on an upholstered sofa, dressed in a dark but plainly decorated dress, sporting a coiffured haircut, and with a wedding ring on her left hand (Plate 6). The picture of a respectable pioneer woman, the image contained little to hint at Canary's famed cross-dressing heroics. The caption, though, was prescient. Highlighting the growing reach of a celebrity status that Canary could not (and did not want to) escape from, it read: "One and Original 'Calamity Jane'." A third photograph, taken at Evanston, Wyoming, sometime in the 1880s, communicated a sense of staging at work: Canary stands in front of a studio diorama of western timberline, suited in highly embroidered buck-skin and with her hand resting nonchalantly on a holstered pistol (Plate 4). Reserved for display at pageants and parades, this visual feast of cowboy flamboyance presented a costumed Calamity in full flourish.

According to the *Sundance Gazette*, Calamity Jane was "a notorious woman who has been the uncrowned queen of a thousand frontier towns and mining camps and who is the heroine of numerous sensational publications." This "world of romance," as the *Gazette* regarded it, saw celebrity spotting of Canary/Calamity emerge as a popular sport in the 1880s and early 1890s. Inspiring a folkloric tornado wherever she touched ground, the paparazzi buzz around Calamity Jane illustrated her super-stardom in the making. The *Livingston Enterprise* reported that "Calamity Jane, the most noted woman of the western frontier and the heroine of many a thrilling nickel novel, is taking in the sights in Livingston today," while the *Cheyenne Daily Leader* related: "after an absence of 10–11 years, notorious Calamity Jane who used to figure so prominently in police courts and circles in this city, has again made her appearance."[45]

What is particularly significant here was the sustained nature of popular interest in Calamity Jane, germane to which was a conspiring of lived and invented experience. Indicating the lines of connection between real life and myth-making, a sighting of Canary frequently turned to an exploration of her canonical deeds, usually followed up with effusive and dramatic claims. The *St. Louis Globe-Democrat* ran with sensationalist themes in an article entitled "A Woman's Reputation," which began by noting that "the original Calamity Jane has located [*sic*]" in Lander, Wyoming, before going on to talk of how she "has drank [*sic*] the cup of vile pleasures to the very degree ... [and] participated in the wildest orgies of the brutish brothels of the Northwestern frontier." Positioning her as "the first woman in that wild section," the paper eagerly described the career paths of Canary as scout and prostitute, identifying her as a "singular" personality with "a reckless spirit, a marvelous coolness and courage and a heart that never beat with one soft or pitying emotion." Often, the spying of Calamity in town served as a prompt for frontier nostalgia, social comment on her lifestyle, a grand reveal, or a comic aside. The *Cheyenne Daily Sun*, for instance, eagerly reported Canary as living

on a ranch in the Yellowstone Valley, "thoroughly regenerated, and ...
intended to live a quiet, domestic, grangers [*sic*] life, only visiting town
occasionally to hear the band play." Renouncing a nomadic existence of
which she had reputedly "become tired," the author (known only as
"Pioneer") found her focused on child-rearing, and "training up little
Calamities for the presidency." Illustrating the affection with which some
locals regarded Canary, as well as her widespread renown, the editorial
pointed out: "Everybody in the Hills, as everybody knows Calamity, will
be pleased to learn of her new life and to know that she enjoys it."[46]

The imaginative landscape inspired by this collective telling of the
Calamity Jane story was compelling. Biography, critique, and mythology
swirled together in an animated cocktail of wild West pageantry.
Expounded on in a *Cheyenne Daily Leader* article, the frontier celebrity
of Calamity Jane allowed for collaborations of journalistic flourish,
regional chatter, and literary fable. Entitled "Calamity Jane. The heroine
of Yellow-back literature appears again. A sketch of the reckless life of
this female bandit," the piece reveled in the juxtaposition of flesh and
fantasy provided by Canary's appearance in town. Though assumed to be
"a heated myth of the disordered brain of some penny-a-liner," the
editorial pointed out that Calamity Jane was "a reality," whose "actual
deeds" far surpassed the "pen of a half crazy imagination." Establishing a
critical distance between dime novel heroine and a "fascinating" and
well-known local hero whose antics personified the old days, the paper
embedded Calamity Jane in a collective pioneer memory. With a mythological cloak of "girlish grittiness" and "great gallantry" under Crook's
command, an insalubrious career as the "inmate of the robber's roost"
and "familiar of the frontier brothel," the "heroine of the plains" nonetheless fell short of attaining anything resembling social acceptability.
With bilious flourish (and with a nod both to an image culture fixated
on normative codes of youthful female beauty and a community glancing
more at its civilized future than its scandalous past), the *Leader* railed:
"As age and exposure has [*sic*] ravaged her beauty and tamed her spirit,

her career has become less notorious but not less vile, and she will go to her grave the hideous ruin in appearance she always was in reality."[47]

As such, the popular imprint of Calamity Jane communicated (at times quite complicated) messages about the nature of fame, suggesting a need to revisit the idea of a monolithic grand fable of the West and think, instead, of the function of play and performance code as important ornaments of frontier mythology. "A gossipy account of New Year's observances" in the *Cheyenne Daily Sun* of January 1890 used the occasion of the arrival of "the real and original, of Black Hills fame" in Wendover, Utah (which Jane reputedly described as much like Deadwood, but with the wood sawn off), to talk up her reputation as "a female holy terror [with] . . . no living superior." With sympathetic air, it mused "Poor, old Calamity, who has not read of thee and wondered at thy strange story?" before ending with a casual reference to the comedy value of her unconventional lifestyle choices:

> Jane wishes it to be known through the public press that there is no truth to the rumor that she is about to sail to England to be presented at court, as the decollete dresses insisted upon by the queen will not meet with her approval.[48]

By the mid-1890s, then, the fixings of the Calamity Jane story seemed at once rigidly set and yet ever more ephemeral. Period expositions on the "real" Calamity were bounded by frontier mythology, on-going chatter in local and literary circles, and the oratorical gestures of Canary herself. According to Cassius Reynolds, a Wyoming rancher, "bushels of chills and fever literature have been written about Calamity Jane . . . but a true story of her has never been given to the world." What remained consistent, however, was an overarching theme of cross-dressing frontier swagger. Contemporaries may have struggled with how to present it, but female masculinity was firmly installed as a foundational referent. Reynolds himself followed up the call for an accurate biographical review with broadcasts of a "good and brave woman" who always wore a buckskin suit and "carried military messages for Custer." From Deadwood to the dime novel, successive versions of the Calamity Jane story were grounded in a contested terrain of gender possibility. These border crossings of the frontier binary encompassed many things—damnation and deification, truth and fiction, hedonism and heresy—each of which became an important element in a mesmerizing tumble of frontier storytelling. Hence, a *Cheyenne Daily Leader* article—entitled "Calamity Jane, the heroine of dime novel tales in town. She gives a sketch of her remarkable career. And tells something about Cheyenne's early days"— flailed theatrically from critique to celebration. Canary appeared first as an obsolete oddity, a "genuine character in Western History . . . [who] will be remembered in the annals of Wyoming long after more useful and better members of society are forgotten." Then, via a "life of shame" exclusive from Canary herself, she eased into the role of spectacular, but trusted storyteller. Offering a rip-roaring tour of saloon shoot-ups, love trysts, a treatise on the freedoms bought from wearing male attire, and even an admission of her weakness for drink, Calamity Jane illuminated her own role in creating a storied past. Pouring scorn on a recent depiction of her in the eastern press, she remonstrated: "it was a pack of lies. I very seldom talk about myself, but when I do, I tell the truth. I can prove every word I've told you by people right in this town." This was characteristic Canary bluster, but also conveyed a sense of marketing savvy (and, perhaps, a hint of self-delusion) in championing herself and members of the local community as authentic eyewitnesses to a frontier past. The *Leader*, for one, was convinced, ending its article with a volte-face and a rousing endorsement of her claims to frontier fame: "she has had a varied career, and it would take volumes to do justice to the history of this remarkable woman."[49]

CHAPTER FOUR

"HEROINE OF A THOUSAND THRILLING ADVENTURES"
CALAMITY JANE AND THE CULTURE OF
FRONTIER CELEBRITY (1895-1903)

Life and Adventures ended with two short paragraphs noting Calamity Jane's triumphant return to Deadwood in October 1895. Canary had left town 17 years previously, and now, as she put it, there was "quite an excitement" among former friends and those who had followed her trail across a landscape of frontier gossip, literature, and newspapers and were eager to make her (re)acquaintance. Notable among these was a group of publicists from the Kohl and Middleton dime museum, who signed her up for a theatrical tour of the urban East (and commissioned her autobiography). Appearing at the Palace Museum, Minneapolis, in January 1896, Calamity Jane was placed before an adoring public keen to apprehend "the Woman Scout who was made so famous through her daring career in the West and Black Hills countries." With a well-placed flourish to her audience—"Hoping that this little history of my life may interest all readers, I remain as in the older days, Yours, Mrs. M. BURK, BETTER KNOWN AS CALAMITY JANE"—Canary at once ended her autobiography and pointed to the latest performance of her story: as live entertainer.[1]

This chapter looks at Canary's career on the stage, exploring the translation of her regional notoriety and pulp fiction presence to a theatrical domain, first in dime museums (1896) and later at the Pan-American Exposition (1901). These years witnessed a woman at the height of her fame, and saw the critical ingredients of her legend as a buckskin-clad "female scout," armed with gun and frontier yarns, firmly imprinted in national popular memory. For her part, Canary cut a determined (if somewhat scattergun) presence, as she flirted with the incendiary fires of frontier celebrity, her heroic persona charging across the folkloric plains alongside other dramatizations of western mythology—from the likes of Pawnee Bill, Dr. W.F. Carver, and Buffalo Bill Cody. As Roger Hall notes in *Performing the American Frontier* (2001), the chance to encounter western heroes "playing" their own histories promised a new kind of sensory experience with the imagined West.[2]

Calamity Jane and her publicists had a strong performance pedigree to draw on, one founded on regional gossip networks, literary imprint, and Canary's own rehearsals of (a now trademark) female masculinity. In seeing how these played out in a theatrical context, a few points of comparison are worth exploring. It was significant, for example, that Canary was hired to perform in the dime museum, a space dominated by freak show performers who exhibited their bodies (and attendant stories of physical and cultural difference) as part of a deviant entertainment culture. Equally relevant, given Canary's adoption of an unorthodox gender identity expressed through sartorial choice, lifestyle, and braggadocio, was the world of the (wildly successful) female-to-male impersonators who trod the boards of the late nineteenth-century music hall. Lastly, it is impossible to think about Calamity Jane's frontier-infused pageantry without thinking of the "wild West" show, and especially how her routine compared to that of superstar sharpshooter Annie Oakley.

Out of the limelight, meanwhile, the life experiences of Martha Canary suggested that the performative cloak of frontier celebrity was becoming increasingly threadbare. Beneath the fiery articulations of a parading pathfinder was an impoverished woman, who struggled to find her place in a female frontier where settled domesticity represented the normative recourse. For reasons of necessity, preference, and performance, she had spent most of her life on the move. Now, though, exhaustion was setting in. Not only did Canary seem to brawl with a sense of her folkloric self and the abjections of everyday life (poverty, loneliness, and alcohol addiction), but the regional climate in the West also seemed to be increasingly fickle. Popular attitudes oscillated between nostalgic recollections of a spectacular and nonconformist heroine and a hackneyed caricature that had no place in a modern West of commerce and conformity. Significantly, on her return to Deadwood in 1895, Canary was keen to present herself as a reformed character, insisting that her principal motivation for coming back was to secure a quiet and comfortable home life for her and daughter Jessie. Months later, however, she was on the train to Chicago to act out her frontier celebrity on a new stage. This tangled story of life and invention said much about Canary's performance identity and the shifting boundaries of gender opportunity and transgression in the West.

INTERVIEWING CALAMITY: THE PRODIGAL DAUGHTER AND IMAGE CULTURE IN DEADWOOD

As soon as she arrived in Deadwood, Calamity Jane met the scrutiny of a journalistic gaze that cast her in the role of frontier artefact-in-residence, the symbol of a West both plain speaking in its vernacular style, and yet ever flamboyant and ripe for creative embellishment. Canary, for her part, seemed in equal part estranged and enraptured with her famous reputation. She reveled in the opportunity for a new performance of frontier bluster, but also insisted on her down-to-earth aspirations for a life of ordered respectability. For the Deadwood *Black Hills Daily Times*, the return of Calamity Jane to her old stomping grounds presented time for reflection. Described as "the fearless Indian fighter and rover of the western plains," the ricochet of Canary back to the epicenter of the "wild and woolly West" conjured up a ghost from the past that warranted front-page news. An animated curiosity and national celebrity—"doubtless the best known character of the primitive Deadwood"—the *Times* alleged that there was "probably not a newspaper nor magazine published in the United States" that had not delved into her story. What was especially intriguing was the fact that, in contrast to her arrival in 1876, Canary appeared without gunfire or parade. She wore not a costume of fringed buckskin, but a simple black dress, her daughter in tow. Prompting a flurry of activity from the offices of the *Times* (and evidently still recognizable outside of her famous attire), she greeted newshounds with a handshake and a "happy cordial manner," before holding court in the sheriff's office. Here Canary told reporters that she was not interested in fame, but merely wanted a quiet life, and the chance to make "respectable employment" and find a good school for Jessie.[3]

It was not long before Canary settled into a performance routine of frontier female masculinity. Talking of scouting days, the daring rescue of Captain Egan, the killing of Hickok, and her timely capture of Jack McCall, she had her canonical deeds down pat. This was, however, a moderated performance that suggested an awareness of the capricious nature of a media gaze. Calamity Jane was, after all, a whimsy from the old West in a region busily being purposed for the new century. Caught somewhere between a desire for settled sobriety and the lure of the frontier imaginary, she regaled the *Times* with tales of a lively past in dance halls and saloons, but insisted that she only ever drank "a little." Playing the role of prodigal daughter with aplomb—once wild, now sober—Canary seemed on her best behavior. The *Times*, for its part, firmly bought into this new story (and rewrote its own back issues). Yes, the paper asserted, the Calamity Jane of yore had certainly dressed in a suit of buckskin. She had, however, "never to our knowledge made a disturbance nor was arrested."[4]

Canary's engagement with the *Times* implied tensions at play between stepping away from the limelight and seizing ownership over her folkloric story. She advised that her life had "never been written up, authentic" and that newspapers had printed many "faked interviews with her." Impersonators in the East were defaming her heroic mantle by pretending to be "the original" Calamity Jane. Possibly she was referring here to Ned Buntline's melodrama, *The Queen of the Plains* (1888–1894), which ran in New York and featured Kate Purssell as avenging lead of a border gang. The actor's life, Canary mused, was not to her taste, but she did admit to thinking of approaching "some good writer" to tell her *true* story. Such a comment at once indicated that Canary was aware of popular interest in her iconic, yet mysterious identity, and also provided a hint as to the process by which her later autobiography came into being. To this suggestion, the *Times* issued an enthusiastic endorsement: "Her life would make one of the most interesting and thrilling stories of western life ever put into type."[5]

We can only guess at Canary's motivations in this exchange. She was undoubtedly unhappy with pretenders to her name. Perhaps she saw the newspaper interview as an opportunity to advertise a memoir she was already working on; or, despite assertions to the contrary, she had every intention of embarking on a theatrical career. Historian James McLaird, for one, contends that Canary had put plans for her autobiography in motion, and that the real reason she returned to Deadwood was to join an acting troupe. She had flirted with theatrical life before, first in the company of John "Liver Eating" Johnson, as part of Tom Hardwick's Great Rocky Mountain Show (1884), and then as part of Harry Oelrichs' Fourth of July extravaganza in the town that bore his name (1887). Living up to her reputation of seemingly inviting calamity, Hardwick's show had folded in the wake of financial troubles. Revelers in Oelrichs' were disappointed, as Canary failed to arrive for her performance, after a morning of heavy drinking, loose gunplay, and a holiday spent sobering up in jail. In spring 1895, meanwhile, representatives from the Diamond Dick and Company Wild West Show had been sighted in Dakota, looking for famous characters to populate their show with authentic western flavor. According to the *Rapid City Daily Journal*, Canary had been due to play "the only and original Calamity Jane" on opening night, but never made her debut.[6]

McLaird may be right to suggest that Canary had already charted a theatrical course when she arrived in Deadwood. She might have seen her *Times* interview as an opportune moment to advertise an embryonic stage career. However, given the hand-to-mouth existence that marked much of her life, this seems less likely to have been a calculated marketing ploy, and more the product of an organic and free-flowing performance code long in the making. In fact, Canary's media presence over subsequent months ably communicated her untidy approach to frontier fame. Drinking in the heady vapors of stardom (and fully conforming to her legendary reputation for wild and unorthodox behavior) she succumbed to intemperate temptations. Reported in the *Lead Daily Call*, a newspaper from a nearby town, a "Bloomer Masquerade Ball" held at a local entertainment venue sparked local interest among residents keen to see the "curiosity" of Calamity Jane. Many, the paper noted, "were anxious to spend 25 cents to dance with her, just to have it to say they had danced with 'Calamity Jane.'" Canary, it seems, easily fell in with old habits, became "howling drunk," and lost all thought of collecting receipts from the event (which had been arranged to raise funds for her daughter's schooling). Other endeavors, meanwhile, saw her grapple more successfully with the pecuniary opportunities of being a frontier artefact-in-residence. In Deadwood, she had photographs taken in different poses (seated, standing, but always wielding a Winchester and in full buckskin regalia) at Locke and Peterson's studio (Plate 1). Generating a brisk trade from old-timers and fans of western fable, Canary made enough to live on, peddling her image on the streets and using it as a calling card in local saloons. The Deadwood *Black Hills Daily Times* recorded her, "selling photos of herself taken in male attire, of buckskin." The souvenir, they agreed, was "a novel picture."[7]

Calamity Jane knew how to draw a crowd. Onlookers in Deadwood reputedly "stared at her in open-mouthed amazement, as though she was one of Barnum's curios." One person said she was definitely worth $5 a view. *Bill Barlow's Budget* indulged in a bit of celebrity spotting, finding Canary (somewhat incongruously) "shopping quietly like any other woman" and holding "impromptu receptions on the street corners and in the stores." According to the *Galveston Daily News*, her fame in Deadwood eclipsed even that of a visiting US president. Significantly, what was striking about media reportage was the lack of reference to any of her dime novel deeds. Instead, press reports focused on the storytelling canon recited by Canary and circulated in local testimonial culture, especially the rescue of Egan and her propensity to be "found at the front whenever there was trouble." For the *Sundance Gazette*, the return of Canary to old haunts provided an opportune moment to reminisce on a career as "checkered as Joseph's coat," as well as to extend the hand of pioneer friendship to the "first woman to enter the dark elevations" of the Black Hills, an individual known for her daring résumé as army scout, her arrest of Jack McCall, and, most of all, her distinctive sartorial identity. Decades spent wandering railroad camps, mining towns, and army posts had embroiled Canary in a western landscape that incorporated the theatrical into the everyday. Now, those performance tracks provided a worthy foundation for a more expansive frontier celebrity. Well rehearsed by 1895, the swaggering gender possibility of Calamity Jane had matured into a raucous but recognizable formula. Accordingly, the *Daily News* celebrated "the most mannish woman the West ever knew ... Fearless and masculine in nearly all her attributes, including the costume she usually chose to wear," but with "a feminine tenderness" in her generosity to others and desire to provide for her daughter. A "conspicuous character," Canary possessed the idealized skill set of the western hero, and successfully navigated a homo-social world "as one of their kind." As the *Rawlins Republican* saw it, "she did all sorts of daring tricks ... she was absolutely fearless and would take any risk." Accustomed to expressing her female masculinity through gesture, costume, and holler, it was but a short step for Calamity Jane to take to the stage.[8]

Several months after Canary returned to Deadwood, a substantive biographical piece appeared in the *Illustrated American*. Written by M.L. Fox, it was based on a personal interview between author and subject, and, most significantly, presented the first dedicated news story on Calamity Jane written by a female journalist. Laid out in the form of a first-person travelogue, Fox carried her readers through the streets of

Deadwood and to a powerful and emotional encounter with the town's most famous resident. Speaking in a frontier dialect and musing on her past, present, and future, this Calamity Jane was raw, seemingly unmediated, and gently choreographed by Fox to reveal a woman of striking complexity.[9]

Fox's account began with a walk through the "new" Deadwood. Once renowned for its ramshackle streets, the town was now on the up, and was noted for its "fruit stands, French cafes, wine-rooms, Chinese chophouses, and laundries." Approaching a "cozy little house set among the pines," Fox was welcomed by Canary, who opened the door with an apology for the house's unkempt quality and her own uncombed hair. Described as "of medium height, robust, rather inclined to stoutness," looking good for her years, with expressive eyes and a "decided" mouth, this Calamity was a handsome woman, sympathetically presented. Playing supporting role in this aspiring domestic drama was a youthful looking Clinton Burke, her well-dressed husband. He was somewhat "out of place" in a room that "would have been quite home-like but for its disorder."[10]

Asked if she was glad to be back in Deadwood, Canary reportedly spoke of her delight at seeing old friends, but added that the town had "growed awfully an' hain't the same." Moving to a familiar narrative stage, she claimed heroic ownership of a frontier-bred female masculinity, and her demeanor grew confident. "I was a regular man in them days. I knew every creek an' holler from the Missouri to the Pacific," she proclaimed. Following a breathless biographical recap, a childhood in Missouri, early years as an orphan in Montana, hand-to-mouth existence in the army camps, and iconic naming, she spoke of her liking for unorthodoxy and itinerancy. She "didn't know nothing 'bout women ner how white folks lived," and even claimed to be "part Injun." At this point, it is worth noting the similarity of Canary's orations to those in *Life and Adventures*. Both sprang from the same source, namely her well-practiced line in storytelling. Importantly, by the time of the interview (likely late December 1895 or early January 1896), Canary *had* signed up with press agents from

Kohl and Middleton and was thinking about her act. It seems too bold to claim, as Linda Jucovy does, that Fox's article was nothing more than a publicity stunt by dime museum bosses to showcase "the real Calamity," in readiness for her first appearance on stage. That said, Canary's adherence to her "script" suggests a keen sense of theatrical timing and attentiveness to creating a consistent (and thus credible) storied past.[11]

The last section of the article makes for particularly interesting reading, as one tries to make sense of Canary's contortions of frontier celebrity. According to historian Richard Etulain, this was a landmark moment in uncovering Calamity Jane's ultimate aspirations for hetero-sexual marriage and motherhood. Her "feminine side" finally unlocked by dialogue with a fellow woman, she talked openly of being "honestly married" to Burke, their attempts to "live decent" through various business ventures, and her hope that Jessie could secure a good education. Pondering a future as a stage entertainer, Calamity Jane spoke not of an opportunity to bask in the glories of the frontier imaginary, but of the last recourse of an unconventional woman hamstrung by poverty and middle age: "I've got lots of chances to go into shows an' the like in the East. I'm g'tting' old an' can't work, an' I ain't anybody now, so I might's well do that as anything else." Fox's presentation *was* significant in its unswervingly compassionate nature, as well as in its illumination of a fragile figure inhabiting a challenging frontier environment. What could be disputed (or at least investigated further), however, is the notion that the exchange between interviewer and interviewee was totally disengaged from the world of performance. Potentially, the domestication of Deadwood's prodigal daughter was actually the bigger act.[12]

Indeed, in many ways, Fox's exposition revealed Calamity Jane in a familiar place of mystery and masquerade. Laid out here was a series of set pieces—a montage of life entangled with legend; raw emotional oratory combined with theatrical gesture. Near the end of the article, Fox explained how Canary broke down during the interview, before introducing her daughter—fresh home from school—with the words:

"I'm glad she's come while you're here, fer I want you to see her. She's all I've got to live fer; she's my only comfort. I had a little boy, but he died." A bristly defense of lifestyle had long been part of Calamity Jane's conversational repertoire—telling anyone who would listen that she was unfairly maligned for her nonconformist ways—and Fox's article illustrated both the plain-speaking style and the flamboyant fixings of her celebrity persona. Their encounter all but over, Canary reportedly grasped Fox's hand, thanked her for giving her the time to talk, and issued an emotional outburst: "I've been tough an' lived a bad life, an' like all them that makes mistakes I see it when it's too late." A tragic celebrity seeking absolution and wrestling with the implications of living in and living up to her boisterous identity, she announced, "I'd like to be respectable, but nobody'll notice me; they say, 'There's old Calamity Jane,' an' I've got enough woman left 'bout me so that it cuts to hear them say it." Fox ended her piece with an affirmation: "When I left her I wondered how much better anyone else would have done, placed in the same position . . . She has a kind heart, or her jolly good-natured manner belies her, and she has done a lot of good in the world."[13]

CALAMITY TAKES TO THE STAGE: THE DIME MUSEUM TOUR

Calamity Jane caught the train to Chicago in mid-January 1896, having installed daughter Jessie in St. Martin's Academy, a convent in nearby Sturgis. She sported a bespoke pair of cowboy boots made by Deadwood cobbler John Sohn (and paid for by the Society of Black Hills Pioneers), and exuded a confidence born of investment in her frontier celebrity by Kohl and Middleton. Ever the performer, Canary had been practicing with her new Winchester, in advance of the trip, doing some "splendid shooting," according to the *Rapid City Daily Journal,* by hitting a six-inch bull's eye at 100 paces five times out of eight, even though she had "not handled a rifle much during the past fifteen years." The Deadwood *Black Hills Daily Times* evinced a sense of pride in its home-grown export, surmising:

We venture the assertion that there isn't a character of the western border who is so well known throughout the United States as Calamity Jane, and whose thrilling experiences have been read and devoured by everybody as much as hers.[14]

The dime museum world that Canary entered was a whirlwind of spectacle that courted the attentions of urban Americans in the latter years of the nineteenth century. From early exemplars, such as Charles Willson Peale's Baltimore Museum (1786) and P.T. Barnum's famed American Museum in New York (1842), these "multi entertainment complexes" had proliferated by the 1880s and 1890s to include venues such as Kimball's Museum (Boston), Eugene Robinson's Museum and Theatre (New Orleans), McGinley's (St. Louis), and Hagar and Campbell's (Philadelphia). Combining truth and fiction, education and whimsy, the dime museum boasted a diverse roster of attractions, from semi-permanent exhibits of artefacts, dioramas, and curios to rotating theatrical shows, talks, and live displays from performers in possession of unusual histories, uncanny abilities, or unique physical characteristics. Kohl and Middleton were key players on the circuit, having started their dime empire in Chicago (first on Madison Street in 1882, and then on Clark Street a year later), before expanding across the mid-West to establish venues in Milwaukee, Cincinnati, Louisville, St. Paul, Minneapolis, and Cleveland. Promising affordable titillation for the masses—in the words of one flyer, "freaks, fun, and frolic"—these museums combined *Wunderkammer* and circus traditions with nineteenth-century affectations for science and moral instruction, technological trickery, and an obsession with the exotic and the eccentric. Cultural historian Rachel Adams describes them as offering "a panoramic view of the most sensational forms of alterity."[15]

Calamity Jane was already a popular character in dime fiction, and had an established reputation as a colorful frontier personality, and so it was no surprise that Kohl and Middleton should see the potential in bringing her to the stage as one of their live acts. She was what George

Middleton termed a fresh and exciting "drawing card." Hired for a touring show of various cities over the spring season, including Minneapolis, Chicago, Cincinnati, Philadelphia, and New York, Canary was to deliver two shows daily on an eight-week contract paying $50 a week, plus expenses (by way of reference, stage actors in the period earned $35–$80). Billboards and press adverts enticed would-be audiences with the opportunity to "See this Famous Woman and Hear her Graphic Description of Her Daring Exploits!" and pictured Canary brandishing a Winchester rifle and clenching a knife between her teeth. Opening at the Palace Museum in Minneapolis in the week beginning 20 January 1896, she appeared as the "female scout," garbed in her hallmark buckskin, armed with revolvers, and seated on a throne. Visitors paid a dime for the "lofty privilege" of "gazing upon her" and hearing her story.[16]

From Minneapolis, the Kohl and Middleton troupe moved to Chicago, where the show played at the Clark Street Dime Museum. Canary was advertised as "Greatest of all Attractions." Combining a sense of western mystique with a performance identity that illustrated shifting gender boundaries in American society, Calamity Jane was given sensational billing as "the most famous of all American women." As well as the usual monikers of frontier adventuring, she attracted plaudits as an advance guard for female emancipation: "The woman who made Buffalo Bill eat his words." Integral to Canary's power in this regard was her sartorial masquerade—someone who "wore man's apparel for 25 years"—as well as a frontier-forged androgyny that meant she boasted the "bravery of a lion" and "the tender heart of a woman." Placed in an urban environment, Canary seemed even more anarchic, holstering a female masculinity with a rough-edged flamboyance both raw and well rehearsed. Rousing the crowd with her oratory and "shooting at flying objects with her Winchester and Colt's '45'," the West was dynamically brought to life. One night in Chicago, she reputedly leapt into the crowd to quieten a heckler with the words: "I'm the real Calamity Jane, General Crook's scout. I'm a howling coyote from Bitter Creek, the further up you go, the bitterer it gets, and I'm from the head end." Ending with a theatrically placed gesture towards her firearm, she added: "Now apologize before I shoot the toes off your damned feet." According to the Deadwood *Black Hills Daily Times*, Canary was "right in her glory now."[17]

Reporting on the show, the *Chicago Inter Ocean* gave Calamity Jane front-page billing. Noting her distinctive prowess on the plains and her scouting career with Crook, the paper emphasized her trademark pluck and hailed her "the most interesting woman in Chicago at the present time." From here, the editorial regurgitated the canonical deeds of an individual who attested to an old West "filled with thrilling experiences, enough to have made a dozen men preeminent." Presenting Calamity Jane as a carrier for the frontier myth, and a character around whom folklore readily gravitated, the newspaper had her killing "scores" of Indians and desperadoes, saving Captain Egan, orphaned in Virginia City, and dispatching justice as part of Deadwood's Vigilance Committee. A large dose of artistic license, meanwhile, meant that Jane not only saved the Deadwood stage ("the only one with courage enough to mount the driver's seat"), but also rescued driver Jack McCall, who—in a neat theatrical conceit—went on to kill Hickok, before being arrested by Jane. Evident here were the layers of a frontier choreography that had built up around Canary since the 1870s, as well as a sense of the power of the press to embellish her legend.[18]

Integral to Calamity's star appeal was the peculiarity of her behavior as a woman operating in a "man's world." As the *Chicago Inter Ocean* put it, she "wears buckskin trousers and is not afraid of a mouse." A frontier education, it suggested, provided useful guidance on various issues from urban crime to stray animals, making Canary a handy addition to the city payroll. Moreover, she delivered important instruction on the question of women's rights, the paper noting that "some day ... she declares her intentions of riding over the boulevards astride her broncho [*sic*]. And showing the new women they are way behind the times in their advanced ideas." Aside from the vivid impression it conjured up, this comment placed Canary firmly in the middle of contemporary discourses about female empowerment. Coined by author Sarah Grand in an article for the *North American Review* (March 1894), the "new woman" channeled independence, self-realization, and agency. Leading the way were literary, artistic, and activist women from an urban world, such as Ella Hepworth Dixon and Jennie Augusta Brownscombe, individuals typically advantaged by wealth, education, or career profile. Martha Canary, as such, was an unlikely addition to these ranks, a point not lost on the *Chicago Inter Ocean* when it crafted its fizzy vignette. That said, beyond the throwaway one-liners about Calamity Jane rounding up coyotes and criminals, the paper issued an important reminder of the political message woven into her performance of female masculinity.[19]

Accompanying Canary's theatrical debut was *Life and Adventures of Calamity Jane, By Herself* (1896), the pamphlet that confirmed her buoyant status as frontier celebrity. Blending lived and invented experience in a rip-roaring showcase of western heroics, this publication placed Canary alongside a canonical cast of masculine heroes whose storied pasts were written up in similar vernacular style (see, for instance, *The Adventures of Buffalo Bill Cody* (1904) or *The Life and Adventures of Colonel David Crockett of Tennessee* (1833)). It was, moreover, part of the entertainment toolkit of the dime museum star. Harry Houdini, a regular on the circuit, peddled copies of his "how to" guides to magic tricks, while a brisk trade emerged in biographies of star performers that laid out their family history, notable feats, and show careers. Canary's offering, in fact, was part script and part souvenir. It at once faithfully reproduced the stage patter of the "female scout" and allowed audiences to take something home from their dime museum encounter for just 15 cents. Most significantly, this Calamity—the Jane of *Life and Adventures* and of the dime museum tour—furnished the essential elements of her lasting folklore. Following her trail west with creative flourish and enough frontier flavor to make it appear believable, Canary's autobiography possessed few airs and graces. It was undoubtedly ghost-written, yet managed to convey a sense of the real. For one thing, the fact that Calamity Jane regularly fell to quoting from her autobiography when meeting press or admirers suggests an implicit sense of authenticity to it. After all, the storytelling swagger on which it was based had been successively articulated around countless campfires and saloon tables since the 1870s. Canary's trademark performance of female masculinity, meanwhile, was not simply a stage act, but an essential part of her identity. No wonder it seemed convincing. As Alex Cunningham, who knew Canary in Wyoming and visited her show in Chicago, put it: "she was the same old Calamity," holding the audience enraptured with her "bright wit." Her claims to fame may well have been erroneous, but Canary played unorthodox frontier heroine with conviction.[20]

FRONTIER CELEBRITY REDUX: THE CALAMITIES OF CALAMITY FROM DEADWOOD TO BUFFALO ... AND BACK

Calamity Jane's dime museum trail went cold after Chicago. Some said she fell off the wagon and quit. According to the Deadwood *Black Hills Daily Times*, Canary's "famesque" qualities had at last been exposed: the "fearless woman of the wild and woolly west," renowned for "nonsensical yarns about her exploits," had "at last lost her charms ... the public has gazed upon her—simply an ordinary woman and she is no longer an attraction." Though evidence remains sketchy, it is equally not beyond the realms of possibility that she honored her contractual obligations to appear in Cincinnati, Philadelphia, and New York during the spring season. What we *do* know is that Canary headed back to the Black Hills in May 1896 to collect her daughter, who had been taken ill. Thereafter, she spent most of the rest of the decade wandering the towns of Wyoming and Montana, falling back on various piecemeal occupations (cooking, laundry, cleaning, hunting, and fishing), as well as the well-worn tracks of frontier performance.[21]

Armed with stories of the old days and a stockpile of *Life and Adventures*, Canary set to as a marketer of herself. The *Butte Weekly Miner* made merry with the idea of a career change for the fabled scout, in an article entitled "Calamity Jane. The One-Time Terror Now a Peaceful Book Agent." Validating her identity as genuine frontier storyteller, it noted:

> Many people have supposed that Calamity Jane never existed, except in the imagination of the writer. But she does exist, and at this particular time she is tramping from house to house in Helena, Mont., selling a book, a book she wrote herself and about herself.

As to the lasting literary qualities of the work, the *Miner* was lukewarm, but, as it pointed out, it served Canary well enough as a vehicle of basic subsistence. Dentist Will Frackelton recalled Canary engaged in similar occupations at the Windsor Hotel, Sheridan, where she received some dental work and took the opportunity of "selling little pamphlet autobiographies." Frackelton noted that she was "discreetly reticent" about some elements of her past (particularly her work as a prostitute), but fully endorsed the veracity of her feats as an army pathfinder and Pony Express rider, as opposed to the "unconventional anecdotes" traded by "romantic writers and railroad press agents" about her.[22]

The movements of Calamity Jane at century's end suggested a woman in possession of a fair degree of marketing savvy. She clearly identified avenues for trading on her fame, and used the power of personal appearance, combined with souvenir photographs and copies of *Life and Adventures*, to capitalize on her celebrity status. Frackelton saw her as a woman well accustomed to living "by her wits and her charms." That she was well known was not in doubt. Nor was her ability to play on the crowd appeal of gender possibility. The Helena *Daily Independent* spoke of how the appearance of a "masculine appearing woman" wearing a sombrero and dark rustic dress "attracted considerable attention" from locals. Her autobiography brought decent returns, it noted, because "everyone had heard of Calamity Jane." Likewise, the *Anaconda Recorder* reported how "The Famous Old-Timer Arrived in the City Yesterday," generating quite a hubbub, based on her unique character appeal. In addition to an eye for performance, Canary had a knack for appearing in places where her star power resonated. In summer 1897, she was to be found in Yellowstone National Park, where she had been granted a special permit to sell postcards and was bedecked in full masculine costume for the tourist season. In preparation, C.E. Finn, a photographer working in nearby Livingston, supplied her with several new photographic prints— each of her in buckskin and grasping a Winchester, and captured from various angles. According to the *Livingston Post*, Canary was also wont to hitch her celebrity wagon to the cause of gender equality, on one occasion "togged" in the garb of the new woman and sporting an "air of up-to-dative-ness about her that was worth coming miles to see." Apparently, she hoped to sell her portrait and pamphlet to "admirers of female emancipation" visiting the park. In summer 1898, she wandered as far as Alaska in search of frontier flavor, reputedly doing a turn on stage as the "original Calamity Jane" for Klondike miners, but otherwise finding the entertainments on offer rather "tame."[23]

Set against this story of agency, mobility, and popular fascination was the daily grind of life for an impoverished and unsettled drifter, living hand to mouth and struggling with the everyday realities and restrictions of gender unorthodoxy. Frackelton described her as a figure "stranded by the march of progress," and noted that talk of old times left her "restless and unhappy." Having ended her on-off relationship with Clinton Burke in 1896/97, she embarked on a fractious and short-lived liaison with Robert Dorsett, a water hauler and casual laborer from Livingston. Gambling, gunplay, and drinking also continued to cause problems. Aside from her studio prints, period photographs show a woman in threadbare clothes, sometimes with horses, drinking with friends or seated for the camera, holding cigar and beer bottle aloft, usually with stoic gaze (Plates 7 and 8). Richard Etulain reads such images as evidence that Canary was a "wannabe traditional pioneer woman," whose inclinations to be a wife and mother were sabotaged by her identification "with a romantic Old West" that she "never broke free from." Read through the lens of gender possibility, however, one might see the domestic costuming of Calamity Jane as a staged presence. Haunting, raw, and harrowing, these images suggest a non hetero-normative woman trying to dress herself for an ill-fitting frontier binary. Female masculinity had brought Canary some freedom of movement and a space for self-expression, but was an increasingly difficult identity to inhabit in a rapidly modernizing West. Meanwhile, the exhausting nature of Canary's peripatetic lifestyle (which saw her rack up nearly a thousand miles of travel in the second half of 1896, when she left Deadwood to wander the towns and tourist sites of Montana and Wyoming) seemed to be catching up with her. Falling ill on a train from Livingston to White Sulphur Springs in February 1901, unable to pay her fare, and disorientated, Canary was disembarked at Bozeman, Montana, and spent a few days recuperating at the Gallatin county poorhouse.[24]

The misfortunes of Calamity Jane, doomed frontier star, generated significant media attention. Under the headline "A Celebrated Woman Scout Unable to Support Herself," the *Cheyenne Daily Leader* spun a tale of romantic tragedy, in which "one of the most picturesque characters in the history of the western border life" had been debilitated by a hard, outdoors life. Drawing a sharp distinction between dime novel imprint and true-life adventure, it pointed out that Canary had "an actual career fully as exciting as the most realistic of writers could conjure up," as well as "more nerve and courage than one man in a hundred." The *Deadwood Daily Pioneer-Times* rallied to her cause, adding a dose of pathos for journalistic impact. Calamity Jane, it noted, had been rendered obsolete in her government service by the conspiring forces of electricity and steam power—the assembled forces of modernity. As a resourceful single mother, who had done everything in her power to support her daughter, she deserved not scorn, but reader sympathy. Canary, for her part, was furious at press reports of her enfeeblement, though mollified by the many charitable donations she received as a result. According to the *Livingston Enterprise*, the tale of her slide into poverty had "stirred up . . . the whole country," prompting gifts from old friends, army officers, and those who thought fondly of pioneer days. Together with pamphlet sales, this financial aid saw her live comfortably over the next few months, though visits to the saloon and wet weather in Yellowstone dented her purse somewhat. As the *Livingston Post* quipped, Calamity Jane would be a millionaire by now, but for the fact that "she is unable to keep the proceeds of her work in this wet weather, when keeping the outside dry does no good unless the inside is kept in exactly a reverse condition."[25]

In fact, Canary's stint in the poorhouse set the stage for another— and, as it turned out, her last—theatrical opportunity. On hearing about her plight, eastern author, journalist, and philanthropist Josephine Brake pledged to bring the "female scout" to New York for a homely life of ease and comfort. According to the local press, Brake was well acquainted with Calamity Jane's illustrious story of "daring, courage and strength," and had become enraptured by the idea of delivering the famed frontier heroine into a life of luxurious retirement. Accordingly, she set off for Montana in early July 1901, enlisted the help of local newspaperman Del Alderson, and together they tracked Canary to a mining camp called Horr, south of Livingston. Here she was found in ailing health, "broken in spirit," and residing in a hut belonging to an African-American woman on the Yellowstone River. Canary was apparently taken aback at Brake's sudden intervention, promptly broke down in tears, agreed to go east, and "promised to be a good girl all the rest of her life."[26]

Press accounts of Calamity Jane's "rescue" tended to favor effusive editorials of quixotic redemption. A few, however, were more critical in tone. The *Billings Times*, for one, saw "some advertising purpose" afoot in the new partnership. Warning that "Calamity will bitterly regret leaving Montana," the paper predicted that Brake would be the major financial beneficiary in this murky business of charity. Indeed, some alleged that she had just completed an (entirely unrelated) romance novel and was counting on Canary to help her shift copy back east. In somewhat caustic tone, the *Helena Evening Herald* suggested that Brake came west "in search of a sensation," only to find a sideshow attraction in the shape of Calamity Jane. Noting that westerners would scarcely miss her, it alluded to the complex layers of performance and personality in Canary's celebrity mantle: "Jane has one recommendation, and that counts for considerable. She is perfectly willing to be what she seems to be and seems what she is." The *Billings Gazette*, too, noted the complicated bargain between Brake and Canary, but this time saw the joke on the former. After all, it mused, the installation of Calamity Jane as a frontier attraction was based entirely on a "famesque" portfolio: a roster of invented deeds and exploits conjured entirely from tall tales and dime novels. Once the East saw the real Martha Canary in all her brawling drunkenness, it concluded, things would be rather less rosy. The *Gazette*'s final comment was particularly intriguing. Stripping away all the fakery, it said, Canary *did* have an important story, one whose nonconformist contours were "no less interesting and amusing than the fictitious ones that have given her fame and renown." This would not, however, be suitable for "circulation in the home and among the people of refined natures."[27]

Brake and Canary certainly made for unusual traveling companions. The urbane philanthropist confessed that she was "extremely nervous" on reaching St. Paul, Minnesota, likely a result of Calamity's Jane's brusque demeanor, as well as her resistance to her chaperone's demand for temperance on the train. At the rest stop, Canary was given new clothes and face powder (which she spilt all over her new shirt), while the remainder of the trip saw her barracking with reporters, smoking black cigars, and being her all-round bristly self. Arriving in Buffalo, New York, in late July, the full force of frontier performance kicked in, and any thoughts of a quiet life of retirement were subsumed by fresh opportunities to act out the western fable. Canary had her photograph taken on a tour of Niagara Falls, and appeared as guest of honor at a gala banquet at the Iroquois Hotel, where a raft of local dignitaries were eager to rub shoulders with the curious cross-dresser, who "had passed through the stirring times of the Far West." Choreographing these appearances were Canary's sponsor, Josephine Brake, and Frederick T. Cummins, ex-prospector, cowboy, and "wild West" showman. Entirely in tune with her tendency to be in the right place at the right time when it came to matters of frontier myth-making, Calamity Jane had arrived in Buffalo in the midst of the Pan-American Exposition, a sprawling world fair that was held on a 350-acre site in the city between May and November 1901. Cummins, who had wowed audiences since 1898 with his Wild West Indian Congress, was always looking for new talent to add to his live-action tableau, featuring 42 indigenous nations (Plate 9). He had already signed up Geronimo, and now added Calamity Jane to the bill.[28]

Canary's career as a Pan-American Exposition performer began on 31 July 1901, when she drove a 100-mule team down Main Street as part of the Elk's Parade and finished the day doing trick riding for the Indian Congress. Her next appearance was on 3 August, Midway Day, when 100,000 Expo attendees were treated to a parade compered by Fred Cummins and featuring a western-flavored smorgasbord, including the Carlisle Indian Band, Apache Chief Geronimo, and "Wenona, the Sioux Sharpshooter," who, as it turned out, had a life that was equally dramatic (and a backstory that was equally fabricated) as Calamity Jane's. Presented in Cummins' show as the 18-year-old Dakota-born daughter of Crazy Horse and a white woman, Wenona was just the latest show personality of Lillian Smith, a 29-year-old from New England, who had toured with William Cody's troupe as the "California Huntress," fallen out with rival Annie Oakley, and escaped her controlling father to inhabit an itinerant existence "playing Indian" in various venues from Hawaii to Virginia. By the time of the Indian Congress, Smith was well practiced as "Princess Wenona," having run her own curio business selling tomahawks. She was in the habit of wearing a full-length fringed tunic, and was blessed with shooting skills that supposedly came from her connection to the Spirit World. Like Calamity Jane, the assumption of an enticing story and a costume to match allowed Smith to claim a new identity (and a sense of personal freedom) through performance.[29]

Billed as "the heroine, who wears a hero's garb," Calamity Jane enthralled visitors to the Congress with displays of horse riding and gunplay (Plate 10). A late arrival to Cummins' show, she did not feature in initial merchandising. Subsequent programs, nevertheless, included the usual roster of her western heroics, added to which was a career masquerading as a man in the Civil War—a pertinent indication of the importance of gender unorthodoxy to Canary's star appeal. Buffalo newspapers eagerly reported that "the arrival of Calamity Jane at the Indian Congress has stirred things to greater activity." At least half of Expo attendees in the week ending 4 August stopped by to see the Indian Congress in all its frontier pageantry. According to Wirt Newcom, a Montana cowboy from the old days, who visited the arena with eastern relatives, Calamity Jane "stole the show." After a curtain call, he stayed behind to introduce his family to the "wonderful woman" they had come to see. Newcom was concerned that Canary would be rude and curmudgeonly, but he need not have worried: she was a model of charisma and charm. As he put it, "Never will I forget poor old Jane, and never was I more amazed . . . I was too delighted with her and she was as polite as any one of the party and entertained them all royally for fifteen or twenty minutes."[30]

Calamity Jane's celebrity bronco, however, was about to buck. Encumbered by both Brake's levy on her earnings (which left her with only 30 cents of her $25 wage, plus meals, for a week's work) and her insistence on sobriety (the latter, as Calamity confessed privately to Newcom, was becoming increasingly hard to stomach), Canary was restless. After a heady dose of performance highs, she reputedly severed her connection to Brake and renegotiated a new contract with Cummins. As soon as she had coin in her pocket, she hit the local saloons. According to the *Buffalo Evening News*, "the aged celebrity" was found inebriated in Amherst Street, just near the gate of the world fair, by a policeman who apprehended her and put her in jail for the night. Canary received a suspended sentence, the paper noted, having hoodwinked the judge into believing "it was the first time she had ever been arrested." Reporting the incident later in the month, the *Livingston Enterprise* presented the tale as a "snag" to Brake's reform program, and pointed out that those "best acquainted" with Calamity Jane would surely conclude it more likely that "she will work a change in Mrs. Brake instead of herself." Canary soon ran into trouble again for excessive drinking, threatening behavior, and profane language, before making fervent enquiries as to when Bill Cody was due at the Buffalo showground. Cody arrived on 26 August, to be greeted by a Calamity Jane eager not to find employment in his show as a famed frontier scout, but to borrow money. Her intention, she told him, was to head back west. "They've got me Buffaloed, and I wanter go back. There is no room for me in the east. Stake me to a railroad ticket and the price of the meals, an' send me home," she pleaded. Cody obliged with a fare to Chicago, where Canary delivered impromptu shows in dime museums and peddled her autobiography to raise further funds.[31]

Calamity Jane slowly made her way back to Montana over the next several months, running the rails, and making stops at various places for shelter and sustenance. She appeared in a dime museum show in Minneapolis, where she reprised her earlier role at the Palace Museum, before spending the winter in South Dakota. Although her arrival in Pierre began rather quietly, before long she was making a name for herself with what one local paper called "hopified elixir" and "pyrotechnic billingsgate," and behaving in a "semi-facetious, semi-serious manner." Tracking her homeward ramblings, the regional press gave the impression of a faded relic, out of sorts in a modernizing West, but a regional treasure nonetheless. The *Cheyenne Daily Leader* reported on her movements in early October, when she was headed "to her haunts in the wild and woolly West," while the *Fergus County Argus* talked of her shaking "the dust off the effete east" and "working her way back to familiar scenes." Editorials in the *Livingston Enterprise* consistently presented her story through the lens of east–west exploitation. Gladly reporting that the "noted heroine, scout, booze fighter and all 'round product of the early days" was "still on Earth," the paper saw deception at work, with an honest broker Canary deceived by a nefarious Josephine Brake into "the undesirable vocation of peddling a blood-curdling tale of western life written by her friend and benefactor." A week later, she was headlined in "Another Tribute to Calamity" as the "Victim of Misplaced Confidence," tricked by an "eastern adventuress ... posing in the guise of a spiritual philanthropist." "Like a true western product," the paper pointed out, "Jane naturally kicked good and hard." By April 1902, Canary was back in old "stamping grounds" in Montana, where, according to the *Livingston Post*, "she sings a song, a song of troubled verse, with a drink and a dirge, a curse and a prayer, a cow horse and a hearse."[32]

FREAKS, MASHERS, AND LADY SHARPSHOOTERS: CELEBRITY, GENDER, AND PERFORMANCE IN THE LATE NINETEENTH-CENTURY ENTERTAINMENT LANDSCAPE

In "A Strange Woman," published for the *Boys of England* magazine in 1881, Calamity Jane had recoiled from the idea of a theatrical career, proclaiming "too much respect for herself to travel with big snakes and double-headed women." In this explicit reference to the world of the freak show, the dime novel heroine drew a sharp distinction between her brand of stardom and the type that involved physical or cultural differences in the spotlight of deviant entertainment. Despite Canary's assertion, however, her stage career in the 1890s might be usefully read in the context of the freak show, a mode of mainstream theatrical entertainment incredibly popular in the late nineteenth and early twentieth centuries. Significantly, the dime museum was the principal venue for such performances, and that (rather than the "wild West" show) was the theatrical landscape in which Calamity Jane first appeared. Period commentators, indeed, used a language of novelty, curiosity, and abnormality to describe her popular appeal. For the Miles City *Yellowstone Journal*, Calamity Jane's fame derived from two sources—deviance and authenticity: "she's a queer freak of nature, and is as well known on the frontier as any living person."[33]

The term "freak" was first used in the mid-nineteenth century, when it was principally invoked to describe something unnatural. By the late 1880s, the industry of the freak show was in full swing, providing exhibitions of human bodily and cultural difference in museums and touring shows that combined interest in the scientific (notably fed from enquiries into evolutionary theory) and the exotic (fueled by colonialism), filtered through a dazzling mass entertainment circuit that traded in the bizarre and the macabre. In the United States, the genre was firmly associated with P.T. Barnum, whose American Museum traded in a roster of "living curiosities" and "strangest human beings"—from the 161-year-old nursemaid of George Washington (1883) to colossal Texas ranchmen (1889) (Plate 14). An essential aspect of freak entertainment culture was the chance to see something exceptional and spectacular, what Barnum called "incredible eccentricities in form and action." Within this broad umbrella, meanwhile, performers were divided into several categories. There were "born" freaks—in other words, individuals noted for their physical attributes (size or stature); "exotics," which usually comprised non-western peoples; "self-made freaks," including tattooed men and women; novelty acts (sword swallowers, fire eaters, and the like); and those who fell under the label of "gaffs," in other words counterfeits and mock-ups. George Middleton wrote in his 1913 memoir of exhibiting "many strange curiosities and some very interesting ones" as part of his dime museum empire. In the Kohl and Middleton show in Minnesota, Calamity Jane thus shared billing with lady sword swallowers, "Big Ella," Goliath "the Strongest Man Alive," and Commodore Speck "The Human Mite." In Chicago, she performed alongside Unzie "the Aboriginal Albino Beauty," Ralston "The Rattlesnake King," William Lee "The Nail King," Adams "The Clever Magician," and Texas Jack "One-armed Whittler."[34]

The nineteenth-century freak show was an uncomfortable terrain of prejudicial assumptions and salacious voyeurism. However, it usefully illustrates the way in which bodily and cultural difference was constructed and contextualized in the period, and sheds light on the nature and function of mass entertainment. Rather than "freaks of nature," here were (as Rosemary Garland Thomson notes) "freaks of culture," whose abnormal bodies were viewed, codified, and consumed according to dominant social values. As such, these sites of whimsy and entertainment communicated important ideas about deviance, morality, and normality. By looking at those of unusual height, size, or strength, or in possession of distinctive traits, audiences measured their own sense of normalcy. At the same time, popular interest in performers suggested a more complicated process at work, one in which viewers were both captivated and challenged by the curious visions before them. As Lillian Craton puts it, the freak show presented "conflicting impulses to reject, exhibit and celebrate the odd body."[35]

Where did Calamity Jane fit in this picture? As a famed cross-dresser and frontier artefact, she was admitted into the freak hall of fame by an unconventional gender profile and an association with a glamorous western past, all wrapped up in the celebrity stardom of sartorial masquerade. Canary had already been labeled a "freak" by the *Cheyenne Daily Leader* in years past for her masculine costuming. A press clipping from the Stockton *Evening Mail*, likewise, pondered the gender identity of Babe Bean in the style of a sideshow billboard as "the mysterious girl-boy, man-woman, or what-is-it?" That the contours of gender performance and possibility were a subject of keen popular fascination was highlighted in the 1891 novel *A Florida Enchantment*, in which leading protagonist Lillian Travers buys African sex-change seeds from a dime museum, swallows them in a fit of rage after an argument with her fiancé, and spends the rest of the book plagued by fears of ending up in a freak show, playing "the woman man." George Middleton saw that it was "a showman's place to supply what the public wants," and the female masculinity with which Calamity Jane was identified was a clear draw. Central to her appeal was the way she straddled the boundaries of the gender binary, already a staple of the freak show universe and exemplified by hermaphrodites and bearded ladies, such as Julia Pastrana and Madame Clofullia. As Thomson puts it, "bodies whose forms appeared to transgress rigid social categories such as race, gender, and personhood were particularly good grist for the freak mill." Moreover, as a charismatic relic of the "wild" West, Canary acquired an additional veneer of exoticism that fitted well into freak show proclivities for exploring the relationship between civilization and "the other," as well as a heady connection to a grand American destiny recently fulfilled. Sharpshooting and buckskin-clad, the dime museum identity of Calamity Jane was expressed via bullet-point prose and affirmed by multiple exclamation marks: "The famous woman scout of the wild west! Heroine of a thousand thrilling adventures! The terror of Evildoers in the Black Hills! The Comrade of Buffalo Bill and Wild Bill!"[36]

Character development was intrinsic to the entertainment culture of the freak show, with each act carefully framed to play to popular interest. As Rachel Adams points out, "freakishness is a historically variable quality, derived less from particular physical attributes than the spectacle of the extraordinary body swathed in theatrical props, promoted by advertising and performative fanfare." From poster and billboard marketing, set design, costume and script, to souvenir memorabilia, the choreography of "enfreakment" was all encompassing. These elements worked together to accentuate the specific and unique attributes of a "living exhibit." A key aspect of the show was the opportunity for audience participation. Not only did the visitor experience focus on "scopophilia" (Laura Mulvey's term for the "love of looking"), but it also included the chance to "know" something of the enfreaked personality by communicating with the character directly. Storytelling was an important element in this exchange, as the audience looked to exhibitors to narrate their personal histories, before engaging in conversation and sometimes touching deviant bodies. As such, the performance of the freak show was co-constituted by show promoter, actor, and viewer. Also important in this regard was an interrogative matrix, in which visitors tested the rightful provenance of an exhibitor. Notable examples of what Marlene Tromp calls "epistemological speculation" were the "What is It?" and the Feejee Mermaid. With such thoughts in mind, Calamity Jane worked as a sideshow act on a number of levels. Not only did she have a strong performance identity that traded in novelty and difference, but also her story was captivating and mysterious. As Laurence Senelick notes, the theatrical allure of cross-dressing combined "divinity, power, class, glamour, stardom, concepts of beauty and spectacle," and toyed with the "visible contrasted with the unseen or concealed." Used to peddling a line in gender unorthodoxy, dealing with hecklers, and playing on an enigmatic identity, the frontier celebrity of Calamity Jane translated well to the freak show universe. Especially interesting in all this was the fact that the fabricated nature of her famous deeds mattered not a jot in an entertainment landscape in which, as Robert Bogdan notes, "in a strict sense of the word, every exhibit was a fraud."[37]

What would the freak show experience have been like for Calamity Jane? In approaching this question, it is impossible to ignore the exploitative context in which performers found themselves. As Thomson notes, "enfreakment emerges from cultural rituals that stylize, silence, differentiate, and distance the persons whose bodies the freak-hunters or showmen colonize and commercialize." Delivering multiple performances a day (sometimes up to 15 shows), often for low pay, and at the mercy of unscrupulous managers and a voyeuristic public, it is hard not to see the life of the itinerant entertainer as a desolate one. Both Canary's fractious relationship with Brake and her alcohol dependency indeed give some hint as to the practical and psychological challenges endured by those trading in deviance as entertainment. That said, for some, the decision to exhibit in a dime museum brought both celebrity status and financial reward. Siamese twins Chang and Eng, and General Tom Thumb, for instance, successfully marketed their bodily difference to achieve high-profile status, buy a property portfolio, and fund business ventures.

Big Winnie, a well-loved act on the Kohl and Middleton circuit, earned $500 a week. Thus, as Nadja Durbach points out, consent, choice, and agency each had a place in the performance landscape of the freak show.[38]

A particularly intriguing character in this landscape of freakery was Milton Matson, arrested in San Jose in 1895 for signing cheques in the name of "Luisa" and imprisoned for two weeks. Fraud charges were dropped when it was discovered that Milton was indeed the legitimate signatory. Born in England, Matson took to dressing in male clothing when her brother died (she said "it seemed natural to me from the first"), and passed as a man for 25 years. On release, things took a theatrical turn, as Matson decided to capitalize on chatter surrounding the gender masquerade to perform as "the bogus man" in a dime museum run by Frank Clifford. Speaking to the *San Francisco Examiner*, Matson explained the financial gains to be had by playing freak: "I'm getting letters from all sorts of showmen offering good salaries if I will exhibit myself. It amuses me very much ... I'm beginning to think it pays to be notorious." The paper remarked that the "part will not be a difficult one," and went on to set the sideshow scene:

> She will be faultlessly attired in patent leathers, a handsome dress suit, embroidered linen and a white tie. She will recline in an easy-chair on a little platform and chat with the socially inclined, but whether she will divulge any of the interesting secrets connected with her numerous love episodes is not definitely known.

Reportedly, a clause in Matson's contract prohibited the wearing of men's clothes off stage, in order to preserve the exclusivity of the show.[39]

In understanding the frontier celebrity of Calamity Jane, some mileage is to be gained from thinking of her as a character who consciously "enfreaked" herself—i.e., assumed a character for the purpose of entertainment. Indeed, Canary actively marketed herself as a cross-dressing curiosity to win popular acclaim (and some pecuniary gain). At the same time, her performance of gender unorthodoxy was a lifestyle choice long in the making, and an important part of who she was. This textured characterization was laid out before dime museum attendees, who, beneath the whimsical flourishes, encountered an authentic and believable figure of gender possibility. The landscape of freak entertainment in the nineteenth century was often a socially conservative one. In the show arena, visitors conjured with the idea of "a world turned upside down," but left with their own sense of normalcy confirmed. A brush with the spectacular provided a message of reassurance, put succinctly by Leslie Fiedler: "*we* are freaks, not you." That said, a more subversive reading of the landscape of deviant entertainment suggests that the sight of enfreaked personalities and their unusual bodies also worked to destabilize normative categories. Various binaries (human–animal, male–female) were regularly and tantalizingly unpicked on the show circuit. According to Durbach, " 'staring at the other' sometimes went both ways," while Fiedler admits that, for some visitors at least, to look at a freak was to see your "secret self." The disruptive potential of Calamity Jane was especially significant, given the empowering associations of the frontier and the power of her personal story. Woven into her nonconformist costume was an opportunity to live out forbidden desires and to ponder the idea of swapping an ordinary life for that promised by a freakish and famous body. As Thomson argues, "fascinated onlookers perhaps longed in some sense to be extraordinary marvels instead of mundane, even banal, democrats in a confusing cultural moment." With her trademark masculine swagger, Calamity Jane delivered a political performance in liminal terrain, underneath her colorful gesticulations of frontier fable a concrete demonstration of gender as an unstable and fluid category. As Jack Halberstam notes:

the very existence of masculine women urges us to reconsider our most basic assumptions about the functions, forms and representations of masculinity and forces us to ask why the bond between men and masculinity has remained relatively secure.[40]

The dime museum freak show was not the only entertainment landscape promising a challenging of normative codes through sartorial revue in the late nineteenth century. In her flamboyant displays of cross-dressing repartee, Calamity Jane might equally be compared to the male impersonators of the music hall and vaudeville circuit. As historian Clare Sears points out, at a time when greater restrictions were being placed on gender-specific dress codes on the streets of American cities, so-called "mashers" on the stage were an enticing draw for theater audiences. As a woman described by the *Cheyenne Daily Leader* as "one of the remarkable women of the West . . . female in sex, but a man in employment and association," Canary shared something with the likes of Annie Hindle, Ella Wesner, and Vesta Tilley—stars who made successful careers from playing out a masculine persona on stage.[41]

Just as in the dime novel and the freak show, the gender-bending routines of music-hall mashers—parading in men's suits and singing of sweethearts and dandy days—both upheld and challenged hetero-normative code. Presented as playfully aberrant, they celebrated masculinity and proclaimed the sanctity of the male–female binary, yet at the same time caricatured its very essence, by showing how women might easily "pass" as men and claim their power. Both on and off stage, the world of the male impersonator also provided a forum for alternative expressions of sexual and gender identity. An important site of same-sex desire and gender masquerade, the music hall was, as Laurence Senelick notes, a place where "the personal predilections of the performers were camouflaged by the contours of the stage."[42]

The career and life of Annie Hindle, the first male impersonator to achieve notable success in the USA, illuminated several of these aspects at play. Born in Hertfordshire, England, in the mid-1840s, she was adopted by Mrs. Anne Hindle and put on the stage at the age of five, wearing male attire and singing of wine, women, and sport. Hindle emigrated to New York in 1867 and forged a successful stage career from the late 1860s until the late 1880s, earning up to $150 a week performing such songs as "Do

Not Put Your Foot on a Man When He's Down." Following a short-lived marriage to actor Charles Vivian (and, possibly, minstrel William W. Long), she disguised herself as a man named Charles and married her dresser, Annie Ryan. Held in 1886 in Michigan, where Hindle was touring, the wedding ceremony featured female impersonator Gilbert Saroney as best man. In common with Canary, press renditions looked in earnest for Hindle's foundational femininity—describing an individual of "medium stature, with a pleasing figure and voice"– yet also reveled in her convincing masculine transformation. "As a male impersonator her sex is so concealed that one is apt to imagine that it is a man who is singing," gushed one show review. In Senelick's judgment, the blurred boundaries between "masculine stage persona" and "masculine personality" gave Hindle a space for personal expression, as well as allowing the possibility of a same-sex relationship. At the same time, however, media interest gloried in freak show-style speculation as to the essence of her gender profile and tawdry tales of her unorthodox lifestyle. The Grand Rapids *Telegram-Herald* exemplified the trend in tabloid sensationalism with the headline "Married Her Maid: The Strange Story of Charles and Annie Hindle, a Man Masquerading as a Woman."[43]

Audience impressions of the male impersonator, equally, throw some light on a performance reading of Calamity Jane. Was cross-dressing an act of celebration or critique? An affirmation of male power or a repudiation of it? Elizabeth Drorbaugh contends that "the theater may have offered spectators some latitude for imagining more elastic social roles." Senelick, too, ponders whether women in the audience found "their hidden desires enacted by the cross-dressing music hall singer." That women were the principal fans of the male impersonator is significant in unpacking the subversive possibilities of the genre. Hindle, after all, received many so-called "mash notes" from women who were romantically attracted to their stage hero(ine). Mimicking male gesture and manner on stage, meanwhile, represented a cogent attack on patriarchal authority (though, as Katie Horowitz points out, the capacity of the cross-dressed woman to challenge male hegemony remained limited by the *actual* power they wielded). What is also worth noting was the changing moral climate of the music hall, which from the 1890s moved away from more masculine routines (what Senelick calls "butchness") to champion acts suggestive of boyish androgyny and family-friendly values. Famed for her performances of "Algy" (1895) and "Burlington Bertie" (1900), Vesta Tilley built up a keen following as a male impersonator, commanding $10 a minute on stage at the height of her fame. In contrast to Hindle, however, she cultivated a conformist image, was married to a man, and asserted the essentially wholesome quality of her repertoire. In "A Plea for Male Impersonators," Tilley was quoted as saying: "the theatre going public of this day . . . like to see a woman don male attire, providing she can do so without showing any sign of vulgarity." One critic took comfort in the finely observed limits to her gender masquerade, musing: "for all her truth to masculine style, you get a sense of the feminine . . . just so much that the truth of the male gesture is made the more piquant by that hint of curving shape."[44]

At a time when gender codes were in flux and sexual categories under renegotiation, the way women dressed and acted on stage was not a matter of idle fancy. Laura Horak rightly cautions against reading the historical landscape of cross-dressing as a mirror of twenty-first-century "concerns and identities" to locate performers as implicitly feminist, lesbian, or transgender in orientation. As she points out, the vaudeville scene continued to thrive, in part, because of the "open meanings" ascribed to its stars. However, with contemporary psychologists creating a new gender paradigm in which "degenerate homosexuals" or "inverts" were seen as holding a "strong preference for male garments" and behaviorisms (including smoking cigars), the holstering of an alternative masculinity assumed great significance. For Calamity Jane, an individual well known for expressions of sartorial and social defiance, this emerging discourse had the potential to disrupt her position in a patriotic frontier imaginary and to curtail her everyday lifeways. As Peter Boag notes, by the end of the century, cross-dressing was associated with "depravity, decadence, and degeneration—the very thing America's frontier past promised the nation it was not." Just as fashions for music-hall mashers began to embrace a more conformist line, so, too, did the fable of "how the West was won." For Clarence Douglas, writing to the *Washington Post*, Wyoming needed investment in schools, rather than a folk culture that elevated Calamity Jane as role model. Chief Justice Corn, in a 1903 lecture on "The Evolution of the State," celebrated the fact that Wyoming no longer featured "short-haired women or long-haired men," but had "a high type of the human race." These prescriptions for a future West had serious implications for a character that consistently inhabited a terrain of gender unorthodoxy. Unlike the masher, of course, Calamity Jane was not only acting as a man, but also acting out a storied version of her own transgressive past. In a world that necessarily blurred politics and play, her performance of female masculinity was increasingly heretical.[45]

Such a conclusion is usefully affirmed by comparing Calamity Jane to her closest rival in the realm of "wild West" entertainment: Annie Oakley. Often assumed to have known each other or to have performed together, in fact only one thing connected the two women—Buffalo Bill Cody. Calamity Jane knew Cody, but the closest she came to starring in his grand staging of western history—what he headlined to show audiences as "America's National Entertainment"—was a line in the 1884 program where she was credited as the savior of the Deadwood stage. In Cody's choreography, of course, it was he who swooped in to save its passengers from ambush. No stranger to frontier celebrity, Buffalo Bill had made his own trail from historical presence to personality of the old West. From his birth in Iowa, he had seen service as a scout and hunter for the US Army, dime novel portrayals, and frontier idolatry to become showman-compere of a wildly popular live-action pageant that appeared across the United States and Europe in the late nineteenth and early twentieth centuries (Plate 12). Interestingly, the staples of Cody's superstardom (scouting career, gun and horse skills, pulp fiction imprint and mantle of frontier heroism) bore more than a passing resemblance to the leitmotifs of the Calamity Jane legend. His showstoppers (including "The Attack on the Settler's Cabin," "Buffalo Hunt," "Custer's Last Stand," and "Pony Express Ride") also found comparison with Canary's oratorical and theatrical performances. Cody, too, had his problems with money and a somewhat tangled personal life, but managed to orchestrate the transition from westerner to western celebrity more easily than Martha Canary: it was a much simpler ride in the frontier imaginary to play an archetypal male hero than a female who wore a hero's garb.[46]

Annie Oakley, who joined Cody's troupe in 1885, highlighted the complex terrain of gender conformity and challenge embedded in performance code. Signed up for a trial run as part of manager Nate Salsbury's marketing strategy, Oakley was hired for her novelty appeal. She also diluted the show's blunt celebration of violent masculinity by adding a dose of the respectably spectacular, what I call here tender, armed femininity. As a "female sharpshooter *and* a symbol of domesticity," historian Louis Warren argues, she projected a very different character to Calamity Jane, "a genuine cross-dressing frontier woman." Born as Phoebe Ann Moses in 1860, in Darke County, Ohio, she sported a backwoods biography that situated her skills with firearms in a homespun vernacular. As Oakley recounted to the Nashville *Barrier*, "I guess the love of a gun must have been born in me." In common with Canary, she too had a "creation story"—located firmly in the midwestern pioneer tradition—which was later reproduced in Cody's show programs. Growing up shooting critters and forging a lucrative business supplying Cincinnati hotels with game meat, Oakley went on to meet trick shooter Frank Butler at a local rifle competition (which she won). The two struck up a romance and married in 1882, before successfully playing as a pistol-packing double act on the vaudeville circuit as the "Great Far West Rifle Shots."[47]

When she joined Cody's entourage, publicity fixed on crafting a useable star. With her four-foot-eleven-inch frame draped in a finely embroidered dress and jacket, "Little Missie" (or "Little Sure Shot," as Sitting

Bull reportedly dubbed her) exuded a sense of feminine charm and domestic sensibility, quite different from the butch and broad-shouldered Canary (Plate 11). Rather than "heroine of the plains," Oakley was hailed by her adoring audience and by press reporters as the "*girl* of the western plains" (emphasis added). She, as manager Nate Salsbury noted, "set the audience at ease" with her respectable demeanor, before taking them on a rip-roaring demonstration of gun-slinging wonder, splitting playing cards in half with well-placed aim, using a mirror to shoot over her shoulder at targets, and sending cigars spinning from the mouths of co-stars (including a future Kaiser Wilhelm II). For the London *Evening News*, Oakley was "The most interesting item on Buffalo Bill's programme ... far and away the best." Traversing the arena with a light-footed skip, and blowing kisses to the audience, she was firmly installed in a hetero-normative home life of devotion and sobriety (despite her husband's recurring role as target). After the curtain went down, show attendees could find her in a tent, surrounded by needlework and baked goods, a world away from Canary's publicly displayed frontier masculinity.[48]

At the same time, both performers sold their routine on the premise of a world upturned. Also, their entertainment personas were a blend of fact and fable. Just as Canary was not a "female scout," so Oakley was not a "true" westerner. Both sought to manipulate their star appeal. In common with Canary, Oakley experimented with a career on the stage (in the show off-season, especially). She starred in a western melodrama in Philadelphia entitled *Deadwood Dick, or Sunbeam of the Sierras* (1888), as well as a frontier romance, *Miss Rora* (1894) and a girl-captures-outlaw adventure *The Western Girl* (1902), the latter two playing to theater audiences on the eastern seaboard, and even touring Great Britain. Dexter Fellows, fellow entertainer, called Oakley a "consummate actress," while her theatrical turn derived much from its fanciful value: a seemingly oxymoronic gender display of firearms acuity and girlish flourish. In public orations, Oakley appeared keen to distance herself from the trappings of first-wave feminism, yet implicit in her act was an invitation for a rethinking of gender expectations. As such, her demonstration of a tender, armed femininity hoisted traditional values, but also illustrated changing times. The British dime novel *The Rifle Queen: Annie Oakley* (1884) judged its star protagonist as presenting firm evidence that "with natural ability and a little encouragement ... courage and perseverance," a woman "can do what any man can do." According to historian Glenda Riley, Oakley served as a "prototype" for a new generation of women embarking on careers in competitive sports, especially rodeo, while many latter-day biographers have presented her as blazing a feminist trail.[49]

Oakley's command performance as a female sharpshooter thus delivered an ambiguous message: one that reveled in the idea of a woman taming a gun (she was, by all accounts, a better shot than Cody), but that took solace in the conservative fixings of its principal lead. Oakley's sartorial choices were incredibly significant in signaling the gender conformist message of "Little Sure Shot." So, too, were her conventional feminine mannerisms and the obvious presence of her husband and manager. Within the theatrical confines of the "cowgirl" performer—a label used by Cody and others to showcase female equestrians and trick shooters from the early 1890s—Oakley represented a contrast to those sporting a muscular physique and riding astride in trouser suits. The latter, significantly, drew crowds for their rebellious look, but also invited a more critical response than Oakley's reassuringly homespun gunplay. As circus performer Fred Stone pointed out,

> There was never a sweeter, more lovable woman than Annie Oakley. It was always amusing to watch people who were meeting her for the first time. They expected to see a big masculine blustering sort of person and then the woman with the quiet voice took them by surprise.

As such, Oakley's brand of frontier celebrity was a lot less subversive than Calamity Jane's. *The Rifle Queen*, for one, expressed unbridled relief that "when the rifle or shotgun is laid aside, she is acknowledged to be an affable, natural and womanly 'American girl' who has by her unusual skill and pleasant, quiet ways made friends with all the sportsmen who have met her."[50]

In their own distinct ways, the popularity of freak show performers, music-hall mashers, and "wild West" sharpshooters suggests an interest among late-nineteenth-century audiences in characters that patrolled the boundaries of gender possibility. A buckskin-clad and enigmatic female scout, Calamity Jane sat in a stage landscape of shock and spectacle, where popular entertainment served as a cathartic site for the bolstering of social conventions, yet provided an opportunity for heretical extrapolations on the "what if?" Canary's theatrical routine was salacious and subversive in its assertions of female masculinity, and championed the frontier as a unique space that allowed for flourishes of unconventional behavior. It posed a significant challenge to the firmament of masculine authority, by appropriating its canonical props of sharp-shooting swagger, story, and costume. Of course, the difficulty in successfully navigating this performance terrain of gender alterity came from the embedded expectations of normativity, both on stage and off. While perfectly happy to find popular amusement in the rambunctious storied past of a quirky pioneer, the world of industrial conformity delivered less and less room to roam for Calamity Jane. Tracked in newspapers from the time of her retreat from the Pan-American Exposition through to summer 1903, she was ever on the move, contesting the exclusivity of male spaces by smoking with men in rail cars, hustling cowboys in saloons, and living a hand-to-mouth existence performing her trademark female masculinity. In June 1902, she was sighted in Livingston, Montana, where the local paper reported her "renewing acquaintances and sustaining her reputation as an all around good fellow" by a night of carousing that culminated in an overnighter in the county jail. Drinking heavily, and in increasingly poor health, Calamity Jane's celebrity status continued to have currency, but was bartered with somewhat wearily. According to the *Butte Inter Mountain*, hers was a tragic and archaic tale:

The successful day of Calamity Jane is past. Her books no longer sell well. Time was when tourists considered it an honor to buy Jane's books and it was considered a lack of progressiveness to make a trip West and not purchase one of these unique souvenirs. Now all is different. The old-timers, many of them, have died, and the younger generation coming up is too busy to pay heed to this woman who helped to blaze the way of the pioneer.[51]

The *Great Falls Tribune* toyed with similar themes, juxtaposing the figure of frontier lore, whom "everyone in the West has known or has heard of" with the woman of today, "old . . . poverty-stricken and wretched," whose drunken sprees had no place in a country that had "outgrown" her. It thus advised readers to think of her in the past tense and with romantic gaze:

It is the Calamity Jane of the old days, the Indian fighter, the scout, the mail carrier, the cow puncher . . . who stands heroic. It is she whom the small boy reads about in the dime novel which he carries hidden beneath his coat.[52]

For a while, it seemed, Canary found a place of personal expression and a source of subsistence playing female scout in the frontier imaginary. Though a well-liked "drawing card," her off-stage drinking, alternative lifestyle, and penchant for taking off into the sunset at a moment's notice did not marry well with the regiment of show timetables or *fin de siècle* anxieties about social norms and rightful pathways to modernity. Annie Oakley she was not. A character that confounded easy categorization, Calamity Jane's stage fortunes thus highlighted both the latitudes and the limits of gender possibility on (and of) a frontier that combined a capacity for rethinking the male–female binary with a heady celebration of patriarchal authority. The *Tribune* showed this mechanism in action, by lionizing *past* Calamity as a "man among men," while falling back on dualistic constructions of *present* Canary as a good-hearted mother seeking to move beyond her colorful past, an ungentle tamer, but a tamer nonetheless: "behind all the rough exterior there is a good deal of the woman to Calamity Jane." An unconventional figure with few support networks and a long-standing problem with alcohol dependency, Canary successfully used the threads and gestures of female masculinity to navigate a West of considerable physical and cultural mobility. Lived and invented experience had seen her constructed as a "pioneer original," renowned for her unorthodox gender identity and famous for being *herself.* Celebrity, however, had never been the same as acceptance, and, as the nineteenth century gave way to the twentieth, the frontier of performance was closing in.[53]

CHAPTER FIVE

"BURY ME NEXT TO WILD BILL"
COMMITTING CALAMITY TO POPULAR
MEMORY (1903-35)

Martha Canary died on 1 August 1903 at the Calloway Hotel, Terry, South Dakota. She had spent the summer moving between various towns in the Black Hills and in late July had hitched a ride on the Burlington rail line from Deadwood to the small mining town located a few miles away. Train engineer Joe Hilton remembered her riding the boxcar with the railroad men, from where she proceeded to a nearby saloon. After collapsing at the bar, Canary was put up by hotel proprietor H.A. Scheffer and his wife, and spent her last days receiving old friends, resisting prescriptions offered by the local doctor, and reporting that she was going to "cross the divide." The official cause of her death was inflammation of the bowels, most likely brought on by alcohol abuse. In her later years, commentators often pictured Calamity Jane as a haggard and eccentric old woman. When she died, though, Canary was just 47.[1]

With her death ended the life and adventures of Calamity Jane; but this was far from the end of her mythological journey. Instead, the stage was set for further inventions of a frontier legend that would continue through the century just begun, and beyond. When Canary died, she left a vibrant testimonial trail crafted by personal rendition, anecdotal account, and artistic flourish. Reporting on Calamity Jane's antics in her final years, the *Livingston Enterprise* described a personality "well known to the people of Livingston, eastern Montana, all of Montana and to the United States in general": a useful allusion to the infectious reach of her frontier celebrity. As Deadwood committed its prodigal daughter to the ground, local press and persons of interest eulogized the "heroine of the plains." In subsequent decades, meanwhile, a new set of cultural representations delivered their own takes on the "female scout."[2]

This chapter explores the posthumous reputation of Calamity Jane, from 1903 to 1935, as her folkloric story was refracted across various formats. In biography, fiction, and silent film, Canary was deployed in the usual mold as a dynamic personification of the wild days of the western frontier. The essential markers of her celebrity persona (scouting with the army, saving the Deadwood stage, capturing Jack McCall, preference for a buckskin costume) were now embellished with fresh vignettes. In the immediate aftermath of her death, a new story emerged that spoke of romantic attachment to Wild Bill Hickok (despite the fact that, in life, the two had known each other for less than two months). Meanwhile, alongside the (mostly) quixotic flourish of early eulogies were hints of puzzlement and critique. Was she a whimsical "heroine in a hero's garb," or a dangerous example of alternative gender expression? Did she *really* do the things claimed of her? Just as in Canary's lifetime, commentators seemed at once entranced and confounded by her enigmatic character, and, specifically, its fixings of female masculinity.

DEATH AND BURIAL: MOUNT MORIAH AND THE CEREMONIAL INTERMENT OF THE OLD WEST

In death, as in life, an air of mystery surrounded Martha Jane Canary. In one narrative, her body was reputedly delivered into the custody of the Society of Black Hills Pioneers, and, in accordance with her dying wishes, transported to Deadwood, to be interred in Mount Moriah Cemetery, next to Hickok. Another story, rather less reverent in design, had a group of old-timers conspiring in a saloon to play a practical joke on Wild Bill beyond the grave, setting him up to "lie with Jane for all eternity." A third, markedly ghoulish, tale suggested that she was roped to a wagon seat and bounced from Terry to Deadwood, delivering well-placed nods to onlookers on the way, and even left outside various watering holes when the driver went in for a drink. Whatever their provenance, these swirls of narrative possibility were significant. Not only did they carry forth the idea of Canary as an unruly personality, but also highlighted the way in which she was being installed as a canonical figure in the town's pioneering past. As Calamity Jane lay in the mortuary parlor at Robinson's Funeral Home, staff kept a watchful eye for zealous visitors who might choose a moment of distraction to purloin a lock of hair, or some such souvenir, from the body of a frontier celebrity. Also notable was the fact that, unlike Hickok, who was buried in his regular clothes and with his favorite rifle, Canary was placed in a full-length white gown. Dressed not in her trademark buckskin, but in the usual garb of a pioneer woman, this posthumous costuming of Calamity starkly illuminated the symbolic and sartorial limits imposed on a female-bodied western idol, even after her passing. Held at the local Methodist church on 4 August, Canary's funeral was reputedly the largest in Deadwood's history. Locals gathered to pay their respects, as Minister Charles Clark spoke about her kind heart, charitable deeds, and her role as a "heroine" in the historical story of the Black Hills. Thereafter, a parade of several hundred people and the town band escorted the funeral cortege to Mount Moriah Cemetery.[3]

Burying Calamity Jane next to Wild Bill had symmetry to it. After all, Canary had ridden into Deadwood with Hickok in 1876—a key moment in her ascent to frontier superstardom. Earlier in her life, and, indeed, in her autobiography, Canary made no allusions to a romantic liaison with Hickok, though it was certainly true that regional chatter had discussed the nature of their association. In her twilight years, however, Calamity Jane took to rewriting her own past to fan the fires of frontier gossip. On her way back west after the Pan-American Exposition, for instance, she told reporters that she and Hickok had been engaged to be married; and in July 1903, just a month before her death, she was photographed paying her respects at Wild Bill's grave (Plate 13). The latter occasion, undertaken at the request of liquor storekeeper and photography buff John Mayo, and recounted later to historian Leonard

Jennewein, communicated both the sublime and the ridiculous threads of Canary performance code in action. On the date of the shoot, Mayo recalled, Calamity Jane was found sitting on a keg behind a Deadwood bar. After stumbling along the track to the cemetery, and nearly tumbling into the adjacent gulch on several occasions, she promptly fell asleep at the gravesite. Mayo woke her up, thrust into her hand an artificial flower (what she called a "phony rose") to place on Bill's grave, and set up his camera. As usual, image was everything. Despite its ad hoc arrangement, the photograph captured by Mayo ably embellished a narrative of Canary and Hickok as irrevocably connected in a sepia-tinted old West.[4]

Central to this developing narrative was Canary's final request, supposedly delivered on her deathbed, that she be buried next to Wild Bill in Mount Moriah Cemetery. On 2 August, the *Deadwood Daily Pioneer-Times* reported her wish to their readers; six days later, it added that Canary and Hickok had lived in the town as husband and wife. According to cowpuncher Teddy "Blue" Abbott, who wrote in his memoir of drinking with Canary at Gilt Edge (though he misdated the rendezvous to 1907), she reputedly avowed: "Blue, why don't the sons of bitches leave me alone and let me go to hell my own route? All I ask is to be allowed to live out the rest of my life with you boys who speak my language. And I hope they lay me beside Bill Hickok when I die." It is also possible that the Society of Black Hills Pioneers had a hand in the plan, mindful of the tourist potential in creating a pantheon of buried frontier heroes. Writing of her life in the town in the late 1800s, Estelline Bennett indeed pointed out that Hickok's grave was already the target of souvenir hunters, many of whom chipped off fragments from his memorial; eventually the city officials enclosed it in a wire cage.[5]

Frontier necro-tourism, in fact, was becoming big business. In Tombstone, Arizona, the City Cemetery (opened in 1878–79 and closed in 1883–84) was refurbished in the mid-1920s, as civic leaders sought to capitalize on the settlement's reputation as a hell-on-wheels cattle town to sell visitors a dose of deadly old West action. The guiding rubric for the restoration of the old cemetery, now named "Boot Hill," was authenticity and work focused on locating the graves of famous denizens and repairing their weathered headstones. However, when that failed to provide sufficient scope for development or pecuniary benefit, organizers switched to a more flexible entertainment remit that added fictive residents and whimsical epitaphs. With signs on the new interstate highway inviting tourists to make a detour to the grisly grandeur of the western past, the San Antonio *Evening Herald* hailed the site as a "paying graveyard." Dodge City, Kansas, underwent a similar makeover from the late 1920s, with its own Boot Hill cemetery (established in 1872 and mothballed several years later) remodeled into a theme park graveyard complete with statues, fake headstones (with rhyming epitaphs), and an accompanying pamphlet entitled *The Thrilling Story of Boot Hill* (1937). Mount Moriah's plans to commemorate two dead frontier celebrities, albeit more pedestrian in design, thus marked the beginnings of a process by which the post-frontier West began to tap into the commercial boon of reveling in their once wild days.[6]

The whys and wherefores of necro-tourism were not always simple. The death and burial of William Cody, Calamity Jane's closest male equivalent in the frontier imaginary, proved a case in point. Buffalo Bill died on 10 January 1917, having gone to Denver to perform a "wild West" show, and suffering kidney failure while staying in the city with his sister. In a will dated 1906, Cody noted his desire to be buried on Cedar Mountain, near Cody, Wyoming, the town that bore his name and that he had founded with business partners in the mid-1890s. Publisher Henry Tammen, however, offered to pay for a lavish funeral befitting the western showman, on condition he was buried in Colorado. Possibly due to financial considerations, pragmatism, or capricious sentiment (the two had a notoriously fractious relationship), Louisa Frederici, Bill's widow, accepted Tammen's offer. In her *Memories of Buffalo Bill* (1919), she claimed that he had come to favor a resting place on Denver's Lookout Mountain, from where he could eternally gaze over four states. Cody stalwarts fought the plan, claiming that Bill had been delirious, duped, or sidestepped. Their protests came to nothing. After lying in state at Denver's Capitol building (during which a reputed 25,000 people filed by), Cody was treated to an elaborate funeral procession on 14 January. Five months later, he was interred at Lookout Mountain, in a steel vault enclosed by a concrete cordon, to stop grave robbers seizing his body. In 1948, American Legion members from Wyoming promised $10,000 to anyone who could repatriate Buffalo Bill to his hometown—an offer that prompted the National Guard of Colorado to post guards at his grave. Even today, some maintain that a crack team of Buffalo Bill faithful stole his corpse from the Denver mortuary to clandestinely bury him at Cedar Mountain. The story seems highly unlikely, but vividly illustrates continuing popular interest in the contested lives and deaths of frontier heroes.[7]

As for Calamity Jane, burial in Mount Moriah served to affirm Deadwood's status as an epicenter of frontier mythology, and made it a critical site of pilgrimage. As the *Belle Fouche Bee* saw it, burying Canary next to her "old consort" conferred on the town "a double attraction to exhibit to visitors from the east." Buffalo Bill himself paid homage at the gravesite in 1914, as did legions of latter-day tourists. The eternal proximity of Hickok and Canary added a new twist to an already imaginative biography, and, in turn, set the stage for two western icons to become posthumous co-stars in a re-making of frontier memory that played out across literature and celluloid (Plate 20). In a somewhat curious demonstration of morbid synchronicity, some commentators even changed Canary's death date to 2 August, to match Hickok's. Performance carried forth into the afterlife.[8]

"A WESTERN HERO GONE": MAKING PEACE WITH CALAMITY

Obituaries spoke of the life and adventures of Martha Jane Canary and her esteemed place in the canon of frontier celebrity. Now that the old West was gone (and so was she), a dedicatory gaze set in, reflecting both genre conventions for respectful oratory and the fact that Black Hills communities no longer had to grapple with her unconventional behavior in their post-frontier present. As old-timers paused to reflect on the gun-slinging, unorthodox raconteur, many cast a roseate glance in her direction. A number, however, dosed their valedictions with caustic judgment on Canary's nonconformist ways. Variations on her age, name, notable activities (especially in her later years), and romantic affairs, meanwhile, attested to the swirling and vibrant storytelling culture that circulated around her.

The *Cheyenne Daily Leader* headlined its 3 August 1903 copy with: "Calamity Jane Dead," before informing readers that the "most noted woman character" in the West had passed away, aged nearly 73 (*sic*). There followed a ticker-tape summary of salient information: "Body Interred Beside That of Wild Bill Hickok—Wore Male Attire and Held Her Own with the Toughest of Men—Tried Refined Life in East and Failed." Illuminated in staccato print, the essential story of Calamity Jane was encapsulated by her female masculinity and, linked to that, her place-ment in an old western landscape, where conventional modes of female decorum were more elastic. The *Leader* identified Calamity Jane as "one of the old border characters who has been famous and notorious for many years on the range and in the frontier towns." Noting how she held her own among "the hardest and toughest of men," it reported how she boasted a dozen bullet scars from Indian fights, and was the "intimate acquaintance" of William Cody, with whom she scouted. The wearing of men's clothes was one of her "most noticeable peculiarities," a habit, the paper believed, that she assumed on arrival in the West. Canary, it alleged, had outlived "husband after husband," made her way selling the "little book of her eventful life," and, in recent years, had lived a quiet existence, "deserting the slums and even . . . refusing to tell the tales of her old life."[9]

Other local press followed a similarly piquant track, furnishing readers with vibrant (and creative) biographies that often repeated the highly fictionalized account associated with *Life and Adventures of*

Calamity Jane, By Herself (1896) or reprinted verbatim from other news-paper tales. The *Rawlins Republican* described Canary as a "noted woman," relaying the potted history offered by the *Cheyenne Daily Leader* and adding a scandalous flavor specific to their town that centered on drinking sprees, jail time, her string of husbands, and a tale that she "stole" a young girl. Conveying a common narrative in eulogies, the *Republican* compensated with a warm ending: "she had many good traits. Even during her wild life she would give her last cent to give assistance where it was needed." It, too, listed her age as 73. The *Livingston Post*, reporting the next morning, summarized the main news of the day thus:

Calamity Jane Dies
　　Famous Female Scout is Put to Rout by Clammy Hand of Death
　　She lived a stormy life
　　Remains to be interred beside those of Wild Bill Hickox [*sic*]—
Close of Career full of much adventure—Many sided character.

Upgraded in legendary status to "the most unique character the great west has produced," Canary was positioned as a cowboy pioneer in vice and virtue, "brave, generous and charitable, yet dissipated and reckless." Judged to be "almost entirely lacking in that high moral sense possessed in great measure by the majority of womankind," she was unceremoniously distanced from her sex, yet honored for "doing a great work on the frontier" as an army scout and nurse of sick soldiers. Also typical of most obituaries, the *Post* offered a potted history that narrated the usual roster of the "famesque," before noting that in her later years she lived off the "bounty of friends of the early days and the curiosity of tourists."[10]

The *Bozeman Avant Courier* offered the lengthiest obituary in the regional press, under a leader that read "Calamity Jane, The Wild West's Wildest Product, Dead." In common with other eulogies, it emphasized her dying wish to be buried next to Wild Bill, before a strident declaration as to her unparalleled status: "Calamity Jane was the most remarkable character the frontier has developed." After a breathless and epigrammatic biographical tour (that extended her activities to scouting in every western state, and prospecting from Mexico to British Columbia), she was hailed as a vivacious creature, enthused by a "passion" for a "free, untrammeled" life. At this point, things took an interesting turn. Not content with printing an in-house valediction, the *Courier* looked to the authority of another frontier icon, Buffalo Bill, who had expounded on the essential character of Calamity Jane in a portrait article the previous year. According to Cody, "Calamity was a character—an odd one. She always was different from any woman I ever knew . . . Only the old days could have produced her. She belongs to a time and a class that are fast disappearing." Here, laid out in full, were the trademarks of Canary's frontier celebrity: her peculiar nature, gender difference, and locatedness in an (increasingly distant) pioneer past. Mixing gender nouns/pronouns and social judgment, he quipped:

> [She was] unique among women so far as I know. Perhaps that is just as well . . . She was a big-hearted woman, generous to a fault, daring as the most recklessly brave men that ever lived, and a prince of good fellows.

On one level, Cody's biographical regurgitation added little to the story of Calamity Jane's cultural representation (though he did have her scouting with him under Crook's command, and killing scores of Indians and desperadoes); but his other comments are worth dwelling on. Evident to Buffalo Bill, at least, were the synchronous connections between gender unorthodoxy, itinerancy, and the tightening strictures of a hetero-normalizing West. As he pointed out: "As soon as a mining camp became a town and the town began to start trying to be respectable Calamity would move." Also in this vignette was a clear sense of Canary's comfort in a homo-social environment, veracity as a frontier witness, and keen sense of performance timing:

There are not many men living who know the West as well as she does. And there are probably few of the old-timers living that have seen more of the lively times in the early days. She was generally in the thick of what was going on.

Adopting the garb and gestures of an alternative gender profile, Calamity Jane had entered the annals of the frontier imaginary for her "masculine appearance" and "man's will and a man's nerve." Significantly, this heretical performance had won fame, but also a defamatory gaze. On this, Cody concluded, she was "eccentric then, and is eccentric now."[11]

Elsewhere in the press imprint were hints of a celebrity culture predicated on the dramatic tensions of celebration and critique. Calamity Jane had been a wondrous personality, but a key target for character assassination. The *Deadwood Daily Pioneer-Times* for 8 August, for instance, talked up her credentials as a "unique feminine character," a staple of "border fiction" who "died as she lived, in defiance of all traditions." Choosing to emphasize her underlying femininity and graceful physique, the *Times* appeared to mash together dime novel Calamity Jane with the storybook of *Life and Adventures*, ending with the comment that her kindly nature meant that local citizens "speak her name almost reverently." The next day, a headline article talked of how "the death of Calamity Jane shoves the wild west still further into the past," and, in subsequent editorials, the paper cast off its romantic veil to express frustration that Deadwood was becoming known only for its association with Canary and Hickok, neither of whom had had a reputation befitting the civilized hue of the modern town. As support for this cause, the paper contained a testimonial from M.L. Fox, author of the 1896 *Illustrated American* piece on Calamity Jane, who fired off a scornful obituary that contested Canary's provenance as scout and Indian fighter. In place of the sympathetic narrative of a pioneer woman trying to get by, Fox now spoke of an "ignorant woman of most unwomanly habits." What had changed in the intervening period? It is hard to say, but the volte-face did illustrate the complex meanings imparted to frontier characters in a West torn between nostalgia for the old days and a future that was understood in terms of propriety and prosperity. It offered, too, a salient reminder of the role of storytelling in the construction of an iconic West, as well as the swirling choreography of indulgence and iniquity that marked popular attitudes towards Calamity Jane. What remained consistent in all this was the signature role of female masculinity as part of Canary's public identity and performance code. As Fox put it, while the veracity of her famous deeds was questionable and her life otherwise "undeserving of notoriety," she absolutely "dressed in the garb of a man, carried revolvers and a knife in her belt and a Winchester rifle." Authenticity came from inhabiting a role as a frontier "original," with Calamity Jane's dubious claims to fame more than substantiated by her everyday demonstrations of gender unorthodoxy.[12]

Writing of the death of Calamity Jane, the *Livingston Enterprise* of 8 August communicated a similarly ambivalent message, noting Canary's connection with the town and her status as a remarkable woman of the frontier, with a mischievous headline that recounted how she had died not with her boots on (in the fashion of the swaggering western hero), but "with her shoes off." Pointing out that local residents would recall her drinking habits, and largely avoided her when she was on one of her sprees, it followed up with a valedictory from Buffalo Bill, this time lifted from a report he delivered while in London on a show tour. Here, Cody's monologue served as a useful vehicle for a narrative trundle through the Calamity Jane story, with added literary flourish. Reflecting on her army career, he pointed out that Crook had appointed her to work in his team, thus making her life "lively all the time." Shoring up his own credentials to frontier heroism, as well as the privileged terrain of hegemonic masculinity, he added that Canary "did not do a man's share of the heavy work," but was liked for her "courage and good fellowship." James McLaird interprets the latter comment as a veiled reference to her role as a prostitute, but *Calamity: The Many Lives of Calamity Jane* reads this differently. One of many references to Canary as a "good fellow," Cody's comment ably illustrates how Calamity Jane used the costume and performance code of female masculinity to successfully operate in a homo-social world.[13]

Obituaries from further afield attested to the successful export of Calamity Jane as a frontier celebrity. Reported on by the *Princeton Press*, she was headlined by the words " 'Calamity Jane' Feared No Man," and presented as "one of the most picturesque and daring characters that has ever romanced the Western plains," and a character of "especial interest" to residents of Mercer County. According to the Princeton *Telegram*, Canary's illustrious life had seen her scout with Cody and work her way through 12 husbands, the first of whom she killed with her "own hands." She also made headline news in the *New York Times*, in an article that described her as the "Woman who Became Famous as an Indian Fighter, Wearing Men's Clothes she served with Gens. Custer and Miles, Most Picturesque Character in the West." Lifting its biographical details largely from *Life and Adventures*, the paper pointed out how Canary's celebrity status led thousands of visitors to travel "miles out of their way to see her." No mention was made of the dime novels about her or of her theatrical career, nor of her unconventional behavior or drinking. Instead, the paper noted, Calamity Jane spent her last days as a captive artefact of frontier unorthodoxy on a Montana ranch, where "speculators fenced in her house and charged an admission fee to tourists."[14]

A signal of her global cachet, the passing of Calamity Jane soon found its way into the British press. On 4 August, just three days after her death, the London *Daily Mail* noted the departure of the "Famous Female Scout and Frontier Warrior," a "Picturesque character" recently retired to a Montana ranch. The London *Star* chose to print an obituary from Buffalo Bill, the contents of which clearly highlighted the obfuscated terrains of memory, authenticity, and star power in the story of Calamity Jane. He spoke of first meeting Canary in 1874, when she was already known by her famous epithet, and had already ridden into Deadwood and avenged Hickok's murder (neither of which events occurred until 1876); he then misdated the Pan-American Exposition to 1891 (rather than 1901). Despite his previous statements to the contrary, Cody issued a damning diatribe that Canary had never worked as a scout, but was instead an army "mascot," prone to drinking. Ending with a comment more astute than he could ever have realized, he pointed out that Calamity Jane was "always up on the firing line," was a dab hand at catching outlaws, and that "everyone knew and liked her." Visibility, a good story, and a striking personality were, indeed, important aspects in Canary's passage to frontier superstardom.[15]

FINDING CALAMITY IN POPULAR ENTERTAINMENT, 1903–20

Canary died the year after Owen Wister published *The Virginian*, popularly seen as the first western novel, and the same year as *The Great Train Robbery*, often cited as the first western movie. With its grand narratives of adventure and nation building in the wide open, the West loomed large in the landscape of popular entertainment unfolding in the early twentieth century. What this period did not deliver, according to recent Canary biographers, was a significant chewing-over of Calamity Jane in popular culture. This, Richard Etulain argues, was down to a convergence of factors: a scarcity of easy-to-gather evidence on her life, the unreliable nature of stories about her, and the hardening of certain myths into actualities (scouting, Indian fighting, romance with Hickok) that left would-be writers reluctant to take on the challenge of depicting her.[16]

Given the elastic approach to mixing fact and folklore that biographers, screenwriters, and novelists adopted towards Calamity Jane throughout her life and afterlife, it feels as if this explanation leaves something out of the picture. For one thing, the vibrant gossip culture that surrounded Canary was contingent on her charismatic and often vivid presence. Her penchant for putting on a good performance and "popping up" in different towns meant that she was a circulating attraction and regular source of media tit-bits. Now that she was gone, it was inevitable

1. This famous image of Calamity Jane as a "female scout"—taken in a Deadwood studio in 1895—graphically illuminates her iconic reputation as a cross-dressing, rifle-toting frontier celebrity.

2. This is the earliest known photograph of Calamity Jane. Taken in the Black Hills as part of the US Army's survey expedition in 1875, it suggests a woman at home in men's clothes and as part of a military train.

3. This rocky outcrop in the Black Hills, named after Calamity Jane, illustrates the developing army gossip culture around the "female scout" in the 1870s.

4. An intensely theatrical photograph, this image depicts Calamity Jane at the height of her fame, dressed in an elaborate embroidered uniform that was probably used for special parades.

5. Deadwood's Main Street in its founding year of '76, a time when the town was marked by gold fever and alive with young prospectors eager to make their fortunes.

6. An unusual image, taken by famous western photographer L.A. Huffman, that presents Calamity Jane in a pose of civilized domesticity and well-to-do ways—not the look we usually associate her with.

7. Taken in the late 1880s, this photograph of Calamity Jane with friend and cowboy Teddy "Blue" Abbott highlights her reputation for drinking. She is dressed here in the usual garb of a pioneer woman.

8. A stark and haunting image of an aging Calamity Jane in her Montana cabin. Far from her frontier celebrity persona, she appears here as a loner struggling with ill health and poverty.

9. The grand entrance of the Indian Congress and Village at the Pan-American Exposition, in front of which stands the performing troupe of Frederick Cummins' wild West show.

10. This photograph, taken at the Pan-American Exposition, shows Calamity Jane "the female scout" mounted and ready to entertain crowds at the Buffalo, New York showgrounds in 1901.

11. Annie Oakley, Calamity Jane's principal competitor in the frontier imaginary, cultivated a much more homespun image, though her demonstrations of sharp-shooting also pointed out that women could excel at "men's work." Oakley, reputedly, was a much better shot than Buffalo Bill Cody.

12. A publicity shot taken to advertise Buffalo Bill's "wild West" show, this image depicts Sitting Bull and William F. Cody, heroic leads in the grand extravaganza of frontier-themed entertainment that Cody took to a global stage.

13. Taken a month before her death, this photograph shows Calamity Jane paying her respects to Wild Bill at Mount Moriah Cemetery, Deadwood. Though the pair only knew each other for a couple of months, the idea of a romance between them dominated Hollywood storylines in the twentieth century.

14. P.T. Barnum, showman extraordinaire, was a leading purveyor of the "freak show" at his American Museum in New York. Dime museums such as his were staples of popular entertainment for urban audiences in the late nineteenth century. Calamity Jane featured on the show ticket for Kohl and Middleton in 1896.

15. Jean Arthur's Calamity Jane wore the buckskin, but offered a toned-down leading lady that left the main action to the men and brought a screen idol femininity to the "heroine of the plains."

16. Left to right: Calamity Jane (Doris Day), Katie Brown (Allyn McLerie) and Wild Bill (Howard Keel). In this still from David Butler's iconic musical, Doris Day's Calamity Jane pulls a trademark frontier pout. Queer readings of the film point out she was much more enamored with Katie Brown than Wild Bill.

17. A dynamic image that clearly communicates the lively appeal of Calamity Jane and Doris Day's athletic performance as the Black Hills heroine who saved the Deadwood Stage. Whip Crack Away!

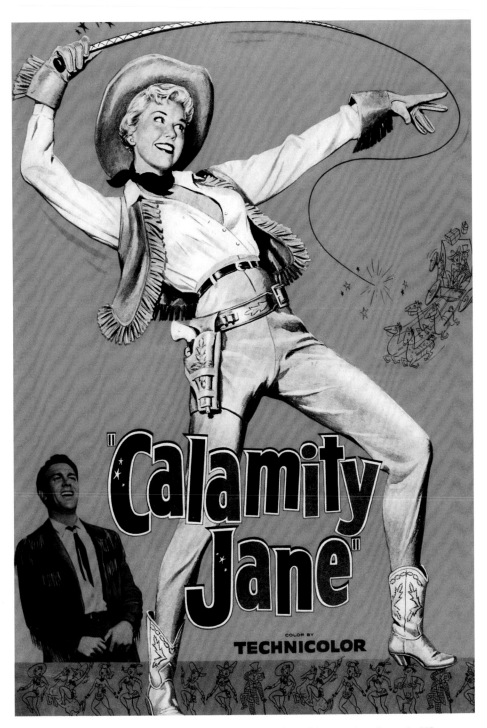

18. A film poster for Butler's 1953 musical. A rousing, feel-good journey into "how the West was sung," it continues to inspire adoration from filmgoers (and the odd sing-a-long).

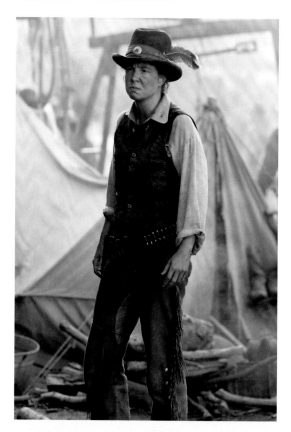

19. A grubby, cursing Calamity Jane for the twenty-first century. Robin Weigert here plays Deadwood's famous raconteur as a buckskin-clad pariah, frontier witness and lesbian.

20. The graves of James Butler "Wild Bill" Hickok (left) and Martha Jane "Calamity Jane" Canary (right). Together for eternity, Wild Bill and Calamity Jane continue to set tongues wagging as to the nature of their relationship. Their interment side by side marks Mount Moriah Cemetery, Deadwood as a key site of "old West" pilgrimage.

that popular chatter should subside somewhat. Thinking more about performance code—and specifically the motif of female masculinity foundational to Canary's identity—might explain her muted posthumous reception. In a patriotic and hetero-normative imagined West, where men were rugged individualists and women were there to be saved, how was one to present "the heroine in a hero's garb?" The focus of media attention, unsurprisingly, zoomed in on a canonical cast of male archetypes, leaving female characters with supporting roles and little room for the subversive swagger of Martha Jane Canary. Josiah Ward's editorial in the *New York Tribune* entitled "Wild West Heroine the Movies Overlook" (1921) shed some light on this issue. Ward argued that the lack of early celluloid coverage of Calamity Jane related to the fact that many considered her to be a creature of fiction, and thus ineligible for biopic review. A folkloric cloak had seemingly obscured the historical tracks of Martha Jane Canary, a character hailed as the "boldest, fiercest, tenderest, most unconventional and best known figure in the old West."[17]

In fact, however, these years *did* present an important scattering of literary and celluloid nuggets that communicated a sense of Calamity Jane's popular appeal and established a "way of seeing" that influenced how she was read by successive commentators. Helpful in this regard are Glenda Riley's comments on the lack of film and book treatments of Annie Oakley in the period 1885–1915—an indication, she says, that media sources were looking for "attention-getters" beyond the domain of the demure lady sharpshooter. While popular culture seemed uneasy about Canary's public demonstrations of female masculinity, there was definitely economic and social capital to be found in the borderlands of the avant-garde (a conclusion corroborated by film scholar Laura Horak, who recently uncovered more than 400 silent films containing female-to-male cross-dressers in the period 1908–34). Dominant social mores may have championed Annie Oakley's tender, armed femininity, but Calamity Jane offered the opportunity for an entertainment encounter that was curious, electrifying, and now contained by a temporal safety net separating her amoral life path from that of the audience. According to Horak, the cross-dressing celluloid excursions of the early twentieth century frequently traded in a dime novel-esque landscape of women posing as men, where concealed female protagonists demonstrated assumed male virtues of bravery, and won over menfolk with sensational, but ultimately wholesome, articulations of white nationalism. Theirs was a "healthy, temporary appropriation of masculinity." Calamity Jane's established presence as a pulp fiction heroine had the potential, at least, to play into this equation, leaving her well placed to ride with the trousered cowgirls of the silent film era (see, for instance, *The Girl Ranchers* (1913) or *The Post Telegrapher* (1912)). What compromised Canary's appeal in this period, ironically, was the same thing that ensured her ultimate longevity as a frontier icon: a reputation for gender unorthodoxy that resisted easy or monolithic resolution.[18]

Stalking Calamity Jane across these years, she was found (invariably in buckskin) as a stock personality in broad-brush histrionic depictions of the westering experience, a bit-part player in pioneer memoirs, a whimsical press artefact of the old days, and a lead protagonist in a (mostly regional) vernacular that dabbled in excavating the truth behind her legend. Presiding over her story was a mixed band of commentators—journalists, memoirists, dime novelists, theatrical agents, and screenwriters—each of whom saw some value in working the "heroine of the plains" into their narratives and cogitating on the meaning of her unconventional life. While not commanding a huge public audience, these various architects of western mythology ensured that Calamity Jane remained a topic of popular conversation, and laid the groundwork for her mid-century installation as frontier superstar.

One of the first in line was William Allen, Billings pioneer and dentist, whose memoir, *Adventures with Indians and Game* (1903), recited a formative encounter with the West. Allen recalled meeting Canary on a remote hunting trail, where there appeared "a white woman riding towards us at full gallop" to warn of an Indian ambush ahead. Thereafter followed a potted biography that positioned Calamity Jane as a "noted female scout" known for "her daring intrepidity, her rapidity of movement and her deadly skill with firearms," reproduced the apocryphal story of how Canary saved Egan to receive her famous moniker, and quoted from Bill Cody on her capture of the runaway Deadwood stage and villain Jack McCall. Allen's testimonial also appeared as a biographical entry in the *Progressive Men of the State of Wyoming* (1903), where Calamity Jane was the only woman to feature in the roll call of regional worthies (though placed right at the end of the list).[19]

Whereas Allen's dramatic introduction of Calamity Jane played on her as a romantic character in a landscape of pioneer adventure, a number of regional figures weighed in to debunk her canonical status. George Hoshier, who had been a pallbearer at her funeral, submitted an interview for the *Norfolk News* (1906) that promised a look at "Women of the Frontier: Stories of Odd Characters of Thirty Years Ago." Identified as an "old-timer" (and therefore credible), Hoshier's testimony presented readers with a tabloid-esque "true story of Calamity's life." This, the paper alleged, was "very different from that which has done the rounds of the press for the last two decades ... because it tells accurately the story of one of the most famous women who ever lived in the West." The article went on to narrate how Hoshier knew Canary in Cheyenne in the mid-1870s, and could say with confidence that she was *never* a scout. Her name came not from saving Egan, but from ripping up frontier towns and getting into trouble. A "wild girl," "booze fighter," and wearer of men's clothes, she was, nonetheless, a striking personality.[20]

Ex-scout and army poet Jack Crawford fired a similar salvo in "The Truth about Calamity." Writing for the *Journalist* in March 1904, he delivered a vitriolic exposé that disputed Canary's claim to frontier celebrity, on the grounds of speaking truth to the dime novel rumor mill. Born in Donegal, Ireland, in 1847, an emigrant to the United States in 1861, Civil War soldier, and Black Hills prospector, Crawford had been one of the military literati who conspired to create Calamity Jane as a figure of frontier gossip; but now his objective focused on setting the record straight. Speaking as a military scout and "one of the earliest pioneers" in the region, with every swipe at Canary's reputation he elevated his own status as authentic witness and frontier hero. This mantle was important. From being an emerging army poet in the 1870s, "Captain Jack" had built a decent literary career, with seven books of poetry, more than a hundred stories, and four plays to his name. At the time of the "Truth" article, the self-styled "poet scout" was entertaining crowds in the East with theatrical and lecture tours. Like Canary, he was an accomplished performer and keenly aware of the dynamics of western showmanship. Boston journalist Nixon Waterman famously called him a "genius in buckskin."[21]

Crawford's first meeting with Canary, he said, had been in Custer City in 1876, when he was a lawman and she was a drunk. While *he* had scouted for the army in the Hills, *she* had been a "camp follower" (prostitute). Nor had she ridden the Pony Express, saved the Deadwood stage, captured McCall, or been christened by Captain Egan. Arguing that Hickok's hallowed name "should not be associated with Calamity Jane," he pointed out that the two had met just a few weeks prior. Wild Bill was a true frontier hero, a stoic individualist cut from the cloth of *The Virginian*, while Canary was a fake and a freak, an aberrant creation of the mining boom, who grew up in a "wild, unnatural manner." Had she been exposed to a more nurturing environment, Crawford believed, Calamity Jane would most certainly have seized the domestic ideal to become "a good wife and mother." In his socially conservative take on the female frontier, he went on to complain that such women had been "glossed over with a glamour of romance" (and awarded both agency and power as potential "role models" for young women), when actually their lives were "wretched and dissolute." On the matter of Canary's masculine costume and characteristics, he was especially bilious. "To a real frontiersman, such statements written about any woman are absurd and would be funny were it not for the harm that accrues from them and other dime novel monstrosities," he railed—a revealing comment on gender politics and the powerfully subversive nature of cross-dressing performance.[22]

Why speak up now? When Canary was alive, Crawford pointed out, she lived off her storytelling gigs and book royalties. A man of honor, he had felt duty bound to refrain from sabotaging her precarious socio-economic situation. Now dead, "the truth deprives her of nothing but her artificial glory," and so "had best be told." At this point, Crawford performed another grand reveal. He, too, had "worshipped the worst kind of a fraud and fake hero until I went through the mill and found out what was genuine and what exaggerated." Specifically, he said, it had been the fault of dime novelists for peddling tall tales of Calamity Jane, and, indeed, of the public for wanting to believe them. "She was simply a notorious character, dissolute and devilish, but possessed a generous streak which made her popular," he concluded.[23]

Crawford's outburst was particularly intriguing when read against one of his most famous poetic offerings, "The Womanhood of Man," which argued for the importance of embracing the necessary threads of femininity within the male psyche. As an army pathfinder, Crawford spoke here of finding respite on the trail in connecting with his emotional self, thereby making a striking border-crossing of the gender binary in wilderness country. Such musings were far removed from the machismo of Theodore Roosevelt and other architects of the strenuous western ideal, in advocating what Darlis Miller calls a "tender masculinity." Like Canary, Crawford was contesting normative gender boundaries and finding new space for homo-social expression in a dynamic frontier landscape. According to Miller, his willingness to explore the "soft male side" helped "redefine masculinity in an age of rapid industrialization." While it was admirable for men to show their feelings, however, the trespass of women on the sacred ground of hegemonic masculinity was apparently something else.[24]

Though not on the scale of her breathless imprint in Wheeler's Deadwood Dick series, Calamity Jane maintained a presence in the world of early-twentieth-century pulp literature. A useful (and largely fictional) character around whom fantastical frontier conceits might be constructed, W.G. Patterson's "Calamity Jane: A Heroine of the Wild West" (1903) cast her as an Indian fighter and fearless carrier of the mail. Prentiss Ingraham hit readers with a dime novel double-header, pairing two frontier icons in "Buffalo Bill and Calamity Jane, or, a Real Lady from the Black Hills" (1916). Famous for his depiction of western heroes, Ingraham had been instrumental in making Buffalo Bill a star across more than a hundred tales. In common with much of Ingraham's work, this story maintained the usual breakneck pace and character contortions of the dime genre, with half of the piece given over to the movements of a man disguised as Calamity Jane, and the other half to tracking her (also in disguise and her usual prickly self) across New Mexico.[25]

Evidence of her star power on the theatrical stage, Calamity Jane featured in various (largely mediocre) stage endeavors, from E.B. Cauthorn's five-act play that bore her name, where she appeared as the good, but amoral, proprietor of the Lone Tree Saloon (also known as the "Bucket of Blood") in a Colorado mining town, to an opera written by Jack Sinclair, born in 1890, a police officer in Colorado and onetime member of the Dodge City Cowboy Band. Sinclair's *The Cowboy's Dream* (1916) included a cowboy serenade to a young girl, whom he remembered eagerly imitating Calamity Jane with a glass of grog and a holler of salutation. Further afield, Calamity Jane was the star of a one-act play at London's Theatre Royal, Drury Lane, and gained top billing in a melodrama written for the British vaudeville scene by Samuel Franklin Cody. Born in Iowa in 1867, Samuel Cowdery (later shortened to Cody) worked as a trick shooter in Adam Forepaugh's Circus and Wild West Show as "Captain Cody: King of the Cowboys." In 1890, he sailed for London, where he embarked on various theatrical ventures, including a "burlesque of the Wild West" on roller skates, and staged races between mounted cowboys and professional cyclists. An inveterate showman, Cody claimed to be from Texas, and the brother of Buffalo Bill (for which William F.

Cody sued him in 1891). In 1898, he tried his hand at music hall, with a melodrama entitled *The Klondyke Nugget*, the runaway success of which prompted him to devote an entire play to Calamity Jane. Pitched as a comedy drama, the action took place in a mining camp in Alaska, where Clarence Russell had ventured on the trail of confederate villain Jake Drince. Lover Mabel Denhan, who happened to have mining claims in the area, had recently joined him. Calamity Jane was first introduced as a rifle-wielding youth and self-reliant tear-away. True to its dime novel styling, the plot soon revealed that Drince had been blackmailing Mabel's father, before throwing in a fight and a marriage proposal. At this point, Calamity Jane made a dramatic entrance through a window, flung Drince to the floor, brandished a poker, and warned him against ever raising a hand to a woman again. Playing with gender ambiguities and codes of honor, Calamity Jane challenged his masculinity, to which Drince replied that he—unlike her—would know a woman when he saw one. Through various plot twists and turns, Calamity Jane was framed as an assassin, found a comic sidekick in the shape of actor Sir Henry Wilson Tree, rescued the hapless Clarence (twice), disguised herself as a member of the outlaw band and a sleeping Indian, and saved Mabel. With the lovers reunited as the curtain fell, the show ended with a toast to Calamity.[26]

In the realms of celluloid, Calamity Jane made her inaugural appearance in a production by the Black Hills Feature Film Company and funded by the citizens of Chadron, Nebraska, who also starred in the film. The *Douglas Enterprise* was effusive in its praise for a movie dubbed "the greatest picture of western life ever produced." *In the Days of '75 and '76* (1915) loosely followed the usual folkloric story, but repositioned its female lead in more of a conformist pose, as sturdy helpmate to Hickok's stalwart scout. She was stripped of the full swagger of female masculinity, to appear instead in a buckskin skirt. The film began in a simple cabin in Butte, Montana, where Calamity Jane was attacked by a villain (Jack McCall), saved by Hickok, and learned to shoot as sensible recourse. From here, the plot revolved around a romance between Hickok and Canary, Jane clandestinely taking up a scouting role to follow her beau on the trail with Custer. Robbed of a romantic future by murderous Jack McCall, Calamity Jane set about seeking righteous retribution to deliver him to the authorities for trial and execution. As Richard Etulain notes, this presentation of Calamity Jane as a domestic and softened heroine set the stage for celluloid treatments in subsequent decades.[27]

A CURIOUS HEROINE: BIOGRAPHY AND MEMORY IN THE 1920s AND EARLY 1930s

Central to the imagined West of popular entertainment in these years was a culture of frontier celebrity that reveled in true-life tales of those who had won, wandered, or wilded the trans-Mississippi theater. Standing pre-eminent in this heroic line-up were scouts, soldiers, lawmen, and outlaws: male leads loaded with guns and rugged machismo. William Cody was valorized in William Visscher's biography *Buffalo Bill's Own Story of his Life and Deeds* (1917), while early film treatments came in the shape of John Ford's *The Iron Horse* (1924) and James Cruze's *The Pony Express* (1925). Cody made top billing as frontier scout in *With Buffalo Bill on the U. P. Trail* (1926) and took a leading role in *The Last Frontier* (1926). Other male icons received similar biographical fanfare. Wild Bill Hickok was treated to a romantic reading in Frank Wilstach's *Wild Bill Hickok: The Prince of Pistoleers* (1926) and William Elsey Connelley's *Wild Bill and His Era* (1933), while Stuart Lake's iconic *Wyatt Earp: Frontier Marshal* (1931) painted its eponymous subject as a noble hero in a book labeled by historian John Mack Faragher "an imaginative hoax." The fact that most of these productions were highly fictionalized (and also wildly popular) offers useful context when thinking about Martha Canary's folkloric pathway in the twenties and early thirties. If, as recent historians argue, Calamity Jane was in danger of being forgotten because of the difficulty in excavating the truth in her heroic story, then why was this not the case with her male equivalents, whose biographical trails were equally laden with romantic license? Such juxtapositions illuminate the workings of a mainstream entertainment culture that lionized hegemonic masculinity and struggled with historical personalities who presented less conventional gender models. Connelley's *Wild Bill and His Era* was illustrative in this regard, describing "plain Calamity Jane" as a canonical figure who could "out-chew, out-smoke, out-swear, and out-drink most of her masculine companions," and would have been liked by Queen Elizabeth I and Catherine the Great (both "great half-masculine, half-feminine queens"), yet who remained a pariah in an idealized wild West of handsome, rugged men and "young, charming" women "of dazzling beauty."[28]

That said, as the rest of this chapter shows, the gender possibilities associated with Martha Jane Canary did invite considerable biopic scrutiny. Although the normative fixings of popular entertainment culture subjected her to a less intense and luminous gaze than her male counterparts, her unusual personal profile and proven frontier pedigree made for a captivating prospect. Calamity Jane made her Hollywood debut in Paramount's *Wild Bill Hickok* (1923), in which Ethel Terry played the female lead, and William S. Hart, Wild Bill. Here Calamity Jane was included in a pantheon of heroic figures, though safely located in silent-film storyboard as a hearty helpmate who harbored an unrequited love for Hickok. The setting was Dodge City, Kansas, where the famed lawman had retired to run a card table, only to be coaxed back into the service of justice by General Custer. Once the errant cowboy band had been safely routed, Hickok fell for a sophisticated, but married, woman just in from the East. He fled the town lovelorn, at which point the would-be target of his affections, Calamity Jane, turned to drink and masculine clothes. As in the dime novel, nonconformist gender behavior could only be the result of romantic or sexual trauma. Necessarily resolved by a wholesome dose of heterosexual resolution, the two leads were reunited in mineral-rush Deadwood, only for Wild Bill to be gunned down by a jealous Jack McCall. The film ended with Calamity Jane crying over Hickok's body: a tragic end to a love story that never really started.[29]

Martha Jane Canary, too, found a bountiful posthumous habitat in a lively regional culture heavy on frontier fancy. Sometime in the 1910s, a sign appeared above the rude shack she had frequented in Livingston: "Once the Home of Calamity Jane." At "Happy Kanyon," a tent city amusement resort established by the American Legion near Casper, Wyoming, in 1921, her name was given to a dance hall that—true to its namesake—offered "mad revelry." Aiming to re-create the mood of "pioneer days," the complex hosted dances in a facsimile pioneer city-scape, complete with jail, saloon, stores, and Chinese laundry. Calamity Jane dolls could be purchased at a concession stand. In Deadwood, the Days of '76 parade was inaugurated in August 1924, featuring horse-drawn wagons and actors dressed as honorable pioneers (including Canary and Hickok) in a mobile pageant of frontier glory that trans-ported visitors back to the old West in immersive style. Reporting on the August 1933 season, the *New York Times* noted that men in Deadwood had boycotted barbershops for weeks to cultivate the proper grizzled look befitting "the raw, blustering life of the pioneer." Poker tables were alive to the noise of flipping cards; town streets regularly dusted up by cavalry re-enactors. Top attractions included "scenes of historical importance," such as the trial of Jack McCall, a Cody-esque set piece of Sioux Indians attacking a settler cabin, and a rodeo show enacted by an all-female troupe. Traditional stories and those of gender possibility both had a space in the frontier imaginary.[30]

With Calamity Jane's "famesque" deeds a recurring source of fascina-tion, the media found much mileage in apprehending her through the lens of frontier nostalgia. A big part of this dialogue involved chewing over the merits (and demerits) of a woman branded a "creature of her time." Writing in the *New York Times*, Seymour Pond regaled readers with tales of a "tough, hard swearing, hard riding, hard drinking and hard headed gunwoman." Sympathetically presented as a character containing equal parts of courage and charity, Canary was an individual forged in challenging days and in possession of a keen moral compass when it came to wrongdoers. "If Calamity Jane was to a certain extent a social outcast," Pond pointed out, "it was not entirely her fault." Syndicated articles appeared under different titles in the *Great Falls Tribune* ("Memories of Calamity Jane's Black Hills Exploits Fading as Sun Sets on Pioneer West"), the *Judith Basin Star* ("Calamity Jane Could Drink and Swear But She Had Many Admirable Traits"), and the *Cody Enterprise* ("Calamity Jane was Handy with a Gun"): a salient example of how regional press culture abetted the dissemination of frontier celebrity.[31]

According to Dan Conway, author of a 1926 news item subtitled "Unique Character of Old Frontier—her Deadwood Romance; 'Wild Bill' was her ideal of man," Calamity Jane was a frontier institution and a "unique character" who (in common with Cody) maintained a "certain nobility." Running through the usual parameters of her life story (birth, life as an emigrant, hand-to-mouth existence as an orphaned young woman, recourse to wearing men's clothes, and capture of the Deadwood stage), he pictured a multi-faceted individual with a confounding gender identity. Canary was, at once, a fearless scout respected by her peers, a serial thrill-seeker (with a life "crowded to the limit with excitement"), and a heart-broken consort of Hickok (described as a "perfect specimen of manhood"). Today, he pointed out, she would be seen as an "undesirable" character; but "in her time, by nature, she was a great deal more than that." Aside from championing her celebrity cause (and safely dodging the issue of social and moral example by placing her firmly in frontier context), Conway offered a couple of particularly intriguing insights. For Conway, at least, an integral part of her popular appeal lay in the fact that she was "a paradox," a rough woman, drinker, and associate of desperadoes, but also someone of an honest disposition who helped those in need, and abided by "the code of the plains." Calamity Jane thus walked assuredly in the boot-steps of the archetypal masculine heroes beginning to swagger across the silver screen. Equally pertinent was Conway's comment as to Canary's mysterious qualities: "She left no personal history. Consequently, no-one can explain her."[32]

A number of newspaper pieces, significantly, pointed to a role for Calamity Jane beyond the realms of frontier fellowship, and firmly in the domain of feminist-in-training. These were only occasional moments in a media landscape more liable to indulge in whimsical, nostalgic, or salacious commentary, but remained important markers of the storied trail that cultural representations took in future years. One such account came from the *New York Times*, which described her as a "pioneer exponent of the idea that a woman's place is wherever she wants to be." The *Casper Daily Tribune* made reference to her story in a section called "Women's Activities," which documented Canary as a "bizarre woman-character of the Far West." A personality in possession of a "picturesque career," and one of the "interesting actors in the drama of the early West," the essential ingredients of her legend (masculine disguise, scouting career) were presented here, alongside a red-herring history that identified her as a well-to-do woman from Pennsylvania named Nell King, who had a muscular build and an impressive line in false mustaches and beards. Most interesting was the way the paper championed Calamity Jane as a pioneer of female agency:

> Although the early history of the nation will always be associated with the deeds of famous men, it should not be forgotten that there were women also who played important parts in the building of this great empire west of the Mississippi.[33]

Canary, it noted, should be placed "in the same category as Buffalo Bill." An equivalently rousing challenge to masculine hegemony was offered in an article from correspondent Myfanwy Thomas Goodnough in the *Rock Springs Miner*, which posed the question "Who was Calamity Jane?" The answer, she surmised, was a complex one. Here stood a "grotesque 'Queen of the Prairie,'" and "picturesque gunwoman of the historic west in the heyday of its wildness," known for her rough and ready demeanor, drinking habits, and tendency for the spectacular. Though not a scout,

Goodnough pointed out, she *did* compete with "the men on an equal footing," and thus cut quite a presence as proto-feminist icon:

Equal rights for woman! She had not heard the phrase, which was being propounded in cities and towns by dignified, educated propagandists. Nor would she have cared for the idea, had such been presented to her in a logical form, as it was only the desire for companionship that had driven her to the places where men were working, in their physical efforts to eke a livelihood from the soil or from the mines. Whimsical as the opinion may appear, Calamity was a pioneer in Equal Rights, so far as the results were concerned, although nonconformist as to the methods involved.[34]

Biographical and memoir literature, in fact, provided the most fertile habitat for the continuing digest of Canary-ana in the twenties and thirties. Here, Calamity Jane served as an important conduit through which westerners committed their own pasts to popular memory and touted their own pioneer credentials. Proximity to frontier celebrity allowed a little of the magic of the old West to settle on their clothing, gold dust style. As the *Bozeman Avant Courier* saw it, Calamity Jane would always be "a real wild west heroine to those who knew her," and someone around whom tall tales would inevitably gather. In his memoir *The Last Frontier* (1930), Lock Sutley made useful reference to the nature of popular chatter:

Any attempt to describe this picturesque character whose name is everywhere an echo of the old frontier is certain to fall short of the truth, for she was a strange mixture of masculine boldness and feminine gentleness. Stories about her can be told, most of them probably true, to prove she was any kind of person one wants to call her.

Presented as unique, generous, and unruly, an animated and enigmatic Calamity was threaded into the biographical fabric of the region. In this collective enactment of frontier pageantry, old-timers committed to posterity both what they remembered and what they *thought* they remembered.[35]

One of the most interesting nuggets in this reminiscence culture was Lewis Freeman's *Down the Yellowstone* (1922), which included a long segment on Calamity Jane, based on his encounter with her in Livingston in 1901. A sense of dramatic portent set the mood, with Freeman proclaiming:

> In every man's life there is one event that transcends all others in the bigness with which it bulks in his memory . . . The thunderbolt of a living, breathing "Calamity Jane" striking at my feet from a clear sky is my biggest thing.

Firmly cast in the role of frontier idol, Calamity Jane represented a "flesh-and-blood heroine," of whom he had dreamed ever since reading the dime novel *The Beautiful White Devil of the Yellowstone.* When played out in real life, the meeting bore the hallmarks of Canary's usual stagger through the heroic everyday. Freeman happened on her in an alley after midnight, where she was propping up a lamppost, wearing cowboy chaps, and too drunk to remember where she was. Having helped her find her bunk, Freeman returned the next morning to find her smoking a cigar and cooking breakfast. Not the dime novel apparition of legend, she was instead a haggard woman, old beyond her years, living hand to mouth, and ever eager to tell her story (Plate 8). Perched on a collection of empty beer barrels at the back of the saloon, Canary swigged some ale, Freeman sat down in the grass, and she began to talk.[36]

Vividly communicating the layering of past experience and personality in her celebrity canon, Canary offered Freeman a slice of oratory straight out of *Life and Adventures*. She spoke of her birth, migration, love of adventure, scouting career, getting used to wearing men's attire, and of her naming by Captain Egan—each a trademark aspect of her legend. Now and then, she punctuated the narrative with interjections to "Short Pants" (her nickname for Freeman). Upon hearing this "matter-of-fact-recital," Freeman asked why elements of her story were so at odds with that depicted in *The Beautiful White Devil*. Did she not save a Major Darkleigh, he asked, and did she not utter valorous cries "for life and love" and "to hell with the redskins," before riding to the fort with the reins gripped between her teeth? Such comments showed the folkloric storm that swirled around Calamity Jane, as well as pointing to the fact that those consuming her mythologies were not always uncritical in matters of storytelling provenance. Canary responded in furious tone, "swearing hard and pointedly," that the literary tales told about her were hokum and that he should listen instead to her *real* story (by which she meant the story delivered by her). A clear sign both of the performance dynamics of her routine and of her difficulty in keeping to a script while under the influence, Canary tripped over her words and went right back to the start of the story with "My maiden name was ..." After she had rattled on through swimming the Platte, riding the Pony Express, and capturing Jack McCall, Freeman interrupted again, this time to query her account of Wild Bill's death, as read against the narrative of pulp literature. Again, Canary became agitated, and once more reverted to the beginning of her spiel. She concluded her talk with the last line from *Life and Adventures*, leading Freeman to note that the one-on-one with his ultimate frontier idol had boiled down to little more than a rehearsal of "her museum tour lecture." Clearly disappointed—he wrote that the Calamity Jane of mythic proportions "vanished" before him—he nonetheless persisted with conversations over the next week, enlivened by the prospect of teasing her out as a "human document, the living page of the most vivid epoch of the north western history." In all this, *Down the Yellowstone* gave an important hint as to how Calamity Jane remained the subject of successive cultural representations. Curious, confounding, she was perennially interesting as a "strange old character" who stood "at close range" to "all the most famous frontier characters of her day."[37]

Expressed in biographical literature and settler testimonials, the memoir culture of the twenties and thirties was hagiographical and hard-nosed, in equal parts. As much as writers gloried in Calamity Jane as an animated buckskin-clad heroine, they relished the possibility of disrobing her to reveal the "true facts" of her life. George Stokes and Howard Driggs' *Deadwood Gold: A Story of the Black Hills* (1926), for instance, portrayed the Hills as a "land of mystery, of adventure, of romance!" and included a section on Calamity Jane as part of a chapter on "Noted Characters of Old Deadwood." Presenting her as a veritable celebrity, the work pointed out to readers that "stories enough, good and bad, have been told about this notorious woman." Often in these texts, the idea of special knowledge was a critical maxim, especially when hoisted by frontier literati to establish an insider/outsider narrative that elevated their status by pitting their own accounts—those of people who *really* knew Canary—against the stories of invention. *The Black Hills Trails* (1924) by Jesse Brown and A.M. Willard, two Black Hills pioneers, noted that, with so much popular chatter about Calamity Jane, it was incumbent on them to "set forth a few of the real facts as to her life and picture her in her true light." As so often, however, stern assertions of objectivity soon fell back on hearsay. Brown and Willard communicated to their readers that Canary was born in Iowa to a Baptist minister, traveled to Nebraska and Salt Lake City, worked as a prostitute in Rawlins and Green River, and acquired a wealthy husband in Denver, all before she even got to the Black Hills. On her scouting career, they were cutting, portraying her not as a heroic pathfinder, but as "nothing more than a common prostitute, drunken, disorderly and wholly devoid of any element or conception of morality." She had, they alleged, saved a man named Antelope Frank from attack by Indians, delivered Deadwood's citizens from a "terrible scourge of smallpox," and was well known for her kindness and generosity. A relationship with Hickok, though, was out of the question because "he was not the kind of man that was attracted to a woman of Jane's class." A good illustration of how Canary folklore was circulated,

revealed, and obscured, the account from Brown and Willard was reproduced in Earl Brininstool's *Fighting Red Cloud's Warriors* (1926), along
with a reprint of *Life and Adventures*. Readers of Brininstool's work
presumably did not notice, or did not care, that these two origin stories
of the "most-talked-of frontier woman" did not match.[38]

Period inclinations for exposé and romantic indulgence were combined
in an extensive and important study of Calamity Jane by Texan journalist
Duncan Aikman. Only the second dedicated biography after Spencer's
1887 treatment, Aikman's *Calamity Jane and the Lady Wildcats* (1927)
expended a third of its text on Canary, and the remainder on other "wild
women," including Cattle Kate, Belle Starr, Madame Mustache, and
Pearl Hart. A good example of popular interest in the extra-domestic
world of nonconformist women, the book cast Canary as a frontier celebrity, fabulously and flamboyantly aberrant, and an important figure of
historical scrutiny. Expressing himself in florid prose, Aikman was more
astute than he realized in having Canary play "the melodramatic role of
Calamity Jane," and thus made important reference to her performance
code. The essential aim of Aikman's work, as he saw it, was to discern the
"truth behind the legend" of Martha Jane Canary, and so he repaired to
Deadwood to talk with old-timers. Unsurprisingly—especially given
what *Calamity: The Many Lives of Calamity Jane* has revealed about
the culture of frontier gossip surrounding Calamity Jane—what he
discovered was "the closer one comes to the actual scene of Jane's heroic
performances, the more they vanish."[39]

In its blend of forensic enquiry and prose flourish, Aikman's biography
was not that different from the work of many commentators who grappled with Canary in life and afterlife. Aikman's quest for the "real"
Calamity Jane saw him trace her movements from Princeton to Virginia
City; but he found no evidence of a scouting career, rescue of the Deadwood stage, capture of McCall, or, indeed, the stories of romance with
Hickok and nursing activity that were otherwise bubbling up in period
reportage. At the same time, when dealing with his leading "lady wildcat,"

Aikman was entirely happy to indulge in artistic license. Suitably remolding his lead actor to fit the narrative choreography, he cast her as a feral and self-destructive figure: drinker, gambler, brawler, and prostitute. Introduced to readers at the age of eight, she was a "wildcat's kitten," remonstrating with local boys who threw corncobs at her in Missouri. Aikman wrote how, on the trail west, "the wild country claimed her . . . It gave her a beautiful, a flamboyant vocation, sensually rich and ecstatic," while Virginia City and the camps of the mining frontier offered up a natural habitat, where Canary ran "like a sprite with the stream of depravity."[40]

Her heroic deeds debunked, Aikman pitched Calamity Jane as a "good-natured camp trollop cruising with the timber bands, handling a pick, hoisting ties on her shoulder, cracking the bull whip." A striking performance of female masculinity, nonetheless, made her a person of significant frontier interest. Combining the threads of celebration and critique that ran through Canary's performance of gender possibility, she was "a grotesque parody on men's serious work," but equally was "delightful." The "macabre splendor" so intrinsic to her appeal, Aikman argued, was consciously cultivated for popular impact. In all its pistol-brandishing, galloping grandeur, the ride into Deadwood in 1876 presented a particularly important moment of folkloric invention. Aikman put it thus: "in a life devoted to distinction as she appraised it, this was the supreme afternoon." The death of Hickok, accordingly, was such a blow to Canary because it removed any opportunity to ride shotgun on Bill's heroic machismo. In true celebrity fashion, thereafter Aikman's Calamity was set for a precipitous fall, crashing down from glory days as "a delectable novelty, a vivid and genial allegory of an era's hearty rowdiness . . . to become a jovial sot." As part of this process, he asserted, she ceased to be a celebrity and became instead a "character," an important shift in nomenclature that attested to her passage into the realms of the passé and the pariah. Black Hills locals only regarded her fondly, he claimed, because of "the condescending amusement she afforded."[41]

Part fact-checking exercise, part fanciful journey, *Calamity Jane and the Lady Wildcats* was a puzzling biographical nugget. Aikman gloried in the subversive possibilities of his eponymous heroine, yet stripped her of a heroic reputation to reveal a deviant and decrepit creature. Enraptured by the hackneyed trope of the "wild woman," he loosely followed the search for her "truth," but digressed into sensational storytelling. Following the familiar tracks of the frontier imaginary, Canary was reprised as a curious artefact of frontier unorthodoxy, a literary sideshow freak. That said, in beginning to conjure with Calamity Jane's place in a culture of manufactured frontier celebrity, Aikman did grapple with ideas of modern superstardom and the "famesque." In many ways a transitional treatment, his imaginative biography channeled various themes running through period commentary—not least the tensions of romance and respectability—while his use of the word *lady* wildcat pointed to a whimsical domestication of Canary that would manifest at mid-century, most notably in Doris Day's musical outing.[42]

Recent historians ascribe little value to *Calamity Jane and the Lady Wildcats* as serious biography. *Calamity: The Many Lives of Calamity Jane*, however, reaches a slightly different conclusion. Despite its fantastical fixings, Aikman's work set an important marker in focusing on Martha Canary as a named subject deserving of biopic review. This historical grounding was significant, not least because, as reviewer Isabel Paterson noted in the *New York Tribune*, though they knew "Calamity Jane" as a "household word," many readers had no idea that she was a real person. According to Stanley Walker, reviewing the book in the *New York Times*, Aikman's heroine may have been "deflated, exploded [and] jeered at," but after reading her tale, he was minded to think favorably of the progressive qualities of such women, who "suffered considerably, but . . . were emancipated and sometimes they had a lot of fun." Paterson was yet more strident in railing at Aikman for writing off folklore as hokum. Offering rare insight into the inspirational quality of Calamity Jane as a powerful feminist role model (and in a striking illumination of how ideas about gender norms and their social construction were being mulled over long before cultural theorists such as Butler and Halberstam provided an explanatory toolkit), she argued thus:

> The name of Calamity Jane connoted a rough and ready feminism, a demonstration that the virtues of adventure, enterprise and independence were not intrinsically masculine. Decent women did not shudder at the name, they were rather wistfully admiring.[43]

Such an assessment suggests a new (and welcome) complexity to reading Calamity Jane outside the confines of mainstream chatter and in the vein of gender possibility. Indeed, the historical imprint of female masculinity provided by Canary was particularly instructive for the second-generation "new women" seeking to renegotiate gender roles in the 1920s. For this group, as for Canary, various performance techniques and the adoption of masculine clothing, gesture, and props (cigarettes, alcohol, etc.) allowed for the presentation of an alternative perspective on questions of social relations, sexual freedom, and bio-politics. While it might be a stretch to see Calamity Jane as a radical gender-fluid hero(ine) along the lines of Virginia Woolf's Orlando or Radclyffe Hall's Stephen Gordon, such period comment, at the least, invites the idea that her folkloric imprint reached beyond the horizons of hetero-normativity and frontier nostalgia.[44]

Two other biographical treatments of the late 1920s and early 1930s are worth noting. Written by female authors, they contributed to a narrative trajectory of women writing about women that began (in the case of Calamity Jane) with M.L. Fox. Both presented sympathetic takes on Canary, and thus suggested the discrete perspective of "women's ways of knowing" in evaluating the life and legacy of Martha Jane Canary. Installed as a figure of gender unorthodoxy, Calamity Jane attracted successive exploration as a trailblazer for alternative modes of female agency. *Old Deadwood Days* (1928), written by Estelline Bennett, took the form of a traditional settler memoir. Based on the author's experiences of growing up in the town in the late 1800s, it indulged readers with a dedicated chapter entitled "When Calamity Jane Came Home." Beginning with a familiar invocation to "a glowing figure in the history of that hectic year of '76," she centered on Canary's understated return to the town in 1895. Dressed in the common garb of the frontier woman, and seeking schooling for her daughter, Canary cut an unremarkable presence—aside, that is, from her heroic backstory. It was this, importantly, that set her apart, started imaginations racing, and piqued old-timers' interest (specifically Bennett's uncle and father, who were desperate to hear her talk, and keen for the young Estelline to meet Canary). Pointing to Canary's buoyant cult of frontier celebrity and singular importance as a personification of pioneer days, Bennett noted, "no one like Calamity Jane ever had come into Deadwood Gulch. She not only was typical of old Deadwood. She was old Deadwood." For many residents, Canary seemed an ephemeral, but very real presence; a figure who assumed an agency courtesy of her colorful tales. For Bennett, she was an iconic woman akin to Joan of Arc or Alice in Wonderland. Equally, she pointed to a "female frontier," where women at the social margins suffered loneliness and hardship. Somewhere between nostalgia and empathy, Bennett summed up the relationship between Calamity Jane and the pioneer collective as one of amnesiac cordiality: "Whatever there was of evil in Calamity's life has been long since forgotten . . . Old Black Hillers seemed never to remember her faults. Certainly they attached no importance to them."[45]

Bennett came from Deadwood's well-to-do contingent of first-generation pioneers, whereas Dora Du Fran's Black Hills profile was rather different. A successful madam running brothels across South Dakota and Montana, Du Fran had reputedly employed Canary as a prostitute in Deadwood in 1895–96 (where the two met), and as cook and laundress in Belle Fouche, just a few months before she died. Writing as "D. Dee," Du Fran sought to capitalize on period interest in the old days and in the vibrant narrative culture surrounding Canary with the pamphlet *Low Down on Calamity Jane* (1932). The foreword read:

> This story of Calamity Jane, one of the famous characters of the Black Hills, was written by one who knew her for many years and was intimately associated with her in the early days in the Hills.

Du Fran thus played on familiar tropes of proximity and authentic witness in the testimonial trail of the frontier. Presented as a "Diamond in the Rough," Canary's life was set out here in a series of typical montages (scouting, freighting, drinking, entertaining). Focused on Calamity's storied past, the pamphlet offered scant details on the actual working relationship between the two women (Du Fran referred, somewhat euphemistically, to dance-hall and restaurant work). Indeed, and in common with most depictions of the time, it was a heroic Calamity Jane that graced the pages of memoir literature. In particular, hers was an unusual gender profile that combined fearless feats and muscular adventuring with a line in rough-hewn good-heartedness: "the men all liked her, being the only woman in camp. She had a good many womanly traits. She mended and washed for the men, cut their hair, and even tried to shave them." At this point, Du Fran took pains to point out to readers that the old West was a landscape where "deeds not words were needed." A world of flux, invention, and socio-economic instability, the conventional boundaries of normativity were necessarily renegotiated in frontier space. Du Fran went on:

> It is easy for a woman to be good when she has been brought up with every protection from the evils of the world and with good associates. Calamity was a product of the wild and woolly West. She was not immoral, but unmoral.

A woman of iron and with a heart of gold, Calamity Jane was metaphorically replete, singular, and spectacular, and "the only original wild woman of the West." Something of a show-woman herself, Du Fran took *Low Down on Calamity Jane* to the Chicago World's Fair in 1933, hoping to make money from a borrowed landscape of frontier celebrity. When sales were not as expected, she burned all remaining copies and returned to Deadwood. Du Fran died of heart failure the following year, and was interred in Mount Moriah Cemetery, alongside her husband and a pet parrot named Fred.[46]

CHAPTER SIX

"HOW THE WEST WAS SUNG"
FEMININITY AND FAKERY ON THE HOLLYWOOD
FRONTIER (1935-60)

In a press piece entitled "Calamity Jane's Own Story is Told Again," the *Buffalo Bulletin* (May 1935) related how Billings resident L.J. Covington had recently unearthed a copy of *Life and Adventures of Calamity Jane, By Herself* (1896). Covington had purchased the pamphlet directly from Canary in 1900, and, for 35 years, it had been gathering dust on a shelf. Reflecting on her life, the editorial related a tragic tale of a fading star selling a rudely constructed narrative (not in the best English, with long paragraphs and poor sentence structure, it said), and a simpler, plain-speaking time in which several pages sufficed to distil the essential elements of a famous life. Calamity Jane, it pointed out, was "perhaps as well known a woman as has ever appeared on the American scene," but struggled to make any money from her fame, working alone and without the assistance of modern-day marketing agents and professional publicists. Today, the *Bulletin* mused: "heavy royalties would await her life story 'told by herself' and she would receive heavy money for the screen rights, serial rights, even the dramatic rights."[1]

As it turned out, the next three decades brought an expansive multimedia treatment of Calamity Jane that catapulted her into the stratosphere of frontier celebrity.

This chapter explores the various takes on her life and legend that appeared from the mid-1930s through to the end of the 1950s—a period that saw the "golden age" of the western and the arresting inscription of the frontier imaginary under a celluloid gaze. Movies narrated "how the

West was won" and wowed cinemagoers with Technicolor vistas of a big-sky landscape roamed by sturdy Stetson-wearing heroes and villains. Of particular importance was the incorporation of Calamity Jane as a subject of the Hollywood canon, from her appearance as a significant character in Cecil DeMille's *The Plainsman* (1936) to a superstar lead in the musical *Calamity Jane* (1953), still the most popular example of Canary-ana to date. As the latest iterations in a folkloric imprint long in the making, cultural representations in these years picked up the trail where their forerunners left off, with an added twist of frontiering fantasy. Retaining her trademark identity as a buckskin-clad curiosity, Calamity Jane also made the (unlikely) transition to stride across the silver screen as a domestic siren for the nuclear family. Feisty, fresh-faced, and resolutely feminine, the mid-century "female scout" communicated the gender politics of containment. She didn't smoke, cuss or drink, and, when under the taming gaze of Bill Hickok, eagerly slipped into the role of adoring romantic companion. As usual, however, there were alternative readings to be made that spoke to the subversive prospects of female masculinity. Thus, while mainstream media applauded celluloid fables of de-wilded conformity on the heterosexual frontier, Doris Day's tomboyish Calamity was outed, adored, and her "butch cut" hair imitated by British gay women in the 1950s, her academy award-winning hit *Secret Love* received with knowing glances. Interestingly, both Jean Arthur and Doris Day saw "their" Calamity Janes as trail-blazers on the frontier of modern feminism.[2]

Alongside a cleaned up "heroine of the plains" was an array of depictions—some old and some new, some expected and some surprising. Mindful of the social (and other forms of) capital to be made from the Calamity Jane brand, a few individuals saw an opportunity to soak up a little frontier celebrity of their own. The most famous of these, Jean McCormick, a middle-aged woman from Billings, generated significant attention in the 1940s and early 1950s when she announced herself as the long-lost daughter of Calamity Jane, and produced an album of letters and various pieces of memorabilia by way of corroboration. Eventually, McCormick's claim was proved to be a hoax, but the fanfare surrounding it cemented the importance of the "famesque" in Canary's folkloric trail. In the written word and world of Calamity Jane, meanwhile, a raft of fictional and non-fictional treatments tangled with a complex character caught between a frontier past and a mid-century landscape of moral compulsion. Canary retained her interest as a conduit for pioneer reminiscence, provoked the attentions of writers who used her as a vehicle for western daydreams, and prompted a swathe of new historical biographies that promised to attend to her life and adventures with forensic vigor. Historian Richard Etulain argues that "no coherent, on-going single image of Calamity Jane had come into focus" by the end of the 1950s—a conclusion unsurprising when considering the fact that enigmatic masquerade had long been a critical feature of her story. A well-worn buckskin cloak, in fact, was a critical factor in explaining the longevity of the Calamity Jane franchise. Holding together all the disparate parts of her folklore was an evocative costume of female masculinity. From fresh-faced screen idol to femme fatale, lovelorn cowgirl to tragic mother, closeted lesbian to hard-boiled crime-fighter, each found room to roam within a well-rehearsed performance of frontier celebrity. As the *Cheyenne State Leader* saw it, Martha Jane Canary had always had a "Hollywood complex. She loved her stage settings and always played to an audience."[3]

CALAMITY JANE AS FILM AND RADIO STAR, 1935–50

Just as they were laid side by side in the frontier imaginary, so Calamity Jane's celluloid trail through the 1930s and 1940s often involved playing co-star to Wild Bill. Developing the narrative for *The Plainsman*, the most significant outing for Calamity Jane in this period, director Cecil B. DeMille had researchers look into the histories of Hickok and Cody, but did not consult on Calamity Jane. As female sidekick to the main attraction, her provenance as a swaggering (and well-known) western personality and a known associate of dead, white, masculine heroes was enough to carry the role. Calamity was there principally to serve as support, plot foil, and (inevitably) romantic interest, and the main consideration for scriptwriter Courtney Ryley Cooper was how to present her as a rough-edged, but suitably womanly suitor. The question then was who might be cast to combine frontier spirit with feminine sexual allure.[4]

Calamity Jane's historical reputation for masculine garb and gesture inevitably played into her entertainment appeal, not least in the context of other period productions that capitalized on the premise of gender disguise. Women were cloaked as men for the purposes of comedic transgression (see, for instance, Katharine Hepburn in *Sylvia Scarlett* (1935)); were toyed with as theatrically sapphic flirts (Marlene Dietrich in *Morocco* (1930)); and appeared in biopic treatments of historically nonconformist characters (Greta Garbo's *Queen Christina* (1933)). Of particular significance here are the findings of film scholar Laura Horak, who documented how Hollywood film from the mid-1930s increasingly favored a presentation of cross-dressing conformity that was "narratively contained, homogenous and visibly feminine." Cultural security in a world marked by economic depression and global conflict came through the reinforcement of traditional gender boundaries. Not only was this a matter of shoring up standards of social conformity, but it was also a reflection of the increasingly strident rules on film censorship under construction in the 1930s. With a heretical line in female masculinity, and a tendency for hard drinking and minor scuffles of violence, a "realistic" Calamity Jane would have likely ended up on the cutting-room floor. *The Plainsman*, hence, cast its heroine in a softer light. As Iron Eyes Cody (a Sicilian actor with his own interesting history of film fakery, and an advisor to DeMille) put it,

it should be mentioned here that if you always suspected *The Plainsman* was complete nonsense from a historical standpoint, you're right. The real Calamity Jane was a vulgar, tobacco-chewing, raw-boned kid who resembled nothing more alluring than an over-sized Huckleberry Finn, minus the charm of innocence.[5]

Similar celluloid remodeling, in fact, could be found in the filmic career of Annie Oakley, whose biopic trace was squeezed and confined to suit screenplay narrative and social message. Barbara Stanwyck's lead in *Annie Oakley* (1935) took titular center stage, but the real action of the piece lay in the "drama of fighting men and red romance," and a plotline focused squarely on her romantic and sharpshooting tête-à-tête with Frank Butler. A homespun career woman, Oakley's biography had never presented the same level of challenge to hegemonic masculinity as Canary's; but even here, the conformist cinematic landscape of the thir-ties demanded the championing of gender hierarchy. In other words, throw a shooting match to get your man, and live happily ever after.[6]

As for the storyboard details of *The Plainsman*, DeMille prefaced his picture with reference to the grand histrionics of the frontier story, noting to viewers "the story that follows compresses many years, many lives, and widely separated events into one narrative—in an attempt to do justice to the courage of the plainsmen of our West." Thereafter, the action focused on Wild Bill and Buffalo Bill, and their attempts to make the West safe from "hostile Indians" and nefarious gun dealers. As romantic foil to Gary Cooper's heroic Hickok, Jean Arthur's Calamity Jane packed a certain amount of "wildness" in cursing, smoking, and twirling a lasso, but wore a fringed buckskin costume with a feminine cut, and sported good looks and immaculate make-up (Plate 15). Her take on the frontier heroine was tomboyish and courageous, and, to be fair, presented a view of the western woman as independent, capable, and existing beyond the male gaze ... to an extent. Ultimately, however, DeMille's main role for his buckskin heroine was to see a "lady wildcat" tamed, educated in womanly graces with the help of Louisa (Cody's sophisticated wife, fresh in from the East with her luggage and new wardrobe options), and running around in pursuit of Hickok's affections.

According to Rebecca Bell-Metereau, Arthur's Calamity Jane was "thoroughly representative of the industry's standard treatment of the masculine heroine of the thirties—a mixture of tomboy features and stereotypically feminine attributes." Accordingly, after various kidnaps, chases, and rescues involving recalcitrant American Indians and noble US cavalrymen (not to mention a cautionary tale on the liability of the "weaker sex" to crack under the pressure of interrogation, especially when a beau is about to be roasted alive), Calamity Jane and Wild Bill meet in Deadwood and settle into a life of contentment on the domestic frontier. Spoiling the party, as ever, Jack McCall takes aim, and Hickok dies in Calamity Jane's arms: a tragic end for two personifications of the wild frontier who could never, in all truth, inhabit a civilized West. According to film scholar Anna Bates, *The Plainsman* provided a cautionary tale as to the torrid life in store for deviant women who resisted conformity.[7]

The press liked the new, pluckily glamorous appearance of Calamity Jane. *Variety* magazine saw Arthur's characterization as "particularly endowed with some punch lines and pungent expletives as the hardy daughter, but softening that historic character of the West, enough for the femme appeal." The *New York Times* was equally impressed, viewing the film as a somewhat contrived epic, "action-crammed, spectacular and inaccurate," but still full of praise for Jean Arthur, who "improved considerably" on the historical figure of Martha Canary, by "taking history by the tail and throwing it out the window." Championing the cause of a clean-living and obviously hetero-normative heroine, it enthused: "She doesn't chew tobacco anymore. She doesn't cuss. She doesn't run around with the boys. She just talks low and husky, is cute when she is being tomboyish, and she loves Wild Bill so much." A subsequent review in the same paper pointed out that the real Calamity Jane "certainly would not recognize herself" in Arthur's "charmingly piquant" portrayal. It also made pleadings for a happier ending. Given the film's comfort with playing "fast and loose" with facts, the paper railed, it should have seen its way to sparing Calamity Jane's anguish, by allowing Wild Bill to live.

Closer to the sites of Canary's former glories, meanwhile, *The Plainsman* earned plaudits and also ignited the fires of frontier memory. One paper reported how the film prompted "a whole new crop of 'Calamity' stories, as pioneer Montanans see the picture and then relate their own reminiscences of the wild capers of this famed woman of the frontier." A salient example of the gossip-circulation culture that had long abetted Canary's celebrity profile, the paper took to picking over the carcass of her life and legend, before noting her trademark performance codes: "Almost anybody could be a cook but not everyone could be the lady wildcat of the frontier … 'Calamity Jane' was a reputation to uphold." The past thoroughly chewed over, the paper conceded that, although not "life-like," Jean Arthur (who earned kudos for the fact that her grandmother hailed from Billings) represented an engaging lead in the mold of Duncan Aikman's *Calamity Jane and the Lady Wildcats* (1927). Closing with pertinent reference to the enigmatic qualities of Canary's star appeal, it mused: "Perhaps no actress could successfully recreate the many-sided, bizarre character of the famed 'Calamity.'"[8]

According to film studies scholar James Card, "DeMille was famous for using historical fact only when it suited his purposes. When history didn't make a good scene, he threw it out." As such, he had much in common with Martha Jane Canary's take on how to tell an enchanting frontier fable. Other celluloid outings in these years followed a similarly selective trail, typically presenting Calamity Jane as a gutsy buckskin-clad aide and aspiring romantic interest. Nowhere did her character gain in-depth scrutiny, historical contextualization, or deeper deconstruction, though the broad brush of the frontier imaginary furnished important referents. In *Caught* (1931), Calamity Jane was cast as an aging bar-owner and part-time cattle rustler who developed a maternal instinct for one of her new saloon girls, while in *Deadwood Dick* (1940) she appeared as part-comic, part-feisty foil to both Hickok and Deadwood Dick. In *Young Bill Hickok* (1940), Sally Payne played partner to Roy Rogers' Hickok within a broader storyboard that conjured with a foreign power conspiring to take California in the Civil War, through the disruption of a gold supply route. Assisted by grizzled sidekick Uncle Gabby, this Calamity Jane was dressed in her customary buckskin, with a feather in her Stetson, and eagerly engaging in schemes to thwart the Overland Raiders gang. Parallel to this, she played incongruous wedding planner for Hickok and his recently reconciled (ex-Confederate) fiancée Louise, fixing up a venue and buying new britches for her bridesmaid duties. The *Badlands of Dakota* (1941) saw her tread the tragic ground of unrequited love, where Frances Farmer starred as a tomboyish stage driver in love with Bob Holliday, roguish owner of the Bella Union saloon in Deadwood. At the film's climax, a distraught Calamity Jane chooses moral code over romantic attachment by shooting Bob (who has fallen in with an outlaw posse) and cradling his dying body. In the final shot she is shown at the saloon, asking the bartender: "Don't you know when a lady needs a drink?"[9]

These tales of puff frontier fancy substantiated Elizabeth Stevenson's comment that Calamity Jane was becoming "a handy peg on which to hang a Western." Indeed, she cropped up in several more films and radio productions through to the early 1950s, none of which actively engaged with the personality of Martha Canary in anything beyond cursory fashion. Running through this media landscape of fantastical romantic adventuring, significantly, was a potent moral corrective. In a 1944 radio episode of *The Lone Ranger*, Calamity Jane appeared as an unruly character, bristling with husky voice and a "headstrong young woman who dressed in men's clothes and scorned the privilege of being a lady." Heading West, she ran with Texan wranglers, played cards, and told tall tales to cowboys in crowded saloons. After saving Hickok with the help of the titular hero and Tonto, she had a sudden romantic realization, declared her undying love for Wild Bill, and vowed to swap her buckskin togs for calico. The next scene opened with an intriguing nod to Calamity Jane's performative nature as the "Queen of the Plains," where she engaged in a fervent competition for frontier celebrity with Hickok, and urged him to keep their marriage secret, so that she could remain in the limelight. As an emasculated Hickok faded into obscurity, Calamity Jane left town to scout for Custer, only to leave a window of opportunity for Jack McCall to shoot his nemesis in the back. In a cautionary tale highlighting the perils of an over-independent woman (as the Lone Ranger put it, "whose thoughtless selfishness helped to destroy the man she loved"), Calamity Jane ended the episode in a conformist gender space, calling herself not by her famous nom de plume, but "Mrs. Bill Hickok."[10]

Also running with a romantic theme, the film *Calamity Jane and Sam Bass* (1949) thrust together two co-star historical characters who had never met in real life. Bass was a famous outlaw and train robber who was killed in a shootout in Texas in 1878. Played by a glamorous Yvonne De Carlo, this Calamity Jane sported red lipstick, a fitted buckskin suit, and a Stetson tipped jauntily to one side. Rough and uncouth she was not. As the story reeled between horse deals, robberies, jail breaks, and competing romantic opportunities, Calamity Jane saved Bass from various scrapes, fought his case with the sheriff, disguised herself as a damsel in distress, and got in between Bass and his local sweetheart Katy. Killed in a final shootout, Hickok style, Bass lay in the arms of Calamity, but his final thoughts were dreams of a domestic life with Katy. In *The Texan Meets Calamity Jane* (1950), Calamity Jane was back in Deadwood, and once more embroiled with Hickok, this time as a keen organizer of a festival to celebrate the memory of her beloved Wild Bill. Played by B-movie and horror film starlet, Evelyn Ankers, she was thoroughly feminized in red blouse and jeans for the daytime, and a blousy dress for the evening. Advertised with the strapline "new adventures of fabulous Calamity Jane," the film played off historical associations with Hickok and Deadwood, but grafted on an entirely fabricated narrative that revolved around ownership of the Prairie Queen bar (given by Frank Mullen to Jane as a thank you for saving his life) and the nefarious plans of a criminal gang. The titular Texan of the movie was a lawyer, Gordon Hastings, who helped Calamity secure her legal claim, learned how to shoot, and provided (lukewarm) love interest along the way.[11]

Things took a mischievous turn in *The Paleface* (1948), in which Jane Russell played Calamity Jane as a voluptuous femme fatale hired by the US Government to find a group of gunrunners, in return for a jail-time pardon. Stripped of her usual buckskin in favor of a masquerade of frilled finery and pistol-packing corsetry, she was, nonetheless, wearing the trousers. A woman who "could take care of herself," she played savvy accomplice to Bob Hope's "Painless" Peter Potter, who stumbled through various set pieces of western-themed slapstick. Choreographed by Calamity Jane into "appearing" to save traveling emigrants from attack and win out in a high-noon shootout, the yarn saw Potter catapulted from greenhorn dentist to heroic gunslinger, a label of some standing which required a new costume (Stetson, gun, and cowboy boots) and the performance staples of frontier masculinity (lowered voice, swaggering walk, penchant for whiskey). By the end of the film, of course, Potter had *really* saved the day, by thwarting Indians and gunrunners, and Calamity Jane had declared her undying love for him. A bubble-gum western comedy, the film highlighted at least the popularity of a genre well known enough to be ripe for parody, as well as the significance of the Calamity Jane name in the mid-century lexicon of frontier mythology.[12]

Read as a body of evidence, the entertainment imprint of Calamity Jane in these years eagerly communicated her allure as a stock carrier for frontier adventure and romance, with just a tease of female unorthodoxy. As such, the media landscape in these years used the Calamity Jane name rather like dime novels had, as a well-known byword for frontier wildness and nonconformist behavior. She was the "best-known" female western idol around, and general aspects of her life or legend could be picked up and discarded as the storyboard required. A dynamic plot driver, love interest, comic foil, and well-known curiosity, the fixings of frontier celebrity could be readily shaped to fit the needs of the mid-century media. Where actual details of her life were covered, things were typically a scattergun affair: a disjointed leap across the territory of Canary's own autobiography, with a smattering of general historical accounts and a shake of other folkloric tales. Significantly, what each of these cultural representations shared was a conversational, and somewhat tense, narrative about appropriate female behavior, attire, and activity. Successively tamed by realizations of domesticity and aspirations for a life with her leading man (usually Hickok), film and radio corralled Calamity Jane to present a softened and contained heroine. Fault lines of gender possibility, however, lay just below the prairie of popular enter-tainment. In most of these pictures, Calamity Jane neither got "her man" nor found a place in the domestic happily-ever-after. Buckskin was, after all, an ill-fitting costume for hetero-normative resolution.

MASQUERADE AND STORYTELLING AT MID-CENTURY: CALAMITY JANE, JEAN MCCORMICK, AND THE TALE OF THE PRODIGAL DAUGHTER

The threads of storytelling and masquerade intrinsic to Calamity Jane's culture of frontier celebrity took a sensational turn in these years, with the revelation of various "long-lost" relations. The first of these, Jessie Elizabeth Murray (Oakes), appeared on the scene in the early 1930s, claiming to be Canary's granddaughter (or sometimes niece). The greatest genealogical reveal of the era, however, was reserved for Jean Hickok McCormick, a 58-year-old woman from Billings, who announced herself as Calamity Jane's daughter in dramatic style. Appearing on the "We the People" national CBS radio broadcast on 6 May 1941, McCormick set out the contours of her famous ancestry as follows. Calamity Jane and Wild Bill Hickok met in Abilene in 1870 and engaged in a turbulent romance, resulting in a shotgun wedding that was later annulled. By September 1873, Canary had become estranged from Hickok, and was living in a cabin at Benson's Landing (near Livingston), where she gave birth to their daughter, Jessie. Struggling with fever and facing the pros-pect of raising the child alone, Canary agreed to Jessie's adoption by a British sea captain, James O'Neil, who passed by her shack when the child was just a few days old (he was in the West, investigating the death of his brother). Several months later, Canary trekked to the railhead at Omaha to deliver Jessie to her new, adoptive parents, James and Helen. Jean, as she came to be known, grew up entirely unaware of her extraordinary past. She recalled meeting Calamity Jane twice in her childhood—once when Canary visited the family in Richmond, Virginia, flush with success from a poker game and brandishing $10,000 for school fees; and the second time, when she performed at Buffalo Bill's "wild West" show in Richmond, after which both Cody's troupe and the O'Neils were booked on a Cunard liner bound for England. Thereafter, McCormick's personal story had been suitably adventuresome. Following a teenage relocation to Liverpool, she gravitated back to Montana in 1898, where she worked for a few years as a schoolteacher, and married a state senator from Virginia. The marriage ended after 18 years, when her husband discovered McCormick's true identity (he supposedly read Canary's diary after finding it stashed away in a flour bin) and promptly filed for divorce, to avoid the scandal of being married to someone with such shameful ancestry. After that, McCormick traveled to France to work as a volunteer nurse in the First World War, married an airman (who died of injuries sustained in combat), and returned to Montana to serve as cook and nurse at various dude ranches. Having lived privately with her illustrious lineage, she had, apparently, been encouraged to "tell all" by friends in the early 1940s.[13]

Corroborating McCormick's claim, and an essential ingredient in her emerging stardom, were papers and related ephemera that had reputedly belonged to Martha Canary. These documents had supposedly been sent to O'Neil on Canary's death in 1903, and had passed to McCormick when her adoptive father died in 1912. The corpus of material consisted of letters between Canary and O'Neil, and a series of diary entries from 1877–1903; the Hickok–Canary marriage certificate (dated 1 September 1870, and inscribed on a page torn out of a Bible); Calamity Jane's "Last Will and Testament" (1898); and a document of "Confession" (1903).

Having discovered these materials, McCormick was plunged into her own frontier story of spectacular revelation—as was an entranced popular audience, when she went public with her claim. Collated in a dog-eared and battered album, these nuggets of testimony seemingly provided proof of a genealogical connection, and served up a fresh instalment of Canary's autobiographical trail. Providing a series of snapshots from the late 1870s until her last days, the tantalizing body of evidence contained references to a heroic West, real-life places and acquaintances, glimpses of travel and campfire life, bristling rants, and heartfelt remonstrations. Writing in the foreword of a collection of the diaries published in 1951, McCormick described a tragic life immortalized in ink, and an enigmatic woman serially misunderstood: "Haunted with loneliness, the old yellow pages stained with tears, symbolic of the misjudged, forsaken woman, Calamity Jane." In time, of course, Jean McCormick's claim, together with her supporting documents, was found to be hokum. Inauthenticity aside, the whole drama remains of interest for a variety of reasons. What motivated a middle-aged woman from Montana to claim an association with the "female scout?" Why did her tale capture the public imagination? And what does the episode tell us about celebrity culture, storytelling, and frontier performance?[14]

The prospects offered by a kinship association with Calamity Jane were various: financial gain, public adoration, and a legion of star appearances. In summer 1941, McCormick took a bus across the plains, appearing at rodeos and shows, giving press interviews, reading from the diaries, and wowing visitors with Hickok's gun. She visited Mount Moriah Cemetery, where she put flowers on her parents' graves, attended the "Wild Bill Frontier" festival in Abilene, and gate-crashed a Hickok family reunion at La Crosse, Wisconsin. As reported in the *La Crosse Tribune*, McCormick cut a striking figure in her ten-gallon hat, cowboy boots, and fringed buckskin skirt. "Soft-spoken, slender, and pretty," she was well attired for a mid-century world of frontier nostalgia and gender containment. Indeed, for someone seeking a borrowed landscape of frontier celebrity, the "heroine of the plains" offered an attractive point of origin. Combining the allure of pioneer days with the radiant iconography of a well-known western character, Canary opened a window of opportunity for 15 minutes of fame. Meanwhile, by moving Calamity away from her trademark reputation for gender unorthodoxy, and towards an image as a tragic mother suffering hard times, McCormick eased the "female scout" into a mainstream vernacular. That information on Canary's historical movements was sparse (and often contradictory) made the task of crafting a believable genealogy somewhat easier. As the *Billings Gazette* put it, "despite literally hundreds of stories concerning Calamity Jane, little is known regarding her life."[15]

McCormick went far, because people were interested in Calamity Jane and a Hollywood-style exposé combining mystery, hidden history, and personal intimacy. According to Vivien Skinner of "We the People," the radio show received many letters from captivated listeners. As one commentator noted, the broadcast inevitably provoked a series of questions: "Where has 'Janie' [the moniker used by Canary to address her daughter in the diaries, though there spelt 'Janey'] been all these years? When did she first learn of the diary? Where has the diary been all these years?" The star power of Calamity Jane had always drawn on her sense of inscrutability, and now there was a hearty appetite for new revelations, with the added benefit of McCormick riding shotgun. In an article entitled "What Kind of a Woman was Calamity Jane?" the *Great Falls Tribune* talked about the key attraction of the letters in revealing her lesser-known "feminine side." Writing to McCormick in 1941, an old resident of Deadwood, now living in New York State, relished this new insight into a "good girl" he knew well, and effused on the domestic qualities of her prodigal daughter: "You resemble your mother very much. You are Jane toned down, refined and well educated, and take after your mother—good and true to your husband and family." Also pertinent was the way in which McCormick's story played to a reminiscence culture with a long-standing interest in Martha Canary. As the

Tribune put it: "Whenever old timers get together, their talk often turns to the spectacular, flamboyant frontierswoman who, since her death, has been cloaked with a thick layer of contradictory legends." Many were enticed by this newly inscribed soap-opera narrative of romance, loss, and tragedy, and were willing to ignore niggling points of contest because they wanted to believe. For one listener from Santa Ana, California: "the whole story of Mrs. McCormick, of her life and of the loneliness her Mother endured through her self-imposed separation from her daughter, is one of the greatest stories in American western history." J. Almus Russell, curator of the Middle Border Museum, Mitchell, South Dakota, hoped that the unearthing of new and "authentic material about this unusual and misunderstood woman" would invite the rehabilitation of a "colorful pioneer." "Coming from her own daughter," he pointed out, "it will have all the more force and truth."[16]

Personality and narrative served McCormick well in crafting a new folkloric layer to Calamity Jane's story. As Vivien Skinner intimated, listeners were struck not only by McCormick's plain-speaking style, but also by the material evidence she provided to back up her story. In inhabiting the role of prodigal daughter, McCormick was intriguing on account of her unlikely genealogy, but also cultivated an all-important veneer of common-sense credibility. A swirling alliance of eyewitnessing and authenticity had abetted in creating Calamity Jane as a "famesque" attraction, and McCormick successfully deployed similar forces. From when the story broke until her death in 1951, she remained at the center of popular discourse, successfully conjuring evocative images of Martha Canary writing by campfire's light in a cathartic act of laying her soul bare. Her delivery was matter of fact (she spoke of carrying around "a pathetic sort of diary written in an old family album in the form of letters to me"), and was usefully embellished by a series of "reveals" of new letters from her mother that kept the fires of frontier celebrity burning brightly. Ever keen to capitalize on public chatter, McCormick started work on a manuscript entitled "Beside Lonely Campfires with Wild Bill Hickok and Calamity Jane," and investigated the building of a "Wild Bill Hickok Lodge" in Deadwood. Both projects ultimately failed to come to fruition, but a successful alliance was forged with Stella and Don Foote, who displayed her memorabilia at their Wonderland Museum in Billings, as part of a "Treasures of the West" exhibition. Key advocates of McCormick's cause, they later bought the letters and published a book edition (that sold in excess of 100,000 copies), and employed McCormick to give visitor talks and readings. McCormick's performance was exceptional and everyday, clunky and compelling. Her DNA may have told a different story, but in building a folkloric trail using creative props and a storied past, she readily channeled the spirit of Martha Jane Canary.[17]

Particularly significant was the fact that the McCormick diaries covered very little of the ground of *Life and Adventures*. There was nothing on scouting for Crook, capturing Jack McCall, or Canary's show career in dime museums or at the Pan-American Exposition. On the face of it, these omissions raised important questions of authenticity. However, their absence also gave substantive space for Calamity Jane as a character to be fleshed out in new ways. According to the *Billings Gazette*, the journals were to be commended for elucidating on "little-known facts." At the heart of this fresh inscription of the "heroine of the plains" was the relationship between her and daughter "Janey" (as Jessie was addressed in the letters). This offered a new storytelling twist, and allowed for an intimate picture of a soul laid bare. Commenting to Clarence Paine, librarian and leading scrutinizer of the McCormick case, Vivien Skinner pondered:

this story certainly has its interesting psychologist sidelights, don't you think? It's not the ordinary type of Western data. There is, of course, the usual rough-and-tumble stuff with plenty of Indians and pioneer hardships and the opening up of our great Northern western country; there is also the fact that a supposed extrovert like Calamity Jane was really, as shown in her diary, a brooding introvert.

As for narrative style, the diaries offered a tumble of sentiments. Reflective and emphatic, bleak and courageous, regretful and romantic, they showed a frontier celebrity examining her past, championing her legitimacy, and pleading for clemency. Reference to specific people and places lent an air of credibility (even those skeptical of McCormick's claim agreed that the letters were composed by someone with an intimate knowledge of Calamity Jane and her world), and purported to be a beguilingly personal rumination from a woman renowned for her taciturn demeanor.[18]

Authentic or not (as it turned out, not), the content of the diaries communicated much about the frontier imaginary and the power of celebrity confessional at mid-century. The first diary entry, supposedly compiled on Janey's fourth birthday (25 September 1877) was self-referential, assuming the reader's basic knowledge of a famous fable. Canary imagined her daughter reading the diary as a complete product in future years, smiling at the photographs of her mother, and digesting her narrative portrait. Thereafter, it followed a consistent formula, in which Calamity Jane appeared as an ailing protagonist in a challenging frontier environment that flashed with the old possibilities of romantic adventuring. The next entry, written three days later, found her at camp-fire with horse Satan, fresh from a visit to the Custer battlefield, listening to wolves, coyotes and (with poetic flourish vastly different from the stilted prose of *Life and Adventures*) "the staccato wail of Indian dogs near their camps," and bivouacked in the same valley as "thousands" of Sioux, who left her alone, thinking she was "a crazy woman." Here, Canary made passing reference to familiar autobiographical terrain (a childhood trip west with her parents from Missouri and the rescue of the Deadwood stage), before speaking of the practicalities of writing a diary on the hoof. Explaining how she tethered the album and pen to her saddle, wrote loose-leaf entries when she traveled light, and perenni-ally grappled with frozen ink, McCormick had her authorial lead clev-erly imprint the surviving textual record with authenticity.[19]

The next series of entries, dated to the early 1880s, tackled a similar tangle of subjects, as well as noting Canary's birth (Princeton, 1 May 1852) and abiding love for Hickok, with whom, she said, she had spent her happiest days. She explained how she had taken to reading the dictionary (a useful put-down to those citing illiteracy as a way of denouncing her diaries), and impressed on Janey the importance of keeping good care of her trinkets, all of which were (conveniently) in McCormick's possession. Recalling the high-minded women of Deadwood who snubbed her, she issued a bristly salvo from the old days: "Keep your chin up Janey, & tell them all to go to hell." Also present were fleeting references to the canonical pillars of her folklore: her naming by Captain Egan, and duties as a scout, freighter, and nurse. As such, the diaries provided enough signposts to Canary's famed deeds to suggest historicity, without re-treading the familiar (even hackneyed) ground of performance. Contained in the journal, instead, was rare insight into a fragile woman trading memories and regrets. She soaked her diary with tears at the death of her horse, and took to drink, in order to forget the pain of giving up her daughter and losing Wild Bill. These tender musings of a misunderstood pioneer mother were ideal fare for the soap-opera landscape of gender containment favored by contemporary audiences.[20]

The third tranche of submissions, from the 1890s, contained the usual jumble of old West crowd-pleasers (including a hailstorm so fierce it split the roof of a stagecoach in two), as well as some unusual digressions. She spoke of marriage to Burke (though still her heart belonged to Hickok), and her impending departure to join Buffalo Bill's show, where she was to "ride a horse bare back, standing up, shoot my old Stetson hat twice after throwing it in the air before it falls back on my head." Somewhat surprisingly, the narrative trail then offered a lengthy exposition on Canary's bush-craft domesticity and her own-brand recipes for "20-year cake" (fruit cake with brandy and spices), the best yeast in the world, horseradish sauce, and omelet with pecan nuts and fried bacon. Thereafter, the tone turned to confessional and traumatic estrangement. Canary implored Janey to ignore all the "lies" told about her mother, before offering an emotional soliloquy on the gap between performance heroics and maternal fulfillment. Writing after her show in Richmond, she spoke of the exhilaration of entertaining an audience with trick riding and shooting, but the anguish of seeing her own daughter approach her with "admiration and wonder" as a distant frontier celebrity. Should Janey have a daughter, Canary vowed, she would steal her to keep as "my most precious possession."[21]

The final group of entries, dated 1902–03, navigated the twilight days of Calamity Jane, a time that saw her confront her own mortality: "I guess my diary is just about finished. I am going blind—can still see to write this yet but I can't keep on to live an avaricious old age. All hope is dead forever." Railing against poverty and the past, she pleaded for forgiveness, but still communicated a sense of performance timing and enigmatic presence:

> I am sick and haven't long to live. I am taking many secrets with me Janey, What I am & what I might have been. I'm not as black as I have been painted. I want you to believe that. If they fail to bury me beside your father will you see that it is done should you ever get this. There is some thing I should confess to you but I just can't. I shall take it to my grave—forgive me & consider I was lonely.

Supplementing these last entries was a "Confession" (dated 3 June 1903), in which Canary expressed a need to "clear up" various matters relating to her life and legend, especially the legitimacy of her romantic liaisons and the diaries themselves. Referencing her tricksterish personality and tendency for dramatic impulse, she noted that she had told tall tales simply "to hear ... tongues wag." Most significantly, she urged that "all letters and information given prior to this are lies except the diary I have kept since 1877."[22]

Several professional historians set about testing the reliability of McCormick's story, the most prominent of whom was Clarence Paine.

He had agreed to write a biography of Calamity Jane with McCormick's endorsement, if her claim was proven; with that in mind, he went through the assembled evidence with painstaking exactitude. His findings were ambivalent. Yes, the ink was consistent with the supposed time of writing, but the handwriting was uncorroborated as Canary's. Certain "facts" remained entirely unproven (her working for Bill Cody; the personage of James O'Neil), others were sketchy (including crossed-out dates in the text), and some otherwise tenable. Something open to particular scrutiny was the Hickok connection, an aspect integral to the narrative thrust of the McCormick case, and one that inspired a number of fiery letters between members of the public, the CBS network, and various historians and historical societies, each proclaiming inside knowledge on the issue. One lambasted Calamity Jane as "an ill-bred, cantankerous, unprepossessing woman who was so given to drink as to make herself a nuisance," and definitely not the companion of Hickok or the mother of his child. Another denied that Canary married Hickok, had a daughter, or, in fact, was the kind of woman "who would keep a diary." One regional commentator invoked the vantage of the "pioneer insider" to assert: "The people out in this country who were well and intimately acquainted with Jane, scoff at the story and look upon it as a bid for notoriety," while Lola Homsher, state archivist for Wyoming, saw an unholy alliance between romantic storytelling and the latest celluloid at work: "I believe that historians of a kind have given way to imagination, Hollywood style, in regard to this relationship."[23]

Even with Hickok's unlikely paternity, many commentators nonetheless leaned towards accepting the broader story at play. Presenting his findings in "The last will and testament of Calamity Jane; or, she laid her pistol down" (1946), Clarence Paine exposed the marriage certificate as fake and doubted some of the material reproduced in the letters, but was initially inclined to believe that McCormick *was* Canary's daughter. To him, the premise was plausible, despite the fact that there were clearly falsified elements and obvious mistakes in the timeline. Holding firm to a baseline position that Canary might well have been literate, and that it was she who, quite possibly, compiled the diary in a single night (dime novelist style), Paine put any narrative failings down to human fallibility or delusion, the act of an author trying to "convince herself and others she had left behind that she was not a failure." As time went on, he became more skeptical, but other historian-biographers (Nolie Mumey, Glenn Clairmonte, Stella Foote) stood firm in their support of McCormick. One particularly intriguing aspect in this was the fact that contradictions and obfuscations in the tale actually seemed to encourage a sense of believability. Puzzled by the mixed picture of evidence before him, Paine concluded, "if the diary is a forgery, it is either the cleverest or the most bungled attempt of which I know. If it is not a forgery we may well ask, what does it prove?" Skinner could not make sense of why "a woman would spend *hours* of her life writing and *embellishing* and *developing* a lie, namely her marriage to Hickok, for all posterity to see." Much like *Life and Adventures*, a jumble of grand illusion, period detail, and peculiarly personal tone lent a certain charm to McCormick's story. With their sense of fuzzy reality and captivating storytelling, the diaries were an excellent fit for Calamity Jane's folkloric canon. While not valuable for their historical accuracy, they nonetheless remained important studies in the power of frontier storytelling, memory, and masquerade. Her claim to daughterhood may have been a fraud, but McCormick's product was a success—not only in convincing many contemporaries of the veracity of her story, but also in informing the shape of the Calamity Jane legend in future years. As for the content of the journals, literary critic Elizabeth Stevenson calls them "believable and haunting," notable for their "frank and lively" style that seemed "to mirror a whole existence." Carried with an "authenticity of art," she notes, the collection of dog-eared scraps of narrative presented Calamity Jane as "a more interesting and complete person than the outward circumstances of her life indicate." Yet more intriguing was the fact that fakery and fabrication failed to dampen their significance. For Stevenson, they remained a "remarkable literary achievement." As ever in the legend of Calamity Jane, a good frontier performance went a long way.[24]

TELLING TALES ON CALAMITY: REMINISCENCE, LITERARY IMAGININGS, AND THE COLLISIONS OF PAST AND PRESENT, 1935-50

Attempts to ride shotgun on Calamity Jane's frontier celebrity were, in fact, happening all across the Black Hills in the 1930s and 1940s. As reminiscence culture entered its most prolific phase, those who remembered Canary in their youth keenly cited her as a leading protagonist in their own storied pasts. The "heroine of the plains" stood center stage in a landscape of collective memory. John S. McClintock's autobiography, *Pioneer Days in the Black Hills, By One of the Early Day Pioneers* (1939), was typical of the genre in positioning Calamity Jane's emerging fame alongside his own western journey. Based on a series of articles written for the local *Deadwood Daily Telegram* in the early twentieth century, his narrative was significant for its skeptical deconstruction of her legend, and for the way in which the author used Canary's fame to vaunt his own authority as frontier witness. An introductory passage read as follows:

> The writer has considerable personal knowledge, as she was well known to me during the periods she resided in the Black Hills ... This account will discredit much of her "own story" of her "life and adventures," published a few years before her death, and many highly fictitious and laudable stories told of her by sensational writers.[25]

In McClintock's estimation, beyond the parade of "heroic parts," Canary was nothing more than a common prostitute. Not a scout, nor a consort of Hickok's (though "seen frequently in his company"), she was "mannish, resourceful and independent" and "plain and unattractive." Frequently appearing in a "man's suit of buckskin, with a belt of 'arsenals'," her reputation for female masculinity was undisputed. Presented as a butch woman drifting between drunkenness and sobriety, prurient fanfare and social exclusion, McClintock's testimony gave a useful illustration of the centrality of gender unorthodoxy to Calamity Jane's identity. Moreover, for all its promises to lay bare the *real* West, *Pioneer Days* effectively illuminated the sinuous threads connecting history and story. In common with many mid-century biographers, McClintock affirmed himself as an "early day pioneer" with a narrative "duty" to tell the truth. In actual fact, by focusing on colorful moments of westering action (Indian raids, murders, and mining fever), as well as celebrities "in action," his sketches of life in the Black Hills instead said more about a folkloric landscape under construction.[26]

Of critical significance was the fact that period memoirists and biographers seemed to wrestle uneasily with a character who belonged to an exceptional and historically important past, but whose unconventional lifestyle raised complicated questions about mid-century moral code. Some responded to this challenge by bending Canary's story to fit conventional parameters (as Hollywood celluloid tended to), while others deployed her as lead actor in narratives both caustic and cautionary. Firmly in the latter vein, Edward Senn, newspaper editor in the Black Hills and author of *Deadwood Dick and Calamity Jane: A Thorough Sifting of Facts from Fiction* (1939), labeled her "a parody on womanhood, shorn of all decency and most womanly attributes," "coarse and unattractive," with a "propensity for romancing and seeking the limelight." Stewart Holbrook's *Annie Oakley and Other Rugged People* (1948) conjured up a similarly critical image of a "mannish" and promiscuous drunk, standing in sharp contrast to Oakley's "merger of feminine charm and lead bullets." For historian Harold Briggs, writing of "The Calamity Jane Myth" in his *Frontiers of the Northwest* (1940), Canary was nothing more than a confidence trickster with a complicated cognitive pathology: "A modern psychologist would find much of interest in the glamour with which Jane, in her later years, overlaid the drab adventures of her youth, when her only claim to fame was her absolute lack of respectability." In a post-war America marked by values of capitalist confidence, modern consumerism and social conservatism, the gender possibilities of Calamity Jane seemed dangerous and anarchic.[27]

The avant-garde quality that defined Canary as a frontier celebrity—in other words, her cross-dressing habits and nonconformist personal life—equally made her a tricky subject for writers. As Richard Etulain notes, the conventional literary formula of the time required "a heroic protagonist; his love interest, the romantic heroine; his competitor, the villainous opponent; and a demanding, almost preternatural, environment." Accordingly, he argues, writers of the fictive West in this period looked elsewhere for inspiration. *Calamity: The Many Lives of Calamity Jane* adds to this interpretation a reference to the powerful vestments of Canary's folkloric canon, which quite possibly limited her scope as a "one-size-fits-all" western storybook heroine. Calamity Jane was just too well known to be crammed into the plot confines of a fictional narrative that required a simpering female protagonist in a supporting role. Hollywood certainly had a stab at this endeavor, though its celluloid renderings often lost something in translation. Meanwhile, for wordsmiths who wanted a hint (often whimsically expressed) of social subversion, Calamity Jane's well-rehearsed performance of female masculinity had much to recommend it.[28]

Ethel Hueston's *Calamity Jane of Deadwood Gulch* (1938) was the second full-length novel to concern itself with the famed heroine of the plains; and, significantly, it was authored by a woman. Already renowned as a writer of western-flavored works, Hueston was not dissuaded by the complexities of taking on Calamity Jane as a heroine. Already accomplished at mixing up historical events, places, and people with an imaginative authorial twist (including *Star of the West* (1935), a fictionalized account of the Lewis and Clark Expedition), Hueston found Calamity an obvious draw. A work considerably more accurate than many of its non-fiction contemporaries, *Calamity Jane of Deadwood Gulch* won applause from the *New York Times* for "sifting the few known facts from the many fictions of Calamity Jane's life" to deliver a work reflective of "conscience and . . . imagination."[29]

True to the canonical imprint, Hueston's Calamity Jane was a wild woman, railing against civilization, and fighting Indians; caring for the sick; holding up grocery shops to get food for ailing miners; sinking bottles of whiskey; reveling in the riot of a cattle stampede; and particularly taken by news gossip, especially when it concerned her. Readers met her on page one, pining for an army sergeant in Wyoming, and headed to the Black Hills with Crook's team. Identified by her "steely muscles, her unerring eye and her vituperative tongue," she bore the familiar markers of female masculinity. A figure in constant motion, she galloped through a series of set pieces in a style reminiscent of *Life and Adventures*: bull-whacking with the army; escorted from the caravan after swimming with men; engaging in the spirited rescue of emigrants; and riding into Deadwood with Hickok. Thereafter, the cursory attention to historical accuracy faded in favor of a plot development that introduced the novel's other central character—Phoebe Norcutt from Boston, orphaned daughter of a missionary, genteel humanitarian, and champion of the Sioux. Highly significant was the fact that this story revolved around two female protagonists, who, as in Spencer's 1887 novel, shaped the narrative arc of the novel through their interactions. Phoebe met Calamity Jane on the trail, during one of the latter's "rampages," leading her to query: "Is—is it a woman?" Cast as polar opposites, Phoebe was devout, sober, and temperate, while Jane "had four passions in her lawless life: first, the savage lewdness of camp; then the exciting but fleet-footed tremors of love; liquor was her permanent, paramount absorption; but the sheer pleasure of running a disaster crowded these others close for honours."[30]

Of particular note was the way that Hueston toyed with the idea of Calamity Jane as an inveterate storyteller. When she related Captain Egan's famous naming, Jack Crawford (scout in the novel) and Phoebe cast doubt on her credibility, to which Jane replied "Well, it's damn' good listenin', ain't it?" Offering a psychological explanation for Canary's "famesque" leanings, Phoebe declared them the result of having the kind of heart that is touched by sorrow, the kind of heart that takes you to where trouble is, and keeps you sober and kind and gentle—until it is over. Probably it is because a calamity makes you good and liquor makes you—different.

Though the heterosexual parameters of the novel were not obviously contested, there were moments of gender possibility. Following Hickok's death, Calamity Jane threw herself into the role of Phoebe's protector, and, along the way (the broader plot concerned treaty negotiations between the army and the Sioux), she "kissed Jane warmly on the lips" and enquired if anyone else had ever done that. The novel ended (somewhat implausibly) with Phoebe settling down with reformed horse thief and Indian killer Len Wade, though she remained keen for Calamity Jane to live with them in Rapid City. Canary, however, rode off into the sunset to tour with William Cody, carousing with the old-timers to recall the "dear, dead, demoniac days."[31]

Elsewhere, the unorthodox threads of Canary's trademark costume delivered the possibility of re-making her as a radical feminist-in-waiting. According to the Federal Writers' Project, *Montana: A State Guidebook* (1939), she was an exemplar of the modern woman who's scouting, equestrian, shooting, and prospecting aptitudes could "not only compete with men in their own field but actually surpass many of them." Glendolin Wagner, likewise, described a much-maligned individual with the "courage to live her own unconventional life," while Billings pioneer W.A. Allen, quoted in Wagner's editorial for the weekly *Choteau Acantha* newspaper, saw her as a decisive trailblazer for gender empowerment:

She swore, she drank, she wore men's clothing. Today nothing would be thought of these peculiarities, for where can you find a woman who doesn't do much the same thing? Then, because standards were different, poor Calamity attracted unsavory attention. Today, she would probably be thought of as "modern." She was just fifty years ahead of her time.[32]

According to the Deadwood *Black Hills Weekly Tribune* (1938), Canary was "a lone soul, daring to do as she pleased in an age when conventions were never more strict or rigid. Years later, she might have been a suffragette leader or a pioneering aviatrix. Calamity Jane was born too soon." Such comments adeptly illustrated a growing complexity to the celebrity persona surrounding Canary/Calamity, as well as the ways in which her signature costume of female masculinity was beginning to take on an activist timbre.[33]

A reframed Calamity played out in interesting ways in the pages of comic books, a graphic medium that seemed to offer an expansive stage on which to conjure her as a vibrant animation of female agency. In three stories from the Green Hornet franchise (1946–47), created by Joe Simon and Jack Kirby, she found herself far from the trappings of frontier geography and working as a film noir private detective. That this comic-book Calamity inhabited an entirely different persona and time period suggested her translatability as an unorthodox, dynamic, and curious character. Here, in the comic-book universe, she shed many of her existing historical and mythological markers, to appear as an empowered and sexually confident woman prospering in the landscape of hardboiled fiction. Standing center stage without the necessity for hetero-normative romantic resolution, this new Calamity was a striking, but not unproblematically constructed, figure of feminist power. On the one hand, she was a strong and independent "lady dick," but also one whose trademark female masculinity had been stripped away in favor of a sexual stereotype of a blonde, buxom private investigator, dressed not in buckskin, but in fur coat, short skirt, and heels. Her inaugural appearance came in "The Case of the Hapless Hackie" (May 1946), where reporter Bill Draut revealed her as Jane Jarvis, known to the cops as "Calamity" for her badass attitude. With lines such as "that female detective is dynamite! . . . and what curves! Her nickname is Calamity! That's short for wildcat!", the series played to the misogynistic tendencies of a pulp fiction genre designed for a young, male market.[34]

"WHIP CRACK AWAY!": DORIS DAY, FEMALE MASCULINITY, AND THE DEFINITIVE CALAMITY JANE

The next milestone in the adventures of a celluloid Calamity—and, in fact, the most important iteration of her across the entire reel of twentieth-century media—was David Butler's 1953 musical, *Calamity Jane*. Undoubtedly the most famous popular cultural product associated with Martha Jane Canary, even today a mention of the film usually precipitates a spontaneous sing-along of "The Deadwood Stage" ("Whip Crack Away!") and sentimental sighs over a movie that, for many, brings back memories of childhood and the nostalgic simplicity of high Hollywood camp. Integral to the charm of the film was its lead, Doris Day, whose "Calam" presented a fresh-faced and feminized heroine to entertain the (thermo)nuclear family (Plate 18). With training as a professional dancer (curtailed by a car accident in her teens) and a back catalogue of singing success ("Sentimental Journey" (1945)) and romantic musicals (*I'll See You in My Dreams* (1951)), she was suited for the physicality and the tunefulness of her role in *Calamity Jane*. A screen identity as "all-American girl next door" also played into a character that channeled a boisterous naivety, as she leapt around in buckskins, falling into dramatic scrapes with Indians, Chicago actresses, and dashing western heroes. Day reputedly had more fun with this role than any of her other acting gigs. As she recalled: "I loved portraying Calamity Jane, who was a rambunctious, pistol-packing, prairie girl (I lowered my voice and stuck out my chin a little)." Catapulted to new heights of superstardom as a 1950s screen starlet, this was, arguably, Calamity Jane's greatest performance sleight of hand.[35]

The idea of creating Deadwood's famous hell-raiser—a woman known for her drunken howls, not her melodious ditties—as a frontier songstress might seem a somewhat unusual choice. However, Warner Brothers' crafting of a rip-roaring account of "how the West was sung" had important precedents. For one thing, in the "golden age" of the western, anything "frontier branded" had popular appeal, especially if it offered a novel take on the Technicolor trans-Mississippi. Mapping a similar genre development was the Hollywood musical. From its early success in *The Jazz Singer* (1927) to the recent hit *Singin' in the Rain* (1952), the medium was looking for new ways to sustain popular interest. Why not put the two together? For one thing, the "singing cowboys" of the 1930s and 1940s had shown the appeal of the cowpoke-crooner formula and had kick-started the careers of Gene Autry and Roy Rogers (even John Wayne tried his hand in *Riders of Destiny* (1933)). Even more pertinent was the recent success of the western/musical crossover, *Annie Get Your Gun* (1950), which starred Betty Hutton as Annie Oakley, and was based on a stage musical written by Irving Berlin in 1946 that ran to more than 1,000 shows in its three years on Broadway. Developed for the cinema by Rodgers and Hammerstein, the film served to reignite popular interest in the character of Annie Oakley as a homespun sharpshooter with Buffalo Bill's "wild West" show. Tracking a biopic trail from a blonde, grubby, backwoods girl with a gun called "grandma" to Oakley's command performance of dazzling gunplay and the "Rescue of the Deadwood Stage" before Queen Victoria (an interesting mixing of Oakley's and Canary's storied pasts), *Annie Get Your Gun* had its lead gambol through her story with musical voice in such numbers as "Doing What Comes Naturally," "Anything You Can Do, I Can Do Better," and "There's No Business Like Show Business." Driving the plot was Oakley's relationship with Frank Butler, self-assured celebrity trick shooter and on-off-on romantic suitor, whom she easily outcompeted. True to the rubric of gender containment, Oakley threw her final match (on Sitting Bull's advice), in order to gain the bigger prize of a life of settled domesticity. With coiffured hair and in embroidered western skirt suit, she skipped within the confines of a gender binary, where men strode pre-eminent and women walked obediently behind. The song "You Can't Get a Man with a Gun" advised: "a man may be hot, but he's not when he's shot."[36]

The movie trailer for *Calamity Jane* set the tenor of the film in depicting Martha Jane Canary as feted raconteur of Deadwood, propping up the bar and regaling customers with tall tales. In this, of course, it was entirely consistent with the historical proclivities of its titular protagonist, though Day's "Calam" only drank snappy "sasperillies." Towering over Calamity Jane as the leading man of the film was Wild Bill Hickok, played by Howard Keel (who also played Frank in *Annie Get Your Gun*). With a buckskin-clad screen idol, twirling weapons and words, in a Technicolor feast of all-action frontier entertainment, the story of Calamity Jane was given a sizeable dose of folkloric license and a decidedly 1950s gloss. The opening credits began with Canary freighting and frolicking on the Deadwood stage, heartily swinging a lasso, clad in boots, cavalry hat, grubby fringed buckskin suit, and sporting a healthy Hollywood glow (Plate 17). Arriving in Deadwood to public fanfare—very much the celebrity of the piece—she threw down various pieces of loot for the townsfolk, before swaggering into the Golden Garter. Amusing her audience with tales of thwarting "painted varmints," and belting out a comically competitive number with Hickok in "I Can Do Without You," Day's lead championed a carefree, bubble-gum take on her character's historical reputation for female masculinity.

Ideas of masquerade and mistaken identity lie at the heart of the film. As such, they trace a direct lineage from the narrative prescriptive of dime novel days to Hollywood celluloid. Integral to this, of course, is the character of Calamity Jane, a buckskin-clad, rough-around-the-edges, frontier gal, who swaggers around a mild, wild West inspiring camaraderie and comic banter. Serving as her logical foil in cross-dressing light entertainment is actor Francis Fryer (whom saloon operator Henry Miller had assumed was an *actress*), who arrives with Calamity on the Deadwood stage, all set to headline that night at the Garter. Fearing a riot in the crowd if "his actress" does not appear, Miller has Fryer take to the stage in drag, where he capably entertains the all-male crowd with his version of "Hive Full of Honey," until a fateful flourish of a band trombone removes his wig. The theatrical disrobing of Fryer, in turn, inspires not only a full-on frontier ruckus in the stalls, but a third masquerade, as Calamity

Jane vows to make amends for the disastrous revue by fetching famed actress Adelaid Adams from Chicago. Plucked from her usual wild frontier habitat and placed in city streets, Calamity's buckskin disguise provokes prurient stares and the odd flirtatious wink from female passers-by. "Calam," for her part, mistakes wigs for scalps in a shop window, a carved Indian for a living breathing one, and, most importantly, in the dressing room of the theater, Katie Brown for Adelaid Adams. Accordingly, when she proudly returns to Deadwood, to the dulcet tones of "Just Blew in from the Windy City," her companion is not a famous actress, but the maid, who had merely been trying on her boss's dresses.

Riding shotgun in *Calamity Jane* were themes of discovery and transformation, expressed through various plot twists in romantic, vocational, and sartorial terms. Katie's real identity is dramatically exposed in her first faltering lines before the Golden Garter, and another mutiny is only prevented by a pistol-packing Calamity asserting that the crowd "give the girl a chance." When she casts off Adams' mantle to give her own crowd-pleasing performance, Katie cements a nascent singing career and invites the attentions of both cavalryman Danny Gilmartin and Bill Hickok, who trip over each other to compete for her affections. Before the romantic denouement, however, Katie abets Calamity Jane in her grand transformation, by moving into her cabin and injecting a floral dose of feminine domesticity, courtesy of "A Woman's Touch." Thrown together as opposites and cabin-mates, the interaction between Katie and Calamity reprises the "taming" narrative that earlier celluloid had bought into as moral safety device. Running through their relationship, too, is the idea of romantic competition—one that is resolved (after a fair share of tears, pistol shots, costume changes, and stagecoach chases) by Calamity Jane and Wild Bill discovering (through their failed pursuit of Danny and Katie) their own "Secret Love." The film ends with a double wedding and the greatest transformation of all: Calamity Jane gives up the grubby buckskin lifestyle to satisfy her innermost, but deeply buried, aspirations for a spick-and-span home, marriage, and "young uns."

Calamity Jane was a huge box-office hit, and won an Academy Award for Best Original Song (for "Secret Love"). *Variety* called it "unimaginative hokum," but enjoyed its "colorful staging and good tunes." Scarcely recognizable from the historical imprint of Martha Canary, the film seemed familiar to the plotlines not only of *Annie Get Your Gun*, but also of the musical tale of cowboy suitors vying for the attentions of Laurey Williams in *Oklahoma!* (a 1943 stage musical that made its movie debut two years after *Calamity Jane*). The *New York Times* labeled Butler's film a "shrill and preposterous musical western," with a script "utterly cheerful and abandoned in tangling a quite unlikely tale." Pointing to the contemporary fixtures of gender conformity, it lambasted the untransformed Calamity Jane as "a frontier female whose indifference to the graces of her sex is both ridiculous and repulsive," and seemed uncomfortable with Day's presentation ("tempestuous to the point of becoming just a bit frightening—a bit terrifying—at times"). Once costumed in dresses and warbling about romantic longings for Wild Bill, however, the heroine was considerably improved: "Everything gets a little better after she takes on the airs of a woman and settles down." "Tomboyishness is not the lady's forte," it concluded. The London *Daily Mail* found Day's depiction more refreshing, somewhere between "dynamite and nightingale," and demonstrating an "unexpected talent for horse, gun, stage coach, and vituperation."[37]

The dominant message of *Calamity Jane*, evident both from its central plotline and media reviews, was of a frontier tomboy tamed, as film critic Linda Mizejewski puts it, "cleaned up, glamorized and sentimentalized." The London *Daily Mail* pointed out that Day's heroine "took the usual quota of ten songs and about the same number of fights to discover that a man likes a girl to behave like a female." Indeed, the fanciful formula of "winning the West" by song and swagger struck a popular (and commercially lucrative) chord. As historian Elaine Tyler May notes in *Homeward Bound: American Families in the Cold War Era* (1988), the 1950s was a time of domestic containment, where at-home women were championed as nurturers of an all-American nuclear family, serving their country from the kitchen counter by baking cookies and fighting communism. This focus on settling down in the domestic interior explained the fact that *Calamity Jane* was, as Eric Savoy puts it, an "oddly indoor western." Moreover, the film told a powerful morality tale of youthful gender transgression in a time and space where gender boundaries were more fluid, necessarily giving way to a pathway of domestic conformity. The raw Calamity offered an appealing brand of female independence, a working woman prospering in a homo-social world, feisty, adaptable, and an actor in her own (and Deadwood's) manifest destiny. At the same time, a rosy future of domestic conformity was an inevitable one once she had met her beau and the frontier had closed. As Calamity Jane confronted her own domestic and patriotic aspirations, her "wild ways" (and buckskin costume) were cast off.[38]

In fact, as film scholar Tamar Jeffers McDonald notes, the dynamics of "normative containment" were clearly visible in the sartorial changes on screen that served to successively feminize Day's character. Dressed in dirty frontier workwear, the uncouth youth Calamity was subject to acerbic judgment from potential suitors, who pointed out that she was not adhering to social expectations. Wild Bill told her to "fix" her hair, and when headed to the city, to get some "female fixings." Adelaid Adams was, in contrast, "everything a woman ought to be." An encounter with the womanly Katie, corseted and coiffured in a Chicago dressing room, meanwhile, precipitated a gender identity crisis, as Canary admitted she looked "a mite strange," and seemed confounded at the idea that anyone might take her to be a man ("course I'm a woman," she bristled). All "Calam" needed, it seemed, was a little guidance in the ways of femininity. This was duly provided by Katie, whose instructional "A Woman's Touch" gave Calamity Jane (and her cabin) a Hollywood makeover and a life lesson in the womanly satisfaction to be had from engaging in household chores ("the magic of a broom can mesmerize a room"), and crafting a home (and a matching feminine identity) to be proud of. By way of two new outfits during the cabin clean-up (first a blue check shirt and shapely buckskins, then a crisp white blouse and long skirt), Calamity's developing path as a homely sweetheart was unveiled. Re-dressed for a new performance in what Yvonne Tasker calls "feminine costumes of restraint," she assumed the full responsibilities of femininity, and presided over the closure of her own frontier adventure. As the film played out, a full-length pink gown, an immaculately clean and tailored brown suede suit, and a delicately buttoned white wedding dress choreographed a process of hetero-normative resolution.[39]

Beneath the simplicity of Doris Day's swaggering "sasperilly"-swigging performance, however, were more subversive prospects. As much as the mainstream message told of the necessary triumph of domestic bliss, the film also provided a space for alternative readings. According to Eric Savoy, *Calamity Jane* was notable for its dismantling of "the western's rigid categories of gender and sexuality"—a reflection, as he sees it, of the fluid performance space provided by "the genre gap" between the musical and the western. Particularly significant was the film's celebration of a dynamic female masculinity that parodied the brash extrapolations of archetypal macho behavior, pointed to other configurations of gender identity, and flirted with the idea of same-sex desire between Calamity and Katie. For Savoy, the "lesbian spectatorial position" of the movie questioned "the possibility, or even the desirability of a coherent gender role." Mandy Merck pointed to its "persistent lesbian overtones." Day's casting in the role, meanwhile, was a perfect fit for readings of gender possibility. As Emma Simmonds notes, Day lacked the "girly allure of Marilyn Monroe, the brazen heterosexuality of Jane Russell, or the 'men come hither' eyes of Rita Hayworth. Her naïve enthusiasm in the role of Calamity and the baggage of her bland all-American persona paradoxically expose her to alternative readings." Not regarded as a definitively straight female role model, and often playing opposite Rock Hudson as her male lead, it was unsurprising that Day garnered a reputation in some circles as a closeted carrier for female homosexuality.[40]

The disruptive nature of Day's performance suggested an American post-war society wrapped up in conformity, but toying with other possibilities, and finding novel ways to explore them under the radar of stringent censorship rules. As Bates points out, "Secret Love" was a big hit in US 1950s gay bars. Important to note is the fact that *Calamity Jane* may well represent the first occasion when the word "gender" was uttered on camera (Henry Miller tellingly comments on Fryer's act: "I may have made a mistake about his gender, but not his talent"). Central to the subversive message of the film, meanwhile, is its message of gender masquerade and performativity. "Calam" has to "learn" to be a woman, and, importantly, successfully carries off a female masculinity that outguns the men on screen and confers on her both agency and confidence. Likewise, in deriding Calamity for crying over Gilmartin, it is not *entirely* clear which aspect of her persona Wild Bill sees as out of step with her identity ("You are a fake, Calam, you dress, shoot, and talk like a man but think like a female . . . a green-eyed, snarling, spittin' female"). Thus, underneath the film's feminine re-dressings, there was a different performance at play.[41]

Substantiating a queer reading of *Calamity Jane* was its decidedly unconvincing hetero-normative ending. For one thing, the mainstream narrative of Calamity Jane casting off her buckskin chrysalis to emerge as a truly realized self did not square with the fact that her most convincing repertoire (and the parts of the movie where she seemed most at home and to be having most fun) involved jumping around in male attire, lasso and pistol at the ready, and hollering "Whip Crack Away!" As one commentator notes, "the promise of marriage cannot cancel out the joyous, life-affirming queer energy of the film's opening, which presents us with the spectacle of Doris Day dressed in buckskin, standing astride the Deadwood stagecoach singing 'The Deadwood Stage'." Yet more telling was the fact that the most plausible romantic relationship in the film took place between Calamity and Katie (Plate 16). On meeting Katie for the first time, "Calam" exclaimed "Gosh almighty, you're the prettiest thing I've ever seen. I never knew a woman could look like that."

This outburst, on one level, spoke of a personal epiphany as to her own concealed femininity; but equally, it might be seen in terms of a different kind of sexual realization. This was particularly worth bearing in mind given the homosexual "hidden histories" of music-hall mashers outlined earlier in *Calamity: The Many Lives of Calamity Jane*. As the film developed, moreover, scenes between Calamity and Katie were dominated by same-sex allusions. Savoy calls their shacking-up in Calamity's cabin a clear example of "a little closet on the prairie," the happy cohabitation of two lesbians living independently of men, singing out the joys of "a woman's touch" (in household economy and bedroom), and inscribing their same-sex union on the cabin door: "Calam and Katie." Further evidence of what the Manchester *Guardian* newspaper called a "hugely enjoyable proto-lesbian musical" could be found in the fact that it was Katie (and not Wild Bill) who first noticed Calamity Jane as "beautiful" (spying her through a freshly cleaned cabin window). "Calam's" heartbreak at the union of Gilmartin and Katie, equally, might be read as a reaction to the loss of the latter, more than the former (who was, it must be said, little more than a walk-on man—a sideshow to the main event). To Barbara Creed, the homosexual dynamics of the film were starkly evident. Here was the story of a lead character giving up a woman "with whom she had set up home and whom she clearly loves."[42]

An enticing artefact of Canary-ana, Butler's film was open to multiple interpretations. Running alongside the story of domestic containment in the all-singing, all-dancing Deadwood Gulch was an alternative narrative of gender fluidity and non-normative expression. This not only reflected the possibilities and prerogatives of a variegated modern entertainment landscape, but also illuminated long-standing tensions over how to apprehend Martha Jane Canary as a historical character in a frontier space, where opportunities for radical reformulations of gender norms sat alongside social conservatism. Beneath all the high-kicking fancy, then, the message of Doris Day's Calamity Jane as a many-sided and colorful character who inspired contested readings was consistent with her folkloric back catalog. Ultimately, of course, what the film (and its enduring success) made clear was the malleability of a lead character whose performance of female masculinity offered expansive possibilities for re-inscription. From bubble-gum gloss to a butch lesbian icon, the possibilities for Martha Jane Canary in the frontier imaginary were seemingly endless.

PAGEANTRY AND STORYTELLING IN FRONTIERLAND, 1953–60

Close to Martha Canary's final resting place, residents were somewhat divided about the fakery of the Hollywood frontier and the inevitable attention that *Calamity Jane* brought to the region. As much as pioneer reminiscence indulged in the folkloric Calamity, the use of the brand name illuminated cultural fissures about remembrance, pecuniary advantage, and moral message. Some in the Black Hills saw possible commercial gains to be had from saddling up with the Butler franchise, and they championed a "Calamity Jane Week" to coincide with the film's release. Deadwood's famous hell-raiser had long featured as part of the annual Days of '76 festival, and a stream of interested visitors continued to make the pilgrimage to Mount Moriah Cemetery, which now boasted concession stands selling trinkets and refreshments. John Sohn, who had made Canary's new boots for her inaugural dime novel stage show, spoke of tourists flocking to Deadwood in the early 1950s, "crazy about Calamity." For his part, he had told a recent group of female tourists who chose to wear shorts and who enquired what Canary had worn around town that "she always dressed like a lady." Particularly caustic was the attitude of South Dakota Governor Sigurd Anderson, who saw no reason to play to Hollywood and to a woman undeserving of posthumous celebration. Quoted in the *Rapid City Daily Journal*, local Bob Lee commented: "If the movie 'Calamity Jane' is as accurate as most Hollywood historical films, it will portray Calamity as a woman and that's about all."[43]

Other places, however, willingly tapped into the greenback and heritage boons of the frontier imaginary by memorializing landmark moments in the life and adventures of Martha Jane Canary. Princeton established Calamity Roadside Park in 1957, situated a few miles north of the town on Highway 65. Sponsored by the American Legion, the dedication of green space to the Calamity Jane brand suggested a community willing to overlook the more complicated sides to her life story, in favor of associating with a frontier celebrity (the dedication came fresh on the heels of Doris Day's performance as a sparkling frontier songstress). Local historian and journalist Doris Thompson declared her delight that "at long last Calamity will have some recognition in her home town," though she admitted that the task of summarizing the history of the town's famous daughter was fraught with complexity. Opened in a formal ceremony on 21 July by G. Morgan, vice chair of the Missouri State Highway Commission, the acre and a quarter site boasted picnic tables, barbeque ovens, trees, and a small pond. Joining civic dignitaries at the event were a local photographer and Tex Allen, showman and movie star (with a penchant himself for cowboy hats and fringed buckskin suits). Allen happened to be passing by on his way to a gig in Tampa, Florida, and obliged with an impromptu knife-throwing display. In a piece for the local *Post Telegraph*, Thompson hailed Princeton's "first attempt to claim fame as the birthplace of this famous woman of the early days," and used the occasion to talk about Canary's upbringing in the town and the local chatter about her cigar-smoking mother; this was followed by a potted biography lifted from *Life and Adventures*. Commenting on the dubious nature of Calamity Jane's scouting claims, she noted: "although Jane's exploits have gone down in history with perhaps more fiction than fact, there is no disputing that as a child she lived near Princeton and was probably born here."[44]

Disneyland, canonical site of all-American entertainment, opened in 1955 with "Frontierland" as one of four themed play worlds. This at once signaled the importance of the old West as a patriotic landscape and linked indirectly to Calamity Jane (though she was not referenced specifically). Harper Goff, who had designed the sets for *Calamity Jane*, also played a key role in fashioning Disneyland's built environment. In fact, the technical layout for the Golden Garter in Butler's film was nearly identical to the Golden Horseshoe Saloon, an important building in Disney's Frontierland section. Meanwhile, across the Atlantic, Calamity Jane was continuing to draw punters as a vibrant sideshow attraction. Yorkshireman William "Texas Bill" Shufflebottom—who claimed to have held a bit part in Cody's troupe—successfully exported frontier mythology (at least until a horse crushed him in the show ring in 1915) to create a family business in "wild West" shows that played across fairgrounds in the North of England from the 1890s to the 1960s. Alongside show staples of snake wrangling, knife throwing, and shooting, granddaughter Florence costumed herself in an outfit of sombrero, neatly fringed buckskin short dungarees, and cowgirl boots. Wowing crowds in the 1950s, she switched show identities between Calamity Jane and Annie Oakley, depending on which character seemed ahead in the frontier celebrity charts.[45]

CALAMITY JANE AND THE TUMBLEWEED OF TRUTH; OR, MARTHA CANARY MEETS THE HISTORIAN-BIOGRAPHERS, 1950–60

In *The Black Hills and their Incredible Characters* (1949), Robert Casey revealed a key problem for the historian: the more one dug into Canary's past, the less one discovered. Lamenting on his own quest for historical certainties in her story, he mused:

> Long ago, somebody asked me "Who was Calamity Jane?" And the answer was simple. I had the legend pat, complete with names, dates, addresses and bibliography. Today if anyone were to ask me the same question the answer would still be simple: "I don't know."

Clarence Paine, likewise, amassed huge amounts of data in his forensic pursuit of the "true" Calamity, but never wrote up his findings in any substantive way. Indeed, the few essays he produced on the subject either fell back on a simplistic invocation of Canary as a freak show hermaphrodite, or became mired in the contested provenance of her name and genealogy. In the end, he pointed out, "Anyone attempting to divine the facts in the life of Calamity Jane is soon impressed by the fact there is as much to be unlearned as to be learned."[46]

It was in the 1950s that the first concerted attempts were made by historians (both amateur and professional) to survey the life of Calamity Jane. These historian-biographers championed the importance of identifying "the facts," and ruminated on Canary's story with a view to necessarily separating lived and invented experience. Unsurprisingly (given what *Calamity: The Many Lives of Calamity Jane* has shown about the entangled nature of Canary's past, personality, and performance), this proved a complex and indeed impossible task. *Calamity Jane, 1852–1903: A History of her Life and Adventures in the West* (1950) was illustrative in this regard, offering as it did a mixture of textual inventory and flag-waving fancy. Written by Nolie Mumey, a Colorado doctor, and with a private print run of just 200 copies, the biography reproduced a number of period newspaper snippets on Canary that had not been collated before, and eagerly reprinted diary entries from the McCormick portfolio. Hailing Calamity Jane as a quixotic frontier original, Mumey effused:

> A part of the great West; a picturesque character who traveled extensively and knew many old pioneers; a strange mixture of the wild; a generous type; unselfish in all her attributes, never posing; a personality of her own; a rough and ready person of frontier days, educated in the school of experience.

In large part, Mumey kept to the safe terrain of inventory, and refrained from substantive reflection on the implications of Canary's unconventional life path. Hence, in this historical biography, she was comely and mannish, homely and flighty. Sympathetic to the plight of a courageous woman fending for herself in a challenging environment, Mumey saw cross-dressing as a pragmatic recourse that allowed her to become "one of the actors on the stage of the West." In fact, he noted, in a modern world where women were "on an equal footing with men," and able to "swear, drink, smoke, and wear men's clothes without becoming outcasts," Martha Canary would "scarcely be noticed."[47]

Another early historical-biography, Glenn Clairmonte's *Calamity Was the Name for Jane* (1959), offered a stylized treatment that also accepted the McCormick narrative, and urgently proclaimed its authentic voice. Playing fast and loose with myth and history, this work scarcely achieved its aim of providing "the only complete life of Calamity Jane." No wonder those trying to track the historical path of Martha Jane Canary found the trail perilous. At every turn were fanciful attempts at biography that drew on each other for supposed facts, and eagerly trumpeted their own accuracy. Alongside several historical photographs of Calamity Jane, Clairmonte included chapters on her wedding to Hickok, and one entitled "Two Tragedies," which mourned the death of Custer and her brother at the Little Bighorn. Critical here was the author's determination to fit together the "truths" of *Life and Adventures* with McCormick's diaries, in order to craft Canary as a courageous, tragic, and morally unambiguous character. The result, less than successful, highlighted the skillfulness of the McCormick corpus in avoiding such a collision, simply by skirting around the familiar autobiographical sign-posts. Eulogized as a "warm-blooded frontierswoman, probably the most independent person who ever lived," Clairmonte's heroine was viewed through a romantic glass, the more complicated elements of her story (unconventional lifestyle, rocky personal life, and performance of female masculinity) ignored in favor of delivering a romp across a frontier landscape with a woman both kindly and brave. According to historian Leonard Jennewein, Clairmonte's work should have been awarded "the prize for the worst biography ever written!"[48]

Alongside these explorations in creative historical biography were two works that signaled the beginning of a more academically credible assessment of Martha Jane Canary: J. Leonard Jennewein's *Calamity*

Jane of the Western Trails (1953) and Roberta Sollid's *Calamity Jane: A Study in Historical Criticism* (1958). Both continued to frame their analysis from the perspective of "fact-finding," and were resolute in their discrediting of McCormick. Most interesting was the way in which they alluded to the importance of performance and symbolism in the Calamity Jane story, though the focus of both remained squarely on the idea of discrediting popular mythology in favor of finding a "true" history.

The product of several years' research, Jennewein's short pamphlet (48 pages) reflected its author's insistence that there were too many gaps in the Canary/Calamity story to make a full biographical manuscript viable. Instead, he confined his survey to a series of set-piece chapters that deconstructed the truths and falsehoods in the life of a character who "followed the man-trails of the old west." With a hint of fascination for the flamboyance of his lead actor, he talked of "a spark of the unforgettable, a flair for the spectacular, an urgency for action, a jigger of Ol' Nick, a touch of the bitters," before turning to the real focus of his enquiry: debunking Calamity Jane's iconic status. Epic reputations, he noted, may well be important, but it "behooves us from time to time to shuck off the grosser husks of a frontier legend and attempt a definition of the grain." This pamphlet, it must be said, was sharply critical of its subject. "Considerable is said in favor of not saying anything about Calamity. She was a disreputable old harridan, a disgrace to womankind," railed its opening paragraph. In a useful insight into the contours of gender containment, both at the time of Canary's life and at mid-century, here was a character whose non-normative position prompted rebuke with a smattering of delight. Thus, *Calamity Jane of the Western Trails* invoked a critical tone to talk of a woman brought up without the moral parameters of a "normal home life," yet in possession of an alluring "factor x . . . the unmeasurable tokens of ancestry from whence came the spark of the unforgettable." Essential to Martha Canary was the strikingly successful way she carried forth her signature line in female masculinity. As Jennewein saw it: "She dressed like a man; she cavorted with men in a manner not usual to her kind. She drank whiskey in saloons with men before such practice was socially acceptable. She wore a gun, she swore, she chewed tobacco; she traveled with bull trains and knew how to crack the whip." This, he noted, was what "set her apart ... [and] made people talk about her."[49]

Roberta Sollid's *Calamity Jane: A Study in Literary Criticism* (1958) presented the first formal academic book-length study of Martha Canary. Authored by a mid-westerner with academic training in psychology and history, the study was based on a 1951 Master's thesis submitted to Montana State University. Driven by a sense of scholarly enquiry, Sollid cultivated a studious and investigative tone that set her apart from earlier pursuits of the "real Calamity." Richard Etulain labels her work the "first well-researched, analytical study" of Canary. Addressing her subject in the introduction, Sollid placed herself within the popular oratory swirling around Martha Canary, recalling how, as a child, she was called "Calamity Jane" by her mother every time she got into scrapes. Equally intriguing was the fact that neither she nor her mother "had the remotest idea of who Calamity Jane was"—a stark illumination of the way in which a colorful folkloric portmanteau had effectively disembodied the "heroine of the plains" from the historical experience of Martha Canary.[50]

Thereafter, Sollid hit readers with a censorious style that suggested little lingering romantic attachment to the character whose nickname she had shared. Using a moralistic tone that demonstrated the codes of gender conformity at play in judgments on Calamity, she asserted "no career is so elusive to the historian as that of a loose woman." Canary's marginal status, moreover, made for a hard prospect in recovering her history: "Like most prostitutes and drunkards she left little behind in the way of tangible evidence which could be used by historians to recon- struct the story of her checkered career." In a similarly pejorative (and also inaccurate) way, Sollid argued that Canary had been "all but forgotten by her contemporaries," her fame only ignited two decades after her death, when, "for some unknown reason, sensation-writers and historians began to take an interest in her." Ultimately, she concluded,

Calamity Jane was a "well-meaning but good for nothing frontiers-woman." Recent Canary historian-biographers regard the work of Sollid (and, indeed, of Jennewein) as representative of a sea change in the treatment of Calamity Jane as a serious topic of historical enquiry. However, from the perspective of modern understandings of gender identity and cultural representations of social deviance, the prejudicial slant to their writing makes them decidedly problematic as guides to action for would-be Canary-ologists.[51]

The work of historian-biographers in the 1950s, then, was not quite the "famesque" gallop of Hollywood makeover; but equally, it fell far short of properly getting to grips with the complexity of Calamity Jane as a historical and folkloric entity. Certainly, many who wrestled with the "heroine of the plains" in her life and afterlife found Canary's performance of female masculinity a challenging subject of study. Tracking her life and legend for the *English Westerners' Brand Book* (1963), Andrew Blewitt argued that Calamity Jane had escaped forensic biographical deconstruction for three principal reasons. First, Canary conspired in her own lifetime to craft a storied past that sabotaged later quests for historical truth. Secondly, anyone who might settle any nagging questions of provenance was, in all likelihood, dead. Thirdly, the precariousness of her existence as a poor, itinerant woman with an alcohol problem made hers "not the type of life which would interest anyone sufficiently to write about." This last observation starkly illustrated the limitations to historical scholarship in an academic canon occupied (in the main) with power politics enacted by "dead white men." Indeed, as *Calamity: The Many Lives of Calamity Jane* has indicated, successive cultural representations of Calamity Jane suggest that she *was* a person of long-standing interest, around whom a weighty costume of gender unorthodoxy had been crafted. Corralled by the narrative architecture of gender containment, and digested as a proto-feminist and lesbian-in-waiting, the buckskin garb of the "female scout" invited diverse mid-century readings. Meanwhile, in true Hollywood fashion, an expansive new West of gender possibility was on the horizon for Calamity Jane.[52]

CHAPTER SEVEN

"A FEMINIST IN BUCKSKIN"
PERFORMANCE, PROFANITY, AND SEXUAL POLITICS ON THE NEW WESTERN FRONTIER (1960-2000)

Calamity Jane in the years 1960–2000 was a roving character, catapulted into all manner of different scenarios. Her storied presence took inspiration from traditional folkloric sources, and also bore witness to a transformed cultural landscape, especially in regard to gender and sexual revolutions, and the reframing of the frontier story according to a countercultural and revisionist canon. Firmly installed as a tantalizing emblem of western wildness, she was conscripted to sell a range of frontier-brand products—from diners to clothing lines, town pageants to cowgirl toys. Courtesy (largely) of Doris Day, she had become a household name, and was now routinely deployed by an expansive multimedia entertainment landscape to evoke pioneer times. A clear indication of her superstar standing, Canary was fabricated in puppetry for the *Muppet Babies* (1990), to play a well-rehearsed role as a stagecoach driver and "wild woman," with whom Skeeter became obsessed. A "famesque" quality long in the making, meanwhile, made her a plot-mobile figure with a powerful, but versatile, folkloric silhouette. In an indication of her performative lure, the British *Beano* comic toyed with Canary's famous nom de plume in its characterization of "Calamity James" (1986), a hapless youth with a pet lemming (Alexander), red jersey imprinted with the number 13, and an uncanny ability to dodge opportunity in the form of diamonds, gold, and money bags.[1]

Most important was the fact that the story of the "female scout" with a long-standing reputation for gender unorthodoxy played out in a late twentieth-century landscape that incorporated radically different readings of the frontier imaginary, cultural values, and sexual politics. The complex mechanics of interpreting an unconventional lifestyle had long played out in her narrative trail. Now, however, the multiplicity of images was extraordinary. Prime-time television westerns employed her as a dynamic lead in tales of domestic morality and heterosexual resolution. Adult novels featured her as a maverick sexual conquest for white strongman heroes roaming a monochrome, misogynistic frontier. Sophisticated theatrical productions presented a modern feminist in a messy and mythically tarnished West that historian Patricia Nelson Limerick described as "a place undergoing conquest and never fully escaping its consequences." The buckskin-clad fixings of her frontier celebrity stayed the same, but the social and moral meanings of Canary's famous costume inspired diverse responses. Historian Richard Etulain dubs these the years of a "new, gray Calamity." In fact, as *Calamity: The Many Lives of Calamity Jane* has demonstrated, the story of Martha Jane Canary was *always* subject to different readings (readings, invariably, that were largely to do with her heretical gender profile). What *was* distinctive about these years was their striking and strident exploration of Canary's female masculinity—something intrinsic to her identity in life and afterlife, but which only received a weighty and philosophical deconstruction at century's end. Striding out in spaghetti western celluloid and artistic productions, a new western "heroine of the plains" swaggered into plain sight as a woman born before her time, whose transgressive performance carried the torch of feminism, gender equality, and queer identity.[2]

TV DINNERS: TECHNICOLOR MORALITY AND AMORALITY IN THE OLD WEST

Initial "versions" of Calamity Jane in the 1960s showed little promise in terms of the journey from female to feminist frontier: they preferred instead to rehash older motifs and showcase a female lead firmly in the genre conventions of a mainstream western vernacular. *The Raiders*

(1963) traded in a tale of irked Texan ranchers and railroad politics in a post-Reconstruction Southwest. Played by petite ex-figure skater Judith Meredith, Calamity Jane appeared 20 minutes in, on the streets of a Kansas cattle town, fending off the unwelcome attentions of three drunk cowpunchers with a well-placed lash of her bull whip and a timely intervention from Bill Cody, who advised the men to lay off "Hickok's girl." Garbed in her ubiquitous buckskin, with a red blouse, confederate hat, pearls, and make-up, Meredith's portrayal was safely in the mold of the feral femme, there principally to play the role of woman out of place and acting up. While Cody and Hickok performed as steely male protectors of the US Army supply train, Jane's purpose in *The Raiders* ran along an equally gendered rail. After being ambushed by outlaws on a freight run, she bristled "one of these days . . . you're gonna treat me like a woman." At the end of the film, Cody suggested that, in order for her to win Hickok's heart, she needed to be more feminine and boast a full purse.[3]

On television, too, emphasis remained on the pursuit of heterosexual romance, and the fortunes of an errant heroine played out as cautionary morality tale. In the *Bonanza* episode "Calamity over the Comstock" (1963), Stephanie Powers' Calamity Jane visits Virginia City, clad in grubby buckskin and riding a buggy. Rescued from Paiute ambush by Little Joe, she is removed to the safe refuge of the Ponderosa ranch, only to fall for the protective charms of her defender. Thereafter, the episode revolves around various gender reveals (to Little Joe and Hoss); a comic rendition of a caricatured Jane who drinks too much whiskey, picks fights, and passes out; and a grand duelling showdown between spurned lover Johnny "Doc" Holliday and Little Joe (in which Calamity saves Joe's honor by faking his winning pistol shot). Likewise, *Death Valley Days* in "A Calamity called Jane" (1966) had its lead joining Wild Bill's western show, only to be told to act more like a lady. Alongside these depictions of a Jane tamed by the love of a good man, *Have Gun Will Travel* (1961) used the wildcat reputation of Martha Jane Canary to issue a modern parable against alcohol abuse. "The Cure" opens in a hotel lobby, with a buckskin-clad rough sleeper on a couch, first mistaken as a man, and then identified as faded trick-shooting star Martha Jane Conroy. The hero of the series, Jack Paladin, fills the audience in on the story of a pistol-twirling legend with Ned Blackstock's troupe who has turned to drink as a result of Ned's philandering. In a nod to the historical trace of Martha Canary, Martha Conroy presents Paladin with a ten-cent pamphlet—"From Deadwood to Buckingham Palace: the True Story of Calamity Jane"—before railing against the fake Calamities in corsetry who have lately filled Ned's show. For all its prime-time TV puff, this was an interesting presentation of Calamity Jane as a washed-up frontier celebrity who had been manufactured by an unscrupulous entertainment industry. She reels off a familiar script of scouting with Custer, catching McCall, and mourning her "darlin'" Hickok, yet seems marooned by the bottle and lost in the social margins between life and legend. A comforting resolution saw Paladin help Canary reclaim her honor and reclaim her debts, while a viewer advisory pointed out that alcohol abuse was now seen as a "sickness."[4]

The most curious iteration of Calamity Jane in these years came from the unlikely landscape of provincial England, and the pen of an ex-army dog trainer, turned postman and fish and chip shop owner, who was introduced to the frontier of Hollywood cinema as a child. Born in 1928, J.D. Edson turned to writing western pulp novels in the 1950s, inspired less by the romance of the West and more by the financial incentives of tapping into the international frontier imaginary. As he put it, "I've never even been on a horse. I've seen those things, and they look highly dangerous at both ends and bloody uncomfortable in the middle." Well proven in the folkloric story of the West (and in the case of Calamity Jane herself), a good yarn was just as important as historical authenticity in convincing a popular audience to buy into the brand. Edson, indeed, hit on a winning formula with his tales of unreconstructed masculine heroes, justice-fueled adventure, and violent gunplay. Channeling his inner dime novelist from a desk in Melton Mowbray, Leicestershire, he produced more than 130 novels for the eager consumption of some 27 million readers. As a bit player in the Floating Outfit novels and a lead character in her own series, Calamity Jane featured in 12 works between 1965 and 1983, making Edson's output the most sustained literary exploration of her since Edward Wheeler.[5]

Inhabiting a grand western landscape populated by normative heroes and conservative values, Edson's Calamity Jane was a curious blend of raw frontier ethics, sexual liberation, and spicy eroticism. With an antipathy to liberalism and a preference for solving problems by capital means of punishment (and capital punishment), his novels conjured a female protagonist placed firmly in the mold of the unconventional and armed western woman, but largely ahistorical in terms of backstory and series plotlines. As he noted in one novel, "this story does not pretend to be a factual account of the life of Martha Jane Canary, but is merely the kind of adventures Calamity Jane might have liked to have." She was here utilized principally as a sidekick or sexual partner for a range of leading men, and was regularly choreographed in fistfights with other women (usually resulting in one or both being disrobed). Repeated across a number of the novels, and delineated first in the series opener *Trouble Trail* (1965), a potted biography of Calamity Jane described a woman in her late teens or early twenties, who had fled from a St. Louis convent aged 16 to join a freighter team headed to Texas. A western education saw her acquire skills as a cook, driver, roper, and sharpshooter, as well as a hard-edged attitude of western bravado, resilience, and independent mindedness. At the same time, Edson was keen to temper her heretical fixings of gender unorthodoxy. His heroine, therefore, was resolutely feminine and lustfully heterosexual. With a mop of red hair cut short, and a mouth "made for laughter and kissing," she was dressed in figure-hugging jeans and a shirt buttoned low to reveal an ample cleavage. In *Troubled Range* (1965), Calamity Jane tussles with Belle Starr (both women had slept with hero Texan Mark Counter earlier in the novel); and in *The Wildcats* (1965) she engages in a fiery feud with saloon matriarch Madame Bullfrog (who later turns out, in time-honored dime novel style, to be Calamity's mother), which results in an hour-long fight. In *The Bull Whip Breed* (1965)—billed as "A blazing novel about the greatest woman in the West"—the action is transported to post-Civil War New Orleans, and the plotline revolves around policeman Philippe St. Andre and a murderer known as "the strangler." Removed from usual frontier context, but in possession of a legend that spanned the Mississippi, the famous Calamity Jane has a boyish silhouette, as she appears in the opening scene; but on closer inspection, she is blessed with a "lack of masculinity." Though she is "a rather unusual product of the times," crime-fighter St. Andre grows to appreciate her matter-of-fact frontier qualities.[6]

Edson's West was a triumphal world of cattle drives, outlaws, army trains, and Indian attacks, in which Calamity Jane played the role of plot-carrier for old West folkloric staples. Accordingly, she was embroiled in set-piece, all-action buffalo hunts (*The Big Hunt*, 1967), tribal wars (*Guns in the Night*, 1968), all-female gang conflicts (*The Bad Bunch*, 1968), stagecoach runs (*Calamity Spells Trouble*, 1968), gambling intrigues (*Cold Deck, Hot Lead*, 1969), ranching disputes (*White Stallion, Red Mare* (also known as *Ranch War*), 1970), and borderland scuffles (*The Whip and the War Lance*, 1979). Dominant in the series was the idea of Calamity Jane as an untamed frontier product, a motif that played out a long-standing (often prurient) intrigue that had tracked through cultural representations since the 1870s. What was particularly notable was the way in which the demands of gender containment that had constrained Canary's opportunities in her lifetime, and that saw the casting of Jean Arthur and Doris Day as feminized "wild women" in tailored buckskin, now reined in the heretical contours of Calamity Jane's identity, by casting her as a sexy and seductive siren.

The distillation of Canary's "wildness" into a simplistic line of sexual objectification and character assassination cropped up in other treatments. Harry Drago's *Notorious Ladies of the Frontier* (1969)—subtitled "the beautiful but shady ladies who kept pace with the advancing frontier"—hailed Canary for her ability to "out curse, outshout and outdrink most of the men with whom she consorted." Betraying a long-standing cultural binary that was enthralled with, but also critical of, Calamity Jane's nonconformist gender identity, Drago went on to savage her as a "coarse, slovenly frontier whore," who would "be largely unknown today were it not for what the fictioneers and the romanticists, bent on presenting her as a tragic, misunderstood, soap-opera heroine, have done with her—mindless of the facts." She transcended the limits of the terrestrial frontier, but not gender conventions, in A. Bertram Chandler's *Rim Worlds* (1961) series, which featured Calamity Jane Arlen as a troubled, "huskily attractive" intergalactic mercenary, who drank whiskey and was suspicious of men. It was, meanwhile, in the genre of the so-called "adult western" that such misogynistic tendencies found their strongest articulation. These empty tales of sex and violence portrayed an intensely problematic West that treated women as subordinates. Martin Nussbaum labeled the medium as reflective of the "inadequacies and psychoses of modern man." In such works as Jake Logan's *Dead Man's Hand* (1979), Jackson Cain's *Hellbreak Country* (1984), and Tabor Evans' *Longarm in Deadwood* (1982), Calamity Jane was sexually voracious and used only to celebrate the agency and libido of the macho strongman. Such treatments were (in Etulain's words) "history lite." They were also deeply troubling in their assumptions about the place of women in frontier life and modern society.[7]

HEROISM AND HAGIOGRAPHY IN THE SIXTIES: CALAMITY JANE'S SITES OF MEMORY

Martha Jane Canary continued to attract attention in these years as part of a regional culture of frontier reminiscence that saw various towns deepen their tourist associations with the "female scout." Across memorials, pageants, and parades, her life and adventures were celebrated and commemorated, with Princeton, Livingston, and Deadwood each burnishing its credentials as a sacred site in the entertainment and folk-loric landscape of the "heroine of the plains."

Princeton built on its roadside park to establish a "Calamity Jane Day" in 1962. Organized by the chamber of commerce, the event featured a plethora of activities over two days. Prizes could be won for guessing the "Mystery Jane" and "Mystery Bill" composite photo-fits, and a lavish homecoming parade provided an opportunity for dress-up and borrowed frontier celebrity, followed by a turkey supper. Paper "flying saucers" were also thrown from a building in the business district: some bore lucky numbers, and could be exchanged for a silver dollar. One local business—McHargue Radio and TV—promoted "Calamity Jane" sales, featuring cut-price ironing-board covers, television antennae, and "what not" shelves; meanwhile Macs Country Store offered festival goers free Coca-Cola and cheese and crackers. By 1966, the event had been extended to three days, and was advertised as "one of North Missouri's largest entertainment attractions," well known for its "old time western atmosphere." The entertainments for the 1966 season included a re-enactment of the robbery of the Deadwood Stage, complete with high-noon shootout, an Indian ambush (thwarted by cavalry troops led by Calamity Jane), a theatrical melodrama, antique stalls, and country music gigs. Central to the festival was a 45-minute parade with 94 entries, and a Calamity Jane beauty contest. Entirely disconnected from anything resembling Martha Canary's historical experience, competitors were judged in street wear, swimsuit, and formal dress rounds. The winner was escorted to supper by her Bill Hickok dream date. A colorful parade of frontier-fifties fusion, the Calamity Jane festival was, by all accounts, a resounding success, and a clear sign of the enduring star power of the "heroine of the plains." Old West nostalgia prompted the widespread adoption of frontier-wear, and a veritable explosion of facial hair among the town's male population. The wooden floor in one packed saloon even collapsed from all the boot-traffic. In honor of the town's most famous daughter, one Princeton restaurant named its eating area "the Calamity Jane dining room," and the civic authorities erected a plaque outside the supposed site of Canary's birth on the periphery of the town. The Mercer County *Pioneer Press* carried a "Calamity Jane Special Issue," charting the ups and downs of Canary's famous trail, and reprinted *Life and Adventures of Calamity Jane, By Herself* in full. Noting that Canary did visit most of the places mentioned in her autobiography, the editorial cannily pointed out: "the role she actually played in each, however, is open to question."[8]

Moves were also afoot further west to memorialize the storied past of Martha Jane Canary. In Livingston, a community campaign was enacted to restore the cabin she lived in and open it as a historical museum. The project failed to get off the ground, but it did provide an occasion for old-timers to share childhood memories. In the *Park County News*, Lou Green remembered walking past the cabin, hoping to catch a glimpse of the famous Canary. Mary Connolly eagerly weighed in on the merits of her notorious neighbor: "One thing Calamity did was to mind her own business ... She may have been rough, but I don't think she was any different from our generation." Though Canary smoked cigars and "drank a little whiskey now and then," the impression gained from Connolly was of a kindly individual who helped the needy and was "not afraid of work." Running concurrently was a plan for a week-long Calamity Jane festival, the brainchild of John Watkins, a Montana State University Masters student. Endorsed by the local chamber of commerce, civic boosters agreed that her story "captures world-wide imagination," and they saw a potential boon to local tourism through the selling of Calamity Jane as a slice of "wholesome entertainment." Significantly, in making his pitch, Watkins had erred on the side of gender containment, noting that while Canary was "rough, tough and knew how to cuss," she was also a humanitarian. The project failed to win sufficient financial backing, but Watkins' Master's dissertation contained a full commentary and script for a theatrical production that pointed to the continuing twists and turns of popular mythology. Entitled "Calamity Jane: A Pageant Drama in Three Acts," this play was the centerpiece of the festival and offered up tragedy as its defining theme. Based around a dramatic telling of local history, the pageant began with a 16-year-old Canary balking at the idea of dressing up as a dance-hall girl, flooring a drunken miner who had tried to manhandle her, and vowing to find work "as a man." From here, Act One moved to the portentous (apocryphal) meeting of Canary and Hickok in Abilene, where she saved him from ambush at the card table and received her famous nom de plume. Thereafter, the two rode as partners, got married, and—reprising the McCormick story—Calamity reluctantly gave up their daughter for adoption by Jim O'Neil. Act Two focused on a chance meeting with Hickok at the post office in 1876, the ride into Deadwood, Hickok's death, and a bereft Canary crying in her cabin. Act Three then rattled through her latter-day drift into insobriety, and closed with Calamity Jane's funeral, where fellow pioneers ruminated on a heroic reputation, her declining health, and otherwise kind-hearted eccentricities.[9]

Deadwood, of course, represented the most important site of folkloric pilgrimage, boasting not only a dose of western-themed tourism, but also a gravesite where people could pay their respects to Canary and Hickok. The entire town-site became a National Historic Landmark in 1961—tellingly, the first community in the country to receive such an accolade. The Days of '76 festival, established in 1924, was still going strong, offering a "mammoth pageant of history and transportation," according to promotions for the 1965 season. An impressive sight, the parade featured 1,500 people, each dressed in authentic period costume and marching in historical sequence. Strict codes barred any advertising or "prettied up" floats. A moving montage of trappers, military teams, miners, freighters, stagecoach riders, and settlers, the pageant was a celebration of Black Hills pioneering. Important in the costumed array were depictions of "the unforgettable history makers," listed by name as General Custer, Wild Bill Hickok, and Calamity Jane. Here was confirmation of Martha Canary's place in an exclusive pantheon of frontier heroes. In its coverage of the annual event, the *Deadwood Daily*

Pioneer-Times located Calamity Jane at the very epicenter of the town's frontier folklore:

> She sleeps, now beside the grave of Wild Bill Hickok, who was said to have been the love of her life. Her funeral was attended by hundreds of persons who came to bury not a sad, unhappy, broken woman, but to lay away a legend.[10]

Read collectively, the celebration of Calamity Jane at these sites reflected a pioneer reminiscence culture long in the making, and one that was entering its final phase in the 1960s and 1970s, with the death of the last generation to recall Canary as a living figure. Evidence of this could be found in such works as Bill and Doris Whithorn's compendium of Livingston press accounts, *Calamity's in Town* (c.1974) and Irma Klock's *Here Comes Calamity Jane* (1979). Both played on Canary as a creature of frontier nostalgia, and balanced reference to her as a rough woman, a drinker, and a prostitute, with sympathetic comments as to her otherwise well-meaning and honest disposition. On this subject, it is worth dwelling on another encounter between local testimonial culture and two historian-biographers that has remained under the radar of Canary-ologists until now. In the early 1960s, retired general, historian, and Wyomingite William C. Rogers embarked on a biographical project with fellow regional historian Virginia Scully. Though it resulted in no publications, the endeavor left an intriguing trail of oral history transcripts and scribbled notes from some 20,000 miles of field work in the Black Hills, along with draft chapters and correspondence about a manuscript dripping with superlatives. "Calamity Jane: Her Life and Times," the authors promised, would be the *only* factual account of Martha Jane Canary, "the FIRST biography of the greatest frontierswoman" and the country's "first genuine heroine."[11]

Dominating the testimonies gathered by Rogers and Scully was an overriding sense of Canary as a good-hearted, if misunderstood, woman who was liked by her peers. George Wolf, a young boy at the time of her death in Terry, South Dakota, bitterly regretted not photographing the room in which she died, as "this picture would have sold forever." He described her as a "humanitarian" with "lots of personality." For Ray Ewing, former mayor of Deadwood, Calamity Jane had been the first drunk woman he had ever seen. He regarded her as a friend to working people and her penchant for the bottle as an unfortunate sickness, asserting that "she was a product of her times." Confirming her hallowed placement in Deadwood's pioneer past, Bill Shikel and Elmer Nelson pointed out that "no one in Deadwood would ever forget Calamity Jane. She was a good woman. Everybody's friend ... She drank too much sometimes ... But she was a good woman." Taken as a whole, this oral history furnished Rogers and Scully with a clear sense of Canary as a memorable figure—"ebullient, high-spirited, voluble, colorful, and irrepressible"—whose charismatic personality lent her an indelible quality in popular memory: "Everyone who saw Martha Jane Canary remembered her for the rest of their lives and talked about her as if they had seen her only five minutes before."[12]

How Rogers and Scully wrote up Canary's history, meanwhile, high-lighted both *her* position in a frontier world in flux and *their* placement in a mid-century marked by the competing contours of gender heresy and containment. On the one hand, here stood a valorous feminist-in-waiting. "An Outline for Calamity Jane—her life and times" (sent to an editor in the mid-1960s) thus identified her as a resourceful young woman who "rode into a man's world" and seized the chance of an independent life free from patriarchal apron strings:

Calamity Jane turned her back on a life of household drudgery in someone else's kitchen, with someone else's children. She didn't become an older man's second wife to rear his brood of children. She didn't tie herself down to slaving for a younger man. She escaped the omnipresent brothel because she learned a trade—teamstering. Soon she made it clear that she had little respect for men because she was a better man than any she met.

According to Rogers and Scully, Calamity Jane could accurately be labeled an army scout by virtue of her traveling with the military in a combat theater. She deserved compassion for striving, in whatever ways she could, to survive in a challenging environment (as they mused, who doesn't drink when times are tough?). "The most famous woman in the West," and a tragic character hampered by daily realities, Calamity Jane was, accordingly, an accessible and resolutely modern heroine.[13]

At the same time, Rogers and Scully seemed to recoil from the implications of placing Canary in a landscape of modern gender politics or fully confronting the gender possibilities intrinsic to her female masculinity. Roaming the prospecting towns of the Rockies, she was resilient and curious, but "no feminist," and always "exuberantly, bubblingly, vitally feminine." Yes, Rogers and Scully argued, the army years saw her dress as a man and serve as a scout; but deep down she remained a plainswoman, striving for domestic security and respectability, and taking on any job she could find as necessary recourse. Elsewhere, Rogers wrote:

It has become "fashionable" to talk in Freudian terms about Calamity Jane's alleged masculinity and the pants she wore. The truth is much simpler: Pants were a convenience and a necessity in the rough open country.

Rogers and Scully emerged with a somewhat ambivalent assessment: they seemed eager to rescue Calamity Jane from a frontier imaginary that obscured her true story; yet they shied away from the radical implications of their findings. Ultimately, it was more comfortable to keep to the well-trod trails of frontier superstardom, in hailing their subject as "the all-time heroine of the West ... the one, the only, the original Calamity Jane of Deadwood, Dakota Territory, in the Black Hills."[14]

A NEW WESTERN (ANTI)HEROINE: AGENCY AND REFLECTION ON A TARNISHED SILVER SCREEN

The late 1960s and early 1970s brought fundamental changes to the socio-political landscape of modern industrialism. A wave of connected protest movements cast a critical gaze over mainstream political values and redefined the landscape of citizen rights. The United States saw growing distrust of government authority, in the shape of activism against the war in Vietnam and the Cold War nuclear bargain, a civil rights movement that pointed to the marginalization of black and indigenous Americans, and feminist and gay rights campaigns for sexual and gender equality. The last of these, in particular, trickled into cultural representations of Martha Jane Canary. Of course, the idea of Calamity Jane as a curmudgeonly and independent woman with a mind of her own was not new to the discourse surrounding her. The challenge she posed to the dominant heterodoxy was a consistent theme in her folkloric story (and an integral part of her frontier celebrity). That said, the theoretical and activist contours of second-wave feminism and the emergence of the LGBT movement provided a vital new space of gender possibility in the Calamity Jane story.

Also part of the equation was the rise of a revisionist historical canon that contested the validity of a global colonial project and called for the incorporation of marginalized voices. Specifically, the rise of a "new western history" in the 1980s that centered not on the triumphal narrative of frontier transformation, but on the complex eco-cultural entanglements between competing groups—a West lost, as well as won—saw a new landscape of critical reflection at play. This close examination of the ideological and material transformation of a region experiencing (as Patricia Nelson Limerick put it in her paradigm-defining 1987 history) a "legacy of conquest" communicated the sense of a fragmented and fraught West, where Turner's glorious frontier was now an "f-word." Played out in Hollywood celluloid, this reversal of folkloric fortune saw hegemonic white masculinity under fire. *Soldier Blue* (1970) rewrote the heroic canon to show the US Army as brutalized and sadistic; while *The Wild Bunch* (1969) and the *Dollars* trilogy (1964–66) blurred the boundaries of morality and manifest destiny, to emphasize avarice, corruption, and violence as critical components in the western story. In this grim and gritty landscape, Calamity Jane was typically found at the margins, a shuffling pariah in dirty buckskins, ruminating on her fading stardom through the bottom of a whiskey bottle. Fed by a fearsome coagulation of feminist and frontier revisionism, a new western (anti)heroine was emerging.

In the realms of Hollywood cinema, the rise of a "gender troubled" Calamity (to borrow Butler's famous phrase, connoting subversive and feminist identities) was a slow-burn process that began with a few tentative inferences. Almost entirely overlooked by film critics and historians, *The Ballad of Josie* (1967) saw Doris Day in her second "horse opera": a comedy-adventure western, in which she faces off against a Wyoming posse of male politicians and cattle ranchers in the cause of sheep farming and women's rights. With posters boasting lines such as "Quick-draw Doris" and "Calamity Josie," and a stand-out scene where Day swaps her feminine dress for Levi's, cowboy boots, and a blue work shirt (causing many slapstick street collisions in the process), the trajectory from *Calamity Jane* and its cross-dressing, woman-in-a-man's-world whimsy is clear. The film tells the story of Josie Minick, downtrodden wife of a drunk, who "accidentally" kills her abusive husband with a pool cue, is exonerated by a Wyoming jury, and promptly decides to take her young son to an abandoned cabin and make a living from ranching. Central to the plot are three lines of interest: the furor generated by a woman not only trying to inhabit a man's role, but also bringing sheep into cattle country (she picks sheep, after being told that raising cattle is too hard for a woman); an equally controversial plan by local politicians to coerce women into giving up their voting rights in the interests of securing statehood for Wyoming Territory; and a brewing love interest between Josie and Jase (played by Peter Graves), a conscientious and lovelorn local cattle rancher. Over the course of the movie, Josie is patronized about "knowing her place," sexually objectified, and stereotyped. Freshly installed as a sheep rancher (with costume and herd in tow) she issues forth with pithy feminist salvos: "I'm not waiting around for some nice man to rescue me. I can think and I can work . . . I don't want a man. I don't need a man. I've got myself and I've got sheep." In time, meanwhile, her impassioned defense of the flock inspires local suffragists to run riot, raise placards aloft, and beat up town menfolk with pool cues. A curious slice of celluloid, the film ends with the cattle-baron villain (Arch, played by George Kennedy) making a deal with Josie to sell her sheep in return for a cut-price prize beef herd, a cheery town parade to celebrate Wyoming Territory becoming a state (where suffragists stride out with confidence in Josie-style britches), and Jase and Josie riding off into the sunset. At the last, gender conformity is safely restored. "Too much independence," Day's character reliably informs a family of skunks that has set up home in her cabin, "is miserable."[15]

Tensions of frontier revisionism and old-school conceits were equally to be found in the inked flourishes of Belgian-French comic book artists, Morris and Goscinny, of Asterix fame. Their *Lucky Luke* series covered Calamity Jane briefly in a 1958 story (*Lucky Luke versus Joss Jamon*, where she appeared as a bit-part criminal), and more fully in a 1967 tale bearing her name. Here she features as a gawky redhead in buckskin, sporting a hillbilly-infused female masculinity, a flower between her teeth, and twirling a rifle. The story begins in heroic fashion, as Calamity rescues Luke from ambush by Apaches, as he bathes in a creek. True to her oddball reputation, Canary seems equally horrified by the idea of taking a bath and being called ma'am. After querying the identity of his campfire companion ("Are you really the famous Calamity Jane? People everywhere are talking about you"), Luke settles down to chew tobacco. Canary, in time-honored fashion, sets down her customary autobiographical signposts, before making a dry addendum: "I'm also a great liar, but wait—I haven't finished yet." With Calamity as a capable, all-action heroine playing foil to a hapless male hero, the book subscribes to the inversion theatrics of historical cross-dressing entertainment, as well as parodying the hegemonic masculinity of the classic Hollywood cowboy. Calamity Jane regales drinkers with tales at the bar, wins the saloon in an arm-wrestle with a local muscleman, and promptly (and with comic incongruity) decides to turn a corner of the bar into a tearoom for ladies. After a series of satirical shots and old western crises—cowboys forced to eat her burned crumpets at gunpoint, a shootout, brawls, desperadoes aplenty, and an attack by the Apache—she apprehends the gunrunners and wins over the Ladies Guild to her culinary cause. The responsibilities of frontier heroism successfully discharged, Canary rides off into the sunset, clothed in her usual buckskin and headed for more adventures. Calamity Jane, the story notes, "occupies a very special place in the legends of the Old West."[16]

Another film where a convoluted Calamity Jane patrolled the margins was *Little Big Man* (1970), a fictionalized biopic featuring Jack Crabb as a 121-year-old reminiscing about his life on the frontier. Based on Thomas Berger's 1964 novel of the same name, the film took the form of a visualized monologue, in which Crabb's life appeared as a serious of snapshots. Offering a window onto a frontier long gone, the film showed his journey west, his parents attacked on the wagon train, a childhood spent with the Cheyenne, and a nomadic existence in which he drifted back and forth between indigenous and settler society. The film begins with Crabb proclaiming his identity as "the sole white survivor of the Battle of the Little Bighorn" to a young historian, eager to ascertain the lifeways of an indigenous culture subjected to "near genocide," rather than hear "tall tales about Custer." Presenting himself as "beyond a doubt, the last of the old timers," Crabb talks the talk of a frontier original, just as Martha Canary had done in her soliloquies in saloons and on stage. Like her, he invokes places and people to conjure an immaculate old western autobiography. He thus appears drinking in Deadwood in 1876; present at the murder of Hickok; mule skinning for the army; and scouting for Custer. Each vignette is placed in a sepia-tinted frontier of transience, adaptation, and cultural relativism. As such, the general flavor of the film references a broader landscape of frontier myth-making and mobility that Canary knew well; a real-life world of extraordinary complexity, set alongside a storied world of imagined identities and performance. Moreover, the specific encounter between Jack Crabb and his sister Caroline—separated in the wagon attack and reunited years later, when he was working with a traveling snake-oil salesman—offers a clear (though uncredited) reference to Calamity Jane. Presented as a brusque drifter with a keen shooting eye, a finely attuned moral compass, and a penchant for men's clothes, Caroline plays Calamity Jane as caricature. Appearing in masquerade, with gun and husky voice, to expose the salesman as a fraud, she offers her brother a "real family life" and a shooting lesson, in preparation for Jack's next cameo as wannabe gunslinger by the name of the Soda Pop Kid.[17]

Explicit celluloid reference to the life of Martha Jane Canary came in the form of two American made-for-television productions. The first, *This is the West That Was* (1974), promised "a light-hearted look at some of the quickest tempers in the West!" Starring Kim Darby as Calamity Jane, an actress with celluloid horse-opera credentials (*Bonanza, Gunsmoke* and *True Grit* (1969)), but a petite boyishness that did not capture Canary's historically butch identity, this NBC offering presented a lead character (almost) in control of her destiny. Darby's "heroine of the plains" was a woman acting with agency to create a heroic mantle of frontier celebrity. In this tale, Canary named herself. At the same time, she struggled to maintain the choreography, and ultimately remained hamstrung by the social realities of the West and its limited opportunities for women. In one scene, Canary points out to Cody how the confinements of the "female frontier" (saloon work, prostitution, or marriage) had encouraged her to dress as a man and take up work as a laborer. *This is the West That Was*, however, could not break free entirely from the Hollywood heartstrings. Though Hickok played only a supporting role, the film's narrative thread continued to run with the idea of Calamity Jane hankering for a romantic liaison with him.[18]

Ten years later, *Calamity Jane* (1984) portrayed a beleaguered lead who combined female empowerment and sorrowful vulnerability. In this TV movie, the new western (anti)heroine appeared more explicitly in a series of montages that illustrated the colorful and convoluted threads of her identity, as well as the revisionist writing of a female frontier that stressed hardship, loneliness, and resilience in women's western experiences. Calamity was portrayed by Jean Alexander as a complex character, wrestling with the competing expectations of settled domesticity and a streak of independent mindedness. The central plot narrative revolved around a romance with Hickok and a daughter given up for adoption (a story that confirmed the continuing vitality of McCormick's story a full half century after her fake revelations). Alexander's buckskin-clad Calamity appeared first sleeping in an abandoned stable, where she witnessed a shootout involving Hickok, before nursing him back to health. Pointing to her forthcoming employment as a scout for the army, she remonstrates "they've gotta know a female can do anything a man can do and better." To Hickok's comment that it must be "awful sad" to go through life as a gender-ambiguous individual, she postulates: "I'm all woman, Bill Hickok, don't you think different." Thereafter, the stage is set for a tempestuous gun-fighting and romantic partnership. Drunken campfire songs of "it's hard to be a woman in the West" preface a hastily contracted marriage and a subsequent parting of the ways. Canary is torn between a desire to "be a good wife" and an army scout. Hickok is smothered by the prospect of family life, and is enticed instead by the allure of acting out past frontier glories in Cody's "wild West" show. The collisions of transformation and tradition, history and performance continued to play out in the western theater. Eventually, Calamity Jane takes charge of the plot and repairs to a remote cabin without announcing her pregnancy, gives birth to—and then gives up—their daughter, Janey. In between classic frontier vignettes of stagecoach runs, Indian raids, the death of Hickok, tall tales of scouting at the saloon table, she sits mournfully in her tent, writing letters to her daughter.[19]

From here, *Calamity Jane* fleshed out McCormick's fictive mother–daughter exchange to create a complicated lead, struggling in a dualistic world. Canary lurches between fame and despair, everyday grind and performance high, independence and insobriety. Attired for Richmond's high society in a full-length dress, she finally meets her long-lost daughter at Captain O'Neil's, and is impressed by her kindness (and her rocking horse). Returning to the West and a precarious life of inebriation and poverty, temporary solace appears to come in the shape of frontier celebrity as a swaggering "wild woman." The film ends with an intimate encounter between Jane and Janey at the Pan-American Exposition, where the latter confesses a desire to be just like the former: "independent . . . strong . . . true to yourself." Suitably touched, Jane advises: "a woman going her own way, what she gets is a hard trade every day of her life and if she ends up with some self-respect come sunset she's damn lucky."

If *This Was the West That Was* and *Calamity Jane* began to grapple with a female frontier marked by powerful women with circumscribed life choices, then Peter Dexter's *Deadwood* (1986) and Larry McMurtry's *Buffalo Girls* (1990) furnished the revisionist frontier (and Calamity Jane) with a more graphic telling. Both these novels presented a messy and maladjusted West. They strayed from the path of heroic or hetero-normative resolution that had marked most literary and film treatments, and played an important role in guiding the trail of cultural representation in subsequent years. Set in the dusty contours of Deadwood city in the 1870s, *Deadwood* was peppered with references to Canary's historical contemporaries, as well as the office of the *Black Hills Daily Times*. It told a tale of the usual suspects, and, with masculine prose style and invocation of sex, violence, and gunplay, was not an obvious contender for revisionist labeling. At the same time, *Deadwood* was distinctly unromantic, its familiar characters aged and estranged from their glorious legends. Far removed from the depictions by Jean Arthur and Doris Day, Dexter's "Calamity Jane Cannary" was a big-boned and bruised outsider, a bull-whacker, prostitute, and drinker, with a tendency for telling tales, mannish ways, a distinctive "eagle scream," and still holding a candle for a has-been Hickok going blind from venereal disease. This was, arguably, the first outing in which female masculinity was advertised upfront as a foundational aspect of her identity. The titular subject of Part Four of the novel, this Calamity was named by herself, was foul-mouthed and foul-bodied (even down to the mold growing on her skin), and was portrayed as a rough, masculine woman who found purpose in the smallpox epidemic as "natural nurse," but ended up spreading the disease to neighboring communities. A throwback to early presentations of a feral Calamity, consciously refracted through a revisionist lens, *Deadwood* offered a bold and striking figure, squarely designed to dislodge the figures of the old West from their heroic afflictions. To this end, Etulain rightly situates the book as an attempt "at countering earlier excessively sentimental images," by presenting "a drunken, filthy, promiscuous antiheroine." However, his criticism of Dexter for stripping Canary of her kind-hearted reputation and desire for marriage and motherhood neglects the radical possibilities presented by Calamity Jane's female masculinity and its message of gender transgression.[20]

Whereas *Deadwood* kept Calamity Jane on the sidelines for the most part, *Buffalo Girls* (1990) placed her center stage, in a humorous and heart-breaking tale that pondered the space between real lives and invented experience in the West. Part of a cast of veteran adventurers whose western habitat had all but disappeared, she was pictured here as a roving traveler, moving across a landscape in which she no longer had a place, and sharing stories and a nostalgic gaze with her friends. Joining Canary on her storied trail was a motley band: beaver trappers Ragg and Bone; 80-year-old Oglala No Ears; and madam and confidante Dora Du Fran. McMurtry's take was tender, thoughtful, and contingent on his readership knowing the frontier canon so well that they could appreciate the irony in a story of aging, tormented heroes who had helped win the West, only to realize that they had been complicit in their own extinction. The *New York Times* called it a novel of "resurrection," uncovering "living human beings" from a voracious "myth machine." An intimate look at attrition and a reflection on a changing frontier, McMurtry's narrative segued between the movements and elegiac musings of its protagonists and the writing of a series of letters by Canary to her daughter. Speaking as narrator—ailing, lonesome, and tearful—McMurtry's Calamity was an individual struggling with her past and her heroic reputation. She reminded herself to write "cheering stories" to Janey, was perpetually mired in psychological and physical discomfort, and seemed caught between her mantle of frontier celebrity and a nagging feeling that, when she put pencil to paper, there was little in her life to be proud of. A character deserving of sympathy, this was a woman whose life had been, in Dora Du Fran's words, "so peculiar, and so lonely," and whose famed deeds were nothing but inventions. As Canary wandered a desolate West, her limbs stiff, and sorrow settling like snow on a shirt, the testimonial trail running through *Buffalo Girls* communicated a stark message of hardship, substance abuse, and limited room for maneuver on the female frontier.[21]

Particularly important is the way in which *Buffalo Girls* wrestles upfront with Martha Jane Canary's gender and sexual identity. Dora Du Fran speaks of how she "lived a life as near to a man's as she could get." Bone and Ragg debate whether she is a woman or not, by trying to recall if she has ever worn a dress or made advances to men (a telling signal of the delimited possibilities for nonconformist women in the West). All three speak of her having an "in-between quality." The relationship, moreover, between Du Fran and Canary is an ambiguous one, always intimate and comradely, sometimes sisterly, and with the occasional suggestion of same-sex romance. Calamity Jane, for her part, reminisced to Janey of dancing with Dora in the guise of a cowboy, and of the ease and acceptance to be found in her company: "I loved her the minute I saw her ... she didn't mind that I chewed tobacco and smoked and cussed. Dora saw the girl in me when I couldn't even see it myself. We're buffalo girls, we'll always be friends, she said." Towards the end of the novel, Canary talks openly about her various reasons for wearing men's clothes: to travel safely, obtain work, and inhabit a homo-social culture in which she feels comfortable. McMurtry here added a biological imperative: Calamity talks of a visit to the doctor and a diagnosis of hermaphroditism (which she confesses to not being able to spell), which serves to explain why she has always felt "stuck in between."[22]

Equally significant is *Buffalo Girls'* engagement with a group of historical characters whose lives, even fictively laid out, communicate important messages about memorialization, storytelling, and frontier celebrity. No Ears points out that if he had named Canary, he would have called her "Helpful," while Ragg and Bone dissect her heroic deeds around the campfire: she was a laundress, not a scout, and a poor shot to boot. Bone recalls telling her on one occasion that she was no Annie Oakley, to which she retorted "nor are you." According to Du Fran, her main claim to fame was wandering "here and there on the plains." Central to this aspect of the novel is a collective wrestling with the idea of saddling up with Buffalo Bill, portrayed in the novel as a hack salesman superstar. In the opening pages, Calamity Jane proclaims: "I *am* the Wild West, Janey, no show about it. I was one of the people that kept it wild, why would I want to make a spectacle of myself before a bunch of toots and dudes?" Before long, however, and with the old West fading fast, she decides to join Cody on his show tour, and, along with the trappers, sails with the troupe to Europe. In Buffalo Bill's grand pageant—Canary calls it "The Pages of Passing History"—Ragg and Bone are cast as Lewis and Clark (anyone can walk to Oregon, they note), and Calamity Jane is written into the set piece "Attack on the Deadwood Stage," but only as coach driver.[23]

Almost immediately, the stage choreography unravels. Calamity Jane stumbles around the ship drunk, fires off a pistol at a London music hall, ends up in jail three times, and falls off the Deadwood stage before Queen Victoria. She is, in short, a failure and a faux celebrity. Missing home and drinking to excess, Canary remains dubious about her place in a world of re-enactment: "It comes to the same thing, Indians and whites pretending to be fighting, shooting at each other with blank shells." She flatly refuses to modify her performance to fit the demands of gender containment, bristling: "if they think I am going to put on a corset and sing a concert they can think again." When the tour ends, their return to a beloved West brings only melancholia and privations: the great frontier drama can only carry so far. In these circumstances, *Buffalo Girls* contends, the only recourse for a woman adrift is to seize on a good story. "Sometimes when I'm drunk I lie, or when people scorn me I exaggerate," Calamity notes, before explaining how a brush with the dime novelist Ned Buntline inspired her to write her memoirs and invent a daughter as a plot device.[24]

Here, then, was the trick in the novel's tale. Having privileged the McCormick account, McMurtry conjured with a figure unable to have children, caught up in a fantasy of public adulation, and 'fessing up to her readers that she wanted Janey so much that she made her up. A liminal figure adrift in a maelstrom of lived and invented experience, this Calamity Jane was a world away from the fresh-faced certainties of her mid-century Hollywood namesakes. Enfeebled and ensnared by her folkloric identity, she noted in the closing pages of the novel: "Perhaps I am only looking for the past . . . how do you find the past?"[25]

WRITING CALAMITY, PLAYING CALAMITY: (AUTO)BIOGRAPHY, FEMINISM, AND FEMALE MASCULINITY ON A LATE TWENTIETH-CENTURY FRONTIER

Calamity Jane dropped out of the landscape of historical biography until the mid-1990s. As the stalled endeavors of Rogers and Scully highlighted, she was a tough historical subject to apprehend, with fragmentary documentary evidence and a convoluted trajectory of invention and masquerade. Meanwhile, as a subject of enquiry for an emerging cadre of new western historians, her story raised particular problems. A tradi-tional fixture of frontier mythology, Calamity Jane represented, for some, little more than a hackneyed icon, part of the dangerous and obsolete folkloric architecture of the old West, and an exceptional case that did not speak to the social realities of an ethnically diverse female frontier. Glenda Riley, for instance, saw little to be gained for the women's West from a scholarship centered on "Calamity Jane syndrome." What was interesting in such an assessment, of course, was the fact that a sensitive and nuanced exploration of the actual life of Martha Jane Canary had never featured in the historical canon. Regarded as a whimsical wild woman by traditional historiography, and passed over by a revisionist scholarship focused on uncovering representative female experience, Calamity Jane had been confined to the margins.[26]

Stella Foote's *A History of Calamity Jane: Our Country's First Liberated Woman* (1995) broke the silence and ushered in an important trend in the interpretive landscape of Calamity Jane. Based on 30 years of research, and resolutely focused (as so much biographical material had been) on discerning fact from fiction, the book promised to "trace chronologically the elusive and fascinating Calamity Jane from birth throughout her entire adventurous, pitiable life." The author had an interesting proximity to her subject, having been born near Canary's cabin in Montana on the anniversary of her death. As such, Foote was definitely part of the pioneer reminiscence culture that connected Canary to a regional collective memory, and that saw her as a "rough ministering angel ... who drank her whiskey straight ... chewed tobacco, smoked cigars and swore a blue streak." Also important was her relationship with Jean McCormick, who had inspired Foote's initial interest in the subject and whose journals had featured in the Wonderland Museum she had created with husband Don in Billings. An uncritical advocate of McCor-mick's story, *A History of Calamity Jane* printed her diaries in full, along with *Life and Adventures*. As well as perpetuating pioneer folk tales and giving airtime to the long-lost daughter thesis, however, Foote's work looked forward, by firmly situating Canary as a trailblazer for modern feminism. Aside from a subtitle touting Canary as the "country's first liberated woman," the dust jacket conjured an activist voice: "Who was Calamity Jane? Male chauvinists wrote unkindly of her. They believed the little woman's place was in the home." In terms of message, meanwhile, the book championed its subject as a pioneer in the world of women's work—a scout and teamster—a sartorial revolutionary, western celebrity, and an individual "truly ahead of her time."[27]

In fact, the distillation of Calamity Jane as a proto-feminist was a decisive aspect of her 1990s entertainment landscape. Canary's life of gender unorthodoxy had long invited comment on her as a figure of female empowerment, but now the conversation was much more vocal and much more visible. Disney entertainment (which had hitherto ignored Calamity Jane), offered her a walk-on part as a stock western figure in the animated production *Tall Tale* (1995), and regaled young readers with an assertive, revisionist, and hetero-normative heroine in *Calamity Jane at Fort Sanders* (1992), friend to the Lakota, and a capable hired hand who championed votes for women, bristled when protagonists told her how she ought to act, and proclaimed a desire to run for the American presidency. Elsewhere, the notion of Calamity Jane as an empowered feminist icon punctuated the 1990s music scene, an association with bristly nonconformism seeing her name used as a hook for various all-women bands, including a punk outfit of "angry young women" out of Portland, Oregon, and a six-piece female harmony group from the California Bay Area, primed and ready to take on the male-dominated a cappella industry.[28]

Hollywood film, too, took on the task of rebranding the frontier, with an array of titles that starred uncompromising female leads who played firmly, if inexplicitly, on the Calamity Jane motif, presenting women inhabiting male roles and costume. *Bad Girls* (1994) used various props of western heroic masculinity (justice, violence, camaraderie) to tell a story of four avenging prostitutes wreaking justice on their male abusers.

Sam Raimi's *The Quick and the Dead* (1995) went further still in presenting the West as a place of "famesque" claims and gender masquerade. Dominating the screen was Sharon Stone's gun-toting drifter, a character fully conversant with frontier code, dressed in cowboy garb, and holding power in a man's world by exemplary performance. Perhaps the most direct indirect reference to Canary's situation came in the form of *The Ballad of Little Jo* (1993), a biopic which explored the life of Josephine Monaghan, a fictional character who fled to the West after being shunned by her family, and adopted a male identity as a survival tactic. A starring role for a celluloid Calamity, meanwhile, came in *Wild Bill* (1995) and *Buffalo Girls* (1995), films based on Dexter's and McMurtry's novels, respectively. In the former, she played confidante to Hickok's aging lawman; in the latter, a stomping Anjelica Huston brought to the screenplay a more explicitly activist voice. Dressed in fringed buckskin (of course), this Calamity railed at the limited possibilities for women on the frontier ("wifin' and whorin'"), and cautiously explored her sexual identity through an intimate friendship with Melanie Griffith's Dora Du Fran.[29]

The most decisive articulation of Calamity Jane as a filmic leader for *fin-de-siècle* feminism came from an animated series produced in France. Played out in 13 episodes, the *Legend of Calamity Jane* (1997–98) cast its star as a fully reconstructed revisionist (anti)heroine. A capable woman in her twenties, with hints of Clint Eastwood, this starkly drawn Calamity used culturally relativist ethics to bull whip bad guys, thwart robberies, reprimand racist ranchers, and stick up for the rights of the Comanche and the Blackfeet. Voiced by Barbara Scaff, she was a red-headed, angular-featured stranger dressed in black, enigmatic, impassioned, and fighting for justice. Accompanied by a Morricone-esque soundtrack and slick graphics, here swaggered a truly cosmopolitan Calamity. As the series pitch explained: "one part action, one part humor … wide open spaces, bad guys, good guys and everything in between. A fast-draw, never stop series that tells stories of the way it was and the way we wish it had been." In a clear homage to the spaghetti western, but one channeled through a European feminist and revisionist vantage, Calamity responded to Hickok's saloon barracking in the first episode ("A Slip of the Whip") with a sharp put-down: "love to stay and chat, Bill, but I have some law-woman-ing to do." Architect of détente between the US Cavalry and plains tribes, she rejected the lore of manifest destiny in favor of a philosophy that "it's a big land we live in, room enough for all of us." Amidst the rout of all-action set pieces, the series also found time to reflect on the theatrical West in a story about a Shakespearian troupe ("The Final Curtain"), in which Calamity Jane noted "what's all the fuss about people pretending to be people they ain't." Meanwhile, in an episode centered on the 1876 Philadelphia Exposition, Jane attended to her eastern fans, foiled a plan to kill President Grant ("I guess I was busy doing something for a change, instead of being helpless"), and inspired Amanda Rothschild to find her inner agency as a woman. The last episode ("Without a Vengeance"), saw her exorcise one of the hoary allusions of her early twentieth-century mythology by shooting an outlaw Wild Bill point-blank, while muttering "it's not about blood, not ... vengeance, it's justice." Especially interesting was the fact that *The Legend of Calamity Jane* only ran for three weeks in the United States, its stylized violence of cartoon slo-mo bullets and swirling rifle smoke apparently regarded as too graphic for televisual display in a society renowned for its endorsement of gun culture.[30]

The Legend of Calamity Jane placed its lead character in a different kind of West—one that was romantic and swaggering, but which allowed space for her to champion the causes of feminism and anti-colonialism. A powerful ambassadorial role for Martha Jane Canary could equally be found in the arena of literary and theatrical performance, where a number of women playwrights read in the life and adventures of Calamity Jane important stories of empowerment, everyday struggle, and non hetero-normative gender identity. Here were the most sophisticated and nuanced interpretations of Canary's unorthodox gender identity and readings of her female masculinity. Particularly significant in this body of work was the (auto)biographical voice. A full century on from Canary's stage turn, the repackaging of her own story provided a natural conduit for many to engage with the testimonies and tribulations of "troublesome" (now lofted as a badge of honor) women across time. Accordingly, these dramatic re-readings of Canary's orations suggested an important folkloric provenance to *Life and Adventures* that transcended the assumptions of most biographers as to its otherwise useless historical value. Channeling the voice of Calamity Jane through first-person monologue, this group of late twentieth-century women playwrights and novelists grappled in erudite ways with issues of frontier celebrity, mythology, and memorialization—in other words, with the entanglements of lived and invented experience in the story of Martha Jane Canary.

Authored by Martine Bellen, the poem "Calamity Jane" (1995) envisages "Marthy Cannary" as an eyewitness roving widely across frontier time and space. Drawing loosely on the narrative of *Life and Adventures*, Bellen follows the contours of Canary's own published testimony, before time-shifting forward to make note of Doris Day, Jane Russell, and Jean Arthur. Situating Canary here as a "sentimentalist scout," part of the grand pageantry of the West, Bellen talks about her many "deeds and miscredits," in a piece which literary critic Anne Browning hailed for its "dazzling associative leaps of logic, image melting into image."[31]

In Sybille Pearson's play *True History and Real Adventures* (1999), a young Scottish woman, Margaret Mackenzie, becomes enraptured with Canary and travels to the United States in pursuit of a better life and her idol, whom she finds—aged and toothless—in Chicago in 1893. On the way, Mackenzie becomes a celebrity herself (she is mistaken for Pearl Hart), rails against corporate culture and racism, and discovers the shifting ground between history and imagination. Through several costume changes and identity masquerades, the enigmatic persona of Calamity, according to Pearson, was purposefully cast to show the way in which truth can be revealed by theatrical conceits. Reviewing the off-Broadway production for the *New York Times*, Anita Gates saw it as a meditation on the links between fiction, reality, and fragile American power in the late nineteenth and late twentieth centuries, though she regarded it as somewhat "lost in a story ... which is trying to say too many things."[32]

An artistic imagining of Canary's psychological reflection and a rumination on memory and mythology equally inform Gillian Robinson's novel, *The Slow Reign of Calamity Jane* (1994), which muses on the complexity of a character living schizophrenically with abjection and adulation, and engaged in various soliloquy conversations with her mother, daughter, Hickok, and Teddy Abbott. Set as a stream-of-consciousness autobiographical tract, the book finds her walking with "restless ghosts" and describing life as a migrant woman in a litany of traumatic episodes (rape, miscarriage, and domestic violence), before pondering the truth of her association with a spectral Hickok: "Did we know each other? Were we lovers? Did we ever have a child? All of these stories are true in this frontier of invention." In Robinson's portrayal, Canary dreams strange dreams and exists as a feral being wandering an ephemeral path: "Calamity Jane lived for a minute ... You will forgive me and remember me anyway you like."[33]

Particularly important in this late twentieth-century vanguard was Carolyn Gage, feminist lesbian playwright, whose one-woman 15-minute monologue offered "a celebration of the survival of the masculine woman, and especially her survival in an era when there was no lesbian or transgendered movement or culture." Dealing with themes of alternative gender identities, repression, and sexual abuse, "Calamity Jane Sends a Message to Her Daughter" presented a powerful piece of activist theatre, designed to be heart-rending and also to incite, in the author's words, "feminist anger" by skillfully adding a new layer to Canary's autobiographical canon. In her rendition of the "heroine of the plains," Gage took the narrative threads of a brusque, brooding, and inebriated Calamity speaking to her dime novel audience, and the themes of mother–daughter exchange and abandonment from McCormick's story, to create a new, first-person encounter with female masculinity. Performed first in 1988 in Oregon, the show played at various international festivals over a 30-year period, drawing considerable praise for its striking cross-century conversation about a female-bodied individual refusing to conform to the normative code. For Gage, the decision to work with Canary as a theatrical subject represented a conscious attempt to explore "behind-the-scenes mechanisms of hetero-normativity" and communicate a powerful message about butch visibility. As she pointed out, the story of Martha Jane Canary offered a potent example of how women's stories had been "hidden, distorted and appropriated," and, moreover, how those who assumed a masculine identity were historically marginalized and often ridiculed by mainstream society. Apprehended in such a context, the sartorial and behavioral practices adopted by Canary marked her out as a valiant resistor to an entrenched patriarchy.[34]

Lurching onto the stage with whiskey bottle in hand, dressed in dirty jeans, battered hat, and threadbare man's shirt, Gage's Calamity communicated an evocative story of hardship, ostracism, and addiction, but also one of survival, subversion, and resistance. As Gage explained, Canary's holstering of a female masculinity reminded her of some members of the generation of older working-class butches whom the playwright encountered when she came out in the 1980s. These masculine women, she noted, had run a similar "gauntlet of contempt" in their daily lives, and had adopted abrasive personalities (and become dependent on alcohol) as part of their coping or survival strategies. Slouching onto a bench and sitting with legs apart, her Calamity spat into a spittoon, before addressing the audience with a rough-voiced request: would they give a message to her daughter? A smorgasbord of folkloric signposts followed. Gage's character spoke of living in Wyoming, bull-whacking, her love of animals, marriage to Wild Bill (Janey's father), giving her daughter up for adoption, riding into Deadwood in 1876, working with the army, and doing "everything a man done, and maybe more." Alternating between wisecracking swagger, gloomy self-reflection, and fiery defiance, she ended with a plea that her daughter should know that she "came from someone famous" and not just a "no-count drunk." Then she staggered off stage. Particularly important in this dramatization was its attention to a culture of frontier celebrity and the conjuring of a character with an (albeit clunky) understanding of her own place in that milieu. Based on the premise of a "proud woman who was realizing that history would deal her a bad hand," Gage had her Calamity engage with the hypocrisy of a myth-making process that lofted hard-living male counterparts as pioneer icons, while lambasting her as a washed-up curiosity. As such, her play offered a nuanced reflection on the double standards of masculine heroism and the everyday limits to acceptance experienced by those living out alternative constructions of gender and sexuality. As part of its narrative track, it playfully teased out the ways in which the historical Martha Canary played trickster with her own caricatured identity. Building on the McCormick saga, and consciously assuming the performance trappings of motherhood—"the only traditional feminine role to which Calamity can lay a claim"—Gage orchestrated a conversation in which her lead "sneaked up on her audience" to "blindside them with her truth, which is that she is nothing less than a superwoman." Interestingly, she pointed out, audiences over the years never queried her presentation of Calamity, though they did sometimes question Hickok's paternity of her daughter.[35]

What these late twentieth-century readings shared was a sense of intimate bonding with Martha Jane Canary: of the power of autobiography and a testimonial trail that connected women's voices. Significantly, in all of this, the traits which had marked Calamity Jane as a freak, outcast, and curiosity in her lifetime were held up a century on as essential aspects of her persona as an inspirational rebel. Championed as a figure of rage, power, and resilience, the female masculinity that had long been a part of her frontier celebrity now became intrinsic to her status as an activist icon. This new configuration of Calamity Jane as role model of female agency and empowerment was seen in various contexts in which performers reflected on, or consciously took on the identity of, Martha Jane Canary—from literary musings and dramatic soliloquies, to a buoyant culture of impersonators who appeared at western heritage days and public events from the late 1980s. Glenda Bell, an ex-teacher and librarian from Colorado who performed up to 150 first-person storytelling revues a year after she took on the role in 1987, saw her subject as a powerful agitant: "Basically, what she did was she put on a pair of britches and she just marched right into the male culture." For Dianne Gleason, a Calamity Jane impersonator working in Montana and the Dakotas, the evocation of a woman making her own way and operating according to her own rules had prompted her own buckskin costuming. Canary had inspired her as an "independent, free-spirited, and liberated" woman. With a degree in cultural anthropology, Gleason approached her muse as a specimen of social interest, and studiously explored archival and photographic records to ensure that her "look" was an exact facsimile. Moreover, as a self-confessed nomad, shooting champion, recovering alcoholic, and woman of formidable stature, Gleason bore more than a passing resemblance to her assumed character. As she put it, "I ain't no Doris Day." Speaking at one of her one-woman shows, she told reporters how she inhabited the role "full-time," and promised a brand-new scoop: "I've written a first-person account of Calamity Jane's life and present historical stories no one has ever heard before. It's fresh and it's new." A century after *Life and Adventures*, the power of storytelling, performance and frontier celebrity were alive and well. Indeed, on one occasion, a spiritualist came up to Gleason after a show in Deadwood and said: "You really *are* the spirit of Calamity Jane. Through you she has been given a second chance to finish out her life."[36]

CONCLUSION

FROM DORIS TO *DEADWOOD* AND BACK
THE CONTINUING LIFE AND ADVENTURES OF
CALAMITY JANE

A quick scan of "Calamity Jane" in an internet search engine reveals a character playing fast and loose in a digital world, a "female scout" who seamlessly traveled from the dusty trails of the late nineteenth-century American West to the electronic frontier of the wild wild Web. Virtual flowers left on Canary's grave at one website number more than 1,100, attached eulogies recording her as an inspiration to all "women's libbers," referencing her abiding love for Bill Hickok, noting the "truth" of the McCormick saga, and celebrating her legendary "service for the nation." Saddled with a bewildering array of cultural representations more than a century in the making, Calamity Jane represents an arresting western artefact-in-residence.[1]

A few aspects of this layered landscape of collective memory strike one at first glance: the international reach of a "heroine of the plains" deployed across many contexts as a synonym for romantic westering; scouting credentials and buckskin uniform as persistent and classic motifs; the enduring popularity of Doris Day's 1953 "Calam" in all her vivacious articulations of musical gusto. Running throughout, most importantly, are long-standing themes of gender possibility, storytelling, and frontier celebrity. Tracked through the chapters of *Calamity: The Many Lives of Calamity Jane*, this long trail of costuming and entanglement, of the knitting together of lived and invented experience, explains the process by which Martha Canary became Calamity Jane, and Calamity Jane became a permanent fixture in the frontier imaginary.

From Doris to *Deadwood* and back, here is a heroine of extraordinary plasticity. Holding her own as a useable wild western nugget, she has been employed in the twenty-first century as a playful framing device for sagas of female friendship (the "Calamity Janes" novels from Sherryl Woods, 2002–03) and for quirky marketing wordplay (My Little Pony's "Calamity Mane" (2012)). Some have seen her as a handy byword for heresy and rebellion (cultural critic Margot Mifflin called her the "Courtney Love of her generation"), or as an auxiliary for misadventure (see solicitor "Calamity" Jane Kennedy in the BBC comedy-drama set in Devon, *The Coroner* (2015)). A frontier personality with a well-signposted legend, she has brought authenticity to western-set productions in the form of cameo appearances. Accordingly, in the Frontierville online game (2010), players were able to purchase a Calamity Jane costume for their virtual character (billed as "the only outfit that allows women to wear the pants"). In Bernard Schopen's *Calamity Jane* (2013), she was a useful "hook" for a novel set in modern Nevada about a female filmmaker seeking out a retired cowboy actor; while Michael Crichton's *Dragon Teeth* (2017) gave her passing mention as a woman boasting of lesbian conquests in his tale of late nineteenth-century competitive paleontology in the Black Hills.[2]

When grappled with up close, meanwhile, the stuff of classic western fable still predominates. John Wayne, it turns out, still rides shotgun on the old frontier well into the twenty-first century. In this realm of Technicolor triumphalism, Calamity Jane continues to deliver a tried and tested formula of boisterous adventuring, in which her famed deeds hold sway as incontrovertible truths. Benedictions of this type can be found in all kinds of places. The Morricone-riffed and dime novel-inflected "White Devil of the Yellowstone" (2007), from Finnish punk band The Micro Girls, for instance, noisily rejoiced in her riding the range, fending off snakes, and resting eternally next to Wild Bill. Likewise, the low-budget Hollywood production *Calamity Jane's Revenge* (2015) saw her embark on a campaign of vengeance for the killing of Wild Bill, tell tales of scouting for Crook, and converse privately with Hickok's ghost. Similar rootin' tootin' fantasies are available for tourist consumption in a series of connected geographies, from Princeton ("Calamity Jane Days" continues to wow crowds) to Brittany, where the Ranch De Calamity Jane, founded by French enthusiasts Fred and Nadine Audo, provides holiday escapes to an old West of cowboys and Indians, bison cook-outs, roping lessons, and saloon dances.[3]

The most widely disseminated example of this bubble-gum frontier smorgasbord has been Butler's 1953 musical, which, 60-plus years after its release, is still regularly reeled out for film-festival showings, audience sing-a-longs, and theatrical adaptations. Inspiring great affection as a vestige of childhood days and cinematic simplicity (the London *Daily Mail* dubbed it "musical comedy innocence"), Doris Day's tuneful taming of the plains remains the principal vision of Calamity Jane in the mind's eye of many people. Played out on stage in the early 2000s by Jerry Hall, Toyah Willcox, and Jodie Prenger (who described her character as "quite a gal ... feisty and very gutsy ... larger than life but with a vulnerable side"), the show wowed a global theater-going audience with its nostalgic feel-good frontier gaze. At the same time, the early twenty-first century has seen various scholars and popular commentators excavate the feminist and queer subtexts hidden in *Calamity Jane*, thereby giving the film an entirely new cultural makeover that brought a new saliency to Doris Day's fresh-faced "Calam," and mapped out a trail to the historical experience of Martha Canary and a nineteenth-century world of gender performance and possibility. Star of a theatrical production in Sydney, Australia, Virginia Gay spoke of the free-spirited and non heteronormative messages of a musical that served up alternative romantic futures and a jocular line in feminist agency. Discussed in a newspaper piece entitled "Why Calamity Jane Matters Now," this continuing conversation about performing *Calamity Jane* illustrates the vitality of its eponymous subject in an age in which, according to Gay, "women are sitting in their power." Meanwhile, some of the more esoteric examples of the film's lasting cultural import include a fierce two-year long dispute between neighbors in Brighton, England, resulting from a committed fan regularly singing "The Deadwood Stage" at unsociable hours and volume, and a junk-removal company in Margate that sports an advertising insignia of a horse-drawn stage and a name founded on a stupendous use of badinage: WhipCrapAway.[4]

Alongside this motley band of whimsical adventures and frontier "outings," these years have seen a deepening examination of Calamity Jane as a worthy subject for historical biography. Largely overlooked by a traditional academic historiography that failed to notice the gendered make-up of the western heroic canon, and by a revisionist camp that read her as non-representative of the ordinary experiences of women on the frontier, Martha Canary finally received proper scrutiny from a cadre of historian-biographers. In 2005, James McLaird published *Calamity Jane: The Woman and the Legend*, a work that successfully achieved the oft-touted goal of excavating the "facts" from Canary's richly textured mythological canopy. With his painstaking (and at times bewildering) assembly of historical accounts, McLaird delivered the most forensic excavation of her actual life to date, to reveal a marginal figure in a prosaic— rather than heroic—space (what McLaird calls "an account of uneventful daily life interrupted by drinking binges"). Linda Jucovy's *Searching for Calamity: The Life and Times of Calamity Jane* (2012) also focused on the tribulations of Canary as woman, rather than legend, to show a complicated figure constantly on the move: an alcoholic pariah who "made history" by refusing to abide by the customary boundaries of the female frontier. For Richard Etulain, too, Calamity Jane's story was one of abjection, his *Life and Legends of Calamity Jane* (2014) advancing the idea of a disjuncture between a mythological "Wild West female" and an "aspiring" pioneer woman whose story needed to be told.[5]

This most recent cultural rendering of the Calamity story, it seems, is all about the human angle. Rough-edged and roving, she was a woman caught up in a West that left her hamstrung by poverty, addiction, and limited choices. Such themes came out strongly in the film *Calamity Jane: Legende De L'Ouest* (2014), the first major historical documentary on the life of Martha Jane Canary. Directed and produced by Gregory Monro, a French film director with a particular interest in his subject (he has authored two French-language books on her, and also purchased Jean McCormick's documents), it presented a woman struggling with changing times, the subject of tall tales, and beset by hardships. Canary's reputation as a frontier heroine was juxtaposed here with her life as orphan, economic migrant, victim of domestic violence, and single mother. Focused around an evocative (and cinematic) landscape of open vistas, film reel footage, and old photographs, *Legende De L'Ouest* delivered a portrait both expansive and intimate. A tale of desperation, told in tandem with the demise of the bison and the American Indian, it shows Calamity Jane as a fellow victim of frontier fantasies, and the perfect embodiment of a West of movement, opportunity, toil, and tragedy.[6]

Constructions of Calamity Jane as a subversive storyteller and eyewitness to the old West had always been foundational aspects of her frontier celebrity. These elements were strikingly aligned in the most important feature film and television treatment in the early twenty-first century: *Deadwood*. Developed by David Milch and running for 36 episodes (2004–06) before its abrupt cancellation, the HBO series presented a grippingly profane, violent, and venomous take on frontier conquest and closure in the Black Hills. Asserting that he didn't want to make a western and never really "understood or cared" for its conventions, Milch focused on challenging a legendary canon by deconstructing the mechanics of law making and breaking in frontier space. Calamity Jane moved on the edges of this captivating pageant of patriarchal power-broking and social conflict. Audiences were treated to very little of her backstory, but she was nonetheless a significant presence, in terms of both her function in the narrative and the way she was depicted. Patrolling the borders of the plot and the settlement (only Hickok was noticed when they arrived in town), Canary popped up to tell stories and help the needy. There, at the margins, she navigated a world of flux, in which social and economic inequity, racialist anger, and cultural uncertainty flourished. For film studies scholar Janet McCabe, this Calamity Jane was a postmodern orator, illuminating, by her experience, the way in which "a sense of history vanishes, amnesia rules, and the past is raided by the present for images." McCabe deemed her a vital "nexus point" that highlighted the inherent tensions in *Deadwood* between fact and fiction, traditional and revisionist histories, and various mediums of storytelling. *Calamity: The Many Lives of Calamity Jane* documents, in the long history of Calamity Jane, a similar mechanism at work. As storyteller and scout, Canary's successive performances in the frontier imaginary pointed to the contortions of history and folklore, contested readings of the grand western fable, and the shifting terrains of modern gender politics.[7]

Implicit in *Deadwood*'s messy narrative was a contesting of hegemonic ideas about masculine heroism, community formation, and the dynamics of frontier fame. Calamity Jane played strongly into all these equations. Portrayed by Robin Weigert as a grubby, cussing, butch woman, she was a world away from celluloid precursors (Plate 19). In her opening scene, Canary made a telling reference to playing in a musical, a notion that she scoffed at. Thereafter, she stumbled through the plot as a part comic, part tragic character, whose female masculinity presented a potent critique of the classic macho contours of the West (and the western), and of the mid-century incarnations of Calamity Jane that championed gender containment, whimsy, and sassy rebellion. Weigert's "heroine of the plains" was also self-referential, fully aware of her folkloric cloak and its limitations. Importantly, by season three she had found her place in town and tale, by stepping out of the shadow of Hickok and embarking on a lesbian relationship with Joannie, the local madam. Film scholar Linda Mizejewski argued that the show was particularly important in highlighting "the presence of diverse bodies and sexualities within the histories and legends of the West." Although themes of same-sex desire and gender fluidity had run through the storied trail of Calamity Jane from Spencer to Gage, this was the first mainstream treatment in which she presented as a lesbian. Dressed in stained and weathered buckskin, Weigert's character found a space to be herself in male costume, yet faced derision, amusement, and pitying glances from townsfolk. Early on, E. B. Farnum called her "Hickok's half-woman friend." As such, Milch's "female scout" authentically communicated the challenging existence faced by those with alternative gender identities in the West. Also significant was the fact that the show made an important notation of Calamity Jane's historical trace as a masculine woman. Richard Etulain criticizes *Deadwood* for downplaying Canary's aspirations for marriage and motherhood—an interpretation that overlooks the importance of gender possibility in her story. Instead, Milch's explorations of a Black Hills community tussling to create itself offered an important acknowledgment of female masculinity as an intrinsic aspect of Calamity Jane's personal and performance identity.[8]

A glance at fan message boards suggests a varied reception for Milch's Calamity. A few advised watching Doris Day ("prettier and cleaner") instead, and questioned the value of giving screen time to a character known only for her sham marriages and "famesque" claims. Most, however, read Canary as a resilient and inspiring woman passing as a man to claim personal power. A number of posts championed her celluloid arrival as a definitively gay woman. One thing was clear: Calamity Jane's "outing" in a prime-time entertainment landscape provoked a good deal of chatter. The subversive possibilities embedded in the story of Martha Jane Canary—a long-standing carrier for gender unorthodoxy—witnessed their most expansive exploration in the early twenty-first century. Cast in the role of activist in action, Calamity Jane took to the stage as a usefully disruptive heroine.[9]

A strong element running through literary and theatrical depictions of this campaigning Calamity was a gruffly articulated, but agile, sense of feminist agency. In "Sonofabitch Stew: The drunken life of Calamity

Jane" (2012), her spirit was emphatically channeled by a modern women's studies professor. Janet Payne saw herself as a maverick campaigner (hard-talking, hard-drinking), who demanded that her students (the show audience) seize a Canary-skill set, instead of languishing in the false security of a university campus and Twittersphere. The steampunk novel *Corsets and Clockwork* (2011), meanwhile, placed her on a hijacked airship over South Dakota, masterminding the saving of Deadwood's children from an outlaw gang of robots bent on enslaving them as mine-workers, and winning the affections of a mysterious sidekick, who turned out to be Jesse James, with her tough-talking charm. J.D. Jordan's *Calamity: Being an Account of Calamity Jane and the Gunslinging Green Man* (2016), a work of speculative fiction (described by a critic as if "Quentin Tarantino wrote a feminist western memoir. With aliens"), told of the journey of a 15-year-old with a fiery temper, running with a "tall, lean and green and terrible" armed extraterrestrial wearing a duster coat and Stetson. Narrated in a western vernacular style, the novel described how Canary found (rather than lost) herself in the persona of Calamity. A roving rider of the plains in masculine attire, she dodged sexual violence and outlaw bullets, discovering on the way that she could "trust no one to save her but herself." Finding pride and purpose in a militant identity, Calamity concluded: "if I'd kept on as Martha, it wouldn't have been a shadow of the life I lived as Jane."[10]

Set in the more familiar stomping grounds of the late nineteenth-century West, but equally embroidered as feminist manifesto, Audry Grant's short e-novel *Calamity Jane: The Masquerade of Masculinity* (2013) advertised a scenario in which a young Canary chose "freedom over marriage," to appear as a reconfigured romantic heroine "who refused to be gendered in a world of men." Masculine costume was firmly positioned here as a political device of gender empowerment. In the French graphic novel, *Calamity Jane: The Calamitous Life of M.J. Cannary, 1852–1903* (2017), the eponymous lead is an independent wanderer, fending off sexual assault to find subsistence and self-expression in an itinerant world of army trails and campfire stories. Created by Christian Perrissin and Matthieu Blanchin, the novel points to an enduring interest in Calamity Jane in France, one which is rooted in an animated tradition stretching from *Lucky Luke* and *The Legend of Calamity Jane* to *Calamity – A Childhood of Martha Jane Cannary* (2020), Rémi Chayé's enchanting animated film that centers on the strong-minded predilections of a young feminist Canary, firmly placed in the role of "a decidedly modern female hero."[11]

Dominating this latest literary and dramaturgical representation of Calamity Jane is the autobiographical voice. Whether displayed as new recitations of *Life and Adventures*, continuing excavations of McCormick's saga, or incantations to Canary as a timeless scout and storyteller, novelists, playwrights, and poets have been inspired by an imaginative quest to let Canary "speak for herself." Threads of authenticity and storytelling have always been intrinsic to her frontier celebrity, and have continued to resonate in early twenty-first century interpretations. Natalee Caple's *In Calamity's Wake* (2013) offers a soporific dance through the narrative testimonies of Martha Canary and daughter Miette. Presenting a procession of characters on a circuitous trail to Deadwood, Caple's magical realist novel conjures a Calamity Jane who was elemental (when her name is mentioned, thunder and hail fall from the sky) and endlessly enigmatic. One traveler tells Miette that her mother was a scout who was killed by a train when drunk, while Dora Du Fran's reminiscence mashes up *Life and Adventures* with McCormick's journals to locate her as a spectacular and sorrowful, self-made and self-ruined, superstar. At the end, Miette is guided by a wolf to find her dying mother at last in Terry, South Dakota, before taking her to Du Fran's in Deadwood to die. For Afro-Native American poet Sea Sharp, meanwhile, the life path of Canary is that of a non-binary Indian fighter who deserves a bold, in-your-face autobiographical curation that defies the structural conventions of line breaks and punctuation. Accordingly, "The Biography of Calamity Jane" runs as one long sentence, recounting a "trigger happy bitch . . . getting buck-rowdy like Wild Bill," no "beauty queen" or "Oakley girl," but an individual with "some dirt on her boots ... grit in her teeth," patrolling "the whole frontier peelin' back scabs from her tiny bruised knuckles." Reprinted as part of the "Dangerous Women Project" (2016) from the Edinburgh Institute of Advanced Studies in the Humanities, Sea Sharp's Calamity featured in an exhibition designed, in the words of historian Mary Beard, "to explore what we expect of women, of how they should behave and of what counts as women 'stepping out of the line'."[12]

Indeed, the swirls of storytelling and masquerade that have already carried Calamity Jane far seem to find a natural place of residency in new readings that depict her as a self-reflexive choreographer of her own celebrity. Thomas Devaney's *Calamity Jane* (2014), an opera in verse, imagines Canary as a performance artiste with a formative past: "Living life doesn't make anyone a hero, but for some, for Jane, it may be heroic simply to survive." Described by critic Cynthia Chris as "epic poetry recast for the drama of daily life," Devaney's Canary talks about the West, mythology, whiskey, Hickok, her daughter, and the authorial power of fame. At the outset she tells her audience "Here's what I know: when you have a name your story is true," before remonstrating on gender code and the fragile contours of hegemonic masculinity. Proclaiming that "no-one knows what it is like to be a man, not even the men," she appears here as part frontier raconteur, part gender theorist, fully cognizant of her own "famesque" contortions: "So there I was, a legend that couldn't live up to her own barking signs, or was living up to them too much ... my name wasn't a stage name. It was the stage." Similar themes graced a theatrical production by M. Heather Carver, whose one-woman show "Will the Real Calamity Jane Please Stand Up" (2003) pondered a life story marked by "multiple levels of performativity." Viewing the story of Canary, at its core, as one of "women's representation, authority and agency," Carver treated her audience to a line of different Calamities, each of which delivered an oration on self-image, identity, and reputation. Seated at a table in a smoky room, the first was a feisty narrator shooting off verbal bullets at her audience: "Hello every-body! I'm a loose woman! I'm a mother! I'm a hero! I'm a troublemaker! I'm a liar! I'm a prostitute! I'm sexually confused! I'm an oddity! I'm drunk! I'm angry! ... oh hell, I'm whatever they say I am." Thereafter, the stage was graced by the "Party Girl" Calamity (who lambasted mid-century biographer Roberta Sollid for calling her a fallen woman), the "Western Hero" (talking herself up as a "Disneyized ... genu-wine legend", like Pocahontas and Annie Oakley), the "Woman's Woman" ("who worked to make the world a better place for us and ours"), and "Jane the Writer" (busily compiling a diary for her daughter). Borrowing from a broad cultural archaeology and the vernacular landscape of *Life and Adventures*, the assembled storytellers converged just before the curtain fell to leave the audience with a set of questions: "So, you tell us, who is the real Calamity ... Could there be some of all of those in us? Would that make us so different from y'all?"[13]

In life and afterlife, the story of Calamity Jane was one of buck-skin-clad gender possibility. Costumed for controversy, she patrolled the borders of female agency, social acceptability, and patriotic myth creation. In this tale of westering and wandering, a journey across an environment marked by extraordinary political, economic, and social changes and a colorful hike into a frontier imaginary of extraordinary reach, Martha Jane Canary earned her stripes as a pathfinder after all. The "female scout" remained a constant presence, armed with a storied past and an enduring mantle of frontier celebrity. As a historical figure, she offered important, if fragmentary, explication on a West that was freer and more open to alternative gender expressions than the East, yet remained corralled by firm limits to action. She was, in common with many pioneers, resilient and resourceful; and, as a poor, itinerant woman, was beset by a litany of daily hardships, as well as debilitating problems with alcohol dependency. A non-normative path marked by the adoption of male clothing, lifestyle and habits became part of a survival strategy that allowed her to make her way as best she could. But, I would argue, it was much more than that. Enacted by costume, gestures, and storytelling, female masculinity became an important way of expressing an alternative gender identity. In this performance, Martha Canary was trying to figure out who she was. Over successive generations, so, too, was her audience. Delving into the obfuscations of her folkloric trail, in all its delights and dangers, popular culture chewed over how to make sense of the "female scout" who flouted the usual rules of propriety. Recent historians have seen the real Martha Jane as lost in the gun-smoking swagger of her famous pseudonym. *Calamity: The Many Lives of Calamity Jane* instead points to a complex choreography of lived and invented experience in understanding the story of Calamity Jane.

Reimagined and retold over the span of a century or more, the "heroine of the plains" has been cast in various roles: curiosity, freak, dangerous aberration, frontier whimsy, and heretical trailblazer. Carrying her frontier celebrity off with aplomb, Canary led her audience across a cultural terrain under radical transformation. Her story communicated important messages about a West of heroics, heresy, and performance; shifting notions of gender identity; and the mechanics of fame in modern celebrity culture. What was most interesting about her journey from frontier curiosity to feminist icon was the fact that the *everyday* story of Martha Jane Canary—nonconformist, defiant, and irrepressible—turned out to be the heroic one. In *Gaga Feminism* (2012), Jack Halberstam pondered on a new era of sexual and gender expression, where provocative role models were to be found in the unexpected and the counterintuitive, at the margins, and with the bold and the outrageous: an environment well suited for Calamity Jane to camp out in. A frontier celebrity, by herself she was unorthodox, enigmatic, and sported a line in buckskin masquerade that invited multiple readings. There are, undoubtedly, more stories to be told of her life and adventures.[14]

NOTES

INTRODUCTION

1. *Calamity Jane* (dir. by David Butler, Warner Bros, USA, 1953).
2. *Cheyenne Daily Leader*, 27 March 1877; *Cheyenne Daily Sun*, 11 July 1877; *Cheyenne Daily Leader*, 15 July 1877.
3. J. Leonard Jennewein, *Calamity Jane of the Western Trails* (Rapid City, SD: Dakota West Books, 1953), 6. In this book I build on the notion of "gender possibility" as explored in film scholar Mair Rigby's non-heteronormative reading of Doris Day's 1953 musical to apply as a useful label for exploring the broader dynamics of Canary's life and legend. See Mair Rigby, "Gender Calamity/Gender Possibility: Calamity Jane (1953)." Available online at: https://purpleprosearchive.wordpress.com/2012/02/06/gender-calamity-gender-possibility-calamity-jane-1953-2 (accessed 18 March 2019).
4. Deadwood *Black Hills Pioneer*, 11 July 1876.
5. Martha Cannary, *Life and Adventures of Calamity Jane, By Herself* (n.p., 1896); Frederick Jackson Turner, "The Significance of the Frontier in American History," in *The Frontier in American History* (New York: Henry Holt, 1920), 1–38.
6. Dee Brown, *The Gentle Tamers: Women of the Old Wild West* (Lincoln: University of Nebraska Press, 1958), 16; Turner, *The Frontier in American History*, 18; Elliott West, "A Longer, Grimmer But More Interesting Story" in Patricia Limerick (ed.), *Trails: Toward a New Western History* (Lawrence: University Press of Kansas, 1991), 104; Susan Armitage, "Through Women's Eyes," in Susan Armitage and Elizabeth Jameson (eds), *The Women's West* (Norman: University of Oklahoma Press, 1987), 9; Evelyn Cameron, "Diary 1895," Box 1, Folder 5, Diaries 1895-6, MC226: Evelyn J. and Ewen S. Cameron Papers, Montana Historical Society, Helena, Montana (henceforth MHS).
7. M. Heather Carver, "Risky Business: Exploring Women's Autobiography and Performance," in Lynn C. Miller, Jacqueline Taylor, and M. Heather Carver (eds), *Voices Made Flesh: Performing Women's Autobiography* (Madison: University of Wisconsin Press, 2003), 16; Duncan Aikman, *Calamity Jane and the Lady Wildcats* (Lincoln: University of Nebraska Press, 1927), 30.
8. J. Leonard Jennewein to Mr. Drake de Kay, 18 February 1958, J. Leonard Jennewein Collection, Dakota Wesleyan University Archives, Mitchell, South Dakota (hereafter Jenn); Linda Jucovy, *Searching for Calamity* (Philadelphia, PA: Stampede Books, 2012), 2; Jennewein, *Calamity Jane*, 7; Lander *Wyoming State Journal*, 2 November 1933.
9. Larry McMurtry, *The Colonel and Little Missie: Buffalo Bill, Annie Oakley and the Beginnings of Superstardom in America* (New York: Simon & Schuster, 2005), 4; *Rapid City Daily Journal*, 20 January 1896; *Livingston Enterprise*, 17 September 1887, "Vertical Files: Calamity Jane," MHS.

10. Aikman, *Calamity Jane*, 59; John E. Hutchens, *One Man's Montana* (New York: J.B. Lippincott, 1964), 80; Richard Etulain, *The Life and Legends of Calamity Jane* (Norman: University of Oklahoma Press, 2014); James McLaird: *Calamity Jane: The Woman and the Legend* (Norman: University of Oklahoma Press, 2005).

11. A useful guide to action has been Annette Kolody's *In Search of First Contact: The Vikings of Vinland and the People of the Dawnland* (Durham, NC: Duke University Press, 2012), which explores the evolving entanglements of storytelling and frontier conquest across Norse saga, Euro-American narrative, and indigenous oral tradition. Frontier biographies which grapple with the tensions of myth-making and life story in the western theater include: Andrew Isenberg, *Wyatt Earp: A Vigilante Life* (New York: Hill & Wang, 2014); Louis Warren, *Buffalo Bill's America: William Cody and the Wild West Show* (New York: Vintage, 2005); McMurtry, *The Colonel and Little Missie*. On the "famesque" and the invention of modern celebrity, I use the general definition of the term as meaning "famous for being famous"—in other words, a notoriety founded less on proven achievements and more on a cultivated performance, but without the pejorative associations often connected with the phrase. See: Amy Argetsinger, "They Must Be Stars Because They Get So Much Press, but What Is It They Do Again?," *Washington Post*, 10 August 2009; Daniel Boorstin, *The Image: A Guide to Pseudo-Events in America* (New York: Atheneum, 1971), and J. Jack Halberstam, *Gaga Feminism: Sex, Gender, and the End of Normal* (Boston, MA: Beacon Press, 2012). On female autobiography and frontier collective memory, see: Shari Benstock, *The Private Self: Theory and Practice of Women's Autobiographical Writings* (Chapel Hill: University of North Carolina Press, 1988), 11; Milner and Boyd quoted in Clyde Milner II, "Afterword: When History Talks Back," in Jessie L. Embry (ed.), *Oral History, Community and Work in the American West* (Tucson: University of Arizona Press, 2013), 336, 329.

12. Glenda Riley, "Images of the Frontierswoman: Iowa as a Case Study," *Western Historical Quarterly*, 8 (April 1977), 189–202; Ray Allen Billington, *Westward Expansionism: A History of the American Frontier* (New York: Macmillan, 1949), 632; Joan Jensen and Darlis Miller, "The Gentle Tamers Revisited: New Approaches to the History of Women in the American West," in Mary Ann Irwin and James Brooks (eds), *Women and Gender in the American West* (Albuquerque: University of New Mexico Press, 2004), 9–15; Richard Etulain, *Calamity Jane: A Reader's Guide* (Norman: University of Oklahoma Press, 2015), 247.

13. Halberstam describes the masculine woman as "a historical fixture" and "a character who has challenged gender systems for at least two centuries": Judith Halberstam, *Female Masculinity* (Durham, NC: Duke University Press, 1998), 45; Jennewein, *Calamity Jane*, 6. See also: Judith Butler, *Gender Trouble: Feminism and the Subversion of Identity* (New York: Routledge, 2006 [1990]). Direct coverage of Calamity Jane in terms of gender, performance, and female masculinity is scant, but instructive comments on her role in the HBO series *Deadwood* are offered by Linda Mizejewski (see: "Calamity Jane and Female Masculinity in *Deadwood*," in Melody Graulich and Nicolas Witschi (eds), *Dirty Words in Deadwood: Literature and the Postwestern* (Lincoln: University of Nebraska Press, 2013), 184–207, and by Catherine McComb's case study of Canary's media imprint in terms of costume theory, gender, and semiotics (see: "Undressing an American Icon: Addressing the Representation of Calamity Jane Through a Critical Study of Her Costume," University of Regina, Saskatchewan, MA thesis, 2016).

14. Aikman, *Calamity Jane*, xii, iv; *The Plainsman* (dir. by Cecil B. DeMille, Paramount Pictures, USA, 1936); Jucovy, *Searching for Calamity*, 1; Stella Foote, *A History of Calamity Jane: Our Country's First Liberated Woman* (New York: Vantage, 1995); *Deadwood* (dir. by David Milch, HBO, USA, 2004–06).

CHAPTER 1

1. "Schedule 1: Free Inhabitants in Ravenna Township, Bureau of the Census, 1860, Mercer County, MO" in "Calamity Jane – Wild Bill Hickok Newspaper Articles," Clarence S. Paine Papers, Box 2, Folder 2, Center for Western Studies, Augustana College, Sioux Falls, South Dakota (hereafter Paine).

2. For detailed genealogies of the Canary family, see McLaird, *Calamity Jane*, 7–17, and Etulain, *Life and Legends*, 5–18.
3. Aikman, *Calamity Jane*, 8, 24, 17–18; Letter from C.W. Ormsbey, Princeton, to W.W. Morrison, Cheyenne, 22 November 1948, Box 7: "Calamity Jane Canary and the Canary Family," W.W. Morrison Papers, American Heritage Center, University of Wyoming Archives, Laramie, Wyoming (hereafter AHC); Doris Thompson, "Princeton Claims Fame as Calamity Jane Birthplace," Princeton *Post Telegraph*, 25 July 1957; Ronald W. Lackmann, *Women of the Western Frontier in Fact, Fiction, and Film* (Jefferson, NC: McFarland, 1997), 21; Jennewein, *Calamity Jane*, 7.
4. Rufus Sage, *Scenes in the Rocky Mountains* (Philadelphia, PA: Carey & Hart, 1846), 122.
5. Richard White, "Trashing the Trails," in Limerick, *Trails*, 26–39; Richard White, *It's Your Misfortune and None of My Own: A New History of the American West* (Norman: University of Oklahoma Press, 1991), 207; Boney Earnest is quoted in McLaird, *Calamity Jane*, 20.
6. Aikman, *Calamity Jane*, 33; Sarah Raymond Herndon, *Days on the Road: Crossing the Plains in 1865* (New York: Burr Printing House, 1902), 67, 78, 99, 106, 127, 138, 162–163.
7. Elliott West, *Growing Up with the Country: Childhood on the Far Western Frontier* (Albuquerque: University of New Mexico Press, 1989), xi–xii; D.B. Ward, *Across the Plains in 1853* (Seattle, WA: Ward, 1911), 52; Sarah J. Cummins, *Autobiography and Reminiscences* (La Grande, OR, 1908), 33–36.
8. Herndon, *Days on the Road*, 260–261.
9. Sarah Royce, *A Frontier Lady: Recollections of the Gold Rush and Early California* (Lincoln: University of Nebraska Press, 1977 [1932]), 79; Herndon, *Days on the Road*, 262.
10. *Montana Post*, 31 December 1864, "Vertical Files: Calamity Jane," MHS.
11. Edwin Ruthven Purple, *Perilous Passage: A Narrative of the Montana Gold Rush, 1862–1863* (Helena, MT: Montana Historical Society Press, 1995), 141–143; see also: "The Women of Virginia City," MHS, available online at http://montanawomenshistory.org/wp-content/uploads/2015/04/Women-of-VA-City_TourMap.pdf (accessed 20 March 2017).
12. Milner, "Afterword," 330–332. See also: W.F. Sanders II and Robert Taylor, *Biscuits and Badmen: The Sanders in their Own Words* (Butte, MT: Editorial Review Press, 1983).
13. Etulain, *Life and Legends*, 26-27.
14. McLaird, *Calamity Jane*, 22; John S. McClintock, *Pioneer Days in the Black Hills* (Norman: University of Oklahoma Press, 2000 [1939]), 117.
15. Ben Arnold, quoted in Lewis Crawford, *Rekindling Camp Fires: The Exploits of Ben Arnold* (Bismarck, ND: Capital Book Co., 1926), 272–273.
16. Etulain, *Life and Legends*, 29; *Cheyenne Daily Leader*, 3 November 1885; *Sioux City Journal*, 25 January 1954; Aikman, *Calamity Jane*, 63.
17. *Lusk Herald*, 28 May 1936.
18. Crawford, *Rekindling Camp Fires*, 272–273; Armitage and Jameson (eds), *The Women's West*, 29, 12.

CHAPTER 2

1. Cannary, *Life and Adventures*.
2. John Hunton, "My Recollections of Calamity Jane," Box 7: "Calamity Jane Canary and the Canary Family," W.W. Morrison Papers, AHC; London *Star*, 7 August 1903.
3. Cannary, *Life and Adventures*; Jennewein, *Calamity Jane*, 8; Roberta Sollid, *Calamity Jane, A Study in Historical Criticism* (Helena, MT: Montana Historical Society, 1958), 36.
4. Argetsinger, "They Must Be Stars"; Sioux Falls *Argus Leader*, 9 July 1906; Crawford, *Rekindling Camp Fires*, 274; Julia McGillycuddy, *McGillycuddy, Agent: A Biography of the Life of Dr. Valentine T. McGillycuddy* (Stanford, CA: Stanford University Press, 1941), 27; George Hoshier, quoted in *Norfolk News*, 13 July 1906.

5. *Billings News*, 13 July 1901; Aikman, *Calamity Jane*, 68–69; *Norfolk News*, 13 July 1906.

6. *Montana Standard*, August 1941, "Calamity Jane file: press clippings," MHS; *Cheyenne Daily Leader*, 28 August 1878.

7. *Rock Springs Miner*, 28 December 1893; Deadwood *Black Hills Daily Times*, 28 October 1878; *Cheyenne Daily Leader*, 30 August 1878; *Cheyenne Daily Sun*, 19 February 1879.

8. *Cheyenne Daily Sun*, 19 February 1879; Denver *Rocky Mountain News*, 27 July 1891.

9. *Cheyenne Daily Leader*, 3 November 1885; *Chicago Inter Ocean*, 27 August 1874; *Chicago Tribune*, 13 January 1878.

10. Annie D. Tallent, *The Black Hills, or the Last Hunting Grounds of the Dakotahs* (St. Louis, MO: Nixon-Jones Printing Co., 1899), 27, 31, 33, 61, 14.

11. Richard White, "Frederick Jackson Turner and Buffalo Bill," in James R. Grossman (ed.), *The Frontier in American Culture* (Berkeley: University of California Press, 1994), 27; M.L. Fox, "Calamity Jane," *Illustrated American*, 7 March 1896, 312.

12. J.R. Lane, "The Gold-Hunters," *Chicago Tribune*, 19 June 1875.

13. Thomas "Mac" Macmillan, "Gold Galore," *Chicago Inter Ocean*, 3 July 1875.

14. "Martha Canary (Calamity Jane), Black Hills, 1875," Jenn; Martha Sandweiss, *Print the Legend: Photography and the American West* (New Haven, CT: Yale University Press, 2004), 2.

15. McGillycuddy, *McGillycuddy, Agent*, 25–39; Harry Young, *Hard Knocks: A Life Story of the Vanishing West* (Portland, OR: Wells & Co., 1915), 80, 169–172; Estelline Bennett, *Old Deadwood Days* (Lincoln: University of Nebraska Press, 1982 [1928]); D. Dee (Dora Du Fran), *Low Down on Calamity Jane* (Rapid City, SD: n.p., 1932).

16. McGillycuddy, *McGillycuddy, Agent*, 25, 27, 33–34, 38; Young, *Hard Knocks*, 170, 171–172.

17. A.W. Spring (ed.), "Diary of Isaac N. Bard (1875–6)," in Alan Swallow (ed.), *1955 Westerners' Brand Book, The Denver Posse* (Denver, CO: Westerners, 1956), 11: 186; Jesse Brown and A.M. Willard, *The Black Hills Trails* (Rapid City, SD: Rapid City Journal Company, 1924), 76.

18. Copies of the Indictment and Bench warrant can be found in "Calamity Jane – Wild Bill Hickok Newspaper Articles," Box 2, Folder 2, Paine; *Cheyenne Daily Leader*, 20 June 1876; Denver *Rocky Mountain News*, 25 June 1876. McLaird suggests that Canary's urgency to reach Fort Laramie may have reflected her desire to tag along on Crook's second campaign to the Black Hills in summer 1876 (McLaird, *Calamity Jane*, 48).

19. J.W. Vaughn, *With Crook at the Rosebud* (Harrisburg, PA: The Stackpole Co., 1956), 12–13; Anson Mills, *My Story* (Washington, DC: Byron S. Adams, 1918), 401.

20. John Bourke, *On the Border with Crook* (New York: Charles Scribner's Sons, 1891), 299–300; "Interview with Samuel Smith, Saratoga, at Laramie, 10 April, 1917: 'Calamity Jane'," Grace Raymond Hebard Papers, Box 32, Folder 17, AHC; Alfred Theodore Andreas, *Andreas' Historical Atlas of Dakota* (Chicago, IL: R.R. Donnelley, 1884), 118; *Cheyenne Daily Leader*, 24 February 1876; Capt. Jack, "News from Black Hills," *Cheyenne Daily Leader*, 24 February 1876; Captain Jack Crawford, "Christmas Day in the Black Hills, 1876" and "The Ranger's Retreat: A Song," in *The Poet Scout: A Book of Song and Story* (New York: Funk & Wagnalls, 1886), 100.

21. Cannary, *Life and Adventures*. See also Evelyn A. Schlatter, "Drag's a Life: Women, Gender, and Cross-Dressing in the Nineteenth-Century West," in Elizabeth Jameson and Susan Armitage (eds), *Writing the Range: Race, Class and Culture in the Women's West* (Norman: University of Oklahoma Press, 1997), 334–348.

22. San Francisco Lesbian and Gay Project, "She Even Chewed Tobacco: A Pictorial Narrative of Passing Women in America," in B. Duberman, M. Vicinus, and G. Chauncey Jnr., *Hidden from History: Reclaiming the Gay and Lesbian Past* (Penguin: London, 1989), 186; L. Sullivan, *Information for the Female-to-Male Cross Dresser and Transsexual* (San Francisco, CA: Haight Street, 1985), 1; Elizabeth Cady Stanton, "Women's Dress," *The Revolution*, 22 July 1869.

23. *New York Times*, 9 January 1880; Peter Boag, *Re-dressing America's Frontier Past* (Berkeley: University of California Press, 2011), 1; *Central City Weekly Register*, 26 July 1878;

Horace Greeley, *An Overland Journey from New York to San Francisco, in the Summer of 1859* (C.M. Saxton, Barker & Co., 1860), 85.

24. Albert D. Richardson, *Beyond the Mississippi: Life and Adventure on the Prairies, Mountains and Pacific Coast* (Hartford, CT: American Publishing Co., 1869), 200; Boag, *Re-dressing America's Frontier Past*, 34; San Francisco Lesbian and Gay Project, "She Even Chewed Tobacco," 184–185; San Francisco *Evening Bulletin*, 22 September 1862.

25. Susan Johnson, "'A Memory Sweet to Soldiers': The Significance of Gender in the History of the 'American West'," in Mary Ann Irwin and James Brooks (eds), *Women and Gender in the American West* (Albuquerque: University of New Mexico Press, 2004), 92; Peter Boag, "Go West Young Man, Go East Young Woman: Searching for the Trans in Western Gender History," *Western Historical Quarterly*, 36/4 (Winter 2005), 477–497; San Francisco Lesbian and Gay Project, "She Even Chewed Tobacco," 183–189; *Daily Alta California*, 16 September 1876.

26. Boag, *Re-dressing America's Frontier Past*, 6; Clare Sears, "Electric Brilliancy: Cross-Dressing Law and Freak Show Displays in 19th Century San Francisco," *Women's Studies Quarterly*, 36 (2008), 170–172; Schlatter, "Drag's a Life," 338.

27. Schlatter, "Drag's a Life," 342–343; Clare Sears, "'A Tremendous Sensation': Cross-Dressing in the 19th Century San Francisco Press," in L. Castaneda and S. Campbell (eds), *News and Sexuality: Media Portrayals of Diversity* (London: Sage, 2006), 18; San Francisco Lesbian and Gay Project, "She Even Chewed Tobacco," 189–191; Stockton *Evening Mail*, 17 September 1897; *San Francisco Sunday Examiner*, 24 October 1900.

28. Johnson, "A Memory Sweet to Soldiers," 93.

29. Bourke, *On the Border with Crook*, 299–300; *Norfolk News*, 13 July 1906; Horace Maguire, *The Coming Empire: A Complete and Reliable Treatise on the Black Hills, Yellowstone, and Big Horn Regions* (Sioux City, IA: Watkins & Smead, 1878), 65.

30. Lou Sullivan, quoted in Nan Alamilla Boyd, "Bodies in Motion: Lesbian and Transsexual Histories," in Susan Stryker and Stephen Whittle (eds), *The Transgender Studies Reader* (New York: Taylor & Francis, 2006), 423–424; Butler, *Gender Trouble*, 25.

31. Halberstam, *Female Masculinity*, 1–21; "Interview with Ernest A. Logan, Sept. 28, 1936," Series III, Box 35, Folder 1, Agnes Spring Papers, AHC.

32. Francis Hilton, "Calamity Jane," *Frontier Magazine* (September 1925), 105–109; Clarence Paine, "Calamity Jane: Man, Woman . . . or Both?," *Westerners' Brand Book, 1945–6* (Chicago, IL: Westerners, 1947), 69; Jucovy, *Searching for Calamity*, 68; Carolyn Gage, "Calamity Jane Sends a Message to her Daughter," available online at http://carolyn-gage.weebly.com/calamity-jane-sends-a-message-to-her-daughter-performance.html (accessed 20 March 2017).

CHAPTER 3

1. Cannary, *Life and Adventures.*

2. Argetsinger, "They Must Be Stars."

3. *Laramie Daily Sentinel*, 28 March 1877.

4. For biographies of Bill Hickok, see: Joseph Rosa, *Wild Bill Hickok: The Man and His Myth* (Lawrence: University Press of Kansas, 1996); Thadd M. Turner, *Wild Bill Hickok: Deadwood City—End of Trail* (Boca Raton, FL: Universal Publishers, 2001); Frank Wilstach, *Wild Bill Hickok: The Prince of Pistoleers* (Garden City, New York: Doubleday, 1926).

5. *Cheyenne Daily Leader*, 14 April 1876.

6. William B. Secrest (ed.), *I Buried Hickok: The Memoirs of White Eye Anderson* (College Station, TX: Creative Publishing, 1980), 93–99.

7. Richard Hughes, *Pioneer Years in the Black Hills* (Glendale, CA: Arthur H. Clark Co., 1957), 159–161; Deadwood *Black Hills Pioneer*, 15 July 1876; Charles W. Bocker, interview by Grace Raymond Hebard, Laramie, Wyoming, 9 August 1927, Grace Hebard Papers, AHC.

8. McLaird, *Calamity Jane*, 56.

9. Secrest, *I Buried Hickok*, 102; Deadwood *Black Hills Daily Times*, 7 May 1892; *Deadwood Daily Pioneer-Times*, 20 December 1899; Young, *Hard Knocks*, 205–206.

10. For competing analysis of prostitution and female agency in the West, see: Anne Butler, *Daughters of Joy, Sisters of Mercy: Prostitutes in the American West, 1865–90* (Urbana: University of Illinois Press, 1985) and Ruth Rosen, *The Lost Sisterhood: Prostitution in America, 1900–1918* (Baltimore, MD: Johns Hopkins University Press, 1982).

11. Young, *Hard Knocks*, 205–206; McGillycuddy, *McGillycuddy, Agent*, 62–64.

12. Bocker, interview; Adrienne Davis, "A Lady Among the Miners: The Experience of a New York Belle in the Black Hills," *New York Graphic*, 11 August 1877; Bullock quoted in McGillycuddy, *McGillycuddy, Agent*, 62.

13. Frank Luther Mott, *American Journalism: A History, 1690–1960* (New York: Macmillan, 1962), 282; McClintock, *Pioneer Days in the Black Hills*, 74.

14. Sally Foreman Griffith, *Home Town News: William Allen White and the Emporia Gazette* (New York: Oxford University Press, 1989), 159.

15. McLaird, *Calamity Jane*, 5; Deadwood *Black Hills Daily Times*, 21 September 1877.

16. *Cheyenne Daily Leader*, 16 August 1876; *Omaha Daily Herald*, 6 August 1876; *Cheyenne Daily Sun*, 11 May 1878.

17. *Cheyenne Weekly Leader*, 23 November 1876; *Cheyenne Daily Leader*, 27 July 1877.

18. *Cheyenne Daily Leader*, 7 July 1877; Lola Homsher, "Wyoming—From the State Archives, Historical Column Release 259," Wyoming State Archives and Historical Department, Box 6, Folder 5, William C. Rogers Papers, 1926–1993, AHC.

19. *Cheyenne Daily Sun*, 9 June 1877; *Cheyenne Daily Sun*, 7 July 1877; Portland *New Northwest*, 7 September 1877.

20. Horace Maguire, *The Black Hills and American Wonderland* (Chicago, IL: Donnelly, Lloyd & Co., 1877), 304.

21. Maguire, *The Coming Empire*, 49, 63–65.

22. Thomas Newson, *Drama of Life in the Black Hills* (Saint Paul, MN: Dodge & Larpenteur, 1878), 2, 35–39.

23. Daryl Jones, *The Dime Novel Western* (Bowling Green, OH: Popular Press, 1978), 26–119. Also see: Albert Johannsen, *The House of Beadle & Adams* (Norman: University of Oklahoma Press, 1950); J. Randolph Cox, *The Dime Novel Companion: A Source Book* (Westport, CT: Greenwood Publishing, 2000); Michael Denning, *Mechanic Accents: Dime Novels and Working-Class Culture in America* (New York: Verso, 1998).

24. Nancy Chu, "Women in the Frontier Dime Novel," *Books at Iowa*, 33 (November 1980), available online at www.lib.uiowa.edu/scua/bai/chu.htm (accessed 14 June 2019); Edward Wheeler, *Hurricane Nell, the Girl Dead Shot; or the Queen of the Saddle and Lasso*, Starr's Ten Cent Pocket Library No. 1 (4 May 1877).

25. Edward Wheeler, *Deadwood Dick, The Prince of the Road; or, The Black Rider of the Black Hills* (15 October 1877, 1/1), 6, 9, 19, 31. For comment as to the moral conservatism of the cross-dressing heroine in the dime novel, see Boag, *Re-dressing America's Frontier Past*, 108–109.

26. Edward Wheeler, *The Double Daggers; or, Deadwood Dick's Defiance* (21 December 1877, 1/20), 10, 18, 31; Edward Wheeler, *Deadwood Dick on Deck; or, Calamity Jane, the Heroine of Whoop-Up* (17 December 1878, 3/73), 1.

27. Wheeler, *Deadwood Dick on Deck*, 2.

28. Wheeler, *Deadwood Dick on Deck*, 3, 4, 24, 23, 31.

29. Edward Wheeler, *Deadwood Dick in Leadville; or, a Strange Stroke for Liberty* (24 June 1879, 4/100), 8, 22.

30. Edward Wheeler, *Deadwood Dick's Device; or, the Sign of the Double Cross* (22 July 1879, 4/104), 6, 17.

31. Edward Wheeler, *Blonde Bill; or, Deadwood Dick's Home Base* (16 March 1880, 6/138), 12; Boag, *Re-dressing America's Frontier Past*, 109.

32. Edward Wheeler, *A Game of Gold; or, Deadwood Dick's Big Strike* (1 June 1880, 6/149), 31; Edward Wheeler, *Deadwood Dick of Deadwood; or, the Picked Party* (20 July 1880,

6/156), 26–27, 32; Edward Wheeler, *Deadwood Dick's Doom; or, Calamity Jane's Last Adventure* (28 June 1881, 8/205), 13, 14.

33. Edward Wheeler, *Captain Crack-Shot, the Girl Brigand* (20 September 1881, 9/217); Edward Wheeler, *Gold Dust Dick, a Romance of Roughs and Toughs* (3 January 1882, 9/232), 30; Edward Wheeler, *Deadwood Dick's Divide; or, the Spirit of Swamp Lake* (8 August 1882, 11/263), 11; Edward Wheeler, *Deadwood Dick's Big Deal; or, the Gold Brick of Oregon* (26 June 1883, 12/309), 15; Edward Wheeler, *Deadwood Dick's Claim; or, the Fairy Face of Faro Flats* (1 July 1884, 14/362); Edward Wheeler, *Deadwood Dick's Diamonds; or, the Mystery of Joan Porter* (2 June 1885, 14/410); Edward Wheeler, *Deadwood Dick's Dust; or, The Chained Hand* (20 October 1885, 15/430).

34. Reckless Ralph, "Calamity Jane: The Queen of the Plains," *Street and Smith's New York Weekly*, 16, 23, 30 January; 20, 27 February; 13 March 1882; *Cheyenne Weekly Leader*, 19 January 1882.

35. "A Strange Woman," *Boys of England: A Journal of Sport, Travel, Fun and Instruction for the Youths of All Nations*, No. 738 (7 January 1881), 176.

36. Henry Llewellyn Williams, *Buffalo Bill* (London: Routledge, 1887); review cited in Ramon Frederick Adams, *Burs Under the Saddle* (Norman: University of Oklahoma Press, 1964), 571.

37. Wheeler, *Deadwood Dick of Deadwood; or, the Picked Party*, 23; Lillian Craton, *The Victorian Freak Show: The Significance of Disability and Physical Differences in 19th-Century Fiction* (New York: Cambria Press, 2009), 124. For discussion of the potential of the cross-dressing heroine to serve as role model in a time of redefined gender roles, see Nina Baym's study of Capitola Black in novelist Eliza Southworth's *The Hidden Hand* (1859), available online at www.english.illinois.edu/-people-/emeritus/baym/essays/southworth.htm#* (accessed 20 November 2017).

38. Mrs. William Loring Spencer, *Calamity Jane: A Story of the Black Hills* (New York: Cassell & Co., 1887), introduction; *Livingston Enterprise*, 17 September 1887; *New York Times*, 11 August 1887.

39. Spencer, *Calamity Jane*, 7, 8, 20, 22–25, 65, 74–79.

40. Spencer, *Calamity Jane*, 80, 82, 132. Also see Sharon Marcus, *Between Women: Friendship, Desire, and Marriage in Victorian England* (Princeton, NJ: Princeton University Press, 2007).

41. Paine, "Calamity Jane, Man, Woman . . . or Both?," 11; Etulain, *Life and Legends*, 141; Etulain, *Calamity Jane*, 199; Jucovy, *Searching for Calamity*, 107.

42. Jucovy, *Searching for Calamity*, 93; *Billings Gazette*, 11 January 1883.

43. *Sundance Gazette* quoted in Etulain, *Life and Legends*, 38; *Livingston Enterprise*, 13 April 1901; Newcom quoted in *Ismay Journal*, 28 June 1934, "Vertical Files: Calamity Jane," MHS.

44. *Rock Springs Miner*, 28 December 1893; *Bighorn Sentinel*, 14 April 1888.

45. *Sundance Gazette*, 10 January 1890; *Livingston Enterprise*, 14 March 1884, reprinted in Bill Whithorn and Doris Whithorn, *Calamity's in Town: The Town was Livingston* (Livingston, MT: Whithorn Publication, n.d.); *Cheyenne Daily Leader*, 12 March 1887.

46. *St. Louis Globe-Democrat*, 4 November 1885; *Cheyenne Daily Sun*, 28 November 1882.

47. *Cheyenne Daily Leader*, 3 November 1885.

48. *Cheyenne Daily Sun*, 3 January 1890.

49. Portland *Morning Oregonian*, 12 June 1890; *Cheyenne Daily Leader*, 21 June 1887.

CHAPTER 4

1. Cannary, *Life and Adventures*.

2. Roger Hall, *Performing the American Frontier, 1876–1906* (Cambridge: Cambridge University Press, 2001), 2.

3. Deadwood *Black Hills Daily Times*, 5 October 1895.

4. Deadwood *Black Hills Daily Times*, 5 October 1895.

5. *New York Times*, 13 May 1888; Hall, *Performing the American Frontier*, 160; Deadwood *Black Hills Daily Times*, 5 October 1895.

6. McLaird, *Calamity Jane*, 146; *Rapid City Daily Journal*, 7 May 1895.

7. *Lead Daily Call*, 9 November 1895; Deadwood *Black Hills Daily Times*, 5 November 1895.

8. Quoted in Foote, *A History of Calamity Jane*, 128; *Bill Barlow's Budget*, 16 October 1895; *Galveston Daily News*, 29 December 1895; *Sundance Gazette*, 18 October 1895; *Rawlins Republican*, 5 August 1903.

9. Fox, "Calamity Jane."

10. Fox, "Calamity Jane."

11. Fox, "Calamity Jane"; Jucovy, cited in Etulain, *Life and Legends*, 323.

12. Etulain, *Life and Legends*, 153–155; Fox, "Calamity Jane."

13. Fox, "Calamity Jane."

14. *Rapid City Daily Journal*, 6 July 1952; Deadwood *Black Hills Daily Times*, 9 January 1896.

15. Andrea Dennett, *Weird and Wonderful: The Dime Museum in America* (New York: New York Press, 1997), 315; Illustration for the "People's Popular Palace of Pleasure and Family Resort, Kohl and Middleton Vine Street Dime Museum, Cincinnati," printed in *The Cincinnati Illustrated Business Directory* (Cincinnati: Spencer and Craig, 1887–88), 47; Rachel Adams, *Sideshow USA: Freaks and the American Cultural Imagination* (Chicago, IL: University of Chicago Press, 2001), 11.

16. George Middleton, *Circus Memoirs* (Los Angeles, CA: G. Rice & Sons, 1913), 74; *Minneapolis Journal*, 20 January 1896; *Custer County Chronicle*, 3 January 1896.

17. *Chicago Inter Ocean*, 27 January 1896; Nolie Mumey, *Calamity Jane, 1852–1903: A History of Her Life and Adventures in the West* (Denver, CO: Range Press, 1950), 129; Deadwood *Black Hills Daily Times*, 30 January 1896.

18. *Chicago Inter Ocean*, 28 January 1896.

19. Sarah Grand, "The New Aspect of the Woman Question," *North American Review*, 158 (March 1894), 270–276; *Chicago Inter Ocean*, 28 January 1896.

20. William F. Cody, *The Adventures of Buffalo Bill Cody* (New York: Harper & Bros., 1904); Davy Crockett, *The Life and Adventures of Colonel David Crockett of Tennessee* (Cincinnati, OH: n.p., 1833); Cunningham, quoted in McLaird, *Calamity Jane*, 157.

21. Argetsinger, "They Must Be Stars"; Deadwood *Black Hills Daily Times*, 9 June 1896; McLaird, *Calamity Jane*, 157; Etulain, *Life and Legends*, 165.

22. *Butte Weekly Miner*, 15 October 1896; Will Frackelton, *Sagebrush Dentist* (Pasadena, CA: Trail's End Publishing Co., 1947), 122, 127, 129.

23. Frackelton, *Sagebrush Dentist*, 129, 130; Helena *Daily Independent*, 18 September 1896; *Anaconda Recorder*, 6 October 1896; *Livingston Post*, 11 August 1898; *Cheyenne Daily Sun*, 9 September 1898.

24. Frackelton, *Sagebrush Dentist*, 125, 126; Etulain, *Life and Legends*, 204; Jucovy, *Searching for Calamity*, 140; *Bozeman Avant Courier*, 16 February 1901.

25. *Cheyenne Daily Leader*, 26 February 1901; *Deadwood Daily Pioneer-Times*, 27 February 1901; *Livingston Enterprise*, 13 April 1901; *Livingston Post*, 13 June 1901.

26. *Livingston Post*, 11 July 1901; *Livingston Enterprise*, 13 July 1901; *Buffalo Evening News*, 12 July 1901; Rawlins *Carbon County Journal*, 13 July 1901. There were contested versions of this story, with Canary located in different western hideouts and less inclined to travel east, see McLaird, *Calamity Jane*, 192–193.

27. *Billings Times*, 18 July 1901; *Helena Evening Herald*, 16 July 1901; *Billings Gazette*, 16 July 1901.

28. *Helena Evening Herald*, 16 July 1901. Press comment on the Buffalo reception quoted in McLaird, *Calamity Jane*, 195.

29. *Cheyenne Daily Leader*, 3 August 1903. For the history of Smith, see Julia Bricklin, *America's Best Female Sharpshooter: The Rise and Fall of Lillian Frances Smith* (Norman: University of Oklahoma Press, 2017). Also see Philip J. Deloria, *Playing Indian* (New Haven, CT: Yale University Press, 1998).

30. *Buffalo Morning Express*, 4 August 1901; *Buffalo Evening News*, 4 August 1901; Cummins' program entry quoted in McLaird, *Calamity Jane*, 196; "Wirt Newcom Writes Interesting Account of His Experience with Frontier Character," *Miles City Daily Star*, 24 May 1934.

31. *Livingston Enterprise*, 21 September 1901; *Buffalo Evening News*, 9 August 1901; *Helena Evening Herald*, 25 September 1901.

32. *Livingston Enterprise*, 12 October 1901; *Cheyenne Daily Leader*, 9 October 1901; *Fergus County Argus*, 2 October 1901; *Livingston Enterprise*, 21 December 1901; *Livingston Enterprise*, 28 December 1901; *Livingston Post*, 24 April 1901.

33. "A Strange Woman," 176; Rosemary Garland Thomson (ed.), *Freakery: Cultural Spectacles of the Extraordinary Body* (New York: New York University Press, 1996), 5; *Miles City Yellowstone Journal*, 8 July 1882.

34. Nadja Durbach, *The Spectacle of Deformity: Freak Shows and Modern British Culture* (Berkeley: University of California Press, 2009), 1, 10; Middleton, *Circus Memoirs*, 70; *Minneapolis Journal*, 20 January 1896; *Chicago Inter Ocean*, 27 January 1896; Robert Bogdan, *Freak Show: Presenting Human Oddities for Amusement and Profit* (Chicago, IL: University of Chicago Press, 1988), 24; Thomson, *Freakery*, 24–32, 315. For cultural histories of freakery, see also: Michael Chemers, *Staging Stigma: A Critical Examination of the American Freak Show* (New York: Palgrave, 2008); Rosemary Garland Thomson, *Extraordinary Bodies: Figuring Disability in American Culture and Literature* (New York: Columbia University Press, 1997).

35. Thomson, *Freakery*, 10; Craton, *The Victorian Freak Show*, 2.

36. *Cheyenne Daily Leader*, 14 June 1877; Stockton *Evening Mail*, 27 August 1897; Archibald Gunter and Fergus Redmond, *A Florida Enchantment* (New York: Hurst, 1891); Middleton, *Circus Memoirs*, 75; Thomson, *Freakery*, 5; *Minneapolis Journal*, 20 January 1896.

37. Adams, *Sideshow USA*, 4–5; Elizabeth Stephens, *Anatomy as Spectacle: Public Exhibitions of the Body from 1700 to the Present* (Liverpool: Liverpool University Press, 2011), 87; Laura Mulvey, "Visual Pleasure and Narrative Cinema," *Screen*, 16 (Fall 1975), 6–18; Marlene Tromp (ed.), *Victorian Freaks: The Social Context of Freakery in Britain* (Columbus: Ohio State University Press, 2008), 8; Laurence Senelick, *The Changing Room: Sex, Drag and Theatre* (London: Routledge, 2000), 10; Thomson, *Freakery*, 25.

38. Thomson, *Freakery*, 10; Durbach, *Spectacle of Deformity*, 12.

39. San Francisco *Morning Call*, 28 January 1895; *San Francisco Examiner*, 7 February 1895.

40. Leslie Fiedler, *Freaks: Myths and Images of the Secret Self* (New York: Touchstone, 1978), 31; Durbach, *Spectacle of Deformity*, 9, 11; Thomson, *Freakery*, 10; Halberstam, *Female Masculinity*, 45.

41. Clare Sears, *Arresting Dress: Cross-Dressing, Law, and Fascination in Nineteenth-Century San Francisco* (Durham, NC: Duke University Press, 2014), 97; *Cheyenne Daily Leader*, 24 April 1901.

42. Senelick, *Changing Room*, 332.

43. Review of a performance at the Metropolitan Music Hall, Washington, D.C. in "Music Halls," New York *Clipper*, 19 December 1868; review of a performance at the Adelphi Theatre, Galveston, Texas in "Variety Halls," New York *Clipper*, 16 December 1876; *Grand Rapids Evening Leader*, 7 June 1886; Senelick, *Changing Room*, 332; Grand Rapids *Telegram-Herald*, 7 June 1886.

44. Elizabeth Drorbaugh, "Sliding Scales," in Lesley Ferris, *Crossing the Stage: Controversies on Cross-Dressing* (London: Routledge, 1993), 136; Senelick, *Changing Room*, 327; Tilley, quoted in Sullivan, *Information for the Female-to-Male Crossdresser*, 5; W.R. Titterton, *From Theatre to Music Hall* (London: Stephen Swift, 1912), 151; Katie Rebecca Horowitz, "The Trouble with 'Queerness': Drag and the Making of Two Cultures," University of California, Berkeley, PhD, 2012, 50–51.

45. Laura Horak, *Girls Will be Boys: Cross-Dressed Women, Lesbians and American Cinema, 1908–1934* (New York: Rutgers University Press, 2016), 2; Carroll Smith-Rosenberg, "Discourses of Sexuality and Subjectivity: The New Woman, 1870–1936," in Duberman

et al., *Hidden from History*, 264–280; Richard von Krafft-Ebing, *Psychopathia Sexualis* (New York: Arcade, 1965 [1886]), 264; Boag, *Re-dressing America's Frontier Past*, 104, 128; Douglas' letter to the *Washington Post* reprinted in the Cheyenne *Wyoming Tribune Eagle*, 17 October 1903; Corn quoted in *Grand Encampment Herald*, 22 July 1903.

46. "Buffalo Bill's Wild West—America's National Entertainment," 1884 Program, 14. Held at the Buffalo Bill Historical Center, Cody, Wyoming (hereafter BBHC). For Cody and the "wild West" show, see Joy S. Kasson, *Buffalo Bill's Wild West: Celebrity, Memory, and Popular History* (New York: Hill & Wang, 2000); L. Moses, *Wild West Shows and the Images of American Indians, 1883–1933* (Albuquerque: University of New Mexico Press, 1996); Paul Reddin, *Wild West Shows* (Chicago: University of Illinois Press, 1999); Robert Rydell and Rob Kroes, *Buffalo Bill in Bologna: The Americanization of the World, 1869–1922* (Chicago, IL: University of Chicago Press, 2005); Richard Slotkin, *Gunfighter Nation: The Myth of the Frontier in Twentieth Century America* (New York: Atheneum, 1992), 63–87; Warren, *Buffalo Bill's America*; White, "Frederick Jackson Turner and Buffalo Bill," 7–65.

47. Warren, *Buffalo Bill's America*, 248; Nashville *Barrier*, 28 March 1891. Biographical treatments of Oakley include: Courtney Ryley Cooper, *Annie Oakley: Woman at Arms* (London: Hurst & Blackett, 1927); Glenda Riley, *The Life and Legacy of Annie Oakley* (Norman: University of Oklahoma Press, 1994); Walter Havighurst, *Annie Oakley of the Wild West* (London: Robert Hale, 1955); Shirl Kasper, *Annie Oakley* (Norman: University of Oklahoma Press, 1992); Isabelle S. Sayers, *Annie Oakley and Buffalo Bill's Wild West* (New York: Dover Publications, 1981); Annie Swartout, *Missie: An Historical Biography of Annie Oakley* (Blanchester, OH: Brown Publishing Co., 1947); McMurtry, *The Colonel and Little Missie*.

48. Riley, *Life and Legacy*, 146; London *Evening News*, 10 May 1884.

49. Oakley recounted her autobiography in *The Story of My Life* (n.p.: NEA Service, 1926); Fellows, quoted in Warren, *Buffalo Bill's America*, 248; Annie Oakley, *The Rifle Queen: Annie Oakley* (London: General Publishing Co., 1884), 3; Riley, *Life and Legacy*, 126.

50. Riley, *Life and Legacy*, 160–161; Fred Stone, quoted in Sayers, *Annie Oakley*, 85; Oakley, *Rifle Queen*, 3. See also Tracey Davis, "Annie Oakley and the Ideal Husband of No Importance," in *Critical Theory and Performance*, ed. Janelle Reinert and Joseph Roach (Ann Arbor: University of Michigan Press, 1992), 299–312; Tracey C. Davis, "Shotgun Wedlock: Annie Oakley's Power Politics in the Wild West," in Laurence Senelick (ed.), *Gender and Performance: The Presentation of Difference in the Performing Arts* (Hanover, NH: University Press of New England, 1992), 153–154.

51. *Livingston Enterprise*, 7 June 1902; *Butte Inter Mountain*, 17 June 1902.

52. *Great Falls Tribune*, 18 January 1903.

53. *Great Falls Tribune*, 18 January 1903.

CHAPTER 5

1. Jennewein, *Calamity Jane*, 8–10; "Calamity Jane to her Last Rest" (undated), Folder 1, "Biographical File—Canary, Martha Jane," Seymour Papers, AHC.

2. *Livingston Enterprise*, 21 June 1902.

3. Mumey, *Calamity Jane*, 133–134; *Deadwood Weekly Pioneer Times*, 6 August 1903.

4. *Aberdeen Daily News*, 16 April 1902; John Mayo to J. Leonard Jennewein, 9 November 1952, Jenn.

5. *Deadwood Daily Pioneer-Times*, 2 August 1903; *Deadwood Daily Pioneer-Times*, 8 August 1903; E.C. Abbott and Helena Huntington Smith, *We Pointed Them North: Recollections of a Cowpuncher* (New York: Smith, Farrar, and Rinehart, 1939), 76; Bennett, *Old Deadwood Days*, 220.

6. San Antonio paper cited in the *Tombstone Epitaph*, 9 April 1936.

7. Don Russell, *The Lives and Legends of Buffalo Bill* (Norman: University of Oklahoma Press, 1960), 469; Louisa Cody and Courtney Ryley Cooper, *Memories of Buffalo Bill* (New York: D. Appleton, 1919), 324; "Buffalo Bill Cody's Burial Mystery Survives

Century Since His Death," *Capital Journal*, 13 January 2017, available at: www.capjournal.com/news/buffalo-bill-cody-s-burial-mystery-survives-century-since-his/article_0ca6b7a4-d966-11e6-8169-dfe16ba92348.html (accessed 25 January 2018); Mark Boardman, "Buffalo Bill Lies Here—Or Here," *True West Magazine*, 7 December 2016, available at: https://truewestmagazine.com/buffalo-bill-lies-here-or-here/ (accessed 25 January 2018).

8. *Belle Fouche Bee*, 6 August 1903.

9. *Cheyenne Daily Leader*, 3 August 1903.

10. *Rawlins Republican*, 5 August 1903; *Livingston Post*, 6 August 1903; Argetsinger, "They Must Be Stars."

11. *Bozeman Avant Courier*, 7 August 1903.

12. *Deadwood Daily Pioneer-Times*, 8 August 1903; *Deadwood Daily Pioneer-Times*, 9 August 1903; *Deadwood Daily Pioneer-Times*, 23 August 1903. For a valuable exploration of authenticity as a critical motif in the western literary canon, see Nathaniel Lewis, *Unsettling the Literary West: Authenticity and Authorship* (Lincoln: University of Nebraska Press, 2003), 1–18.

13. *Livingston Enterprise*, 8 August 1903.

14. *Princeton Press*, 12 August 1903; Princeton *Telegram*, 12 August 1903; *New York Times*, 2 August 1903.

15. London *Daily Mail*, 4 August 1903; London *Star*, 7 August 1903.

16. Etulain, *Life and Legends*, 216–218; McLaird, *Calamity Jane*, 221.

17. Josiah Ward, "Wild West Heroine the Movies Overlook," *New York Tribune*, 16 October 1921.

18. Riley, *Life and Legacy*, 163, 171; Horak, *Girls Will Be Boys*, 2, 13–14.

19. William Allen, *Adventures with Indians and Game* (New York: A.W. Bowen, 1903), 32–33; entry from *Progressive Men of the State of Wyoming* (New York: A.W. Bowen, 1903), Box 8, Folder 3, William C. Rogers Papers, AHC; Mumey, *Calamity Jane*, 133.

20. George Hoshier, "Women of the Frontier: Stories of Odd Characters of Thirty Years Ago," *Norfolk News*, 13 July 1906.

21. Jack Crawford, "The Truth about Calamity," *The Journalist*, 5 March 1904, "Clippings (books, newspapers, etc.) Calamity Jane, 1856–1903," MS322 John Wallace Crawford Collection, McCracken Library, BBHC; Darlis Miller, *Captain Jack Crawford: Buckskin Poet, Scout, and Showman* (Albuquerque: University of New Mexico Press, 1993), 247.

22. Crawford, "The Truth."

23. Crawford, "The Truth"; *Anaconda Standard*, 19 April 1904.

24. Jack Crawford, "The Womanhood of Man," poem by Jack Crawford, John Wallace Crawford Collection, BBHC; Miller, *Captain Jack Crawford*, 263.

25. W.G. Patterson, "Calamity Jane: A Heroine of the Wild West," *Wild World*, 11 (September 1903), 450–457; Prentiss Ingraham, "Buffalo Bill and Calamity Jane, or, a Real Lady from the Black Hills," *New Buffalo Bill Weekly*, No. 177 (New York: Street & Smith, 1916).

26. Robert McReynolds, *Where Strongest Tide Winds Blew* (Colorado Springs, CO: Gowdy-Symonds, 1907); Jack Sinclair, "The Cowboy's Dream" (1916), MIMSY 88.101, Autry National Center, Los Angeles (hereafter Autry); London *Times*, 8 January 1912; Samuel F. Cody, "Calamity Jane," Samuel Franklin Cody Papers, 1888–1913, Autry.

27. *In the Days of '75 and '76* (Black Hills Feature Film Co., USA, 1915); *Douglas Enterprise*, 12 October 1915; Etulain, *Life and Legends*, 220.

28. William Visscher, *Buffalo Bill's Own Story of his Life and Deeds* (Chicago, IL: Homewood Press, 1917), 339; Wilstach, *Wild Bill Hickok*; William Elsey Connelley, *Wild Bill and His Era* (New York: Press of the Pioneers, 1933); Stuart Lake, *Wyatt Earp: Frontier Marshal* (New York: Houghton Mifflin, 1931); John Mack Faragher, "The Tale of Wyatt Earp," in M.C. Carnes (ed.), *Past Imperfect* (New York: Henry Holt, 1996), 154–161; Connelley, *Wild Bill and His Era*, 184. For a critical biographical history of Earp that examines his life with precision and situates him in a western context, see Isenberg, *Wyatt Earp*.

29. *Wild Bill Hickok* (dir. by Clifford Smith, Paramount Pictures, USA, 1923).
30. Whithorn and Whithorn, *Calamity's in Town*, 24; *Casper Herald*, 8 April 1921; *Casper Daily Tribune*, 7 April 1921; *New York Times*, 4 August 1933.
31. Seymour Pond, "Frontier Still Recalls 'Calamity Jane'," *New York Times*, 18 October 1925; *Great Falls Tribune*, 25 October 1925; *Judith Basin Star*, 5 November 1925; *Cody Enterprise*, 18 November 1925.
32. Dan Conway, "Calamity Jane: Unique Character of Old Frontier—her Deadwood Romance; 'Wild Bill' was her ideal of man," Montana News Association, 4 October 1926, MHS.
33. *New York Times*, 12 January 1927; *Casper Daily Tribune*, 25 November 1921.
34. *Casper Daily Tribune*, 25 November 1921; *Rock Springs Miner*, 20 October 1933.
35. *Bozeman Avant Courier*, 17 May 1929; Lock Sutley, *The Last Frontier* (New York, Macmillan, 1930), 267.
36. Lewis Freeman, *Down the Yellowstone* (New York: Dodd, Mead & Co., 1922), 70–90.
37. Freeman, *Down the Yellowstone*, 70–90.
38. George Stokes & Howard Driggs, *Deadwood Gold: A Story of the Black Hills* (London: George Harrap & Co., 1926), v, 75, 77; Brown and Willard, *The Black Hills Trails*, 411–418; Earl Brininstool, *Fighting Red Cloud's Warriors* (Columbus, OH: The Hunter-Trader-Trapper, 1926), 333.
39. Aikman, *Calamity Jane*, xii, xv–xviii, 59.
40. Aikman, *Calamity Jane*, 4–5, 12, 33, 37.
41. Aikman, *Calamity Jane*, 53, 68, 85, 90–94.
42. "She was a 'Lady Wildcat,' undated clipping, Folder 2, "Biographical File," AHC; Argetsinger, "They Must Be Stars."
43. *New York Tribune*, 11 December 1927; *New York Times*, 11 January 1928.
44. On gender renegotiation and the "new woman" of the interwar period, see: Smith-Rosenberg, "Diseases of Sexuality and Subjectivity," 265, 278; Susan Gubar, "Blessings in Disguise: Cross-dressing as Redressing for Female Modernists," *Massachusetts Review*, 22/3 (1981), 477–508.
45. M.F. Belenky, B.M. Clinchy, N.R. Goldberger and J.M. Tarule, *Women's Ways of Knowing* (New York: Basic Books, 1986); Bennett, *Old Deadwood Days*, 217–243.
46. Dee, *Low Down on Calamity Jane*, front and back covers, 1–12.

CHAPTER 6

1. *Buffalo Bulletin*, 2 May 1935.
2. Jackie Stacey surveyed women's responses to Hollywood stars in the 1940s and 1950s for *Star Gazing: Hollywood Cinema and Female Spectatorship* (London: Routledge, 1994), 203.
3. Etulain, *Life and Legends*, 271; *Cheyenne State Leader*, 9 March 1936; Argetsinger, "They Must Be Stars."
4. *The Plainsman* (1936). For details on discussions between DeMille and scriptwriters as to preparation, film actors and content, see Etulain, *Life and Legends*, 262–263.
5. Horak, *Girls Will Be Boys*, 223; Iron Eyes Cody and Collin Perry, *Iron Eyes: My Life as a Hollywood Indian* (London: Frederick Muller, 1982), 198.
6. *Annie Oakley* (USA, dir. by George Stephens, RKO Pictures, 1935).
7. Rebecca Bell-Metereau, *Hollywood Androgyny* (New York: Columbia University Press, 1985), 82; Anna Louise Bates, "Calamity Jane and the Social Construction of Gender in the 1930s and 1950s," *Popular Culture Review*, 16/2 (2005), 70.
8. *Variety*, 20 January 1937; *New York Times*, 14 January 1937; *New York Times*, 17 January 1937; unknown newspaper, 5 August 1937, "Vertical Files: Calamity Jane," MHS.
9. *Caught* (dir. by Edward Sloman, Paramount Pictures, USA, 1931); *Deadwood Dick* (dir. by James W. Horne, Columbia Pictures, USA, 1940); *Young Bill Hickok* (dir. by Joseph Kane, Republic, USA,1940); *Badlands of Dakota* (dir. by Alfred E. Green, Universal, USA,1941); James Card, *Seductive Cinema* (New York: Alfred Knopf, 1994), 215.

10. Elizabeth Stevenson, *Figures in a Western Landscape* (Baltimore, MD: Johns Hopkins University Press, 1994), 149; "Frank Brown/The Lone Ranger Meets Calamity Jane," Program #1751/971, Air date 10 April 1944, available online at www.otrcat.net/otr6/LR-440410-0971-Calamity-Jane-7o16-OTRCAT.com.mp3 (accessed 4 May 2018).

11. *Calamity Jane and Sam Bass* (dir. by George Sherman, Universal, USA, 1949); *The Texan Meets Calamity Jane* (dir. by Ande Lamb, Columbia Pictures, USA, 1950).

12. *The Paleface* (dir. by Norman Z. McLeod, Paramount Pictures, USA, 1948).

13. McLaird and Etulain both cite Oakes as the biological daughter of Calamity Jane, her father most likely being Bill Steers. For correspondence on her, see: Box 2, Folder 22: "Correspondence with Jean Hickok McCormick," Paine; Etulain, *Life and Legends*, 139–140, 236–239; McLaird, *Calamity Jane*, 249; "Report of an Interview with Mrs. Jean McCormick, Self-Styled Daughter of Jane Hickok, 'Calamity Jane,' Chicago, May 11, 1941," Box 2, Folder 22, Paine.

14. "Calamity Jane's Diary and Letters, taken for an exhibit at the Wonderland Museum, Billings, MT," (c.1951), Autry. This material was published in various forums, including: Mumey, *Calamity Jane* and Martha Jane Cannary Hickok, *Calamity Jane's Letters to Her Daughter* (San Lorenzo, CA: Shameless Hussy Press, 1976).

15. *La Crosse Tribune*, 15 September 1941; *Rapid City Daily Journal*, 12 September 1941; *Abilene Daily Chronicle*, 13 June 1941; *Billings Gazette*, 14 June 1941.

16. Letter (and encs.) from Vivien Skinner, We the People, to Marion Schumacher, Yellowstone County Dept. of Welfare, 6 August 1941: Box 2, Folder 20: "Calamity Jane C.S. Paine Correspondence," Paine; *Great Falls Tribune*, 20 November 1941; letter from William Lull to Jean McCormick, 4 July 1941, Box 2, Folder 22, Paine; letter from J. Almus Russell to Jean McCormick, 12 February 1942, Box 25: "Calamity Jane/McCormick," Jenn.

17. Letter from Vivien Skinner to Carl Anderson, 15 September: Box 2, Folder 20, Paine; letter from Jean McCormick to J. Almus Russell, 8 February 1942, Box 25, Jenn; Letter to Charles Bovey from Jean McCormick, 23 June 1937, MHS; Argetsinger, "They Must Be Stars."

18. *Billings Gazette*, 14 June 1941; Letter from Vivien Skinner to Clarence Paine, 15 September 1942, Box 2, Folder 20, Paine. Also see: James McLaird, "Calamity Jane's Diary and Letters: The Story of Fraud," *Montana: The Magazine of Western History*, 45 (1995), 20.

19. Clarence Paine typed and annotated copies of the diary entries, confession, and last will and testament. See: Box 2, Folder 20 and Box 3, Folder 12: "Manuscript/Original Newspaper Copies, Articles of Calamity," Paine. See also: Mumey, *Calamity Jane* and Cannary Hickok, *Calamity Jane's Letters to Her Daughter*.

20. For the diary and associated documents, see: Box 2, Folder 20 and Box 3, Folder 12, Paine.

21. Box 2, Folder 20 and Box 3, Folder 12, Paine.

22. Box 2, Folder 20 and Box 3, Folder 12, Paine.

23. Letter from Will G. Robinson, Secretary, South Dakota Historical Society to George Simmons, Cedar Rapids, Iowa, 5 February 1952, MHS; Letter from A.O. Burton to Gale Heatter, We the People, 9 May 1941; Letter from John Milek to Clarence Paine, 17 April 1945 and other related correspondence. All in Box 2, Folder 20, Paine; Letter from Lola Homsher, Wyoming State Archivist, to George Simmons, Cedar Rapids, Iowa, 15 February 1952, MHS.

24. "The last will and testament of Calamity Jane; or, she laid her pistol down" (1946), Box 3, Folder 14: "Misc Calamity Jane," Paine; Letter from Clarence Paine to Helen Smith, Port Jefferson, New York, 1 December 1954, Box 2, Folder 22, Paine; Letter from Clarence Paine to John Milek, 20 April 1945, Box 2, Folder 20, Paine; Letter from Vivien Skinner to Clarence Paine, 15 September 1942, Box 2, Folder 20, Paine; Stevenson, *Figures in a Western Landscape*, 172, 170, 164.

25. Examples include Abbott and Smith, *We Pointed Them North*; McGillyguddy, *McGilly-cuddy, Agent*; Frackelton, *Sagebrush Dentist*; McClintock, *Pioneer Days in the Black Hills*, 115.
26. McClintock, *Pioneer Days in the Black Hills*, 117, 115, 1.
27. Edward Senn, *Deadwood Dick and Calamity Jane: A Thorough Sifting of Facts from Fiction* (Deadwood, SD: n.p., 1939), 10, 13; Stewart Holbrook, *Annie Oakley and Other Rugged People* (New York: Macmillan, 1948), 31–36; Harold E. Briggs, "The Calamity Jane Myth," in *Frontiers of the Northwest: A History of the Upper Missouri Valley* (New York: Peter Smith, 1950 [1940]), 78–79.
28. Etulain, *Life and Legends*, 258.
29. Ethel Hueston, *Calamity Jane of Deadwood Gulch* (London: Hodder & Stoughton, 1938), 9; *New York Times*, 3 October 1937.
30. Hueston, *Calamity Jane*, 73, 82
31. Hueston, *Calamity Jane*, 133, 245, 280.
32. Federal Writers' Project, *Montana: A State Guide Book* (New York: Hastings House, 1939), 194; Glendolin Wagner, "Calamity Jane," *Choteau Acantha* (c.1936), MHS.
33. Deadwood *Black Hills Weekly Tribune*, 29 July 1938.
34. Joe Simon and Jack Kirby, "The Case of the Hapless Hackie," *Green Hornet: Boy's Explorer 1* (May 1946), 39–46.
35. *Calamity Jane* (1953); A.E. Hotchner, *Doris Day: Her Own Story* (New York: Morrow, 1976), 131.
36. *Annie Get Your Gun* (dir. by George Sidney, Metro-Goldwyn-Mayer, USA, 1950).
37. *Variety*, 21 October 1953; *New York Times*, 5 November 1953; London *Daily Mail*, 5 February 1954.
38. Mizejewski, "Calamity Jane and Female Masculinity in *Deadwood*," 185; London *Daily Mail*, 5 February 1954; Elaine Tyler May, *Homeward Bound: American Families in the Cold War Era* (New York: Basic Books, 1988); Eric Savoy, "That Ain't All She Ain't: Doris Day and Queer Performativity," in Ellis Hanson (ed.), *Outtakes: Essays on Queer Theory and Film* (New York: Duke University Press, 1999), 152.
39. Tamar Jeffers McDonald, *Hollywood Catwalk* (London: I.B. Tauris, 2010), 141–66; Yvonne Tasker, *Working Girls: Gender and Sexuality in Popular Cinema* (London: Routledge, 2002), 58–59. See also Tamar Jeffers McDonald, "Carrying Concealed Weapons: Gendered Makeover in *Calamity Jane*," *Journal of Film and Popular Television*, 34 (2007), 179–187.
40. Savoy, "That Ain't All She Ain't," 161, 151, 153; Mandy Merck, "Travesty on the Old Frontier," in Jane Clarke and Diana Symonds (eds), *Move Over Misconceptions* (London: BFI, 1980), 47; Emma Simmonds, "Calamity Jane: Creating a Myth," London Lesbian and Film Festival, Features Archive, 2006. Available online at: www.llgff.org.uk (accessed 29 June 2018). For queer readings of the film, see also Vito Russo, *The Celluloid Closet: Homosexuality in the Movies* (New York: Harper, 1987).
41. Bates, "Calamity Jane," 76; Armond White, "The First Gay Anthem: Secret Love," *Out Magazine*, 29 June 2017. Available online at: www.out.com/armond-white/2017/6/29/first-gay-anthem-calamity-janes-secret-love (accessed 17 June 2019).
42. Mair Rigby, "Gender Possibility/Gender Calamity: *Calamity Jane* (1953)." Available online at: https://purpleprosearchive.wordpress.com/2012/02/06/gender-calamitygen-der-possibility-calamity-jane-1953-2 (accessed 18 March 2019); Savoy, "That Ain't All She Ain't," 173; Barbara Creed, "Lesbian Bodies," in Elizabeth Grosz and Elspeth Probyn (eds), *Sexy Bodies: The Strange Carnalities of Feminism* (London: Routledge, 2013), 95; Manchester *Guardian*, 7 April 2016.
43. *Rapid City Daily Journal*, 6 July 1952; Anderson, quoted in McLaird, *Calamity Jane*, 236; *Rapid City Daily Journal*, 18 October 1953.
44. Letter from Doris Thompson to Clarence Paine, 11 July 1957 and "Calamity Jane Roadside Park Dedicated" (undated clipping), see: Box 2, Folder 23: "Reprints of Newspaper Articles," Paine; Doris Thompson, "Princeton Claims Fame as Calamity Jane Birth-

place," Princeton *Post Telegraph*, 25 July 1957; "Mercer County, Missouri Historical Markers," available online at: www.waymarking.com/waymarks/WMJA0W_Mercer_County (accessed 17 March 2017); brief details of the site contained in "Notes: Field Trip," William C. Rogers Papers, Box 8, Folder 2, AHC.

45. For the story of the Shufflebottom family, see entry at the National Fairground and Circus Archive, Sheffield, UK, available online at: www.sheffield.ac.uk/nfca/researchan-darticles/wildwestshows (accessed 20 March 2018).

46. Robert Casey, *The Black Hills and their Incredible Characters* (Indianapolis, IN: Bobbs Merrill, 1949), 175–176; Paine, "Calamity Jane: Man, Woman . . . or Both?," 69–82.

47. Mumey, *Calamity Jane*, xvii, xviii, 21, 38–39, 30–31.

48. Glenn Clairmonte, *Calamity Was the Name for Jane* (Denver, CO: Sage Books, 1959), 5, 1; Jennewein quoted in Etulain, *Life and Legends*, 250.

49. Jennewein, *Calamity Jane*, 6–7.

50. Etulain, *Life and Legends*, 252; McLaird, *Calamity Jane*, 253; Sollid, *Calamity Jane*, xiii.

51. Sollid, *Calamity Jane*, xvii, xviii.

52. Argetsinger, "They Must Be Stars"; Andrew Blewitt, "Calamity Jane," *The English Westerners' Brand Book*, 5/2 (January 1963), 1.

CHAPTER 7

1. *Muppet Babies*, Episode 709: "Buckskin Babies," 22 September 1990; *Beano*, 1 November 1986; Argetsinger, "They Must Be Stars."

2. Etulain, *Life and Legends*, 24; Patricia Limerick, *Legacy of Conquest: The Unbroken Past of the American West* (New York: W.W. Norton, 2011 [1987]), 26.

3. *The Raiders* (dir. by Herschel Daugherty, Universal, USA, 1963).

4. *Bonanza*, "Calamity Over the Comstock," 5/7 (November 1963); *Death Valley Days*, "A Calamity Called Jane" (29 December 1966); *Have Gun Will Travel*, "The Cure," 4/35 (20 May 1961).

5. London *Daily Telegraph*, 25 July 2014.

6. J.T. Edson, *Trouble Trail* (London: Brown & Watson, 1965), 6; J.T. Edson, *The Bull Whip Breed* (London: Brown & Watson, 1965), 4, 11, 15, 20.

7. Harry Drago, *Notorious Ladies of the Frontier* (New York: Dodd & Mead, 1969); A. Bertram Chandler, *Rim of Space* (New York: Avalon, 1961). Available online at https://books.google.co.uk/books?id=1ULFCgAAQBAJ&pg=PT7&lpg=PT7&dq=the+rim+of+space+-chandler+huskily+attractive&source=bl&ots=8AIqIgjETW&sig=lsTDciw9Bd7QkXQF_gVBTCZ-PyM&hl=en&sa=X&ved=0ahUKEwjkss3HkqvbAhUMBsAKHVL-jC3oQ6AEIODAC#v=onepage&q=the%20rim%20of%20space%20chandler%20huskily%20attractive&f=false (accessed 14 August 2017); Martin Nussbaum, "Sociological Symbolism of the 'Adult Western'," *Social Forces*, 39/1 (1960), 25–28; Etulain, *Calamity Jane*, 195.

8. Mercer County *Pioneer Press*, 1 October 1966; Princeton *Post Telegraph*, 18 October 1962; "6th Annual Calamity Jane Day," Program, Box 6, Folder 3, William C. Rogers Papers, 1926–1993, AHC; Princeton *Post Telegraph*, 22 September 1966; Princeton *Post Telegraph*, 6 October 1966.

9. Livingston *Park County News*, 2 December 1960; Livingston *Park County News*, 8 December 1960; Livingston *Park County News*, 29 December 1960; Livingston *Park County News*, 1 December 1960; John McLain Watkins, "Calamity Jane: A Pageant Drama in Three Acts," Montana State University, Masters thesis, 1961.

10. *Deadwood Daily Pioneer-Times*, 30 July 1965.

11. Irma Klock, *Here Comes Calamity Jane* (Deadwood, SD: Dakota Graphics, 1979); Whithorn and Whithorn, *Calamity's in Town*; "Calamity Jane—Her Life and Times" (n.d.), Box 7, Folder 78, William C. Rogers Papers, AHC; Letter from Virginia Scully to Elizabeth Otis, 6 November 1965, Box 2, Folder 1, William C. Rogers Papers, AHC.

12. Interview with George Wolf, 29 December 1964; Interview with Ray Ewing, 18 December 1964; Interview with Bill Shikel and Elmer Nelson, 28 December 1964: All

held in Box 1, Folder 6, William C. Rogers Papers, AHC; "Second Draft" (n.d.), Box 1, Folder 7, William C. Rogers Papers, AHC.

13. "An Outline for Calamity Jane—Her Life and Times" (n.d.), Box 2, Folder 1, William C. Rogers Papers, AHC.

14. Letter from William C. Rogers to James McCormack, 18 January 1865; "Calamity Jane," (n.d.); "Synopsis Beginning Chapter 2" (n.d.). Held in Box 2, Folder 1, William C. Rogers Papers, AHC.

15. *The Ballad of Josie* (dir. by Andrew V. McLaglen, Universal, USA, 1967); Butler, *Gender Trouble.*

16. Morris and Goscinny, *Calamity Jane: A Lucky Luke Adventure No. 8* (Paris: Dargaud, 1971 [1967]), 5, 6, 46.

17. *Little Big Man* (dir. by Arthur Penn, National General Pictures, USA, 1970).

18. *This Is the West That Was* (dir. by Fielder Cook, NBC-TV, USA, 1974).

19. *Calamity Jane* (dir. by James Goldstone, CBS-TV, USA, 1984).

20. Peter Dexter, *Deadwood* (New York: Penguin, 1986); Etulain, *Life and Legends*, 286; Etulain, *Calamity Jane*, 179.

21. Larry McMurtry, *Buffalo Girls* (New York: Simon & Schuster, 1990), 6, 14, 30; *New York Times*, 7 October 1990.

22. McMurtry, *Buffalo Girls*, 30, 109–110, 66–67.

23. McMurtry, *Buffalo Girls*, 40–41, 72, 31, 6, 187.

24. McMurtry, *Buffalo Girls*, 153, 334.

25. McMurtry, *Buffalo Girls*, 330.

26. Riley, "Images of the Frontierswoman," 189–202.

27. Foote, *History of Calamity Jane*, ix, 66, 53.

28. Ron Fontes and Justine Korman, *Calamity Jane at Fort Sanders* (New York: Disney Press, 1992); *Tall Tale* (dir. by Jeremiah S. Chechik, Walt Disney Pictures, USA, 1995).

29. *Bad Girls* (dir. by Jonathan Kaplan, Twentieth Century Fox, USA, 1994); *The Quick and the Dead* (dir. by Sam Raimi, TriStar Pictures, USA, 1995); *The Ballad of Little Jo* (dir. by Maggie Greenwald, Fine Line Features, USA, 1993); *Wild Bill* (dir. by Walter Hill, United Artists, USA, 1995); *Buffalo Girls* (dir. by Rod Hardy, CBS-TV, USA, 1995).

30. *Legend of Calamity Jane* (dir. by Pascal Morelli, Canal +/France 3, France, 1997–98).

31. Martine Bellen, "Calamity Jane," *Conjunctions*, 24 (1995), 277–286; Anne Browning, "Kaleidoscopic Poetry," *American Book Review*, 37/5 (July/August 2016), 25.

32. Sybille Pearson, *True History and Real Adventures* (Vineyard Theatre, New York, 1999). Details available online at: www.vineyardtheatre.org/true-history-real-adventures/ (accessed 27 June 2019); Anita Gates, "Review: *True History and Real Adventures*," *New York Times*, 20 December 1999.

33. Gillian Robinson, *The Slow Reign of Calamity Jane* (Kingston, ON: Quarry Press, 1994), 8, 37, 122, 123.

34. Carolyn Gage, *The Second Coming of Joan of Arc and Selected Plays* (Denver, CO: Outskirts Press, 2008), vi, ii; author's correspondence with Carolyn Gage, 10 May 2018.

35. Gage, *Second Coming*, vi, 76, 77; author's correspondence with Carolyn Gage, 10 May 2018.

36. Forrest Hartman, "Myth Versus Truth in the Life of Calamity Jane: Ask Glenda Bell," *Humanities*, 36/4 (July/August 2015). Available online at: www.neh.gov/human ities/2015/julyaugust/statement/myth-versus-truth-in-the-life-calamity-jane-ask-glen da-bell (accessed 10 April 2018); "Here Comes Calamity!," *Deadwood Magazine* (n.d.). Available online at: www.deadwoodmagazine.com/archivedsite/Archives/Calamity Jane.htm (accessed 24 May 2018); Gleason, quoted in Laura Browder, *Her Best Shot: Women and Guns in America* (Chapel Hill: University of North Carolina Press, 2006), 18; Genevieve Schmitt, " 'Calamity Jane' Returns to Montana," Montana Living website, 3 October 2004. Available online at: www.montanaliving.com/blogs/people/calamity -jane-returns-to-montana (accessed 24 May 2018).

CONCLUSION

1. "Find a Grave." Available online at: www.findagrave.com/memorial/166/martha-jane-canary (accessed 7 June 2018).
2. Margot Mifflin, "The Real Calamity Jane," *Salon Magazine*, 5 December 2005, available online at: www.salon.com/2005/12/06/mclaird/ (accessed 22 March 2017); "Pioneer Party: Frontierville Blog." Available online at: https://pioneerparty.wordpress.com/2010/07/02/pioneer-fashion-calamity-jane/ (accessed 29 June 2019); Bernard Schopen, *Calamity Jane* (Reno, NV: Baobab Press, 2013); Michael Crichton, *Dragon's Teeth* (New York: HarperCollins, 2017), 267–268.
3. The Microgirls, "White Devil of the Yellowstone" (2007); Correspondence with Fred Audo, 8 October 2016; *Calamity Jane's Revenge* (dir. by Henrique Couto, ITN Distribution, USA, 2015).
4. *Calamity Jane* (1953); London *Daily Mail*, 27 June 2003; Leeds *Yorkshire Post*, 25 January 2015; Sonia Harford, "Women are Sitting in their Power: Virginia Gay on why Calamity Jane Matters Now," *Sydney Morning Herald*, 15 February 2018; London *Daily Mail*, 11 July 1997; "WhipCrapAway," company website available online at: www.jackieraines.co.uk/whipcrapaway/ (accessed 30 May 2018).
5. McLaird, *Calamity Jane*, 5; Jucovy, *Searching for Calamity*, 2, 14, 67, 68; Etulain, *Life and Legends*, 344, 4.
6. *Calamity Jane: Legende De L'Ouest* (dir. by Gregory Monro, Arte France & Temps Noir, France, 2014). See also Gregory Monro, *Calamity Jane: Mémoires de L'Ouest* (Paris: Hoebeke, 2010) and *Calamity Jane, Aventurière* (Lyon: Amaterra, 2017).
7. *Deadwood* (2004–06); Graulich and Witschi, *Dirty Words in Deadwood*, xii; Janet McCabe, "Myth Maketh the Woman: Calamity Jane, Frontier Mythology and Creating (Media) Historical Imaginings," in David Lavery (ed.), *Reading Deadwood: A Western to Swear By* (London: I.B. Tauris, 2006), 61, 76.
8. Mizejewski, "Calamity Jane and Female Masculinity in *Deadwood*," 185–186.
9. "HBO's *Deadwood*: Democratic Underground," available online at: www.democraticunderground.com/discuss/duboard.php?az=view_all&address=105x5531692 (accessed 10 June 2017); Argetsinger, "They Must Be Stars."
10. Libby Simon, "Sonofabitch Stew: The Drunken Life of Calamity Jane at FemFest, 2012," available online at: www.geist.com/blogs/libby-simons-blog/sonofabitch-stew%3A-the-drunken-life-of-calamity-jane-at-femfest-2012 (accessed 14 October 2017); Michael Scott, "Deadwood" in Trisha Telep, (ed.), *Corsets and Clockwork* (Boulder, CO: Perseus Books, 2011); J.D. Jordan, *Calamity: Being an Account of Calamity Jane and the Gunslinging Green Man* (San Diego, CA: Heliosphere, 2016), 15, back cover, 297. Reviews of Jordan's book available online at: www.o-jd.com/calamity-praise (accessed 10 February 2018).
11. For the publicity blurb on Audry Grant's *Calamity Jane: The Masquerade of Masculinity*, a 14-page short story self-published on the Kindle format in 2013 (but no longer available), see: www.goodreads.com/book/show/20558484-calamity-jane (accessed 10 April 2018); Christian Perrissin and Matthieu Blanchin, *Calamity Jane: The Calamitous Life of M.J. Cannary, 1852–1903* (San Diego, CA: IDW, 2017); *Calamity – A Childhood of Martha Jane Cannary* (dir. by Rémi Chayé, Gebeka, France, 2020); Eleanor Coleman, Head of Animated Acquisitions, Indie Sales, quoted in Carlos Aguilar, "Rémi Chayé's New Feature *Calamity – A Childhood of Martha Jane Cannary* acquired up by Indie Sales," *Cartoon Brew*, 5 June 2019. Available online at: www.cartoonbrew.com/feature-film/remi-chayes-new-feature-calamity-the-childhood-of-martha-jane-cannary-acquired-up-by-indie-sales-173380.html (accessed 4 July 2019).
12. Natalee Caple, *In Calamity's Wake* (New York: Bloomsbury, 2013), 208; Sea Sharp, "The Biography of Calamity Jane," 9 May 2016, available online at: http://dangerouswomenproject.org/2016/05/27/calamity-jane/ (accessed 29 June 2017); Beard, cited at: http://dangerouswomenproject.org/2016/03/07/year-dangerous-women-begins/ (accessed 7 August 2017).

13. Thomas Devaney, *Calamity Jane* (Baltimore, MD: Furniture Press, 2014), 3, back cover, 28, 26, 32, 37; M. Heather Carver, "Too Wild for Her Own Good: Searching for the Real Calamity Jane," in Lynn C. Miller, Jacqueline Taylor and M. Heather Carver (eds), *Voices Made Flesh: Performing Women's Autobiography* (Madison: University of Wisconsin Press, 2003), 96–102; Argetsinger, "They Must Be Stars."
14. Halberstam, *Gaga Feminism*, 5, 27–29.

BIBLIOGRAPHY

ARCHIVES

American Heritage Center, University of Wyoming Archives, Laramie, Wyoming (AHC)
Autry National Center, Los Angeles, California (Autry)
Buffalo Bill Historical Center, Cody, Wyoming (BBHC)
Center for Western Studies, Augustana College, Sioux Falls, South Dakota
Dakota Wesleyan University Archives, Mitchell, South Dakota
Huntington Library, San Marino, California
Montana Historical Society, Helena, Montana (MHS)
Special Collections and University Archives, Stanford University, Stanford, California

NEWSPAPERS

Aberdeen Daily News
Abilene Daily Chronicle
Anaconda Recorder
Anaconda Standard
Belle Fouche Bee
Bighorn Sentinel
Bill Barlow's Budget
Billings Gazette
Billings News
Billings Times
Bozeman Avant Courier
Buffalo Bulletin
Buffalo Evening News
Buffalo Morning Express
Butte Inter Mountain
Butte Weekly Miner
Casper Daily Tribune
Casper Herald
Casper Tribune–Herald
Central City Weekly Register
Cheyenne Daily Leader
Cheyenne Daily Sun
Cheyenne State Leader
Cheyenne Weekly Leader
Cheyenne *Wyoming Tribune Eagle*
Chicago Inter Ocean

BIBLIOGRAPHY

Chicago Tribune
Choteau Acantha
Cody Enterprise
Custer County Chronicle
Daily Alta California
Deadwood *Black Hills Daily Times*
Deadwood *Black Hills Pioneer*
Deadwood *Black Hills Weekly Tribune*
Deadwood Daily Pioneer-Times
Deadwood Daily Telegram
Deadwood Weekly Pioneer Times
Denver *Rocky Mountain News*
Douglas Budget
Douglas Enterprise
Emporia Gazette
Fergus County Argus
Galveston Daily News
Grand Encampment Herald
Grand Rapids Evening Leader
Grand Rapids *Telegram-Herald*
Great Falls Tribune
Harper's New Monthly Magazine
Helena *Daily Independent*
Helena Evening Herald
Helena *Independent Record*
Ismay Journal
Judith Basin Star
La Crosse Tribune
Lander *Wyoming State Journal*
Laramie Daily Sentinel
Lead Daily Call
Leeds *Yorkshire Post*
Livingston Enterprise
Livingston *Park County News*
Livingston Post
London *Daily Mail*
London *Daily Telegraph*
London *Evening News*
London *Star*
London *Times*
Lusk Herald
Manchester *Guardian*
Mercer County *Pioneer Press*
Miles City Daily Star
Miles City *Yellowstone Journal*
Milwaukee Sentinel
Minneapolis Journal
Montana Post
Montana Standard
Nashville *Barrier*
New York *Clipper*
New York Graphic
New York Times
New York Tribune

Norfolk News
Northern Wyoming Daily News
Omaha Daily Herald
Portland *Morning Oregonian*
Portland *New Northwest*
Princeton *Post Telegraph*
Princeton Press
Princeton *Telegram*
Rapid City Daily Journal
Rawlins *Carbon County Journal*
Rawlins Republican
Rock Springs Miner
San Antonio *Evening Herald*
San Francisco *Evening Bulletin*
San Francisco Examiner
San Francisco *Morning Call*
San Francisco Sunday Examiner
Sheridan Journal
Sioux City Journal
Sioux Falls *Argus Leader*
St. Louis Globe-Democrat
Stockton *Evening Mail*
Sundance Gazette
Sydney Morning Herald
Tombstone Epitaph
Variety
Washington Post
Wheatland World

DIME NOVELS AND COMICS

Ingraham, Prentiss, "Buffalo Bill and Calamity Jane, or, a Real Lady from the Black Hills," *New Buffalo Bill Weekly*, No. 177 (New York: Street & Smith, 1916)
Morris and Goscinny, *Calamity Jane: A Lucky Luke Adventure No. 8* (Paris: Dargaud, 1971 [1967])
"Reckless Ralph," "Calamity Jane: The Queen of the Plains," *Street and Smith's New York Weekly*, 16, 23, 30 January; 20, 27 February; 13 March 1882
Simon, Joe and Jack Kirby, "The Case of the Hapless Hackie," *Green Hornet: Boy's Explorer*, 1 (May 1946), 39–46
Wheeler, Edward, *Hurricane Nell, the Girl Dead Shot; or, the Queen of the Saddle and Lasso*, Starr's Ten Cent Pocket Library No. 1 (4 May 1877)
——*Deadwood Dick, The Prince of the Road; or, The Black Rider of the Black Hills* (15 October 1877, 1/1)
——*The Double Daggers; or, Deadwood Dick's Defiance* (21 December 1877, 1/20)
——*Deadwood Dick on Deck; or, Calamity Jane, the Heroine of Whoop-Up* (17 December 1878, 3/73)
——*Deadwood Dick in Leadville; or, a Strange Stroke for Liberty* (24 June 1879, 4/100)
——*Deadwood Dick's Device; or, the Sign of the Double Cross* (22 July 1879, 4/104)
——*Blonde Bill; or, Deadwood Dick's Home Base* (16 March 1880, 6/138)
——*A Game of Gold; or, Deadwood Dick's Big Strike* (1 June 1880, 6/149)
——*Deadwood Dick of Deadwood; or, the Picked Party* (20 July 1880, 6/156)
——*Deadwood Dick's Doom; or, Calamity Jane's Last Adventure* (28 June 1881, 8/205)
——*Captain Crack-Shot, the Girl Brigand* (20 September 1881, 9/217)
——*Gold Dust Dick, a Romance of Roughs and Toughs* (3 January 1882, 9/232)

——*Deadwood Dick's Divide; or, the Spirit of Swamp Lake* (8 August 1882, 11/263)
——*Deadwood Dick's Big Deal; or, the Gold Brick of Oregon* (26 June 1883, 12/309)
——*Deadwood Dick's Claim, or, the Fairy Face of Faro Flats* (1 July 1884, 14/362)
——*Deadwood Dick's Diamonds; or, the Mystery of Joan Porter* (2 June 1885, 14/410)
——*Deadwood Dick's Dust; or, The Chained Hand* (20 October 1885, 15/430)
"A Strange Woman," *Boys of England: A Journal of Sport, Travel, Fun and Instruction for the Youths of All Nations*, No. 738 (7 January 1881)

FILM, RADIO, AND TELEVISION (IN CHRONOLOGICAL ORDER)

In the Days of '75 and '76 (Black Hills Feature Film Co., USA, 1915)
Wild Bill Hickok (dir. by Clifford Smith, Paramount Pictures, USA, 1923)
Caught (dir. by Edward Sloman, Paramount Pictures, USA, 1931)
The Lone Ranger (created by George Trendle and Fran Striker, WXYZ Radio, Detroit, USA, 1933–56)
Annie Oakley (dir. by George Stephens, RKO Pictures, USA, 1935)
The Plainsman (dir. by Cecil B. DeMille, Paramount Pictures, USA, 1936)
Deadwood Dick (dir. by James W. Horne, Columbia Pictures, USA, 1940)
Young Bill Hickok (dir. by Joseph Kane, Republic, USA, 1940)
Badlands of Dakota (dir. by Alfred E. Green, Universal, USA, 1941)
The Paleface (dir. by Norman Z. McLeod, Paramount Pictures, USA, 1948)
Calamity Jane and Sam Bass (dir. by George Sherman, Universal, USA, 1949)
The Texan Meets Calamity Jane (dir. by Ande Lamb, Columbia Pictures, USA, 1950)
Annie Get Your Gun (dir. by George Sidney, Metro-Goldwyn-Mayer, USA, 1950)
Death Valley Days (created by Ruth Woodman, syndicated TV, USA, 1952–70)
Calamity Jane (dir. by David Butler, Warner Bros, USA, 1953)
Have Gun Will Travel (created by Herb Meadow, CBS-TV, USA, 1957–63)
Bonanza (created by David Dortort, NBC-TV, USA, 1959–83)
The Raiders (dir. by Herschel Daugherty, Universal, USA, 1963)
The Plainsman (dir. by David Lowell Rich, Universal, USA, 1966)
The Ballad of Josie (dir. by Andrew V. McLaglen, Universal, USA, 1967)
Little Big Man (dir. by Arthur Penn, National General Pictures, USA, 1970)
This Is the West That Was (dir. by Fielder Cook, NBC-TV, USA, 1974)
Calamity Jane (dir. by James Goldstone, CBS-TV, USA, 1984)
The Ballad of Little Jo (dir. by Maggie Greenwald, Fine Line Features, USA, 1993)
Bad Girls (dir. by Jonathan Kaplan, Twentieth Century Fox, USA, 1994)
The Quick and the Dead (dir. by Sam Raimi, TriStar Pictures, USA, 1995)
Wild Bill (dir. by Walter Hill, United Artists, USA, 1995)
Buffalo Girls (dir. by Rod Hardy, CBS-TV, USA, 1995)
Tall Tale (dir. by Jeremiah S. Chechik, Walt Disney Pictures, USA, 1995)
Legend of Calamity Jane (dir. by Pascal Morelli, Canal +/France 3, France, 1997–98)
Deadwood (dir. by David Milch, HBO, USA, 2004–06)
Calamity Jane: Legende De L'Ouest (dir. by Gregory Monro, Arte France & Temps Noir, France, 2014)
Calamity Jane's Revenge (dir. by Henrique Couto, ITN Distribution, USA, 2015)
Calamity – A Childhood of Martha Jane Cannary (dir. by Rémi Chayé, Gebeka, France, 2020)

MA/PHD THESES

Horowitz, Katie Rebecca, "The Trouble with 'Queerness': Drag and the Making of Two Cultures," University of California, Berkeley, PhD, 2012
McComb, Catherine, "Undressing an American Icon: Addressing the Representation of Calamity Jane Through a Critical Study of Her Costume," University of Regina, Saskatchewan, Masters, 2016
Watkins, John McLain, "Calamity Jane: A Pageant Drama in Three Acts," Montana State University, Masters, 1961

PUBLISHED BOOKS AND ARTICLES

Abbott, E.C. and Helena Huntington Smith, *We Pointed Them North: Recollections of a Cowpuncher* (New York: Smith, Farrar, and Rinehart, 1939)

Adams, Rachel, *Sideshow USA: Freaks and the American Cultural Imagination* (Chicago, IL: University of Chicago Press, 2001)

Adams, Ramon Frederick, *Burs Under the Saddle* (Norman: University of Oklahoma Press, 1964)

Aikman, Duncan, *Calamity Jane and the Lady Wildcats* (Lincoln: University of Nebraska Press, 1927)

Allen, William, *Adventures with Indians and Game* (New York: A.W. Bowen, 1903)

Andreas, Alfred Theodore, *Andreas' Historical Atlas of Dakota* (Chicago, IL: R.R. Donnelley, 1884)

Argetsinger, Amy, "They Must Be Stars Because They Get So Much Press, but What Is It They Do Again?," *Washington Post*, 10 August 2009

Armitage, Susan, "Through Women's Eyes," in Susan Armitage and Elizabeth Jameson (eds), *The Women's West* (Norman: University of Oklahoma Press, 1987)

Armitage, Susan and Elizabeth Jameson (eds), *The Women's West* (Norman: University of Oklahoma Press, 1987)

Bates, Anna Louise, "Calamity Jane and the Social Construction of Gender in the 1930s and 1950s," *Popular Culture Review*, 16/2 (2005), 69–82

Belenky, M.F., B.M. Clinchy, N.R. Goldberger and J.M. Tarule, *Women's Ways of Knowing* (New York: Basic Books, 1986)

Bellen, Martine, "Calamity Jane," *Conjunctions*, 24 (1995), 277–286

Bell-Metereau, Rebecca, *Hollywood Androgyny* (New York: Columbia University Press, 1985)

Bennett, Estelline, *Old Deadwood Days* (Lincoln: University of Nebraska Press, 1982 [1928])

Benstock, Shari, *The Private Self: Theory and Practice of Women's Autobiographical Writings* (Chapel Hill: University of North Carolina Press, 1988)

Billington, Ray Allen, *Westward Expansionism: A History of the American Frontier* (New York: Macmillan, 1949)

Blewitt, Andrew, "Calamity Jane," *The English Westerners' Brand Book*, 5/2 (January 1963), 1–9

Boag, Peter, "Go West Young Man, Go East Young Woman: Searching for the Trans in Western Gender History," *Western Historical Quarterly*, 36/4 (Winter 2005), 477–497

——*Re-dressing America's Frontier Past* (Berkeley: University of California Press, 2011)

Bogdan, Robert, *Freak Show: Presenting Human Oddities for Amusement and Profit* (Chicago, IL: University of Chicago Press, 1988)

Boorstin, Daniel, *The Image: A Guide to Pseudo-Events in America* (New York: Atheneum, 1971)

Bourke, John, *On the Border with Crook* (New York: Charles Scribner's Sons, 1891)

Boyd, Nan Alamilla, "Bodies in Motion: Lesbian and Transsexual Histories," in Susan Stryker and Stephen Whittle (eds), *The Transgender Studies Reader* (New York: Taylor & Francis, 2006), 420–433

Bricklin, Julia, *America's Best Female Sharpshooter: The Rise and Fall of Lillian Frances Smith* (Norman: University of Oklahoma Press, 2017)

Briggs, Harold E., *Frontiers of the Northwest: A History of the Upper Missouri Valley* (New York: Peter Smith, 1950 [1940])

Brininstool, Earl, *Fighting Red Cloud's Warriors* (Columbus, OH: The Hunter-Trader-Trapper, 1926)

Browder, Laura, *Her Best Shot: Women and Guns in America* (Chapel Hill: University of North Carolina Press, 2006)

Brown, Dee, *The Gentle Tamers: Women of the Old Wild West* (Lincoln: University of Nebraska Press, 1958)

Brown, Jesse and A.M. Willard, *The Black Hills Trails* (Rapid City, SD: Rapid City Journal Company, 1924)

Browning, Anne, "Kaleidoscopic Poetry," *American Book Review*, 37/5 (July/August 2016), 25

Butler, Anne, *Daughters of Joy, Sisters of Mercy: Prostitutes in the American West, 1865–90* (Urbana: University of Illinois Press, 1985)

Butler, Judith, *Gender Trouble: Feminism and the Subversion of Identity* (New York: Routledge, 2006 [1990])

Cain, Jackson, *Hellbreak County* (New York: Warner Books, 1984)

Cannary, Martha, *Life and Adventures of Calamity Jane, By Herself* (n.p., 1896)

Cannary Hickok, Martha Jane, *Calamity Jane's Letters to Her Daughter* (San Lorenzo, CA: Shameless Hussy Press, 1976)

Caple, Natalee, *In Calamity's Wake* (New York: Bloomsbury, 2013)

Card, James, *Seductive Cinema* (New York: Alfred Knopf, 1994)

Carver, M. Heather, "Risky Business: Exploring Women's Autobiography and Performance," in Lynn C. Miller, Jacqueline Taylor, and M. Heather Carver (eds), *Voices Made Flesh: Performing Women's Autobiography* (Madison: University of Wisconsin Press, 2003), 15–29

——"Too Wild for Her Own Good: Searching for the Real Calamity Jane," in Lynn C. Miller, Jacqueline Taylor, and M. Heather Carver (eds), *Voices Made Flesh: Performing Women's Autobiography* (Madison: University of Wisconsin Press, 2003), 96–102

Casey, Robert, *The Black Hills and Their Incredible Characters* (Indianapolis, IN: Bobbs Merrill, 1949)

Chandler, A. Bertram, *Rim of Space* (New York: Avalon, 1961)

Chemers, Michael, *Staging Stigma: A Critical Examination of the American Freak Show* (New York: Palgrave, 2008)

Clairmonte, Glenn, *Calamity Was the Name for Jane* (Denver, CO: Sage Books, 1959)

Clarke Jane and Diana Symonds (eds), *Move Over Misconceptions* (London: BFI, 1980)

Cody, Iron Eyes and Collin Perry, *Iron Eyes: My Life as a Hollywood Indian* (London: Frederick Muller, 1982)

Cody, Louisa and Courtney Ryley Cooper, *Memories of Buffalo Bill* (New York: D. Appleton, 1919)

Cody, William F., *The Adventures of Buffalo Bill Cody* (New York: Harper & Bros., 1904)

Connelley, William Elsey, *Wild Bill and His Era* (New York: Press of the Pioneers, 1933)

Cooper, Courtney Ryley, *Annie Oakley: Woman at Arms* (London: Hurst & Blackett, 1927)

Cox, J. Randolph, *The Dime Novel Companion: A Source Book* (Westport, CT: Greenwood Publishing, 2000)

Craton, Lillian, *The Victorian Freak Show: The Significance of Disability and Physical Differences in 19th-Century Fiction* (New York: Cambria Press, 2009)

Crawford, Jack, *The Poet Scout: A Book of Song and Story* (New York: Funk & Wagnalls, 1886)

Crawford, Lewis, *Rekindling Camp Fires: The Exploits of Ben Arnold* (Bismarck, ND: Capital Book Co., 1926)

Creed, Barbara, "Lesbian Bodies," in Elizabeth Grosz and Elspeth Probyn (eds), *Sexy Bodies: The Strange Carnalities of Feminism* (London: Routledge, 2013), 86–103

Crichton, Michael, *Dragon's Teeth* (New York: HarperCollins, 2017)

Crockett, Davy, *The Life and Adventures of Colonel David Crockett of Tennessee* (Cincinnati, OH: n.p., 1833)

Cummins, Sarah J., *Autobiography and Reminiscences* (La Grande, OR, 1908)

Davis, Adrienne, "A Lady Among the Miners: The Experience of a New York Belle in the Black Hills," *New York Graphic*, 11 August 1877

Davis, Tracey, "Annie Oakley and the Ideal Husband of No Importance," in Janelle Reinert and Joseph Roach (eds), *Critical Theory and Performance* (Ann Arbor: University of Michigan Press, 1992), 299–312

——"Shotgun Wedlock: Annie Oakley's Power Politics in the Wild West," in Laurence Senelick (ed.), *Gender and Performance: The Presentation of Difference in the Performing Arts* (Hanover, NH: University Press of New England, 1992), 141–157

Dee, D. (Dora Du Fran), *Low Down on Calamity Jane* (Rapid City, SD: n.p., 1932)

Deloria, Philip J., *Playing Indian* (New Haven, CT: Yale University Press, 1998)

Dennett, Andrea, *Weird and Wonderful: The Dime Museum in America* (New York: New York Press, 1997)

Denning, Michael, *Mechanic Accents: Dime Novels and Working-Class Culture in America* (New York: Verso, 1998)

Devaney, Thomas, *Calamity Jane* (Baltimore, MD: Furniture Press, 2014)

Dexter, Peter, *Deadwood* (New York: Penguin, 1986)

Drago, Harry, *Notorious Ladies of the Frontier* (New York: Dodd & Mead, 1969)

Elizabeth Drorbaugh, "Sliding Scales," in Lesley Ferris, *Crossing the Stage: Controversies on Cross-Dressing* (London: Routledge, 1993), 120–143

Duberman, B., M. Vicinus, and G. Chauncey Jnr. (eds), *Hidden from History: Reclaiming the Gay and Lesbian Past* (London: Penguin, 1989)

Durbach, Nadja, *The Spectacle of Deformity: Freak Shows and Modern British Culture* (Berkeley: University of California Press, 2009)

Edson, J.T., *The Bull Whip Breed* (London: Brown & Watson, 1965)

——*Trouble Trail* (London: Brown & Watson, 1965)

——*Troubled Range* (London: Brown & Watson, 1965)

——*The Wildcats* (London: Brown & Watson, 1965)

Embry, Jessie (ed.), *Oral History, Community and Work in the American West* (Tucson: University of Arizona Press, 2013)

Etulain, Richard, *The Life and Legends of Calamity Jane* (Norman: University of Oklahoma Press, 2014)

——*Calamity Jane: A Reader's Guide* (Norman: University of Oklahoma Press, 2015)

Evans, Tabor, *Longarm in Deadwood* (New York: Jove Books, 1982)

Faragher, John Mack, "The Tale of Wyatt Earp," in M.C. Carnes (ed.), *Past Imperfect* (New York: Henry Holt, 1996), 154–161

Federal Writers' Project, *Montana: A State Guide Book* (New York: Hastings House, 1939)

Ferris, Lesley, *Crossing the Stage: Controversies on Cross-Dressing* (London: Routledge, 1993)

Fiedler, Leslie, *Freaks: Myths and Images of the Secret Self* (New York: Touchstone, 1978)

Fontes, Ron and Justine Korman, *Calamity Jane at Fort Sanders* (New York: Disney Press, 1992)

Foote, Stella, *A History of Calamity Jane: Our Country's First Liberated Woman* (New York: Vantage, 1995)

Fox, M.L., "Calamity Jane," *Illustrated American*, 7 March 1896

Frackelton, Will, *Sagebrush Dentist* (Pasadena, CA: Trail's End Publishing Co., 1947)

Freeman, Lewis, *Down the Yellowstone* (New York: Dodd, Mead & Co., 1922)

Gage, Carolyn, *The Second Coming of Joan of Arc and Selected Plays* (Denver, CO: Outskirts Press, 2008)

Grand, Sarah, "The New Aspect of the Woman Question," *North American Review*, 158 (March 1894), 270–276

Graulich, Melody and Nicolas Witschi (eds), *Dirty Words in Deadwood: Literature and the Postwestern* (Lincoln: University of Nebraska Press, 2013)

Greeley, Horace, *An Overland Journey from New York to San Francisco, in the Summer of 1859* (New York: C.M. Saxton, Barker & Co., 1860)

Griffith, Sally Foreman, *Home Town News: William Allen White and the Emporia Gazette* (New York: Oxford University Press, 1989)

Grossman, James (ed.), *The Frontier in American Culture* (Berkeley: University of California Press, 1994)

Grosz, Elizabeth and Elspeth Probyn (eds), *Sexy Bodies: The Strange Carnalities of Feminism* (London: Routledge, 2013)

Gubar, Susan, "Blessings in Disguise: Cross-dressing as Redressing for Female Modernists," *Massachusetts Review*, 22/3 (1981), 477–508

Gunter, Archibald and Fergus Redmond, *A Florida Enchantment* (New York: Hurst, 1891)

Halberstam, J. Jack, *Gaga Feminism: Sex, Gender, and the End of Normal* (Boston, MA: Beacon Press, 2012)

Halberstam, Judith, *Female Masculinity* (Durham, NC: Duke University Press, 1998)

Hall, Roger, *Performing the American Frontier, 1876–1906* (Cambridge: Cambridge University Press, 2001)

Hartman, Forrest, "Myth Versus Truth in the Life of Calamity Jane: Ask Glenda Bell," *Humanities*, 36/4 (July/August 2015)

Havighurst, Walter, *Annie Oakley of the Wild West* (London: Robert Hale, 1955)

Herndon, Sarah Raymond, *Days on the Road: Crossing the Plains in 1865* (New York: Burr Printing House, 1902)

Hilton, Francis, "Calamity Jane," *Frontier Magazine* (September 1925), 105–109

Holbrook, Stewart, *Annie Oakley and Other Rugged People* (New York: Macmillan, 1948)

Horak, Laura, *Girls Will be Boys: Cross-Dressed Women, Lesbians and American Cinema, 1908–1934* (New York: Rutgers University Press, 2016)

Hoshier, George, "Women of the Frontier: Stories of Odd Characters of Thirty Years Ago," *Norfolk News*, 13 July 1906

Hotchner, A.E., *Doris Day: Her Own Story* (New York: Morrow, 1976)

Hueston, Ethel, *Calamity Jane of Deadwood Gulch* (London: Hodder & Stoughton, 1938)

Hughes, Richard, *Pioneer Years in the Black Hills* (Glendale, CA: Arthur H. Clark Co., 1957)

Hutchens, John E., *One Man's Montana* (New York: J.B. Lippincott, 1964)

Irwin, Mary Ann and James Brooks (eds), *Women and Gender in the American West* (Albuquerque: University of New Mexico Press, 2004)

Isenberg, Andrew, *Wyatt Earp: A Vigilante Life* (New York: Hill & Wang, 2014)

Jameson, Elizabeth and Susan Armitage (eds), *Writing the Range: Race, Class, and Culture in the Women's West* (Norman: University of Oklahoma Press, 1997)

Jeffers McDonald, Tamar, "Carrying Concealed Weapons: Gendered Makeover in *Calamity Jane*," *Journal of Film and Popular Television*, 34 (2007), 179–187

——*Hollywood Catwalk* (London: I.B. Tauris, 2010)

Jennewein, J. Leonard, *Calamity Jane of the Western Trails* (Rapid City, SD: Dakota West Books, 1953)

Jensen, Joan and Darlis Miller, "The Gentle Tamers Revisited: New Approaches to the History of Women in the American West," in Mary Ann Irwin and James Brooks (eds), *Women and Gender in the American West* (Albuquerque: University of New Mexico Press, 2004)

Johanssen, Albert, *The House of Beadle & Adams* (Norman: University of Oklahoma Press, 1950)

Johnson, Susan, " 'A Memory Sweet to Soldiers': The Significance of Gender in the History of the 'American West'," in Mary Ann Irwin and James Brooks (eds), *Women and Gender in the American West* (Albuquerque: University of New Mexico Press, 2004)

Jones, Daryl, *The Dime Novel Western* (Bowling Green, OH: Popular Press, 1978)

Jordan, J.D., *Calamity: Being an Account of Calamity Jane and the Gunslinging Green Man* (San Diego, CA: Heliosphere, 2016)

Jucovy, Linda, *Searching for Calamity: The Life and Times of Calamity Jane* (Philadelphia, PA: Stampede Books, 2012)

Kasper, Shirl, *Annie Oakley* (Norman: University of Oklahoma Press, 1992)

Kasson, Joy S., *Buffalo Bill's Wild West: Celebrity, Memory, and Popular History* (New York: Hill & Wang, 2000)

Klock, Irma, *Here Comes Calamity Jane* (Deadwood, SD: Dakota Graphics, 1979)

Kolody, Annette, *In Search of First Contact: The Vikings of Vinland and the People of the Dawnland* (Durham, NC: Duke University Press, 2012)

Krafft-Ebing, Richard von, *Psychopathia Sexualis* (New York: Arcade, 1965 [1886])

Lackmann, Ronald W., *Women of the Western Frontier in Fact, Fiction, and Film* (Jefferson, NC: McFarland, 1997)

Lake, Stuart, *Wyatt Earp: Frontier Marshal* (New York: Houghton Mifflin, 1931)

Lane, J.R., "The Gold-Hunters," *Chicago Tribune*, 19 June 1875

Lavery, David (ed.), *Reading Deadwood: A Western to Swear By* (London: I.B. Tauris, 2006)

Lewis, Nathaniel, *Unsettling the Literary West: Authenticity and Authorship* (Lincoln: University of Nebraska Press, 2003)

Limerick, Patricia (ed.), *Trails: Toward a New Western History* (Lawrence: University Press of Kansas, 1991)

——*Legacy of Conquest: The Unbroken Past of the American West* (New York: W.W. Norton, 2011 [1987])

Logan, Jake, *Dead Man's Hand* (New York: Playboy Press, 1979)

Macmillan, Thomas "Mac", "Gold Galore," *Chicago Inter Ocean*, 3 July 1875

Maguire, Horace, *The Black Hills and American Wonderland* (Chicago, IL: Donnelly, Lloyd & Co., 1877)

——*The Coming Empire: A Complete and Reliable Treatise on the Black Hills, Yellowstone, and Big Horn Regions* (Sioux City, IA: Watkins & Smead, 1878)

Marcus, Sharon, *Between Women: Friendship, Desire, and Marriage in Victorian England* (Princeton, NJ: Princeton University Press, 2007)

May, Elaine Tyler, *Homeward Bound: American Families in the Cold War Era* (New York: Basic Books, 1988)

McCabe, Janet, "Myth Maketh the Woman: Calamity Jane, Frontier Mythology and Creating (Media) Historical Imaginings," in David Lavery (ed.), *Reading Deadwood: A Western to Swear By* (London: I.B. Tauris, 2006)

McClintock, John S., *Pioneer Days in the Black Hills* (Norman: University of Oklahoma Press, 2000 [1939])

McGillycuddy, Julia, *McGillycuddy, Agent: A Biography of the Life of Dr. Valentine T. McGillycuddy* (Stanford, CA: Stanford University Press, 1941)

McLaird, James, "Calamity Jane's Diary and Letters: The Story of Fraud," *Montana: The Magazine of Western History*, 45 (1995), 20–35

——*Calamity Jane: The Woman and the Legend* (Norman: University of Oklahoma Press, 2005)

McMurtry, Larry, *Buffalo Girls* (New York: Simon & Schuster, 1990)

——*The Colonel and Little Missie: Buffalo Bill, Annie Oakley, and the Beginnings of Superstardom in America* (New York: Simon & Schuster, 2005)

McReynolds, Robert, *Where Strongest Tide Winds Blew* (Colorado Springs, CO: Gowdy-Symonds, 1907)

Merck, Mandy, "Travesty on the Old Frontier," in Jane Clarke and Diana Symonds (eds), *Move Over Misconceptions* (London: BFI, 1980), 21–28

Middleton, George, *Circus Memoirs* (Los Angeles, CA: G. Rice & Sons, 1913)

Miller, Darlis, *Captain Jack Crawford: Buckskin Poet, Scout, and Showman* (Albuquerque: University of New Mexico Press, 1993)

Miller, Lynn, Jacqueline Taylor, and Heather Carver (eds), *Voices Made Flesh: Performing Women's Autobiography* (Madison: University of Wisconsin Press, 2003)

Mills, Anson, *My Story* (Washington, DC: Byron S. Adams, 1918)

Milner II, Clyde, "Afterword: When History Talks Back," in Jessie L. Embry (ed.), *Oral History, Community and Work in the American West* (Tucson: University of Arizona Press, 2013), 327–337

Mizejewski, Linda, "Calamity Jane and Female Masculinity in *Deadwood*," in Melody Graulich and Nicolas Witschi (eds), *Dirty Words in Deadwood: Literature and the Postwestern* (Lincoln: University of Nebraska Press, 2013), 184–207

Monro, Gregory, *Calamity Jane: Mémoires de L'Ouest* (Paris: Hoebeke, 2010)

——*Calamity Jane, Aventurière* (Lyon: Amaterra, 2017)

Moses, L., *Wild West Shows and the Images of American Indians, 1883–1933* (Albuquerque: University of New Mexico Press, 1996)

Mott, Frank Luther, *American Journalism: A History, 1690–1960* (New York: Macmillan, 1962)

Mulvey, Laura, "Visual Pleasure and Narrative Cinema," *Screen*, 16 (Autumn 1975), 6–18

Mumey, Nolie, *Calamity Jane, 1852–1903: A History of Her Life and Adventures in the West* (Denver, CO: Range Press, 1950)

Newson, Thomas, *Drama of Life in the Black Hills* (Saint Paul, MN: Dodge & Larpenteur, 1878)

Nussbaum, Martin, "Sociological Symbolism of the 'Adult Western'," *Social Forces*, 39/1 (1960), 25–28

Oakley, Annie, *The Rifle Queen: Annie Oakley* (London: General Publishing Co., 1884)

——*The Story of My Life* (n.p.: NEA Service, 1926)

Paine, Clarence, "Calamity Jane: Man, Woman . . . or Both?," *Westerners' Brand Book, 1945–6* (Chicago, IL: Westerners, 1947), 69–82

Patterson, W.G., "Calamity Jane: A Heroine of the Wild West," *Wild World*, 11 (September 1903), 450–457

Perrissin, Christian and Matthieu Blanchin, *Calamity Jane: The Calamitous Life of M.J. Cannary, 1852–1903* (San Diego, CA: IDW, 2017)

Picton, Thomas, *Wild Bill the Indian Slayer: A Tale of Forest and Prairie Life* (New York: R. De Witt, 1867)

Pond, Seymour, "Frontier Still Recalls 'Calamity Jane'," *New York Times*, 18 October 1925

Purple, Edwin Ruthven, *Perilous Passage: A Narrative of the Montana Gold Rush, 1862–1863* (Helena, MT: Montana Historical Society Press, 1995)

Reddin, Paul, *Wild West Shows* (Chicago: University of Illinois Press, 1999)

Richardson, Albert D., *Beyond the Mississippi: Life and Adventure on the Prairies, Mountains, and Pacific Coast* (Hartford, CT: American Publishing Co., 1869)

Riley, Glenda, "Images of the Frontierswoman: Iowa as a Case Study," *Western Historical Quarterly*, 8 (April 1977), 189–202

——*The Life and Legacy of Annie Oakley* (Norman: University of Oklahoma Press, 1994)

Robinson, Gillian, *The Slow Reign of Calamity Jane* (Kingston, ON: Quarry Press, 1994)

Rosa, Joseph, *Wild Bill Hickok: The Man and His Myth* (Lawrence: University Press of Kansas, 1996)

Rosen, Ruth, *The Lost Sisterhood: Prostitution in America, 1900–1918* (Baltimore, MD: Johns Hopkins University Press, 1982)

Royce, Sarah, *A Frontier Lady: Recollections of the Gold Rush and Early California* (Lincoln: University of Nebraska Press, 1977 [1932])

Russell, Don, *The Lives and Legends of Buffalo Bill* (Norman: University of Oklahoma Press, 1960)

Russo, Vito, *The Celluloid Closet: Homosexuality in the Movies* (New York: Harper, 1987)

Rydell, Robert and Rob Kroes, *Buffalo Bill in Bologna: The Americanization of the World, 1869–1922* (Chicago, IL: University of Chicago Press, 2005)

Sage, Rufus, *Scenes in the Rocky Mountains* (Philadelphia, PA: Carey & Hart, 1846)

San Francisco Lesbian and Gay Project, "She Even Chewed Tobacco: A Pictorial Narrative of Passing Women in America," in B. Duberman, M. Vicinus, and G. Chauncey Jnr., *Hidden from History: Reclaiming the Gay and Lesbian Past* (Penguin: London, 1989), 183–194

Sanders II, W.F. and Robert Taylor, *Biscuits and Badmen: The Sanders in their Own Words* (Butte, MT: Editorial Review Press, 1983)

Sandweiss, Martha, *Print the Legend: Photography and the American West* (New Haven, CT: Yale University Press, 2004)

Savoy, Eric, "That Ain't All She Ain't: Doris Day and Queer Performativity," in Ellis Hanson (ed.), *Outtakes: Essays on Queer Theory and Film* (New York: Duke University Press, 1999), 151–182

Sayers, Isabelle S., *Annie Oakley and Buffalo Bill's Wild West* (New York: Dover Publications, 1981)

Schlatter, Evelyn A., "Drag's a Life: Women, Gender, and Cross-Dressing in the Nineteenth-Century West," in Elizabeth Jameson and Susan Armitage (eds), *Writing the Range: Race, Class and Culture in the Women's West* (Norman: University of Oklahoma Press, 1997), 334–348

Schopen, Bernard, *Calamity Jane* (Reno, NV: Baobab Press, 2013)

Scott, Michael, "Deadwood," in Trisha Telep (ed.), *Corsets and Clockwork* (Boulder, CO: Perseus Books, 2011)

Sears, Clare, " 'A Tremendous Sensation': Cross-Dressing in the 19th Century San Francisco Press," in L. Castaneda and S. Campbell (eds), *News and Sexuality: Media Portrayals of Diversity* (London: Sage, 2006), 1–19

——"Electric Brilliancy: Cross-Dressing Law and Freak Show Displays in 19th Century San Francisco," *Women's Studies Quarterly*, 36 (2008), 170–187

——*Arresting Dress: Cross-Dressing, Law, and Fascination in Nineteenth-Century San Francisco* (Durham, NC: Duke University Press, 2014)

Secrest, William B. (ed.), *I Buried Hickok: The Memoirs of White Eye Anderson* (College Station, TX: Creative Publishing, 1980)

Senelick, Laurence, *The Changing Room: Sex, Drag and Theatre* (London: Routledge, 2000)

Senn, Edward, *Deadwood Dick and Calamity Jane: A Thorough Sifting of Facts from Fiction* (Deadwood, SD: n.p., 1939)

Slotkin, Richard, *Gunfighter Nation: The Myth of the Frontier in Twentieth Century America* (New York: Atheneum, 1992)

Smith-Rosenberg, Carroll, "Discourses of Sexuality and Subjectivity: The New Woman, 1870–1936," in B. Duberman, M. Vicinus, and G. Chauncey Jnr., *Hidden from History: Reclaiming the Gay and Lesbian Past* (Penguin: London, 1989), 264–280

Sollid, Roberta, *Calamity Jane: A Study in Historical Criticism* (Helena, MT: Montana Historical Society, 1958)

Spencer, Mrs. William Loring, *Calamity Jane: A Story of the Black Hills* (New York: Cassell & Co., 1887)

Spring, A.W. (ed.), "Diary of Isaac N. Bard (1875–6)," in Alan Swallow (ed.), *1955 Westerners' Brand Book, The Denver Posse* (Denver, CO: Westerners, 1956), 171–204

Stacey, Jackie, *Star Gazing: Hollywood Cinema and Female Spectatorship* (London: Routledge, 1994)

Stanton, Elizabeth Cady, "Women's Dress," *The Revolution*, 22 July 1869

Stephens, Elizabeth, *Anatomy as Spectacle: Public Exhibitions of the Body from 1700 to the Present* (Liverpool: Liverpool University Press, 2011)

Stevenson, Elizabeth, *Figures in a Western Landscape* (Baltimore, MD: Johns Hopkins University Press, 1994)

Stokes, George and Howard Driggs, *Deadwood Gold: A Story of the Black Hills* (London: George Harrap & Co., 1926)

Stryker, Susan and Stephen Whittle (eds), *The Transgender Studies Reader* (New York: Taylor & Francis, 2006)

Sullivan, L., *Information for the Female-to-Male Cross Dresser and Transsexual* (San Francisco, CA: Haight Street, 1985)

Sutley, Lock, *The Last Frontier* (New York: Macmillan, 1930)

Swallow, Alan (ed.), *1955 Westerners' Brand Book, The Denver Posse* (Denver, CO: Westerners, 1956)

Swartout, Annie, *Missie: An Historical Biography of Annie Oakley* (Blanchester, OH: Brown Publishing Co., 1947)

Tallent, Annie D., *The Black Hills, or the Last Hunting Grounds of the Dakotahs* (St. Louis, MO: Nixon-Jones Printing Co.,1899)

Tasker, Yvonne, *Working Girls: Gender and Sexuality in Popular Cinema* (London: Routledge, 2002)

Thomson, Rosemary Garland (ed.), *Freakery: Cultural Spectacles of the Extraordinary Body* (New York: New York University Press, 1996)

——*Extraordinary Bodies: Figuring Disability in American Culture and Literature* (New York: Columbia University Press, 1997)

Titterton, W.R., *From Theatre to Music Hall* (London: Stephen Swift, 1912)

Tromp, Marlene (ed.), *Victorian Freaks: The Social Context of Freakery in Britain* (Columbus: Ohio State University Press, 2008)

Turner, Frederick Jackson, *The Frontier in American History* (New York: Henry Holt, 1920)

Turner, Thadd M., *Wild Bill Hickok: Deadwood City—End of Trail* (Boca Raton, FL: Universal Publishers, 2001)

Vaughn, J.W., *With Crook at the Rosebud* (Harrisburg, PA: The Stackpole Co., 1956)

Visscher, William, *Buffalo Bill's Own Story of his Life and Deeds* (Chicago, IL: Homewood Press, 1917)

Ward, D.B., *Across the Plains in 1853* (Seattle, WA: Ward, 1911)

Ward, Josiah, "Wild West Heroine the Movies Overlook," *New York Tribune*, 16 October 1921

Warren, Louis, *Buffalo Bill's America: William Cody and the Wild West Show* (New York: Vintage, 2005)

West, Elliott, *Growing Up with the Country: Childhood on the Far Western Frontier* (Albuquerque: University of New Mexico Press, 1989)

——"A Longer, Grimmer but More Interesting Story," in Patricia Limerick (ed.), *Trails: Toward a New Western History* (Lawrence: University Press of Kansas, 1991), 72–76

White, Richard, *It's Your Misfortune and None of My Own: A New History of the American West* (Norman: University of Oklahoma Press, 1991)

——"Trashing the Trails," in Patricia Limerick (ed.), *Trails: Toward a New Western History* (Lawrence: University Press of Kansas, 1991), 26–39

——"Frederick Jackson Turner and Buffalo Bill," in James R. Grossman (ed.), *The Frontier in American Culture* (Berkeley: University of California Press, 1994), 7–68

Whithorn, Bill and Doris Whithorn, *Calamity's in Town: The Town was Livingston* (Livingston, MT: Whithorn Publication, n.d.)

Williams, Henry Llewellyn, *Buffalo Bill* (London: Routledge, 1887)

Wilstach, Frank, *Wild Bill Hickok: The Prince of Pistoleers* (Garden City, New York: Doubleday, 1926).

Young, Harry, *Hard Knocks: A Life Story of the Vanishing West* (Portland, OR: Wells & Co., 1915)

INDEX

women in the West: opportunities and constraints on the female frontier, 2, 11, 19–21, 36–37, 39, 235; stereotypes, 3, 6, 10, 27; diaries, 5–6; as subject of study, 5; in mining towns, 21–4; prostitution, 2, 25, 49, 58, 62–64; photographers, 40; "passing" women and gender disruption, 46–55, 128–130, 135; film representations of, 151–152

Wonderland Museum, Billings, Montana, 189, 242
Woods, Sherryl, 252
Wyatt Earp: Frontier Marshal (1931), 158

Yellowstone National Park, 114
Young Bill Hickok (1940), 180–181
Young, Harry, 40–42, 62, 64
Young, Mattie, 34